FAITH
A COMMENTARY ON JAMES

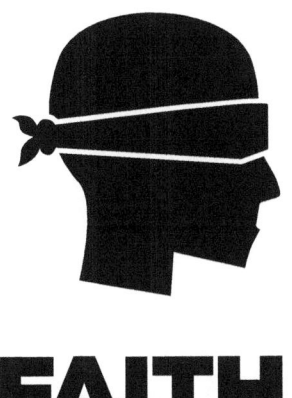

FAITH
A COMMENTARY ON JAMES

BY JACOB ABSHIRE

Truth411
Houston, Texas
www.t411.com

Faith: A Commentary on James
© 2012 by Jacob Abshire

Published by Truth411
12907 Chalfield Cir., Houston, TX 77044
www.t411.com

All rights reserved. No part of this publication may be reproduced, stored, in a retrieval system, or transmitted in any form by any means, electronic, mechanical, photocopy, recording, or otherwise, without the prior permission of the publisher, except as provided for by USA copyright law.

Design and typeset: Resolute Creative, Inc., Houston, TX
First printing 2012
Printed in the United States of America

Unless otherwise indicated, scripture quotations are from the ESV Bible® (The Holy Bible, English Standard Version®), copyright © 2001 by Crossway Bibles, a publishing ministry of Good News Publishers. Used by permission. All rights reserved.

ISBN: 978-0-9837153-5-1
Kindle ISBN: 978-0-9837153-6-8
ePub ISBN: 978-0-9837153-7-5
Nook ISBN: 978-0-9837153-8-2
Library of Congress Control Number: 2012947151
  Religion / Biblical Commentary / New Testament

TO KATHY,
my wife and unequalled helper, who surrendered countless hours to me in order to see this book completed, much of my life accomplishments are to her credit.

CONTENTS

Acknowledgements 11
Preface 13
Introduction 15
1. The Test of Faith 17
2. The Trial of Response 51
3. The Trial of Partiality 67
4. The Trial of Works 107
5. The Trial of Speech 135
6. The Trial of Wisdom 167
7. The Trial of Loyalty 215
8. The Trial of Planning 263
9. The Trial of Wealth 281
10. The Trial of Suffering 313
11. The Prayer of Faith 341
Appendix: James, The Brother of Jesus 383
Study Guide 385
General Index 397
Scripture Index 401
About the Author 413

ACKNOWLEDGEMENTS

This book would have killed me if it took any longer. Moreover, I would have died long ago had I not had the help that I did. For this purpose, I now set acknowledgements to print.

Budget is my dear friend. He introduced me to Sara Moseley, and her mother, Shirley Moseley. It was their generosity and editorial expertise that has turned this mess of words into something worth reading. They were kind enough to set aside time and energy in order to dot the i's and cross the t's, and a great many other things. To them both I say, "Thank you."

It was the subtle, though sometimes forceful, nudges my friends gave me that helped me push through this lengthy work. My prior book (*Forgiveness: A Commentary on Philemon*) was rather brief and awarded me a great deal of excitement for the next one. Thinking a tougher book, like James, would be a better challenge, I got started and quickly felt the weight of laborious writing. Midway through the book, I wanted to quit. There is no doubt that the prayers of Rudy Rocha and Dennis Rogers carried me to the end. Their time to discuss and contemplate the more gaping truths with me enabled me to keep forging ahead. They also deserve my thanks.

The book of James required me to work harder than ever before. There were Jewish customs, Hebraic nuances, and rare parts of speech that stumped me time and time again. For this reason, I relied on the scholarly minds of a few individuals. One is Dr. John Garr, the Chancellor of Hebraic Heritage Christian College. Another is Dr. Bill Klein, a professor of Biblical Greek at the Master's Graduate School of Divinity. Both men made themselves available to answer my questions and supply me with resources that would otherwise cost an arm and a leg. And though we have never met in person, Dr. William Varner, a professor of Bible and Greek at The Master's College and author of *The Book of James: A New Perspective* was kind enough to make a contribution. Of course, there a number of others whose material kept me from drowning in the deep, most of which I will thank when I see them in heaven.

I dedicate this book to my wife. She was a mother of three when I first sat before my computer and began fleshing out this book. When I finished, she was a mother of four. With an abundance of patience and strength, she endured pregnancy and all the headaches that come with child rearing, four times over. Each week, she relinquished hours of her time for me to close the office door and write. I can make my way through some of the most complex doctrines of the Bible, but I cannot grasp how she does what she does with our household. Few do it as well. Thank you, Kathy.

PREFACE

An old Cajun man once instructed his young grandson to, "Wait for dem birds to fly all up togetter before ya sqeeze dat dere trigger—hit three or four, or even two, of dem birds with one shot and save dem bullets." From the sounds of it, the aged hunter understood the principle of killing two birds with one stone and took it nearly literally.

On the heels of completion of *Forgiveness: A Commentary on Philemon*, the birds aligned and I took a shot—so to say. Wrapping up the book gave me a new sense of energy so much so that I was eager to start my next writing project—my second reader's commentary. I was already thinking about the book of James. At the same time, the home-group Bible study that I facilitated was coming to an end in our current study and was looking to start something else. Also at the same time, my pastor asked me consider developing a series of lessons for our corporate mid-week Bible study. I happily obliged, thinking that I could do all three at one time—my Cajun roots, no doubt.

From this came a study guide on James. I called it, *Tried and True: Painful Trials and Maturing Faith*. There is a common thread woven throughout the epistle of James. It is the subject of trials. Over and over James lays on his readers a number of evaluations in the form of hardships and temptations. His purpose is to cause professing believers to examine their lives and see if what they profess is actually true. It reminded me of those pop quizzes that teachers would lay on us in school. It was their way of seeing what we actually understood, and to help us know where we needed to grow in our understanding. In James, trials are described as spiritual pop quizzes to assess our spiritual growth and ultimately to develop our spiritual faith.

The common thread of James had two colors. Yet it was one thread. On one hand, the subject is trials. On the other hand, the subject is faith. Therefore, the title was rendered in such a way that we communicated both colors of the thread: one negative, one positive. Christians who are tried by the hardships and temptations of life are found true as Christ-followers and people of faith. And, as we discover early on in James, the more trials we endure, the more mature our faith becomes. We are being tried and made true by going through painful trials and maturing our faith.

Though this made for a good sermon series and Bible study series, it didn't quite jive with my plans for the book series. My idea was to have each book focus on a characteristic of the Christian life. Trials are definitely characteristic of our lives, but "trials" are not as strong as "faith" when appealing to what matters in the Christian life. Both exist, but one is more supremely valuable and helpful as our focus. Besides, how many people want to read a lengthy book on drawbacks, inconveniences and hardships? Not very many.

For this purpose, I chose the word *faith* as my focus. Still, eight out of eleven chapters are titled with the word *trial* as you can see. In each chapter, I highlight what characteristics of faith we find when enduring each particular trial. This way, we build a number of qualities of faith in order that we might come to a better understanding of what faith is. However, I never set aside a moment to develop a thorough explanation of the concept of faith. I purposely unpack its features in order to stay within the confines of James' letter. Maybe in future writings, I will divert more attention to defining faith more exhaustively. For this book, I believe that James wants us to know what faith looks like, not what faith is, and that is my aim.

On another note, it may be argued that trials and faith are not the main focus of the epistle (though both are mentioned frequently). Some might say that *wisdom* is the main focus. I am definitely sensitive to this argument and would agree with it to some extent. James does describe wisdom as the root of all life decisions. Depending on the source of the wisdom, we pass or fail the tests we face. The double-minded man is double-minded because he is adheres to both worldly wisdom and heavenly wisdom. He has two masters when he can have only one. I unpack this premise in chapter six more deeply. Still, while wisdom is the root, faith is the flower.

My hope is that you adopt the wisdom of God through James, plant it deeply within the soil of your heart and let faith grow and mature in your life so that you might enjoy the wondrous assurance of salvation.

Jacob Abshire
October 25, 2012

INTRODUCTION

In the summer of 1967, a young teenage girl dove into a lake not knowing just how shallow it really was. The plunge snapped her neck instantly, paralyzing her body from the neck down. She spent the next two years plagued with regret over the consequences of her youthful exuberance and grieving the loss of her mobility. She suffered depression and struggled with life, God, and her paralysis.

Her Christian friends, as sincere as they were, annoyed her by trivializing her plight and giving her advice and counsel that she really didn't want to hear. She grew tired of it all. Her heart was growing fearful and her emotions were numbing. Desperately wanting to understand her circumstances, she cornered a friend and asked, "I just don't get it, I trusted God before my accident. If God is supposed to be all loving and all powerful, then how does this demonstrate His love and power?"

Her friend responded by asking, "Whose will do you think was the cross?" She answered him confidently, "God's will, everybody knows that." He continued, "Think this through carefully, who entered the heart of Judas Iscariot and handed Jesus over for 30 pieces of silver? Who instigated the mob on the streets to clamor for Jesus' crucifixion? Who prodded those Roman soldiers to spit on Jesus and slap Him and mock him? What about Pontius Pilate, who caused him to desire political popularity above all and give mock justice to Jesus? Treason, injustice, murder, torture, how can any of these be God's will?"

In order to help her understand, he turned to Acts and read, "For truly in this city there were gathered together against your holy servant Jesus, whom you anointed, both Herod and Pontius Pilate, along with the Gentiles and the peoples of Israel, to do whatever your hand and your plan had predestined to take place" (Acts 4:27-28).

This young woman never regained her ability to use her body completely. However, by God's grace, she has grown wise in the theology of suffering and the knowledge that God, in His power and love, sovereignly perfects His children through the agony of trials.

Today, as a quadriplegic, she is one of the most popular Christian teachers. She has written over 14 books, a curriculum for Dallas

Theological Seminary, and she speaks regularly at a variety of events—building the body of Christ. We know her as Joni Eareckson Tada.[1]

Joni's story typifies the book of James. It is about painful trials and the maturing of our faith. On the surface trials might appear to be pointless, unnecessary and even surprises to God, but they are none of these things. As Joni's friend so wonderfully illustrated, things happen according to God's divine plan—a plan that has purpose. For the Christian, the purpose of trials is the perfecting of our faith.

In the following chapters, we will introduce ourselves to some rather hard-hitting trials and what they can tell us about our faith in God. In the short run, trials will ultimately reveal to us whether or not we really have true faith or whether we think we do. In the long run, trials will be used to develop and mature our faith and thereby stir up the joy of our assurance of salvation. One writer from the poetic prayer entitled *The Divine Will* said:

> For if I do not walk holily before thee,
> > how can I be assured of my salvation?
> It is the meek and humble
> > who are shown they covenant,
> > know thy will,
> > are pardoned and healed,
> > who by faith are sanctified and quickened,
> > who evidence thy love.[2]

The journey ahead of us will be terribly rough. God's word will indeed cut deeply to our souls and uncover sins that we never thought to exist. We will find grief and sorrow, shame and uncertainty, conviction and repentance. But in the end, and I do hope you make it to the end, we will find inexpressible joy and gladness. May God be with you during this journey. I am confident that He will.

---

[1] Story was derived from a presentation given by Joni at Biola University for its Centennial Chapel Series on September 19, 2007. Some portions are actual quotes. Joni Eareckson Tada. "Joni Earekson Tada Story." Life Story. 2009. Life Story Foundation. October 13, 2009. <http://joniearecksontadastory.com>

[2] Bennett, Arthur. "Man a Nothing." *The Valley of Vision: a Collection of Puritan Prayers & Devotions*. Edinburgh: Banner of Truth Trust, 2002. 14-15. Print.

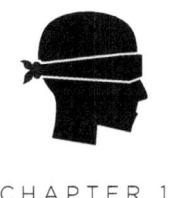

CHAPTER 1

THE TEST OF FAITH

JAMES 1:1-18

"the testing of your faith produces steadfastness"

"Come quietly, or there will be trouble." I've always loved that line. It was uttered by the robotic humanoid cop leering at the criminal with gun in hand. Trouble came. It does to us all. And most of us scoff at the warning to come quietly. We come kicking and screaming. Then we wallow in self-pity. What can we say? We are criminals.

The truth is, troubles are used as instruments in the hands of God. He uses them to chisel us, shape us, and make us more presentable both to Him and us. And by looking at you, I'd say you need some good trouble!

Like it or not, this is the reality in which we live. Troubles come. But our view of them in light of God's greater purpose will transform the way *we* come. We can kick and scream and fight and complain, or we can trust in the Lord and His sovereign plan to work out as He sees fit. I think it is worth it to do so. Moreover, God says that it is for our benefit. And that, my friend, makes it worth it. If you agree then the book of James is the place to start. It is a series of practical lessons on troubles, their purpose in God's greater plan, and your most beneficial response to them—not mention your reasonable and Biblical response to them. So sit tight and let it unfold. Just don't fight it. Trust me, it will be worth it.

To begin with, we will set a context by which we will view and understand the rest of the book. It is like setting the table before dinner. You could have a mess on your hands if you did it the other way around. Do you have your thinking cap on? If not, grab it and pull it tight. If you are restless, grab a "chill pill," whatever that is. You will be confronting some serious things about yourself and you need to know that. So, consider the words of G.K. Chesterton as your mantra, "I believe in getting into hot water. I think it keeps you clean." Let's not just get in. Let's dive in!

The People of Trials

Troubles seem to find their way to all people. Job observed that "Man who is born of a woman is few of days and full of trouble" (Job 14:1). Another writer said, "For all his days are full of sorrow, and his work is a vexation. Even in the night his heart does not rest" (Ecc. 2:23). Of course, there is that passage our spouses love to recite, "those who marry will have worldly troubles" (1 Cor. 7:28).

Troubles are all around us. This is especially true of Christians since we are inevitably an offense to the world if we are obeying God. In fact, Jesus made the connection of being His disciple and being in a world of trouble. To begin with, Jesus was purposed for trouble (Jn. 12:27) which came from even His friends (Jn. 13:21). And so He made the point, "a servant is not greater than his master, nor is a messenger greater than the one who sent him" (Jn. 13:16). This means that Christians are not entitled to a life better than His. To further this point, consider Jesus' words in John 15:18-21:

> **Christians are not entitled to a life better than His.**

> "If the world hates you, know that it has hated me before it hated you. If you were of the world, the world would love you as its own; but because you are not of the world, but I chose you out of the world, therefore the world hates you. Remember the word that I said to you: 'A servant is not greater than his master.' If they persecuted me, they will also persecute you. If they kept my word, they will also keep yours. But all these things they will do to you on account of my name, because they do not know him who sent me."

The early church had their share of severe troubles. Many of them were martyred in the most grotesque of ways. Even the first disciples suffered evils and death. The same is true of us today. If you are alive, you will face troubles. And, if you have been made alive in Christ, you will face it doubly.

For the sake of James' letter, the people of trials have been specified as James and the twelve tribes of the dispersion. However, the implications are quite relevant to us all—sometimes even those reading who do not believe. Let's look at our people of trials.

James, a Servant of God

My wife and her best friend were once grabbing some drive-thru at a popular fast-food joint. It was founded by Dave Thomas, who named this national chain of restaurants after his daughter, Wendy. The girls were in a rush. They were busy teenagers. Believe me, there was much to do. Needless to say, they wanted their "fast" food ... fast.

They placed their order and moved ahead to pick it up. At the window, they handed over the cash and observed a rather rude waitstaff. "You have to wait a minute," one unapologetically told the girls. Contrary to her statement, several minutes passed before the window reopened. The same grumpy teller holding two bags of food extended her arms.

My wife's friend was not excited about the service, but she was in no position to make management changes that might help morale. She was just another hungry customer. However, to her it was worth it to try and, at least, lighten the air some.

> **For James, a brother made a big difference in big ways.**

"Do you know who I am?" She said to the testy teller who stared back as if no one was speaking to her. There was a slight pause to gather some thoughts. She is quick on her feet. So what came next was bold. "I'm Wendy!" Yeah, that will show them.

Sometimes, who you know means the world to your circumstances. On the other hand, sometimes it is as useless as an ashtray on a motorbike. For James, a brother made a big difference in big ways. He was the brother of Jesus, the Son of God.[1]

Of course, this does not mean that James was also a son of God. Rather, they were half-brothers. Jesus had no biological father. James did. His father was Joseph. Still, both Jesus and James were born of

---

[1] For an argument for James being the brother of Jesus, see the appendix article: *James, the Brother of Jesus*.

Mary.

If this is borderline heresy for you, consider a few things before throwing this book in the fire. First of all, the Bible tells us that when Mary conceived our Lord, she was a virgin (Matt. 1:23; Lk. 1:34) and that God would miraculously make her pregnant with His Son (Lk. 1:35). Jesus was therefore "from heaven" and not "from the earth" (1 Cor. 15:47). In fact, Matthew records that Joseph was not intimate with her "until she had given birth" to Jesus (Matt. 1:25). Clearly, Jesus was *the* Son of God (note the emphasis).

None of this precludes the possibility of Joseph and Mary joining together afterward in order to have more children. In fact, there are several places in Scripture where Christ is said to have brothers and sisters.

Take Matthew 13:54-56 for example. When Jesus was visiting his hometown and teaching in the synagogue, the people were astonished and said, "Where did this man get this wisdom and these mighty works? Is not this the carpenter's son? Is not his mother called Mary? And are his brothers James and Joseph and Simon and Judas? And are not his sisters with us?" Other passages like Matthew 12:46, Mark 3:31, Luke 18:19 and John 7:1-10 mention Jesus' brothers and sisters. Again, after the resurrection, they are found "devoting themselves to prayer" with the disciples in Jerusalem (Acts 1:14).

The evidence is clear—Mary had more children after she gave birth to the Lord. For this reason, Jesus is called Mary's "firstborn son" (Lk. 2:7). If this were not true, Jesus would have been called Mary's "only son" but was not.

Yes, James knew somebody with pull. It might have been much like being Wendy in a Wendy's fast-food line (but in a really trivial sense).

James grew up with the Lord. He saw the perfections of God in a human brother. He sat in the same pew, ate the same food, and played many of the same games. So, if anyone could drop names it was James —second born of Mary and brother of Jesus the Son of God.

Yet, there is no mention of kin in his entire letter. Rather, he calls himself **"a servant of God and of the Lord Jesus Christ"** (Ja. 1:1). This might imply that James was already well known by his audience. But you and I both know, at least from our modern perspective, even if a person is known for something they will still hang it over your head to make sure you don't forget it. This was not true of James. I'm sure that the people knew that he was the Lord's brother, but there is something deeper to why he doesn't mention it. I think it reveals to us a rich truth about James' faith. It was proven to be real.

It will be tempting to me to go into the many characteristics of faith in the next few paragraphs. But, that would render the rest of this book redundant. Rather, I'll touch briefly on a few things that suggest a genuine and considerably godly change in the life of James.

James, the Sinner

We should first look at James before his conversion because it is a strong contrast to the time after. Remember that James was raised alongside of Jesus. They shared the same upbringing and parental guidance. Yet they were dynamically different by the time Jesus began his ministry.

James, along with his other brothers, didn't believe that Jesus was the Son of God (Jn. 7:5). Instead of loving him, they mocked him. They told him to go be with the disciples, those who listened to and liked him, and to give proof of his claims openly (Jn. 7:3-4). This was like saying, "Go be with your 'yes' men!" James was infused with the carnal Messianic misconceptions of the Jews and was probably tired of Jesus' innocence before his parents and others. Can you imagine growing up with the sibling who never does wrong?

Then, as if things could not make him more disgusted with his brother, James witnesses the crucifixion. Although it may have softened his heart since the kind of death was so gruesome and his brother was so innocent, it likely deepened his doubt. "A god who condemns himself to death is certainly not one who could rule the world," might have been his thinking.

James, the Saint

The cross provided some assurance of James' doubt. It was the lid to the bottle sealing the idea that his brother was tragically confused even with his good intentions. However, it was the resurrection from this cross that turned James one-eighty degrees. After his death and resurrection, Jesus personally and specifically appeared to James and he believed (1 Cor. 15:7).

In hindsight, Jesus was shaping his half-brother for years of strong ministry. By the many trials he faced and with the consummation of revelation at the appearing of the Lord, James became the intercessor of the Jews leading "the disciples of Moses gently to Christ." [2] Called from the Jewish misconceptions, James becomes the witness to those Jews still misconceived.

James, the Leader

Jesus was a famous person from His youth to His death. Remember that King Herod tried to kill Him as a child. In fact, he murdered all children under two years of age in order to ensure Jesus' death (Matt. 2:16-18). When Jesus was twelve, He amazed the teachers of Jerusalem (Lk. 2:47). During the time of His ministry He attracted crowds on numerous occasions, one of which sentenced him to His death on the cross. After this, the two disciples on the road to Emmaus were astonished that someone had not heard about Jesus (Lk. 24:18-24).

For this reason, James' conversion was nothing small. He grew up with Jesus. He was His earthly brother. He rejected Him. But now he has become a believer in Him. By the time he penned his letter, he was nearly as popular as Jesus was, but this was due to Jesus. This reality made James quite the follower of Christ so much so that he was promoted to leadership in the Jerusalem church.

We discover this in one of Paul's letters. Paul is defending his apostleship and uses James as the proof. He says that he "went up to Jerusalem to visit Cephas [Peter] and remained with him fifteen days. But I saw none of the other apostles except James the Lord's brother" (Gal. 1:18-19). Although, James was not one of the twelve, Paul calls him an apostle. Further in the same epistle, Paul refers to him as one of the three pillars including Peter and John (Gal. 2:9). Apparently, James was prominent enough to validate Paul's apostleship. (This was an excellent moment for dropping names by the way.)

Also, in Acts 15:13, James is mentioned as the pastor of the Jerusalem church and therefore, "the ecumenical leader of Jewish Christianity" as one historian put it.[3] When disputes over Mosaic customs of circumcision threatened the unity of the Church, James

---

[2] Schaff, Philip. *History of the Christian Church*. Peabody, MA: Hendrickson Publishers, Inc., 2006. p.265.

[3] Ibid., 265.

proposed a compromise that saved it. In addition, he most likely prepared the synodical letter to all believers on behalf of the Council (Acts 15:23). Jerusalem was the theocratic metropolis and James was in the oval office. You could call him the president of the United Christians of Earth (if there would have been such a organized nation).

Lastly, although there is quite more evidence than just this, the angel of the Lord tells Peter to "tell these things to James and to the brothers" (Acts 12:17). The "things" he was to tell included that the Lord freed Peter from imprisonment. Peter was to report the news to James. He needed to know above others.

Evidently, he had the most prominent leadership role in Jerusalem—even among the apostles. However, we have no reason to believe that it was because he was the brother of Jesus. Rather, we have reason to believe that it was because of his godliness and wisdom—both of which came from his brother. His big brother brought about a big change in his heart which promoted him to a big role in the church.

> **His big brother brought about a big change in his heart.**

James, the Slave

When all of the facts settle, the most astonishing thing that we know about James is what he says in the first few words of his epistle, "**a servant of God and of the Lord Jesus Christ**" (Ja. 1:1).

The word translated "servant" here is the Greek word *doulos* which means most literally "slave". In order to be less offensive to American readers, most of our Bible translations render it as "servant" which is the Greek word *desmios* which is not used in this passage. James is calling himself a slave and not a servant. There is a difference. A slave was bound to his owner. He lived to please his master-owner. A servant was a hired hand who could quit at any time and negotiate his labor and wages. A servant had a choice; a slave had no choice.

James is doing more than just refraining from name-dropping to impress his readers. He is going far beyond that to lower himself to the lowest state.[4] It is like being the CEO of a major corporation and introducing yourself as an office janitor.

---

[4] For information on the use of *doulos* in the Bible, refer to my appendix article, *Slaves and Scriptures*, found in my book, *Forgiveness: A Commentary on Philemon*. It is available at http://www.t411.com.

James was a slave of God and a slave of the Lord Jesus Christ. I guess you can say that he did drop a name. But it was not like how we do it. He mentions the name of Jesus, but not as "my brother." In Greek, it is *kurious* which means "master". A slave is not a slave if he has no master. And so he draws our attention to the greatest master of all and one who used to be his brother.

There is another relationship communicated here. It would have been evident to his Jewish readers. By referring to himself as a "slave of God," he is using an honorable title. Luminaries of the Old Testament, such as Abraham (Gen. 26:24), Isaac (Gen. 24:14), Jacob (Ezek. 28:25), Job (Job 1:8), Mozes (Ex. 14:31), Joshua (Josh. 24:29), Caleb (Num. 14:24), David (2 Sam. 3:18), Isaiah (Is. 20:3) and Daniel (Dan. 6:20), were called slaves of God to imply great honor. In the New Testament, Epaphras (Col. 4:12), Timothy (Phil. 1:1), Paul (Rom. 1:1) Peter (2 Pet. 1:1), Jude (Jude 1), John (Rev. 1:1), and even Jesus (Acts 3:13) bore the title *doulos*. Though a slave was a social substandard to the culture, it was an honorable label to those who knew God.

Imagine pulling into a fast-food drive thru with James. When your food is slow and your anxieties are high, dropping the name of God might get you your meal quicker than the next guy. (On the other hand, it might also get you some unpleasant surprises underneath your bread.) But James did not flaunt who he was or who he was related to. He did the opposite. This is likely due to the fact that he was very humble. I think this is true. Besides, I can't think of anything more humbling then growing up with Jesus—the only perfect human!

> **James went from sinner to saint to supervisor to slave.**

James, the Humble

I use these titles on purpose. Traditionally we hear him called *James, the Just*.[5] And there is reason for this. However, in this portion of his epistle, what appears to be most evident is that he is James the Humble. He went from sinner to saint to supervisor to slave.

This is the progression of the Christian life is it not? We are born sinners who are depraved and lost. And, when Christ appears to us through His word, we become saint. Then, God sanctifies us and

---

[5] Schaff, Philip. *History of the Christian Church*. Peabody, MA: Hendrickson Publishers, Inc., 2006. p.265.

moves us into mature leadership roles where we are instrumental in leading others to the same gospel that saved us. But, in the end, we look back and see that it was all by God's sovereign grace. We were only doing what we ought and what He did through us. We cannot take credit.

This is true transformation. And, with the help of some more historical details, we will discover that James' life was one of great paradox. Before he was converted, he was somebody drifting with the stream of the world. He was a Jew with the most common Jewish misconceptions. He was self-confident, high and lifted up. He shunned the obedience of Jesus and criticized His workings. He was every bit a good person by the opinion of the world, but quite the opposite by the opinion of God.

However, he came face to face with the reality of who Jesus was. He faced the Truth and humbly submitted. He considered the value of the world useless and became someone of value in the Kingdom of God. As he became more popular among the Christians, he became more of an outcast to the world. So much so that he was eventually killed. The paradox is that he was loved by the world and hated by God until Jesus saved him and made him loved by God and hated by the world. He went from worldly approval to worldly refusal. His life went from proud to humble.

James went from worldly approval to worldly refusal.

His life is an ironic tale of brotherhood. Consider the words of Jesus in Matthew 12:46-50:

> "While [Jesus] was still speaking to the people, behold, his mother and his brothers stood outside, asking to speak to him. But he replied to the man who told him, 'Who is my mother, and who are my brothers?' And stretching out his hand toward his disciples, he said, 'Here are my mother and my brothers! For whoever does the will of my Father in heaven is my brother and sister and mother.'"

Jesus was a new kind of brother to James. In times past, they wrestled in the dirt and labored with the wood and nails together. He knew Jesus to be the one who sat near him at the dinner table and in the synagogue. He grew up to know him as the seemingly powerless criminal who hung on the cross while the other Jews threw up their fists in anger. Afterward, he knew him as the one who died and was buried in a borrowed tomb.

But these things changed. By the time of writing this letter, James knows Jesus as the one holding the world on its axis (Ps. 89:11; Matt. 19:28; Mk. 14:61-62). The spiritual brother who laughs at those who are confident in their own power (Ps. 2:4). The head of every ruler and authority (Col. 2:9-10) as Lord of all who will not be mocked (Gal. 6:7). Now, he understands Him to be the One who ordained all of His own troubles while living on earth—even the evil done to Him (Acts 4:27-28).

James saw his brother in a whole new light—literally. Therefore, he could not call Jesus "my brother" with a good conscience. It lacked the reverence that Christ alone deserves. Rather, he calls Him, Lord.

Diaspora, the Scattered of God

Ever stomped on a giant ant bed to see a rush of little insects frantically run amok? I have. I learned, however, that this doesn't rid the yard of ants. Rather, it scatters them throughout it. Most of the time, stomping out one pile caused several more to pop up a day later. I was young when I learned this principle and it made my life miserable since I was the keeper of the yard, according to my dad.

There is something strangely similar about ants and Jews—I mean that respectfully. Let me explain. Since the early days of the Israelites, God has been sovereignly "kicking the ant pile" and scattering His chosen people throughout the known world.

Some point to the year of 926 B.C. when Shishak, the king of Egypt, invaded Jerusalem and "took away everything" (1 Kings 14:25-28). If it was not during this time, then it was definitely just two hundred years after when God, who was angered with their sin, "uprooted them from their land in anger and fury and great wrath, and cast them into another land" (Deut. 29:27-28).

Just more than two hundred years later, the Jews were deported by the Babylonians and again by Pompey which was closer to the time of Jesus' birth (about 63 B.C.). According to historians, there were as many as one million Jews in the city of Alexandria and at least ten thousand were massacred in Damascus. They were also all over Asia Minor and the Mediterranean. First-century Jewish historian, Josephus, wrote, "There is not one city, Greek or barbarian, nor a single nation where the custom of the seventh day, on which we rest from all work, and the fasts, and the lighting of candles, are not observed."[6] Jews permeated the world.

You wonder, "Where is the respect in that?" Behind all of the scattering was the providential hand of God. Yes, it was often a form of judgment. But in the end, it was purposed by God for something much greater. Far from my own purposes, God's design was to scatter His chosen people into the world so that the gospel would reach the ends of the earth.

Remember that on the Day of Pentecost, as recorded in Acts 2, "there were dwelling in Jerusalem Jews, devout men from every nation under heaven" (Acts 2:5). It says that they were hearing the disciples speak "in his own language" (Acts 2:6). Meaning, that the scattered Jews were gathered from various nations where they spoke different languages. There were "Parthians and Medes and Elamites and residents of Mesopotamia, Judea and Cappadocia, Pontus and Asia, Phrygia and Pamphylia, Egypt and the parts of Libyaa belonging to Cyrene, and visitors from Rome, both Jews and proselytes, Cretan and Arabians" (Acts 2:9-11). These were Jewish people from all over the known world hearing the gospel first preached by the disciples.

After this event, we read that Paul, the evangelist to the Gentiles, would travel from city to city to preach the gospel. Upon entering the city, he first visited the Jewish synagogues to give the gospel. And, when the Lord willed, he would use Jews to help him preach to the people there. This is why the scattering of the Jews throughout history was something very good in the grand scheme of things. From our standpoint, looking back that is, we can see God's hand all over it. However, to the people experiencing the scattering, it was sometimes full of suffering and sorrow. For this reason, I don't mean to trivialize their tragedies and losses. Still, I can't help but notice the sovereignty of God throughout it all. Even the worst of times will ultimately end in the goodness of God. This is true especially here. Evangelism began with the scattering of God's people.

Remember that the worst of all sins, the murder of Jesus, was a ordained and designed by God (Lk. 24:27, 46). It was a terrible sin.

---

[6] Against Apion, 2.282

Yet, it resulted in the greatest of things. Was Satan at work here? Sure he was. But even Satan is a tool of the Lord. Acts reads, "For truly in this city there were gathered together against your holy servant Jesus, whom you anointed, both Herod and Pontius Pilate, along with the Gentiles and the peoples of Israel, to do whatever your hand and your plan had predestined to take place" (Acts. 4:27-28). Yes, even Satan contributes to God's glory one way or another.

In regards to the ant pile, God's purpose was far different than mine. I might have been closer to illustrating the devil in this case (shame on me), because I tried to snuff them out. Surely, this was Satan's plan as well. But after smashing their homeland, they simply appeared elsewhere almost as quick as I stomped. There was no eternal purpose in my mind. However, God had one that would touch the entire planet with eternal consequences. By scattering the Jews, He was spreading the gospel.

> **By scattering the Jews, He was spreading the gospel.**

This is the idea behind the words **"to the twelve tribes in Dispersion"** (Ja. 1:1). The term "twelve tribes" was a common name for the Jews (Matt. 19:28; Acts 26:7; Rev. 7:4). They understood it to refer to themselves. It was based largely on the twelve tribes listed in the Old Testament (Gen. 35:23-26; Ex. 1:2-5; Num. 1:20-43; 1 Chron. 2:2) and rekindled in the twelve apostles of the New Testament.

The Greek word *diaspora*, from where we translate "dispersion," literally means to scatter seed. And, from an eternal perspective, that is the most appropriate name for the Jews spread out all over the world. By the time James was penning this letter, the Jews were dwelling in every part of the known world. Those outside of their homeland in Palestine were considered to be the Diaspora, the scattered seeds.

James writes to these people. He says, **"Greetings"** (Ja. 1:1). This was a common Jewish salutation translated from the word *chairein* which is an verb meaning "to rejoice, be glad." Although these scattered Christians were suffering various trials (Ja. 1:2), it was time to rejoice and be glad. This is the setting of the tone. Rejoice. It is the exhortation of James' letter. "Blessed is the man who remains steadfast under trial, for when he has stood the test he will receive the crown of life" (Ja. 1:12). Be glad. Be blessed. Greetings.

The Purpose of Trials

Whether you are dispersed or still under the roof of your parents, you will face troubles. There is nowhere to run and no way to hide. It is not unlike the game small children play when they close their eyes and ask if you can see them. Troubles can see you even if you close your eyes. This might be the reason that James wrote "*when* you meet trials" and not "*if* you meet trials." The meeting of trials is certain. The times and types of trials are not. If you are not certain about much, you can be about this: Trouble will find you—there is no need to go looking.

James thought this was good news. And no, he wasn't crazy. He said, "Be glad! Rejoice!" Then, continuing his train of thought, **"Consider it pure joy, my brothers, when you meet trials of various kinds"** (Ja. 1:2). You might compare it to telling Chris Carrier,[7] a young boy stabbed, shot and left for dead on the side of the road, "Don't worry, be happy!" Or to those young Amish students of West Nickel Mines School[8] who survived a hostage situation where five girls were shot and killed by a suicidal gunman, "You are blessed!"

> Joy is not due to the freedom from trials, but the victory over trials.

Sound insensitive? It's not. Rather, it is quite sensitive and hope-bringing. This is the purpose of trials. James says, **"you know, that the testing of your faith produces steadfastness. And let steadfastness have its full effect, that you may be perfect and complete, lacking nothing"** (Ja. 1:3). Joy is not due to the *freedom from* trials, but the *victory over* trials.

This is not to imply that we should never be sad, mourning, or even angry. It doesn't mean we should falsify our smiles and become some strange form of *The Stepford Wives*. Maybe quoting Bobby McFerrin's popular song title was a tad too strong. But still, underneath all trials is a spiritual gem that exceeds any trouble we may face—and I mean that literally. If I were a betting man, I would wage that at some

---

[7] Read more about Chris Carrier and his courages forgiveness of his attempted killer at http://www.christianity.com/Christian-Living/Features/11622274

[8] For more on the West Nickel Mines School shooting see http://en.wikipedia.org/wiki/Amish_school_shooting. I would also recommend reading *Forgiveness: A Legacy of the West Nickel Mines Amish School* by John L. Ruth (Harrisonburg, VA: Vision Publishers, 2007).

point in this chapter you do as James says to do, "count it all joy when you meet trials" (Ja. 1:2). I guess if you don't, it will mean that I didn't explain it well enough. But I pray that you do.

When we understand trials the way that God understands them, we start to no longer see them as trials, but something greater. Oh, and for the record, I am not leading you into some metaphysical, mind-over-matter stuff. This is truth triumphant. It is overcoming pride. It is the death of selfishness and a key to unlocking heavenly perspectives. And it begins with knowing the purpose of trials.

Yes, trials have a purpose. Paul taught us not to be disturbed by our afflictions "for you yourself know that we are destined for this" (1 Thess. 3:3). The word "destined" here is the Greek verb *cheimetha* which means "to lay or to put in a place." He was teaching that God literally positions us for trials. He ordains that we "meet trials of various kinds" as James put it (Ja. 1:2). Peter acknowledged this as well. He wrote, "do not be surprised at the fiery trial when it comes upon you to test you, as though something strange were happening to you" (1 Pet. 4:12). Accordingly, suffering is not just expected, it is purposed. James and Peter collectively say we should rejoice in our trials and "suffer according to God's will" (1 Pet. 4:6, 19).

> **Suffering is not just expected, it is purposed.**

But why? What is the purpose of trials? Simply put, trials are for the **"testing of your faith"** (Ja. 1:3). That is to say that your faith is put through all kinds of experiments in order to make a certain determination. Its like those dreaded tests you had to take in school. They measure your knowledge. Likewise, trials measure your faith.

I love a good assessment. Tests are fun exercises to me—especially on subjects that I'm passionate about. However, I always find it peculiar that no matter how sure I was about my answers, and even confident about my outcome, I am usually surprised at the questions I get wrong. Often, this is true of my spiritual assessment. Maybe I am far too confident in myself!

The idea of testing our spirituality is a biblical concept. It can be found all throughout the Bible. The Psalmist wrote to God, "You have tried my heart, you have visited me by night, you have tested me" (Ps. 17:3). In return, the Lord has said, "Consider your ways" which means "examine yourself" (Hag. 1:5). Paul wrote, "let each one test his own work" (Gal. 6:4) and to "examine himself" (1 Cor. 11:28) before the Lord.

So troubles should not disturb or surprise us. They are God's will. They are ordained and put in place. And we are dropped in the middle of them for the purpose of testing our faith. Now, why is that good news and what does it prove? Sit tight. This is where it gets crazy good.

The Proving of Trials

I don't carry around much cash. I'm a debit kind of guy. But I do recall a time when I paid a cashier with a one hundred dollar bill. Rather than slipping it into the register, she first held it up in the air. I had an idea of what she was doing but asked anyway. Apparently, there is a security thread embedded in the bill that can only be seen and read in the light. "Just making sure," she said to me.

Anything that has intrinsic value is subjected to tests in order to affirm its true worth. The cashier needed to make sure that the bill I handed her was really worth one hundred dollars. Had it been denied, the bill would not have been worth the printing costs. It would have been useless.

> **When our faith is held up against the light of trials, the value of our faith is revealed.**

The same is true of our faith. It has intrinsic value and worth and is sometimes counterfeited. When our faith is held up against the light of trials, the value of our faith is revealed.

Consider some passages from other biblical writers. The Psalmist wrote, "Vindicate me, O LORD, for I have walked in my integrity, and I have trusted in the Lord without wavering. Prove me, O LORD, and try me; test my heart and my mind" (Ps. 26:1-2). Paul said it this way, "Examine yourselves, to see whether you are in the faith. Test yourselves. Or do you not realize this about yourselves, that Jesus Christ is in you?—unless you fail to meet the test!" (2 Cor. 13:5). Peter wrote, "brothers, be all the more diligent to make your calling and election sure" (2 Pet. 1:10).

The testing of our faith proves our faith to be genuine or false. We will look at this more closely later in the book but it is worth mentioning that there are two kinds of faith: one that is natural to man and one that is not. James will later distinguish the two but it would be helpful at this point to note that one faith saves and the other does not. The faith that saves is supernatural faith. It comes from the Lord (Eph. 2:8). Testing the faith that we profess to have is the process by which we determine the kind of faith we really possess—the saving kind or not.

Let's be honest, God knows already. We don't. And this is why Paul instructs us to "work out your own salvation with fear and trembling." Why? Because "it is God who works in you, both to will and to work for his good pleasure" (Phil. 2:12-13). Saving faith is given to us by the Lord and He works this faith in us so that it is evident and proven. "He who began a good work in you will bring it to completion at the day of Jesus Christ" (Phil. 1:6). God's gift of faith will stand during trials and until the end. God will see to it. Tests will affirm it.

Again, this is why tests are purposed. They meet a need. They are divinely designed to expose true and false faith. Let me remind you of a passage where Paul encourages us during our troubles:

> "And we know that for those who love God all things work together for good, for those who are called according to his purpose. For those whom he foreknew he also predestined to be conformed to the image of his Son, in order that we might be the firstborn among many brothers. And those whom he predestined he also called, and those whom he called he also justified, and those whom he justified he also glorified." (Rom. 8:28-30)

Of course, troubles don't always point out to us that we have genuine faith. To some people, trials reveal quite the opposite. One preacher said that trials make the Christian better, but make the non-Christian bitter. Underneath it all is this important reality—trials tell us the truth. This is what it means to have your faith tested. A positive result can be very encouraging to a troubled Christian. However, a negative one will stir up the soul to seek forgiveness or affirm a hardened heart.

> **Trials make the Christian better, but the non-Christian bitter.**

Jude's letter is a good example of this. He wrote to Christians being troubled by the imaginations of false teachers. He calls them "ungodly people, who pervert the grace of our God into sensuality" (Jude 4). He compares them to Sodom and Gomorrah (Jude 5-7), Cain, Balaam, and Korah's rebellion (Jude 11). He says that they are grumblers, malcontents, sinful, loud-mouthed boasters, worldly, divisive, and devoid of the Spirit. The concern of Jude's audience was this: "What if I fall to their deception?" And Jude encouraged them by pointing out that God is able to keep them "from stumbling and to present you blameless before the presence of his glory with great joy" (Jude 24). He calls them the "beloved in God the Father and kept for Jesus Christ" (Jude 1).

This is the working of saving faith. It is God finishing the good work that He started. Faith triumphs over all troubles—even those of false teachers. When tested, it proves itself genuine.

How does it prove itself? Jude encouraged the Christians to be "building yourselves up in your most holy faith and praying in the Holy Spirit, keep yourselves in the love of God, waiting for the mercy of our Lord Jesus Christ that leads to eternal life" (Jude 20-21). Genuine faith draws itself to God expressing a love for Him above everything else.

This is what John had in mind when he taught us to test the spirit of others. He argues that those born of the Spirit of Christ will prove to be Christ-like. The true gift behind faith is the Spirit Himself. Faith is His virtue and He lives within us. "Anyone who does not love does not know God, because God is love" (1 Jn. 4:8). This is synonymous with the test of faith. If our affections are on the Lord and of the Lord, then our faith parallels. So we know that we have genuine faith if we find a godly love because we know that godly love and faith are "given us of his Spirit" (1 Jo. 4:13). And His love "is perfected in us" (1 Jo. 4:12) through various trials. Thus, "we know the Spirit of truth and the spirit of error" (1 Jo. 4:6).

> **Faith triumphs over all troubles.**

Let's go back to James and continue. **"The testing of your faith produces steadfastness. And let steadfastness have its full effect, that you may be perfect and complete, lacking in nothing"** (Ja. 1:3-4). Hopefully, this is starting to fit together now. The testing of our faith produces endurance. It works patience in us. It keeps us and carries us through trials so that we are victorious on the other side. The faith that God has so graciously given us shines through our troubles and proves to be genuine. Then, once our testing brings about patience, overtime we are matured and perfected so that we lack nothing.

My friends, that is the crazy good news I was referring to. This is the victorious end. Trials make the Christian better, not bitter. They make us more like Christ and more pleasing to the Lord. They conform us to Him and prepare us for heaven. For this reason, we should consider it joy when we are troubled in various ways. It is proof that God is doing something in us. He is building us up in holiness and making us godly. If you can allow that to settle in your heart you might not see trials as your enemy any longer. "Bring it on!" I say.

The Payoff of Trials

I hope that I am not exaggerating the point here. I really don't like the hard-pressed troubles I must endure while testing my faith but that is far from my mind when I think about the wondrous work being done in my heart through it all. Still, the reality is, I sometimes do not remember. All of us have this tendency. We are not perfect yet. We are still being tested and purified.

James understood this. After pointing out how trials are God's way of perfecting us so that we are "lacking in nothing," he continues, **"If any of you lacks wisdom"** (Ja. 1:4-5). The reality is that until God's work of maturing is complete, we will be lacking. In this case, James calls out those who lack wisdom.

Wisdom is the ability to see things the way God sees them. In regards to trials, we sometimes lack the ability to see the trials as God does. Sometimes we forget that they are testing our faith and for the good of our spirituality. Other times we simply do not see the godly response to the circumstances that the trials have brought. We are usually faced with many choices. One is the right choice. The many others are the wrong ones. Discerning which choice is which is a matter of wisdom.

> **Wisdom is the ability to see things the way God see them.**

Put yourself in King Saul's shoes for example. God's prophet, Samuel, gives you some instructions on behalf of the Lord. He tells you to go down to Gilgal and wait seven days until he appears so that he can offer burnt offerings and sacrifice peace offerings unto the Lord (1

Sam. 10:8). Now, you know that only Samuel can do that sort of thing —God forbade everyone else. So you do as he says. You go down to Gilgal confident that the Lord is with you.

But, when you arrive, you find "thirty thousand chariots and six thousand horsemen and troops like the sand on the seashore in multitude" (1 Sam. 13:5). Your army gets scared and hides. Wanting to obey the Lord, you patiently wait for Samuel to arrive. It is the seventh day and your enemies are before you. Samuel isn't there but the materials for the offerings are.

What do you think? What do you feel? What should you do? Remember that you are near powerless and a fierce army is breathing down your neck wanting to kill you. God's prophet said wait for him because offerings made by anyone else are forbidden.

You have at least two choices. You make the offerings and go to war or you wait and hope that Samuel comes through before it is too late.

This was a test for King Saul. Unfortunately, he failed the test and brought judgement against himself for making the offerings. Samuel arrived right on schedule but the offerings were already made. "What have you done?" Samuel said. "When I saw that the people were scattering from me, and that you did not come ... wine, wine, wine, poor me, poor me ... so I forced myself, and offered the burnt offering" (1 Sam. 13:11-13, more or less). Samuel said to him, "You have done foolishly," and now "your kingdom shall not continue" (1 Sam. 13:13-14).

> **Do not seek pity for your special temptation because it is not all that special.**

Saul's highest affections were not on the Lord. He did not fear God more than he feared for his own life and it was evident by what he did. Essentially, his trust in the Lord was questionable.

Sadly, this is our story in so many ways and at many times. Granted, you are probably not a king and I doubt that you are offering Old Testament sacrificial offerings. But the illustration is almost a one-to-one to many of our life situations.

What about your taxes? You really need to get that extra bit of return and you can, if you only smudge your numbers a little. Maybe it is your work. The company won't crumble if you tack on a few extra hours in your timesheet. Or maybe it is that dadgum speed limit. It is far too slow and you are running late. Do you get the idea? We are being tested all the time and in many ways. Some are more tragic and serious than others. But they are all tests.

Fortunately for us, God always provides a way out. The Bible says that "no temptation has overtaken you that is not common to man." This means that your test is nothing new. Others have been there, done that, and won the t-shirt. Do not seek pity for your special temptation because it is not all that special. "God is faithful, and he will not let you be tempted beyond your ability, but with the temptation he will also provide the way of escape, that you may be able to endure it" (1 Cor. 10:13). There it is again—endurance of trials. Don't you just love how the Bible interprets itself!

Ask for Wisdom

God gives us a way out to each and every temptation. Guess what? If you don't know the way out, you should **"ask God, who gives generously to all without reproach, and it will be given him"** (Ja. 1:5). Wisdom is our ticket out of tests. If we are troubled and seeking the godly way to endure and we cannot quite figure it out, we should ask God for wisdom.

I like how James brings confidence to us here. He says that God **"gives generously to all without reproach"** (Ja. 1:5). It is encouraging because we are full of reasons for reproach. We are sinners and we don't deserve any of His good gifts. Yet, "God is faithful," as Paul worded it (1 Cor. 1:9). He doesn't express disapproval and withhold His grace. Rather, He gives with liberty and generosity. He loves to give and we can be confident that He will.

There is a caution though. James adds that we should **"ask in faith, with no doubting"** (Ja. 1:6). I take this to refer to the doubting of God's wisdom and not the grace to give it. I don't think James is saying we should be confident that God will give wisdom. He cleared that up in the prior verse. Rather, he is telling us not to doubt that God's wisdom is right. To use the story of King Saul again, the wisdom of God was to trust Samuel would arrive as the Lord promised so that the offerings would be made appropriately. Saul doubted God's word, God's wisdom. He gave into his own wisdom that said, "If you want to live, you need to make the offering yourself—God won't mind." In thinking such, he chose the wrong wisdom. (We will talk later in the book about right and wrong wisdom.)

I think this is what James means by asking in faith. It makes more sense when you consider the rest of the passage. "**For the one who doubts is like a wave of the sea that is driven and tossed by the wind**" (Ja. 1:6). He is saying that the doubting person is a Johnny Fencerider.[9] He rides the fence of trust. He trusts in the Lord and then he trusts in himself. He goes back and forth. The only thing that drives him either way is the wind.

"**For that person must not suppose that he will receive anything from the Lord; he is a double-minded man, unstable in all his ways**" (Ja. 1:7-8). There it is. Asking for wisdom without faith, or trust in God's word, is pointless and therefore, unrewarded. Why would God give you something that you don't really want? See, often we make professions of things like our faith in God, but when the rubber hits the road, we do otherwise. By doing so, we are essentially expressing that we really don't want it.

In John Bunyan's classic book, *The Pilgrim's Progress*, a character who symbolized double-mindedness was called Mr. Facing Bothways because he tried to be both worldly and godly at the same time. Such a man cannot see the purpose of trials as he ought. He is confused by them since the world influences and clouds his godly thinking. For him there is no payoff to trials accept for a bitter end. On the other hand, for those who love the Lord, ask for wisdom in faith, and endure, the payoff is grand. It is wisdom—seeing things the way God sees them. This is one-step closer toward our spiritual perfection.

The Power of Trials

Trials are purposed by God and prove the condition of our faith. For the genuine believer, the payoff of trials is invaluable. In case it is not obvious by now, trials are powerful. They will humble the proud and exalt the lowly.

James has just mentioned how the person who waivers between the world and the Lord, claiming to be a Christian but trusting in what he thinks is best rather than what God says, is double-minded. He is

---

[9] It is never good to insert inside-jokes in a public writing, but I couldn't resist. *Johnny Fencerider* was a song performed by an old Christian pop group called Fresh Fish. If you are lucky, you can still find their music online.

unstable in all his ways, not just some. Now, James gets very practical.

Apparently, the polarization of the poor and the rich was a strong test for his readers because he speaks to the issue more than once in his letter. The times must not have been so different than they are here in America in our present age. Although we are a land who proudly speaks of "equal" opportunity, we have a wide separation between those who are poor and those who are rich.

In America, the poor are shunned and viewed as a nuisance, while the wealthy are revered as models of success and placed on a pedestal of worship. Our country's people are led by pop culture, which celebrates excess, exalts money, encourages self-indulgence and excuses immorality in favor of pursuing whatever you desire. One could say the American dream has morphed into the American nightmare.

Unfortunately, this dream has captivated the hearts of many Christians. Like the Pharisees of the New Testament, some leaders argue that wealth is an indicator of spirituality and God's favor. The more wealth you have, the more spiritual and blessed you are.

In Jesus' sermon contrasting these "spiritual" people, He taught us not to be like those hypocrites. "Do not lay up for yourselves treasures on earth, where moth and rust destroy and where thieves break in and steal; but lay up for yourselves treasures in heaven, where neither moth nor rust destroys and where thieves do not break in and steal. For where your treasure is, there your heart will be also" (Matt. 6:19-21). In the same sermon, He reminds believers to "seek first the kingdom of God and his righteousness, and all these things will be added to you" (Matt. 6:33). Jesus encouraged believers by reminding them that God is our provider and our focus should be on Him and not worldly things.

> **The American dream has morphed into the American nightmare.**

Nevertheless, money has a strange way of becoming our provider at times. So much so that we tend to have two masters when we are not careful. How we handle money, then, is a test. Some pursue riches in hopes of relinquishing themselves from the normal trials of life. But, if you have ever known a wealthy person, you will know them to be full of troubles. For example, they have troubles trusting friends, troubles of being robbed, and especially troubles of feeding their desires.

James has something to say to this. **"Let the lowly brother boast in his exaltation, and the rich in his humiliation"** (Ja. 1:9-10). There is an interesting thing here found in the Greek language. Bear with me, this might get a little technical. But it will pay off. Trust me.

Being Humble

The words translated "lowly" and "humiliation" are the same stem words. One is an adjective and the other is a noun. They refer to a state of being low to the ground. This was often said of slaves in their day. They were to sit at the foot or on the floor. They were low people who lived just above the ground. In verse 9 it means "low, humble" and in verse 10 it means "made low, made humble." Some translations have translated it "poor" so that the verses would read, "Let the poor brother boast in his exaltation and the rich in his being made poor." They simply substitute both words out with "low" or "humble" with the meanings provided above.

This brings a deeper sense to the passage. It reminds me of Jesus' words in the Sermon on the Mount, "Blessed are the poor in Spirit, for theirs is the kingdom of heaven." And, "Blessed are the meek, for they shall inherit the earth" (Matt. 5:3, 5). In this sermon, Jesus is contrasting the Pharisaical righteousness to that of genuine righteousness. He is teaching what it means to have true salvation—something that the most Pharisees lacked. The accumulation of things didn't mean that you were saved by God. In their case, it meant the opposite. It proved their faith to be in their own works and accomplishments. But Jesus throws it back in their faces and says that heaven belongs to the poor.

> The *humble* inherit the riches of salvation.

In the Sermon on the Mount, the word "blessed" could easily be switched out with "saved" so that it reads, "Saved are those." This was the point of the sermon. Jesus was teaching on who inherits the kingdom of heaven. It was those who were poor and meek.

Now, before you get carried away with this. Don't run off and tell you pastor that I said you are going to heaven because you don't make as much as the next guy. Remember that "poor" is a reference to humility. The *humble* inherit the riches of salvation. The *humble* are blessed beyond measure because of the Lord's provisions. This is indifferent to the income check you receive each week. You can make one million dollars or one dollar and it would make no difference to your eternal destination.

James' point here is that our trials are powerful enough to bring about salvation. Those who are already poor, financially speaking, are generally already humble. Why? Because they are humiliated by their needs. The rich, on the other hand, have no needs. They are not humbled. Therefore, they must *be made* humble.

Being Made Humble

The rich will be humbled by the removal of their things. James continues, **"like a flower of the grass he will pass away. For the sun rises with its scorching heat and withers the grass; its flower falls, and its beauty perishes. So also will the rich man fade away in the midst of his pursuits"** (Ja. 1:10-11). On one hand this is a good reminder God will humble the rich so that they are made perfect in trials. On the other hand it is a strong warning to the rich—trust not in your stuff! A good friend of mine has this philosophy about money: Get rid of it quickly or it will get rid of you! I like his thinking.

Do you remember the passage in Matthew 19 where Jesus is approached by the rich young man? He asks our Lord, "Teacher, what good deed must I do to have eternal life?" Jesus, knowing that this man's heart was set on his riches, said, "Sell what you posses and give to the poor, and you will have treasure in heaven; and come, follow me." The man was saddened because he loved his riches and could not part with them. So he left sorrowfully and without salvation.

With God all things are possible.

Jesus then seizes the opportunity to teach his disciples. "Truly, I say to you, only with difficulty will a rich person enter the kingdom of heaven. Again I tell you, it is easier for a camel to go through the eye of a needle than for a rich person to enter the kingdom of God." The disciples were troubled by this and wondered if anyone could be saved at all. Jesus confronted their wondering by saying, "With man this is impossible, but with God all things are possible" (Matt. 19:16-30).

The truth of the matter is this, a camel cannot go through the eye of a needle. It is so difficult that it is impossible, as Jesus puts it. This is why it is a work of God. Faith comes from God. Faith is worked by God. We are matured by God. Riches are not to be trusted. They cannot save us. Rather, as James says, they are here today and gone tomorrow. They look pretty and glossy today. But time will consume them. They are temporal and have no value in eternity. For this reason, a rich man who pursues these temporal things will fade away with them. He and his eternity.

The Profit of Trials

There is even more good news underway. For those who are poor in this lifetime, there is hope for future profit in the life to come. **"Blessed is the man who remains steadfast under trial, for when he has stood the test he will receive the crown of life, which God has promised to those who love him"** (Ja. 1:12). In comparison to the crown to come, one that is worn at the feet of Christ, everyone is poor in this lifetime.

In a sense, James is revisiting an idea that he had in the prior verses. He said that the testing of your faith produces steadfastness and steadfastness brings about perfection and godly maturity (Ja. 1:2-4). However, he adds to this some extra polish by emphasizing a doctrine known as "The Perseverance of the Saints." The Westminster Confession of Faith describes it this way:

> They, whom God hath accepted in his Beloved, effectually called and sanctified by his Spirit, can neither totally nor finally fall away from the state of grace; but shall certainly persevere therein to the end, and be eternally saved. [10]

The reality of salvation is the most superior blessing and it is guaranteed for those who persevere or, in James' words, remain steadfast under trial. Of course, those who will remain steadfast are those who have the Lord's gift of saving faith. For it is by this faith that they are able to persevere. Consequently, tests reveal to us whether we have that faith or not.

This is easily understood, especially in light of the prior passages.

---

[10] *The Westminster Conffession of Faith.* Chapter XVII. Of the Perseverance of the Saints. Accessed February 18, 2010. http://www.reformed.org/documents/index.html?mainframe=http://www.reformed.org/documents/westminster_conf_of_faith.html

However, it begs the question that may have been lingering since the beginning. What about when we fail the tests? What if we do not endure? There are two matters to consider here: *failing temporarily* and *failing finally*.

Failing Temporarily

Let us look at the matter of failing temporarily first. If we are honest with ourselves, we fail our tests more often than not and certainly more than we know or wish. We are sinful creatures. We were born sinners and sin remains in our bodies even after we are born again. James was not ignorant of this fact. He mentions in verses 2-4 that steadfastness is a constant refining work. It is not a one-time event. When we are reborn of God, we are not suddenly perfect. We require the transforming work of the Spirit to chip away and reshape us. This is called sanctification. It is the process of being made holy. James said that perfection would come, but until it does, we will be worked. Again, the Westminster Confession speaks to this end:

> **We require the transforming wok of the Spirit to chip away and reshape us.**

> Nevertheless they may, through the temptations of Satan and of the world, the prevalancy of corruption remaining in them, and the neglect of the means of their perseverance, fall into grievous sins; ad for a time continue therein: whereby they incur God's displeasure, and grieve his Holy Spirit; come to be deprived of some measure of their graces and comforts; have their hearts hardened, and their consciences wounded; hurt and prevalancy others, and bring temporal judgments upon themselves.

It is beautiful literacy, but sometimes a tad confusing. I'll explain. Christians, with saving faith, may fall to temptations and even remain in them for a time and for various reasons. They may hurt others in their sin and suffer the judgements of God on earth. However, this does not mean that they will *totally* or *finally* fall away. The idea here is that Christians, even genuinely saved ones, will sin but they will repent of their sin and return to a love for the Lord. In other words, they do not totally and finally reject God and turn back to their sinful life before they believed.

Failing Finally

This leads me to the others who will fail tests totally and finally. These are those who once professed to love the Lord and might even have a testimony, but they later turn away from God and never repent in their heart. These are the ones who do not endure to the end. They are not saints who persevere. John says this about them, "They went out from us, but they were not of us; for if they had been of us, they would have continued with us. But they went out, that it might become plain that they all are not of us" (1 Jo. 2:19).

John uses the word "continue" to mean persevere, endure, and remain. These are all synonyms that refer to staying in the love of Christ. Those who "went out from us" are those who totally and finally fail. They fall away, and then return to the life before their public profession of faith. It is key to understand that "they were not of us" from the get-go. These people were never born again. It only took some time to show. As one pastor said, "no one is secure who doesn't endure."

Why can John make such an assumption? Because he understood saving faith to be of God and by implication eternal, powerful, and persevering. He knew that God would not give a faith that was unable to keep His children. It is a virtue of the Spirit and therefore, it must and it will endure.

The Big Wall

In case I just lost you, welcome back. I know that it was somewhat of a deep thing to consider, but it is necessary to understand if we are to get the bigger picture and really appreciate our responsibility within God's powerful hand. Allow me to put it illustratively.

In summer camps, there was usually this obstacle course that included a big wall with a level at the top to stand inside. Dangling from the top of the wall was a rope. The object of the course was to get your entire team up the rope and on to the upper level. It was not easy at all. At least one person would have to go first and make it there on his own. Then, he could stand on the upper deck, lean over and reach down to help the next person. But there was ten feet between you and his hand. So you would have to climb the rope to make it most of the way.

The aim was to build endurance, strength, and team unity. The team would holler encouraging words in order to motivate you along the way. They were also there to help you get started and help you cross over. But the majority of the work was yours to do.

People would agonize up the wall and find great satisfaction once they grabbed the upper level and flipped themselves over to lay down on the other side in exhaustion. Every person would experience the hardship of the course and fall numerous times before making it to the top. Occasionally, there were people who, no matter how much others cheered them on, would not make it. They would try and try and then give up and walk away. In doing so, they proved that they did not have what it took to conquer the obstacle.

This is to say that we are surrounded by people who are doers and sayers. Some acknowledge that they are on the team and have what it takes. But during the obstacle course, they prove otherwise. We do not know either way. We too are finding out as we climb. If we are like many who after several failed attempts get frustrated and quit, then we have proven that we did not have what it takes.

On the other hand, if we have genuine, divinely given, virtuous, effectual, powerful faith, we will endure the big wall and stand the tests of life. And by doing so, we will **"receive the crown of life"** (Ja. 1:12). as our reward.

The Crown of Life

In the Jewish mind, the crown of life stirred up a picture of the ancient races. Paul alluded to them in a very popular passage: "Every athlete exercises self-control in all things. They do it to receive a perishable wreath, but we an imperishable. So I do not run aimlessly; I do not box as one beating the air. But I discipline my body and keep in under control, lest after preaching to others I myself should be disqualified" (1 Cor. 9:25-27). The writer of Hebrews exalted us "to run with endurance the race that is set before us, looking to Jesus, the founder and perfecter of our faith" (Heb. 12:1-2). The crown is the reward for a lifetime of endurance that only God can bring about. (It is like getting a reward for God's work! It is a win-win for us!)

> **The crown is the reward for a lifetime of endurance that only God can bring about.**

The crown is awarded to those who endure to the end—not necessarily those who endure to the end *first*. We are not in competition. I am not trying to reach heaven before you. There has been many before us both. We have no chance if that were so. Rather, we endure to win the crown that has our own unique name on it. It is waiting for us in heaven. It is polished up and the exact fit. God made it for each one of us who endure. And only He knows who will. You can bank on this because James says that these are what **"God has promised to those who love him"** (Ja. 1:12).

Do you love him? Then you will not give up after falling. Do you have the faith that only He gives? Then you will endure the hardships of life until the end. This is a promise to you and me. If you really love God, you will endure until the crown of life is placed on your noggin. What a great day that will be when we throw ourselves over the top of the big wall and fall to our rest on the upper level. We look up and see that it was Jesus who went before us and who was pulling us up along the way.

Likewise, we will look to our side and see the many who went before us who encouraged us and cheered us on (Heb. 12:1-2). There will be Paul, Peter and even James, and so many more. Looking back over the wall we will see the Spirit of God who was our invisible and faithful arm who carried us each time we grabbed ahold of the rope and tugged ourselves upward. What a day that will be!

Trials vs. Temptations

The sound of footsteps startled Adam after he ate from the forbidden tree. He faced a trial and failed miserably. His shortcoming led him to another. "Adam, where are you?" God said to him in a holy voice. "Have you eaten of the tree?" Adam replied, "The woman whom you gave to be with me, she gave me fruit of the tree, and I ate" (Gen. 3:8-12).

Do you know what Adam was thinking? He did not want to face up to what he did. He was trying to weasel out of responsibility knowing full well that he was the head of the marriage, the one whom God gave His command, and the one who stood next to his wife while she was deceived (Gen. 3:6). He was the one to blame for his actions. But you know what crossed his mind? I bet he thought that he was the victim. He says that it was God's fault for giving him Eve! This is probably what he thought:

> "You know, I did not ask to be made. God made everything. He made all this food to eat. He put the tree there and told me not to eat it when He could have easily left the tree out of the garden. On top of that, he gave me this beauty and I cannot deny her anything! It is His fault."

I do not want to add to the Holy Scriptures, but I like to fill in the blanks at times—just to help me understand things better. We do not know if those were the exact words that crossed Adam's mind, but they certainly seem like it once you read his accusation.

There is some level of truth here. God made everything—including the tree that was forbidden, the wife that was lovely, and the serpent that was deceiving. He did not have to, but He did. He chose to make what He made and whom He made. He also chose to make them in the way that He made them. He put them in a specific setting with certain smells, tastes, sights, and so forth. Every thing made in this story was made by God. The key here is the word "thing." Evil, a word of description, is not a *thing* that is made. It is a way of thinking or doing. The serpent, though made by God, acted wickedly and volitionally when it spoke deceptively to Eve thereby making itself responsible for its own actions and incurring the judgement of God (Gen. 3:14-15). Plainly put, God made the serpent. The serpent acted evilly. Eve acted evilly. Adam acted evilly. And so the story goes. God is absolved from all guilt of sin. Yet, in all of this, God sovereignly used these evil actions to glorify Himself and continues to do so today.

Of course, we can only speculate the answers to why God made all that He made and in the way that He made it (Rom. 11:33-34). We do know that He did so to bring glory to Himself and express the excellencies of His nature. Nothing could be greater. No other reason could be more perfect. This leads us back to the question, "Is God to blame for evil?" When I am put in the midst of a trial that God could have otherwise removed, should God be blamed for my temptation? Is it His fault that I fall? Certainly not! Although God sovereignly uses evil for His own purposes, He Himself is not evil, nor is He the immediate cause of evil. He restrains it, restricts it, and he uses it to accomplish His good.

James sets the matter straight by saying, **"Let no one say when he is** tempted, 'I am being tempted by God,' for God cannot be tempted with evil, and he himself tempts no one. But each person is tempted when he is lured and enticed by his own desire" (Ja. 1:13-14).

The words *tests, trials, troubles* and *temptations* have been used quite a bit now without a great deal of qualifications. I did this on purpose. I wanted to keep with James and not get ahead. So, if you have been waiting for it, now is the time.

The Bible makes a distinction between two kinds of temptations: one is external and one is internal. External temptations are usually translated as "tests" or "trials" since they are not necessarily tempting to all people. Yet, they can fall among everyone. This is the kind of "temptation" that Jesus faced. Hebrews 4:15 says that He was "one who in every respect has been tempted as we are."

One person asked me once if Jesus had sexual desires for women according to this text. But this is not what it means. The writer is referring to the external kind of temptation. I like to call it a test. We have to qualify it this way because Jesus was tested, "yet without sin." And, according to Jesus, it is sin to have such a desire (Matt. 5:28). If we connect the dots, that Jesus never sinned but was "tempted" as we are, then the temptation was not that of inner lusts, since Jesus did not have them.

> **A temptation leads you to sin and makes you fail, but a trial leads you to strength and makes you firm.**

This leads us to the other kind of temptation which is from within. This is the one that deals with our desires. James describes this kind of temptation as the one that all sinners have and it comes from our sinful heart. "**Each person is tempted when he is** *lured and enticed by his own desire*" (Ja. 1:14, emphasis mine).

The desires of sinful man is never that of the Lord. Paul wrote that "No one seeks God. All have turned aside; together they have become worthless; no one does good, not even one" (Rom. 3:11-12). Again, he speaks all inclusively, "All have sinned and fall short of the glory of God" (Rom. 3:23). When we are lured and enticed by our desires, we are essentially giving into sin. We are yielding to our depravity and not the Lord. These desires are sinful and so to follow them is sinful as well. Therefore, it is a grave error to say, "I am being tempted by God."

A temptation leads you to sin and makes you fail, but a trial leads you to strength and makes you firm. This is the essential difference between the two ideas. One is purposed and ordained by God. The other originates in our sinful hearts.

James' final point on this matter is important. In verse 15 he wrote, **"Then desire when it has conceived gives birth to sin, and sin when it is fully grown brings forth death."** Notice the progression and how it relates to trials. Twelve verses earlier James said that trials bring about steadfastness and steadfastness, when it is complete, brings about perfection. The difference between the two kinds of temptations is their chief end. Understanding them will help you steer clear from falling into sin and keep you persevering toward the profit of trials—the crown of life. It also equips you to have a better perspective on trials. To make it personal, my trials exist to perfect me, but when I fail at them, it is because of my own inner lusts that tempt me.

The Provision of Trials

So far, James has taught us that trials are purposed by God for His children in order to prove his work in their life which brings about spiritual maturity. They are powerful and will do the job. In the end, once trials have ran their course and the Christian has endured, the profit is eternal life—a crown in heaven. Finally, James points out that trials are provisioned.

"Do not be deceived, my beloved brothers." In other words, "Do not fool yourself." I take this as a good attention getter. Does it not make you wonder what you could be possibly fooling yourself about? Did you ask yourself, "Do not fool yourself of what?" As if James heard us, he adds, **"Every good gift and every perfect gift is from above, coming down from the Father of lights with whom there is no variation or shadow due to change"** (Ja. 1:16-17). It appears that James does not want us to be fooled about the origin of good and perfect gifts. If this is the case, and I think it is, then it seems a little too easy of a challenge. But I suggest to you that some people are in fact deceived.

This is a popular verse in the Bible. You may have heard it quoted more than once. I certainly have and thank God for it. But I fear that some who quote it so often misunderstand the broader context that shapes the meaning of the verse. If so, they are missing a truth that is life-shaping. Let me explain.

Keep in mind what we have learned so far. First, Christians ought to count it all joy when facing trials because we know that trials are used by God to mature our faith and reveal our sin. But, we are not to count our temptations as something godly. The inner lust is from us. The perfecting grace is from God. But where does that leave the trials?

Although verse 17 tells us that every good gift and every perfect gift comes from God, the primary emphasis is on the quality of the gift, not its source. James wants us to know that what God gives is good and perfect. (This is why we can exclude our inner lusts as gifts from God.) But, we cannot exclude our trials. They, as instruments of God, are included in what is considered good and perfect. Think of them as the gifts of circumstances. You are given a situation that will bring about the greater gift of grace.

Did you catch that? I will put it in other words. Trials are given to you as gifts from God because they come with God's perfecting power. Yes, a trial is your gift wrapped in a bow and handed to you for your growing in the Lord.

> **A trial is your gift wrapped in a bow and handed to you for your growing in the Lord.**

Now that is radical thinking. This does not imply that troubles are inherently righteous, but that it is good for God to give it and good for you to go through it. Therefore, it is a good gift "from above" (Ja. 1:16). Think in those terms next time someone recites the verse to you.

I remember preaching on this subject one evening. I began by asking for the audience to show their hands if they faced trials of various kinds the past week. Hands went up across the audience. I then asked them to keep their hands raised if they appreciated the blessing. No hand was lifted. Hopefully, by the time I finished, they saw the verse in a new light—pun intended.

Do you feel the full turn here? Count it all joy when your faith is tested. Count it all joy when you are placed among trials. Count it all joy when you suffer troubles. These things are the gifts of God and they are good and perfect because of their chief end.

This is key to understanding trials. And it is necessary if we are to grasp the final verse in this section, **"Of his own will he brought us forth by the word of truth, that we should be a kind of firstfruits of**

his creatures" (Ja. 1:18). The imagery here of firstfruits is the idea of giving back to God. Those who endure to the end are the ones who are given to the Lord from among all the creatures. The big 'aha' here is that the who, what, when, and how are all due to His own will and by His own word.

In light of this we can say nothing else but "Soli deo gloria!" (To God be the glory!) There is no boasting for us to do except to boast in what He has done in and through us. Did you ever think that trials and tribulations would be this sweet to the ear?

Things to Come

In the following chapters we will be guided through various trials that we face more often than you might think. James does not pull any punches. He does not keep one hand behind his back. He throws it all out there and it will be quite a ride.

In doing so, we will learn a lot about the nature of God's gift of faith. We will look at it from many different angles and through many different lenses that we now understand to be gifts of God. We call them trials.

I am confident that the words of James, inspired by God Himself, will be as challenging to you as they were to me. And that, in the end, you will have a brand new outlook on your troubles and how they relate to your faith.

> God help us as we journey through this practical and challenging book of trials. Teach us the nature of faith and mature it in our hearts and minds. Amen.

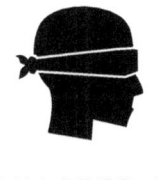

CHAPTER 2

THE TRIAL OF RESPONSE

JAMES 1:19-27

"be doers of the word, and not hearers only"

Ever heard of a *shift change*? It's that moment of the day when you have twice the help. I remember the time my wife and I spent in the hospital with our firstborn. There were some minor complications and the doctors wanted to keep an eye on him. Plus, the hospital was kind enough to help train us on handling this new life. Over the three days we stayed there, we saw at least six shift changes. One group of nurses would end their work day as another group began theirs, thus the schedules would overlap for a time and we would have two nurses in the room instead of one—or twice the help.

The same is true for James 1:19-27, only in this case it is an overlapping of thoughts. The author is finishing one idea (the nature of trials), and shifting into the first example of a trial. On one hand, this passage is about trials. On the other hand, it is our first test and practical challenge, giving us twice the benefit, like two nurses on duty at the same time. Thus we have twice the richness and twice the guidance due to double the truths. (And as I told the church, this means twice the time to get through one sermon!)

Already James has introduced a concept radically different from what we would naturally think. He taught us that trials are good for the Christian because they accomplish two things. First, they prove the existence of genuine faith. That is to say, they tell us if our trust in God is real. Trials either assure us of our salvation or they warn us of our self-deception.

Secondly, James teaches that if our faith is truly of God (Eph. 2:8), trials will bring spiritual maturity. For this reason, we are to be joyful when we face trials. To the true Christian, trials mean only good things (Rom. 8:28). Spiritual maturity, as James describes it, is the cultivation of wisdom (Ja. 1:5-8) and humility (Ja. 1:9-11), so it is no surprise that he calls trials a good gift of God (Ja. 1:17).

James transitions from teaching believers how to perceive trials to explaining how to respond to trials. He then shares the process of how to become spiritually mature during trials. When we experience trials, how should we respond in order to bring about our spiritual perfection? The answer to this question was introduced in verse 18, "Of his own will he brought us forth by the word of truth." God gives us His word to see us through our trials and by doing so, He brings us forth. So, James continues:

> Know this, my beloved brothers: let every person be quick to hear, slow to speak, slow to anger; for the anger of man does not produce the righteousness of God. Therefore put away all filthiness and rampant wickedness and receive with meekness the implanted word, which is able to save your souls.
>
> But be doers of the word, and not hearers only, deceiving yourselves. For if anyone is a hearer of the word and not a doer, he is like a man who looks intently at his natural face in a mirror. For he looks at himself and goes away and at once forgets what he was like. But the one who looks into the perfect law, the law of liberty, and perseveres, being no hearer who forgets but a doer who acts, he will be blessed in his doing.
>
> If anyone thinks he is religious and does not bridle his tongue but deceives his heart, this person's religion is worthless. Religion that is pure and undefiled before God, the Father, is this: to visit orphans and widows in their affliction, and to keep oneself unstained from the world. (James 1:19-27)

True Faith is Receptive

"Can you dig it?" This was my way of asking my son if he understood what I just said. I thought it was pretty complex and certainly long-winded and so I wanted to stop and make sure that he got it. I thought it was funny when I said it, but he was only six years old and didn't understand the reference to the old movie, *The Warriors*.

James was much more careful when he wrote something similar. **"Know this, my beloved brothers"** (Ja. 1:19). Some translations render "know this" as a bridge word between verse 18 and 19 so that it reads, "So then," or something similar. Whatever the case, it appears to be referring to the teachings leading up to verse 19 and so it might be best to read as "Knowing this" or "with that in mind." The recipients weren't thrown for a loop like my son. They got the point.

We should, too. Consider all that we have discussed about trials (I'll spare you another reminder for the sake of time). James gives us some practical direction in light of it. **"Let every person be quick to hear, slow to speak, slow to anger; for the anger of man does not produce the righteousness of God"** (Ja. 1:19-20). Again, He is writing, "In light of what we have learned about trials, let every person be quick to hear, slow to speak, slow to anger."

This reminds me of a rather funny story that took place in the middle of a baseball game where a man lost his temper and expressed all kinds of anger—it was historical.

His name was Phillip Wellman. He was the manager of the Mississippi Braves, a minor-league baseball team. One summer day in 2007, he threw a major-league fit. A call was made by the home plate umpire that rattled him deeply.

Wellman charged out of the dugout and stood nose-to-nose with the umpire, screaming at the top of his lungs in what first appeared to be a typical baseball argument. After emphatically shaking his hands just inches from the umpire's face, he stormed toward home plate to make his point visually.

He got down on one knee and completely covered the home plate in dirt. Then, he traced a giant home plate in the dirt with his finger, exaggerating its size. Next, he marched down to the third base umpire to chew him out, too.

After that tirade, Wellman stole third base—literally. He ripped it out of the ground, tucked it under his arm and walked to second base before hurling it into the outfield.

Next, he made his way to the pitcher's mound, where he proceeded to crawl on his belly, like a soldier in a foxhole. He picked up the rosin bag and, acting like it was a grenade, pulled an imaginary pin and threw it at the home plate umpire.

He was still not done with his rage.

He then walked over and uprooted second base and strutted over to where he had tossed third base, taking both bases with him as he proceeded toward the outfield exit. In the final throws of his tantrum, he tossed both bases one last time, turned and blew kisses to the crowd, shook his fist in the air, and left through a door in the outfield wall.

After reflecting on it, maybe it was not as funny as I thought—at least not for Wellman. His temper that day earned him a three-game suspension. But the fans enjoyed it. They screamed and cheered him all the way. This was entertainment!

In actuality, and unfortunately for Wellman, God is angered by such shenanigans. He is partial to no man, according to James, who says, "You know better than that. You know what trials are for and you know how you should respond."

The Anger of Man

We are to be quick to hear, slow to speak, slow to anger. These three phrases ring of the same principle—never react in a worldly way. The world would have us rant, take it personally, pity ourselves, complain, scream and maybe even throw a few bases around. Moreover they would have us sue—to garner some reward for our haughtiness.

All of these responses are carnal and self-seeking. They miss the point which is to shut up and listen. This is because **"the anger of man does not produce the righteousness of God"** (Ja. 1:20).

If you allow God's words to lodge in your heart, you will have the right ammunition to war against the worldly tendency to express yourself when trying things happen.

To begin with, the anger of man is what we express when we handle things the way the world would. It is our worldly reaction and manifestation of frustration. Someone bumps our bumper and we become all hot under the collar and try to sneak the dent on the front hubcap into the insurance premium. Or, we are late for church and speed and a policeman [doing his job] has the nerve to pull us over. What was he thinking?

No, what are *we* thinking? We are definitely not thinking about what our anger produces. If we would remember everything James has taught us so far, we would have been cautioned before letting our flesh take over. We would remember that getting all worked up is not going to produce spiritual maturity which is the righteousness of God. James told us that God does not use our anger to produce such perfection in us. If our expressions do anything, they are having the reverse effect. They are making us more like the world we live in, professing the sinful nature we once had (2 Cor. 5:17).

The Implanted Word

Rather than our anger, God uses trials and "**the implanted word**" (Ja. 1:21). Were you not expecting this? It is exactly where James goes next. But before getting there, he tells us to "**Therefore put away all filthiness and rampant wickedness**" (Ja. 1:21). The action "put away" is from the Greek word, *apothemenoi* which means "put off, lay aside." It serves as an excellent illustration to what God would have you inscribe in your heart.

> **Getting all worked up is not going to produce spiritual maturity.**

Picture being a worker of the field during those times. You cultivated the ground and harvested the crops. Day by day you pushed and pulled and struggled and lifted until you and your clothes were drenched with sweat and dirt. And you walk into your home where your wife has cleaned and prepared food. The first thing you would do is shed your clothes and put on clean ones. (If you cared for your wife, you would shower too.)

This is the idea behind the verb. Put the dirty clothes away. Take them off and cast them aside. But the imagery doesn't stop there. The word "**filthiness**" (Ja. 1:21) comes from a word that meant "ear wax." Does that sound out of place? It shouldn't. Let's read the passage again with our new context. We will paraphrase, of course. "Let every person be quick to hear, slow to speak ... put away all the dirty ear wax." Is it starting to make more sense to you?

The word "filthiness" actually refers to any moral defilement or impurity. James understood these things to be like wax in your ear impairing your hearing. It is the moral sins that cloud your hearing and understanding, confusing your judgment and reception. They are the stain of guilt and shame that weigh on your heart and mind after committing such crimes against the Lord. These things clog your hearing because your mind and heart are dividing their attention two ways—to the Lord, but more so to the sin.

When counseling a friend who once asked me about his problem with understanding and retaining the truths of the Bible, I brought him to this very passage and asked him if he was struggling with a particular sin—perhaps a habitual one. It might be lying to your parents, cheating on your homework or even an addiction to pornography. Since these are sins that we have great difficulty overcoming, we find ourselves struggling with the guilt they bring us each time we give in to them. Most of the time, this guilt hangs over us long after the sin is committed and it acts as a fog that lingers in our mind, preventing us from thinking deeply of God's rich truths.

On the other hand, there is another kind of sin that James mentions which has the same effect on us. It is "**rampant wickedness**" (Ja. 1:21) which means evil in abundance. One preacher related it to the storage of sin, the buildup of evilness that you keep hidden in order to prevent accountability. It is the secret things we have deep in our heart that only we know about and hold onto. Like any other, these sins rob you from thinking and meditating on the Lord and His goodness. It is difficult to focus our attention on Him when we know that secretly (though not to Him) we have sins that follow us around. They have grown like weeds among the flowers of our heart's garden. They creep and intermingle and go unresolved by accountable agents. These might be sins of bitterness accumulated over time by withholding forgiveness of others. It could be accrued grudges and gossip. On the other hand, it could be something as terrible as murder or adultery. It is whatever sin you have bottled up inside your heart.

> **In order to grab hold of the knowledge of His word, we must first let go of the things that weigh us down.**

I have often wondered if God withholds the deep truths from our contemplation as a way of chastising us for our lenience with sin. Jesus withheld the truths of God from the Pharisees due to their sinful hearts. This was one of His purposes in using parables (Mk. 4:10-12). Since we Christians long to understand God's Word, we reach up to Him with great expectation. Yet, we often keep our other hand gripped tightly to the ground. In order for us to enjoy the peace that He so graciously gives through the knowledge of His word, we must first let go of the things that weigh us down (1 Cor. 2:14).

James tells us to shed both of these kinds of sins, to rid ourselves of them. The reason is that we cannot hear the word of God. Once you shed these things, you can "**receive with meekness the implanted word**" (Ja. 1:21). This is how God matures and perfects us when trials occur.

I like how this breaks down. To begin with, we are to receive the word "**with meekness.**" This is having humility. (We will cover this word more deeply in chapter six.) Have you ever known someone to be in need and when someone else is there to meet the need, the needy person begins making demands? This happened to me once. A man drove up next to me in a parking lot one night. He asked me for money to get some gas because he could not afford it and needed to get home. I was happy to oblige. I pulled out a five dollar bill and gave it to him. He looked at it and said to me, "Is that it? Do you not have a ten?"

Not to sound insensitive, but this man was not being humble. I did not tell him this, but he should have taken what was given to him and not made demands—especially when he was in need. Neither should we. I hear time and time again how Christians are struggling with everyday troubles and they turn to God for one particular thing, like they know exactly what they need. Except they don't and neither do we. Rather than telling God what to give us, we should open our hands and take whatever He provides. We should not refuse the word of truth as if we know better. This is arrogance. We should be like a child in need. We should tell the Lord our troubles and expect what He gives us is for our own good.

> **We should not refuse the word of truth as if we know better.**

Secondly, we are to receive the implanted word and not the word the world offers. Believe it or not, the word you receive is just as important, if not more so, than the way you receive it.

It is the implanted word. The word "**implanted**" is no stranger to us today—especially here in America. We know much about implants. We can get all types of implants. In fact, there is a new craze for male implants. We can now get them in the strangest places—the strangest to me being the calf.

There are guys who wear shorts in public who are concerned about the size of their calf muscles. They want the girls to notice them and so they add a bit of diameter to their lower legs. That wins the ladies every time, supposedly. (If you could see me right now you would notice my sarcastic facial expression—made without any surgical assistance, I might add.) Maybe the girls do like it. But it does not win the praise of God.

Rather, God is pleased when we have the implanted word. And the good news is that all who have been born again have been implanted with the word of God. When we are converted, Jesus comes to take up residence in our hearts. He is the living Word. So if we have Christ, we already have the word implanted. Our problem is not that we do not have it; rather it is that we have not learned to listen to it, to listen to Him. However, we would do well to do so since the Word **"is able to save your souls"** (Ja. 1:21).

For this reason our first characteristic of genuine faith is our reception of the Word of Truth. True faith is receptive. It quiets the mind, humbles the heart, sheds the sin, and receives whatever God teaches.

True Faith is Submissive

G.I. Joe was my favorite cartoon as a young boy. I hated to miss an episode. (In fact, I have almost the entire collection on DVD today!) At the end of every show, there was a short public service announcement where the Joes would teach us boys good things, such as staying safe distances from downed power lines. (That was my most memorable one.) The stories and teachings always changed but the way the show ended did not. It occurred each time with one of the Joes saying, "Now you know, and knowing is half the battle."

Funny thing about it was they never mentioned what the other half is. But I think I know. It is doing. At least, that is the case here in James. Faith is receptive to "the implanted word, which is able to save your souls" (Ja. 1:21). But receiving is ... well, only half the battle.

James adds to that, **"be doers of the word, and not hearers only, deceiving yourselves"** (Ja. 1:22). The word here is a reference back to the "implanted word" in verse 21. It is the word of truth (Ja. 1:18). For this word we are to put away our sins and evil behavior and be humbly receptive. And after we have received, we are to *do* what we have learned. We are to put the principles the Word of God teaches into action.

The command is in direct opposition to the phrase that follows it. We are to be doers, **"and not hearers only"** (Ja. 1:22). In other words, we should not hear and do nothing with what we have heard. We should hear and obey. This is because those who do not obey are **"deceiving yourselves"** (Ja. 1:22).

These are strong words but they cut right to the root of the issue. True faith is living and active and cannot be hidden under a lazy attitude. "Faith apart from works is dead" according to James 2:26. Jesus elevated doers above His own mother saying, "Blessed rather are those who hear the word of God and keep it!" (Lk. 11:27-28). Also, to His disciples He said, "If you love me, you will keep my commandments" (Jn. 14:15; 1 Jn. 5:3). Paul had this in mind when he wrote, "My beloved, as you have always obeyed, so now, not only as in my presence but much more in my absence, work out your own salvation with fear and trembling" (Phil. 2:12).

Our obedience is connected to our love for God which is the root of our belief. If we love and believe Him, we will obey His word. To do otherwise is to lull us into a false sense of faith. We may not love God like we think we do. That is a staggering thought and a warning for all who are lax in their obedience.

> **True faith is living and active and cannot be hidden under a lazy attitude.**

Hear and Do

Well then, what does it mean to hear *and not* do? What does it mean to hear *and* do? James gives us an example of both. First, **"if anyone is a hearer of the word and not a doer, he is like a man who looks intently at his natural face in a mirror. For he looks at himself and goes away and at once forgets what he was like"** (Ja. 1:23-24).

Haven't we all done that before? Have you ever shaved and nicked yourself a few times and, rather than bleeding all over your collar, you throw a small piece of tissue on it and hurry off to breakfast? Because you are running late, you forget to look in the mirror one last time. You hop in the car and head to work. Or, like my wife who was readying herself for church one Sunday morning and forgot one earring because she'd been interrupted by the children. We've all done something like that before.

During the times of James' letter, they did not have mirrors like we have today. They were simply polished metals like silver or brass. Those who were wealthy might have had one made out of gold. They were not that clear in producing one's image, but most people were able to get an idea of what they looked like. James is saying that the man who hears only, is like a man who sees himself briefly and then walks off and forgets what he saw in the mirror. This type of man does not intend to remember. He's indifferent to the reality of his appearance. He walks away without any resolve.

On the other hand, **"the one who looks into the perfect law, the law of liberty, and perseveres, being no hearer who forgets but a doer who acts, he will be blessed in his doing"** (Ja. 1:25). This man is quite different from the first one. He looks into the mirror with the intent to remember. It is worth noting that the Greek words translated "look into" are different from those in verses 23 and 24 where "look" is rendered. Here it means "to stoop down" as if one is getting into position to examine his image in detail. In the prior verses it was more of a casual glance and consideration. The same way you view your reflection in a store window when you pass. However, when the doer sees his reflection, he is concerned about his own reality and tends to investigate as a detective would.

> **When the doer sees his reflection, he is concerned about his own reality.**

The man who stops to examine and look into the perfect law, the law of liberty, is the one who is submissive to the word. Here, James calls the word of God a **"perfect law"** and a **"law of liberty"** (Ja. 1:25). When accompanied by the gospel of Christ, the law is a wonderful reflection of our true filth. We are blemished by sin and need a washing of regeneration by the Holy Spirit (Tit. 3:5). This law is perfect and liberating when the whole counsel is observed. The Psalmist wrote, "Oh how I love your law! It is my meditation all the day" (Ps. 119:97). And so is the heart of the doer of the word of truth. The condemnation of God's Law stirs the heart toward God's gospel. Thus, to the genuine believer, the Law is one of liberty. It condemns and saves (hearing and doing).

He does not walk away and forget. Nor does he fall away after learning of his own sin. He perseveres. He is steadfast and so he is blessed (Ja. 1:12, 25) and saved (Ja. 1:3-4). This is the one who grows mature. God produces righteousness in him until the final day where he is perfect before the Lord.

True faith does not only hear, but obeys. The first characteristic of living faith is eager reception of the Word of God. The second characteristic is eager submission to the word of God. True faith is submissive. It seeks. It investigates and examines. Then it obeys.

True Faith is Pure

If you have children, especially boys, then you are quite familiar with impurities. You may not think of your child that way, but it is true at times. My son is a builder. He builds inside and outside with wires and boxes and cables. He loves these things and he loves to make things with them. Outside, we have one of those "big toys" as I called them when I was young. It is sort of a clubhouse, swing set, slide, rope, and obstacle course all wrapped in one. I think this is one of my son's favorite places to be. He can spend an entire day outside making his "shop" where he works as the Master Electrician (no worries, there is no electricity out there).

After a good day of shop work, Justus will come inside and flop on the recliner. His hair is glued to his face with sweat. His cheeks are no longer pink, but brown and black. His clothes appear to be painted with dirt and grass. And the funny thing is, you don't have to see him to know he is not the same boy who went outside earlier. He has morphed into a catalyst of stench. He is sweaty and dirty. He is my boy mixed with some outside care. This is the idea of impurity—something mixed with another.

It should be easy then to define the word "pure" as James uses it in verse 27. It is "unmixed with anything else." Spiritually speaking, it is used in the Bible to refer to the soul washed from its sin and the truth unmarred by error. Jesus said that "Blessed are the pure in heart, for they shall see God" (Matt. 5:8). Paul taught that the deacons of the church should "hold the mystery of the faith with a [pure] conscience" (1 Tim. 3:9). It is to be "undefiled" by sin which is the synonym used by James in the same verse.

Things that are pure are untouched. They are altogether clean and free of contamination. They need not be washed or altered. They are in their clearest and perfect form. It would be appropriate then to describe the divine gift of faith as such. Since it is of God's nature, it is by necessity pure. Therefore, a trial, such as one of response, should reveal genuine faith to be clean and undefiled.

Since James has called us forth in our response to trials and our response to the implanted word of truth, he now helps us to discern what we have observed. He writes, **"If anyone thinks he is religious and does not bridle his tongue but deceives his heart, this person's religion is worthless"** (Ja. 1:26). This is basically the conclusion of all he has taught us so far in this passage.

Let's recap to make certain. He first said that we should "be quick to hear, slow to speak, slow to anger" (Ja. 1:19) when trials come. This is to say that we should not express our sin but humbly receive the instruction of God through His word. He then adds that receiving the truth is only half the response. We should also obey it because we are deceiving ourselves into thinking we are saved if we don't.

So this first part is like a summary statement. It reminds us that anyone who thinks that he is religious but does not hush, listen, or obey is thereby deceiving himself. His religion is worth less than a heater in Texas (where heaters are generally not required). Actually, the Greek word translated **"worthless"** suggests something far less than worth little. It is worth nothing. The word is *mataios*, which means "vain, empty and profitless." It implies that it really has no value and is capable of doing nothing. (At least heaters have *some* value in Texas, however small.) James says that your faith is *mataios* if it is not pure. It is a tall glass of nothing; you can't even drink it. This is the opposite of true religion.

Good Religion

"Religion that is pure and undefiled before God, the Father, is this: to visit orphans and widows in their affliction and to keep oneself unstained from the world" (Ja. 1:27). The word "religion" is not like what is meant today. It doesn't mean unwarranted, man-made rules and regulations used to cultivate spirituality. It is not a bad thing. Rather, it refers to our worship of God in the virtue of our beliefs and reverence. It can easily be substituted with the word "faith" if we use it to refer to our set of beliefs. So there is a good religion. You can be religious in this sense and it is noble.

James qualifies this good religion as something that motivates good works and godly living. However, we shouldn't get too hung up on visiting the orphans and widows in order to assure ourselves of our faith while neglecting other people and other things. These are good things and we should do them, but James means something much more grandiose.

Both orphans and widows were considered to be a lower-class citizen since they generally required assistance and rarely contributed to society. They were needy and often lost in the civil systems. There were no life insurance or adoption plans in the early church. Few would find it in their hearts to support them, since there was no reciprocation. This is still true of our day—even with our welfare systems. Caring for them required a special kind of love which can be found in God.

When the Lord instituted the nation's tithe, He commanded them to equally provide for the orphans and widows. "At the end of every three years you shall bring out all the tithe of your produce in the same year and lay it up within your towns. And the Levite, because he has no portion or inheritance with you, and the sojourner, the fatherless, and the widow, who are within your towns, shall come and eat and be filled, that the Lord your God may bless you in all the work of your hands that you do" (Deut. 14:28-29). There was also a strong consequence for disobeying this command, "Cursed be anyone who perverts the justice due to the sojourner, the fatherless, and the widow" (Deut. 27:19).

Paul taught this in the New Testament as well. In his instructions to the church, he told us to "honor widows who are truly widows" (1 Tim. 5:3) and if someone doesn't, "he has denied the faith and is worse than an unbeliever" (1 Tim. 5:8). This kind of instruction is in line with the character of God and therefore, a characteristic of the fruit of His Spirit that we should have if we are truly saved. It is not the specific work of caring for the orphans and widows only, but the love and care for anyone in real need and especially those who cannot give back. John explained it this way, "By this we know love, that he laid down his life for us, and we ought to lay down our lives for the brothers" (1 Jn. 3:16).

As somewhat of a sidebar, consider the implications of this. We are called to sacrificially give to those who cannot give back. This is essentially putting a value on those who have no inherent value. And the value of our religion (faith) is measured accordingly. What does this say about Jesus who gave of Himself for our benefit? We can give nothing in return since we have nothing to give (Rom. 14:23). We have no intrinsic value (Rom. 3:9-10). Yet we have been valued by God. None of us are valuable in and of ourselves. We only have worth when the Lord chooses us. (This principle will be important in the following chapter.)

There is another virtue mentioned here in James. It is **"to keep oneself unstained from the world"** (Ja. 1:27). This is a continuous action. It is an ongoing work of keeping oneself unstained, which is synonymous with being pure and unblemished. It is the word used to describe Jesus when He was sacrificed as a propitiating lamb. He was spotless (1 Pet. 1:19).

The idea here is that those who have a genuine faith will be discontent with the reality of their existing sin and the failure to not always victor over it. It is being like Paul, who upsettingly wrote, "For I know that nothing good dwells in me, that is, in my flesh. For I have the desire to do what is right, but not the ability to carry it out. For I do not do the good I want, but the evil I do not want is what I keep on doing" (Rom. 7:18-19).

The person of true faith is one who lives in a way to kill sin in his life (Rom. 8:13). He is always at war with the flesh and desires to be victorious each time. He seeks to be separate from the fallen world and not conformed by it. Genuine faith, then, is also characterized by its spotless character. True faith is pure.

Conclusion

If you have made it this far, you have tasted what is to come in the following chapters. We will continue to look at how we should respond to various trials and hopefully pull out some positive characteristics of true faith so that we can be sure of what it looks like. This way, we can work toward the goal that God has for us—namely, the perfecting of our souls, the maturing of our spirituality.

For now, we can be confident that when we are put in the midst of trials, God will bring us through them by the living power of His word. Therefore, we should resist the temptation to express ourselves in a sinful way and learn to be quiet and listen to God's instruction. We should not forget that hearing His Word is only the first of two steps. We must also obey it. This is true faith. It is receptive and submissive to God's wisdom and pure and sacrificial in its obedience.

CHAPTER 3

THE TRIAL OF PARTIALITY

JAMES 2:1-13

"show no partiality as you hold the faith"

"A dollar fifty," the lady said at the checkout. I handed her two dollars and told her to keep the change. She smiled, and I was pleased by the love I'd demonstrated. But what happened immediately afterward would be the true test. I walked away, feeling rather good about myself, and made my way to the cafeteria tables.

You might remember the scene. Seemingly endless rows of tables full of young chatterboxes and juvenile stages of segregation. Everyone belonged somewhere in the oversized room. Yet, there was always that one table where that one boy sat alone. No, I was not that kid. But looking back, I wish I had been.

Here, my love was examined—at least in my own heart. Before me was this opportunity to be a friend to someone who needed one. I could do as Jesus did and befriend one from whom others distanced themselves. I was a regular churchgoer and openly Christian. Yet the love I professed was worth no more than the fifty cents I'd given away moments before. Maybe I did it in order to feel better about myself, a sort of modern day exercise straight from the desk of a psychiatrist. Or maybe I was simply impatient and did not want to wait for the change. I do not know what my heart's intent was, but what I do know is that I failed the test of true faith by not loving as Jesus loved.

The test was well-worded by John: "But if anyone has the world's goods and sees his brother in need, yet closes his heart against him, how does God's love abide in him?" (1 Jn. 3:17). An excellent question, and one I should have asked myself each day I saw him sitting alone. It was not that he needed money for lunch or clothes for his back. It was that he needed acceptance and for someone to see him as a real person. That was the underlying problem. So John continues, "Little children, let us not love in word or talk but in deed and in truth" (1 Jn. 3:18).

I never did sit next to the boy. I cannot recall the reason, but I am confident that it had something to do with him being him and me being me. We did not belong together according to the world. There were reputations on the line. I had my pride (both literally and metaphorically). There was no advantage to my sitting next to him or being the one to carry the conversation.

Peter did something similar. (Not to let myself off the hook, but to give a biblical example.) He was gladly eating "with the Gentiles; but when they came he drew back and separated himself, fearing the circumcision party" (Gal. 2:12). In their time, the Jews were the "pride" and the Gentiles were the "castaways." And although Peter believed the gospel was good news for those outside the pride as much as it was for those inside, he did what he thought was to his own advantage.

Whereas Peter had Paul to rebuke him (Gal. 2:11), I had no one, or so I thought, since the company I surrounded myself with was just like me. However, there is always someone to oppose me—and you as well. And he will continue to oppose us until we act like we love the Lord whom we say we love. His name is James and he brought a sword to mortify our sin of partiality. He wrote this:

> My brothers, show no partiality as you hold the faith in our Lord Jesus Christ, the Lord of glory. For if a man wearing a gold ring and fine clothing comes into your assembly, and a poor man in shabby clothing also comes in, and if you pay attention to the one who wears the fine clothing and say, "You sit here in a good place," while you say to the poor man, "You stand over there," or, "Sit down at my feet," have you not then made distinctions among yourselves and become judges with evil thoughts? Listen, my beloved brothers, has not God chosen those who are poor in the world to be rich in faith and heirs of the kingdom, which he has promised to those who love him? But you have dishonored the poor man. Are not the rich the ones who oppress you, and the ones who drag you into court? Are they not the ones who blaspheme the honorable name by which you were called?
>
> If you really fulfill the royal law according to the Scripture, "You

shall love your neighbor as yourself," you are doing well. But if you show partiality, you are committing sin and are convicted by the law as transgressors. For whoever keeps the whole law but fails in one point has become accountable for all of it. For he who said, "Do not commit adultery," also said, "Do not murder." If you do not commit adultery but do murder, you have become a transgressor of the law. So speak and so act as those who are to be judged under the law of liberty. For judgment is without mercy to one who has shown no mercy. Mercy triumphs over judgment. (James 2:1-13)

True Faith is Impartial

We typically talk about God being all knowing and powerful, nearby and transcendent. We say that He is forgiving and righteous, merciful and gracious, perfect and holy. But we sometimes forget that He is equally impartial in every way. He is not a respecter of persons.

Moses described Him as "God of Gods and Lord of Lords, the great, the mighty, and the awesome God, who is not partial and takes no bribe" (Deut. 10:17). This is quite a thing to consider. When Moses desires to express God's greatness, he doesn't turn to the characteristics mentioned earlier. He says that God is impartial. This is not because Moses thought less of God in other ways or because he was not acquainted with God's other characteristics. Moses was quite familiar with God in many informative ways. God taught him audibly and personally as well as inwardly and through real-life lessons.

> **God judges men based on what matters and not on face value.**

Moses knew the Lord. He didn't think God was less of a being in any one quality. That is why Moses' description is so intriguing. Out of all the reasons why he can refer to God as "the great, the mighty, and the awesome God," he chose impartiality. This is significant. God is celebrated, powerful and magnificent because He judges men based on what matters and not on face value. This is why He is great!

There is more. A similar passage found in 2 Chronicles 19:7 reads, "Let the fear of the Lord be upon you. Be careful what you do, for there is no injustice with the Lord your God, or partiality or taking bribes." Both of these passages refer to God's dealings with mankind. Although He elected the Israelites and brought them out of slavery in Egypt, they were still held to the Law of God. They were still required to obey and live reverently in God's sight. His act of choosing them gave them no advantage over other people as it related to their morality. Both verses admonish the people to live in fear because God's judgment is just. He takes no bribes. He holds no one higher or lower than what is just. This is true even for those God has chosen to be His own. So "be mindful of God's impartiality" is the idea. He judges all without discrimination. This is a reason to call Him great.

The New Testament echoes this. Peter wrote, "If you call on him as Father who judges impartially according to each one's deeds, conduct yourself with fear" (1 Pet. 1:17). Paul, in his own words, wrote, "There will be tribulation and distress for every human being who does evil, the Jew first and also the Greek, but glory and honor and peace for everyone who does good, the Jew first and also the Greek. For God shows no partiality" (Rom. 2:9-11). This tells us that God deals with all people the same way. If you sin, you will be punished for your sin. If you obey the Lord, you will be blessed for your obedience. Both are true no matter your social or economic status, or living condition or ethnicity. You cannot bribe the Lord with money or good things. Nor can you be excused for your poverty or uncertain circumstances. Each man will be judged on the basis of his soul, not his pocketbook.

> **God judges all without discrimination.**

There is also no partiality where God is concerned regarding salvation. Peter was convinced of this in Acts 10:34 when he witnessed the salvation of the Gentiles: "truly I understand that God shows no partiality." This was a big lesson to learn for the Jews, even those who were Christians. They believed that Gentiles had to be proselytized before they could enjoy the benefits of God's salvation. But this was not so with God.

God is impartial regarding discipline, as well. Pastors and other leaders receive no privileges concerning sin. Rather, they are to be rebuked publicly if their sin is public, just as the lay people are rebuked (2 Tim. 5:20). Paul encouraged Timothy to "keep these rules without prejudging, doing nothing from partiality" (2 Tim. 5:21). This means that not even God's appointed leaders receive special freedoms over the congregation (Matt. 18:15-20). Church discipline is commanded for the entire church body, not just the parishioners.

FAITH

So God is impartial when dealing with mankind in matters of judgment, salvation, sin, discipline, and chastening. He is impartial in all His dealings. This is to say that God does not judge you based on your position at work, your marital status, your social status, your wages, your property, your car, your personality, your ethnicity, or your geographical location. All of these things are inconsequential to Him.

We, on the other hand, make most of our decisions based on these things. We will slight someone based on their appearance, clothing style, and even race.

I recall a time as a young teenager when I had it in mind to shave my head. I preferred the bald look as a hardcore basketball player. It was not as common as it is today and so the older people in the worship services tended to be standoffish at times, especially those who didn't know me well. One Sunday morning I sat on the pew next to an old lady who took one look at me, left the pew, and seated herself some distance behind me. Later, my mother told me of the disapproving expression she witnessed on the lady's face. Apparently she'd watched the whole thing unfold and was unhappy to the say the least.

> **God does not judge you based on your position.**

I was not offended even if the old lady was. (Frankly, it made me feel all the more comfortable with my bald head—a clever way to ward off old ladies who liked to pinch cheeks!) The story is funny in hindsight though, since I received offensive looks from others that day, as well. The point remains that this is how we all live to some degree. In fact, it's no stretch of the imagination to consider how we, the church, are prone to exhibit the exact opposite qualities of God regarding choice. Those who are higher up the ladder tend to receive more privileges than others. It might be the ladder of success, education, style, relation, or a number of other things. These people generally receive more favors and attention. While less is required of them, more is available to them. When they sin, it is easier to overlook than it is for others. We tend to think of these people as more sophisticated, more upright. Whereas someone farther down the ladder is far more easily rebuked.

Am I wrong? How often do you delight in talking to the pastor or the "cool" guy, to the extent that you can carry on a rich conversation? Yet, you can't seem to find the words to start a simple conversation with an obscure youth. What about the homeless man who begs for food in the underpass? Do you wonder if he will waste your money on some cheap liquor? Yet, you feel benevolent toward a pal who borrows from you and loves to gamble, never questioning the use of the loan. Do you ever consider criticism from a person who is not a close friend? Are there some with whom you will not share the gospel because you do not think they will receive it? When someone nearly hits you on the highway, are you frustrated when you see their nationality? If you are a man, how do you treat women? If you are young, how do you treat the elderly? What about those who live in low-rent housing, or those who prefer different music, or those who dress poorly? How do you relate to those who are from other countries or different ethnicities?

> **We are guilty of righteous neglect.**

Should I go on? The reality is that we are all guilty of righteous neglect. In fact we are all so guilty that we have grown accustomed to it. We don't even know that we are guilty of it most of the time. What's worse than not knowing is that we don't even blush when we finally realize it. Even more disgusting is the fact that we are partial with our sins. Some sins are actually okay with us, especially when they're our own sins.

But James shows us no partiality in this passage. He gives it to us straight. He does not care where we live, what we do for a living, how much money we make, what car we drive or how well we dress. He tells us plainly, "if you show partiality, you are committing sin" (Ja. 2:9). How is that for impartiality?

The Heart of Impartiality

God is unlike us. (Thank God!) As mentioned, He is impartial. And he commands us to be the same. John wrote under the inspiration of God, "if God so loved us, we also ought to love one another" (1 Jn. 4:11). At the heart of this matter is the concept of love. It is the idea of how we accept and consider others. Does that sound too obvious? Could it be that we are so prone to partiality, we did not even know it was unloving? Have we missed it in even the clearest teachings of the Bible?

I know that I have.

Consider what is commonly called the Great Commandment. In Matthew 22, we read of a Pharisee who asks Jesus, "Teacher, which is the great commandment in the Law?" Jesus responds with, "You shall love the Lord your God with all your heart and with all your soul and with all your mind. This is the great and first commandment. And a second is like it: You shall love your neighbor as yourself." He concludes with: "On these two commandments depend all the Law and the Prophets" (Matt. 22:34-40).

By His answer, it appears that Jesus might not have heard the question correctly. The teachers asked Him for the greatest single commandment, and He gave them two. But He understood the question. His response was exact and, in my opinion, profound. Two commandments were cited, but I think the answer is in their connection. Do you see it?

The Greatest Commandment is the Connection of Two

Some people understand the Ten Commandments to be grouped into two categories: love for God and love for man. With the same emphasis, many people understand that the Ten are an explanation of just one command, "Love your God," which is based on the reality that God exists (Ex. 20:2; Deut. 5:6). I believe the latter is the connection. Since God exists, He is our Lord. Since God is our Lord, we must love Him. Since we love Him, we must do what pleases him. Since impartiality pleases Him, we must be impartial. Since we must be impartial, we must love our neighbors. This is the connection. It is love. If we love God, then we will love what God loves. He loves people. So we, too, should love people.

If we love God, then we will love what God loves.

To put it plainly, "If you love me, you will keep my commandments," Jesus said (Jn. 14:15). Love is the root and the fuel of impartiality. In contrast, hate is the root and the fuel of partiality. Allow me to draw your attention to one last passage on this matter so that we really understand the depth of this sin. It is Matthew 5:21-26. Jesus is clarifying the meaning of the Law when it says that we should not murder. He says:

"You have heard that it was said to those of old, 'You shall not murder; and whoever murders will be liable to judgment.' But I say to you that everyone who is angry with his brother will be liable to judgment; whoever insults his brother will be liable to the council; and whoever says, 'You fool!' will be liable to the hell of fire."

So the Law says not to murder. Jesus, helping us understand the spirit of the Law, explains that murder is the end of hatred and hatred is the beginning of partiality. This brief passage says a whole lot, but let me work through this as succinctly as I can. (I realize that I might sound passionately technical, but bear with me.)

Remember the three grades of church discipline? If someone is in sin, go to him with correction. If he rejects you, go to him with another and try again. If he rejects both of you, take him before the church. Likewise, Jesus mentions three levels of sin with consequential punishment. The first is the sin of anger. This is unwarranted anger since anger in and of itself is not sin (Eph. 4:26).

The second is the sin of insult. The Greek literally says "saying to someone, 'Raca!'" which really has no English equivalent. It is a Jewish word of vilification that means empty-headed and worthless.

The third is summed up in "You fool!" which is quite a strong word when you really look at it. Jesus addressed two of His followers as "foolish men" and was without sin (Lk. 24:25). James also does this later in 2:20. One who is foolish is one who is not putting the spiritual truth together. They don't get it. Here in Matthew's record, calling a man "You fool!" is an unwarranted insult of the worst kind. It is calling someone godless when that might not be the case at all.

To put it briefly, these three sins are inner feelings that are unwarranted toward another. That is to say they have no reason or are based on things that are inconsequential. They are partialities at their core. And Jesus' point here is that these things lead to murder. If they are committed, you have already murdered in your heart before you ever carried out a real execution.

By any honest person's admission, Hitler was a murderer. He actually killed Jews for reasons that were vain. But before he mortified them, he was stirred with anger because they were Jews. His anger brought about contempt for their intellectual capacity and then contempt for their religious character. In the end Hitler was a murderer because in the beginning he was partial. So, to Jesus' point, partiality is murder.

Should anything else be said of this sin?

The Objections to Impartiality

Two Christian men were having an enthusiastic debate over the infallible Word of God. Gradually the debate took on an unpleasant tone as one of the men, who was drinking at the time, said angrily, "I'm offended by what you just said!" The other Christian responded, "It must be the alcohol talking."

I am not new to the life of sin. Like everyone else I was born into it and then cultivated by it. So I understand that one might have some objection to what I am saying and might even be offended, like the inebriated man in the debate. That is likely because the sin is talking. I do not say that in a judgmental way. I have been there, too. And, occasionally I go back there.

I want to quickly look at three objections to this high calling of being impartial. They will help in the transition to chapter two of James.

The first objection is that Jesus said we must love our neighbors *but not all mankind*. Actually, He never said that, but that is what people think He implied (cf: Matt. 19:19; Mk. 12:31).

We use the term "neighbor" today in a very restrictive way. Generally, it refers to those who live next door to us. But this was not so in biblical times. The word carried two main thoughts with it: proximity and need. Your neighbor was anyone near you whom you were able to reach. A neighbor is any person who is a possible recipient of your love and care. John said it this way, "By this we know love, that he laid down his life for us, and we ought to lay down our lives for the brothers" (1 Jn. 3:16).

> **A neighbor is any person who is a possible recipient of your love and care.**

Consider Jesus' description in Luke 10. A lawyer asked Him, "Who is my neighbor?" He replied with a parable of a man who had been robbed and was left to die on the road. A priest happened to be traveling down that road and when he saw the man who had been robbed, he passed him by on the opposite side of the road. Likewise, a

Levite came and went. But, a Samaritan came and saw the man who had been robbed and had compassion. He cared for his wounds, gave him a ride on the back of his own animal and brought him to an inn where he saw that the man was cared for, even to the extent of buying him whatever he needed to get back to his life.

Then Jesus asked the lawyer to whom He told the parable, "Which of these three, do you think, proved to be a neighbor to the man who fell among the robbers?" The lawyer answered him correctly, "The one who showed him mercy" (Lk. 10:29-37). So, according to Jesus, your neighbor is one who is in need of your care. The proximity is in reference to your ability to meet that need. The only time that someone is not your neighbor is when you cannot meet their need due to distance. In other words, your neighbor is everyone you know. The moment you become aware of someone, they become your neighbor. Nice to meet you, neighbor!

The second objection is over the idea of how you love yourself. This one frustrates me! I've heard too much about how we should love ourselves in order to be better people. Psychologists, and even some preachers today, will tell you that you must first love yourself if you expect to make anything out of your life. We are a culture of self-esteem. Some even teach that low self-esteem is sin and believing that you're important is the way to salvation. They claim that Christ died so you could feel better about yourself. Haven't you heard it said, "Nobody comes in last, there are only second- and third-place winners"?

> **Loving yourself is not the way to love others.**

Our problem today is not that we love ourselves too little. It is that we love ourselves too much. In fact, this has been our problem for years. Do not be fooled. Self-pity is self-love, and is simply glorifying ourselves in a different way. Loving yourself is not the way to love others. It is the exact opposite. Loving yourself requires you to not love others. Why? Because the object of your love is the thing you place first. If you love yourself, you are putting yourself first. And in the real world, there is only one first-place winner. The commandment to "love your neighbor as yourself" assumes you are realistic and the Bible is true when it says that "no one ever hated his own flesh, but nourishes and cherishes it" (Eph. 5:29). It supposes by nature you realize that you put yourself first all of the time.

Let us think of it in this way. Who is the first person you feed when you are hungry? Who is the first person you clothe in the morning? Do you let yourself slide when you make a mistake? Do you spare yourself? Do you tell others good things about yourself? Do you praise own work? Do you meet your own needs? Of course you do. We all do. This is because we love ourselves.

This is precisely why the commandment is to do unto others as you would do unto yourself. Love them like you love yourself. When someone is hungry, feed them because you would feed yourself if you were hungry. When someone needs clothes, clothe them because you would clothe yourself. When someone needs compassion, give them compassion like you do yourself every moment of your life. Consider others before yourself. This is the commandment. As Paul wrote, "Love does no wrong to a neighbor; therefore love is the fulfilling of the law" (Rom. 13:10).

Now, in order to cover all the bases of loving your neighbor as yourself, let us also consider our enemy. Are we to love them, too? Really, this sort of combines the first two objections. I would first wonder what would define someone as my enemy. I am not sure I know how to do that. If everyone is my neighbor than who is my enemy? I suppose my enemy is one who persecutes me, violates my body or attacks me. Maybe my enemy is someone who hates me and wants me dead? I am not certain if there is such a thing as an enemy to me. I know there are enemies of the state and nation. I know of terrorists and criminals and other civil classifications. But I actually have no knowledge of any personal, mortal enemies. Even so, be forewarned that personal enemies do exist, just as they did in Jesus' time, whether we're aware of them or not, which explains the command the Lord gave concerning our treatment of them. He said:

> "You have heard that it was said, 'You shall love your neighbor and hate your enemy.' But I say to you, Love your enemies and pray for those who persecute you, so that you may be sons of your Father who is in heaven. For he makes his sun rise on the evil and on the good, and sends rain on the just and on the unjust. For if you love those who love you, what

If everyone is my neighbor than who is my enemy?

reward do you have? Do not even the tax collectors do the same? And if you greet your brothers, what more are you doing than others? Do not even the Gentiles do the same? You therefore must be perfect, as your heavenly Father is perfect." (Matt. 5:43-48)

Being perfect is being absolutely impartial, which leads me to the third objection. What is partiality? (If you say it with condescension, you will feel the objection that is not necessarily noticeable in print.) To be honest, I understand this objection when it is broached with a sincere heart. In other words, how can we avoid partiality if we do not understand exactly what it is? In fact, when I began my preparation for James 2, I wondered about it myself.

Many of us use the word in our everyday language and do not really know what it means. The word itself is abstract and complex. To lend a meaning in one way or another will ultimately change the word altogether, even implying terrible things. For example, if being partial is showing affection to some people more than others, then God would be guilty of partiality. He chose the Jews to reveal His gospel. He also chose the elect to be saved. If God is guilty of partiality then He is no God at all. But He is not partial because choice, in and of itself, is not partiality. God chose the Jews and the elect based on the counsel of His own will alone and it was decided before anything was created. It was not based on human value or any kind of social status (Eph. 1:4-11; Rom. 9:11).

We must be careful of how broadly we define partiality. If we see it as receiving one type of advice over another, then we have made discernment a sin. If it is guiding our children to select specific friends over others, then we have made wisdom a sin. And what about choosing strawberry ice cream over vanilla? Is this too a sin? (My daughter says no, while putting another spoon of strawberry in her mouth.)

My theory is that we have confused the meaning of the word by misusing it in our contemporary conversation. Maybe you have heard something like, "I am partial to Pepsi, not Sprite." We say that we are partial to this and that, but what we mean to say is that we *prefer* these things. We are not partial to them, and preference alone does not require partiality.

Like a rock sculptor, I chiseled away at the word until I was able to understand it independently of other uses. Thus, I think I have nailed down a solid definition.

First, let me mention a few things about the word and its usage in the Bible. James chose the noun *prosopolepsia* in verse 1 and the verb form in verse 9 to communicate his point. It is a matter of the heart even before it is witnessed by the eye. Partial people will show partiality. The word literally means "to accept or judge according to face."[1] It is to take someone at face value and nothing more.[2] It is shallow, snobbish and self-seeking. The concept is wrapped up in the old phrase, "Don't judge a book by its cover." When you do, you are demonstrating your partiality.

Depending on your translation, you might have an English synonym for showing partiality in verse 4 where James asks the rhetorical question, **"have you not then *made distinctions* among yourselves?"** This is the Greek word *diakrino* and means "to make a separation." In the context of partiality, it refers to the act of withdrawing or dividing. Standing alone, the word should be understood as the act of preferring—which is not a sin in and of itself. But, if preference exists based on face value, it is definitely a sin.

Throughout the Bible, these and other terms like them are consistently used. They are always used with regard to the sinful preferences of people and often in connection to the rich and more socially accepted. So, biblically speaking, you cannot be partial to ice cream flavors. (That is good news for my daughter!)

Still, by merely understanding the word as "accepting or judging according to face," I worry that we do not really capture the essence of the word. Let me offer some hypothetical situations to show you why.

Suppose you walked into a restaurant and noticed two people sitting inside but on opposite ends of the room. One is your good friend. The other is a stranger.

1) In our first case, you walk in and sit next to your friend because you were delighted to talk to him. You have then preferred a seat in the room over another but you have not been partial.

---

[1] *The ESV Study Bible, English Standard Version (ESV)*. Wheaton, IL. Crossway, 2008. Print.

[2] Thayer's Lexicon defines *partiality* as "the fault of one who when called on to requite or to give judgment has respect to the outward circumstances of men and not to their intrinsic merits, and so prefers, as the more worthy, one who is rich, high-born, or powerful, to another who is destitute of such gifts."

2) In our second case, you walk in and sit next to your friend because the stranger is a known terrorist and has a handgun on the table and a smug look on his face. Now you are showing wisdom and have not exercised partiality.

3) In our third case, you walk in and sit next to your friend because the stranger is from Iraq and you disdain people of the Islamic religion. *Now, you have shown partiality.*

In each of these three cases, you are making a preference based on face value. You have judged these people by their appearance. In the first case, you preferred your friend for the delight of friendly fellowship, unintentionally ignoring the other. In the second, you intentionally preferred your friend over the other to prevent any possible tragedy. In the third, you preferred your friend because of your hatred of the Arabic nationality. Your friendship was inconsequential.

Putting my head together with a dear friend, we defined partiality as *the intentional choice of people whereby less mercy or grace is shown for selfish benefit and for reasons that are unimportant to God.* I believe it to be a precise definition. This is because partiality requires choice, intention, selfishness, and hate.

We are partial when we show less mercy or grace to someone for reasons that are not important to God. Although we cannot write an exhaustive list of what things are considered unreasonable preference, some that we are familiar with: social status, economic ranking, political association, nationality, age, gender, attire, language, lifestyle, education, etc. These things, when used as a means to establish the value of human life, are sinful reasons and are considered to be an act of partiality.

Holding One Thing or the Other

I am not a fan of moving, particularly now that I have a large library. In my experience, books are among the most difficult objects to move because they weigh so much.

The last time we moved, I had two medium-sized boxes of books left to load then we would be finished. Not wanting to waste a trip, I knelt down and wrapped my arms around both boxes—planning to

FAITH

carry them simultaneously. But when I stood up, one of the boxes slipped and crashed to the floor. I tried again and the other box crashed to the floor.

Call me stubborn, I kept at it until one of the boxes began to break open. My back and arms hurt and I was worn out. What's more, the reality that I could have made twenty trips during the time I'd wasted trying to make one finally sunk in.

In comparison, when James considered impartiality and faith, he knew better. You can hold one or the other, but not two at the same time. **"My brothers, show no partiality as you hold the faith in our Lord Jesus Christ, the Lord of Glory"** (Ja. 2:1). In other words, do not hold the box of partiality and the box of faith at the same time. Together they are too weighty.

In the Greek, James' emphasis is on partialities (meaning all forms of partiality). He is literally drawing your attention to partiality first. It would say something like this to the Greek reader, "My brothers, have no partialities concerning faith in our Lord Jesus Christ, the glory." He is not saying to have no faith with partiality. Rather, since he is writing to **"my brothers,"** he is saying to not have partiality with faith. There is a big difference here.

> **Do not hold the box of partiality and the box of faith at the same time.**

Those who are genuinely saved must not have partialities of any kind. It is inconsistent with faith. The two do not coexist. So, faith, which is the more realistic, must exist only. To draw from my earlier illustration, Christians are already carriers of the box of faith and they cannot carry the box of partiality. There is no room for it. Partiality is inconsistent with faith because of whom we place our faith in, and by whom it is given. James makes it a point to add to the obvious. Partiality is inconsistent with faith because faith is held in reference to **"our Lord Jesus Christ, the glory."** Now, this may not make a whole lot of sense to us Americans. But to the Jew, this was clear. The phrase and apposition "the glory" speaks of Jesus being the glory of God revealed. We know that God is not a respecter of persons. He is not partial in any way. Therefore, Jesus, whom we call Lord, is not partial because He is the Son of God.

The Jews understood **"the glory"** (or *doxa*) to refer to the divine presence of God, the *Shekinah*. In Old Testament terms, this was a reference to God's majestic presence or manifestation among men. It is God's dwelling. Exodus 25:8 records the Lord saying, "Let them make me a sanctuary, that I may dwell in their midst." Numbers 35:34 warns His people saying, "You shall not defile the land in which you live, in the midst of which I dwell, for I the Lord dwell in the midst of the people of Israel." These and many others[3] show how God has called a tabernacle and a gathering of people His dwelling place. Occasionally, this is true of the name of God.[4] Nehemiah 1:9 records God saying, "If you return to me and keep my commandments and do them, though your outcasts are in the uttermost parts of heaven, from there I will gather them and bring them to the place that I have chosen, to make my name dwell there." God is also said to have dwelled in the burning bush (Deut. 33:16), and on Mount Sinai (Ex. 24:16) among other places.

The Jews identified with the concept of God's dwelling among man. They understood that God descended in some way to show His divine glory among them. This has been true for past generations and was true for the Jews at the time this letter was written. The writer of Hebrews says it like this:

> "Long ago, at many times and in many ways, God spoke to our fathers by the prophets, but in these last days he has spoken to us by his Son, whom he appointed the heir of all things, through whom also he created the world. He is the radiance of the glory of God and the exact imprint of his nature, and he upholds the universe by the word of his power." (Heb. 1:1-3)

Jesus is the *Shekinah* of the Lord. He is the divine glory of God dwelling among man. To hold faith in Him is to hold faith in God the Father. It is also true that Jesus, since He is the divine dwelling of God, would manifest the same kind of impartiality. He did. Even the Pharisees noticed it, "Teacher, we know that you are true and teach the way of God truthfully, and you do not care about anyone's opinion, for you are not swayed by appearances" (Matt. 22:16).

Jesus taught His disciples the same thing. In an illustration, He tells

---

[3] Exodus 29:45-46; Numbers 5:3; 1 Kings 6:13; Ezekiel 43:9; Zechariah 2:14.

[4] Deuteronomy 12:11; 14:23; 16:6,11; 26:2.

a story of a master who owned a vineyard. One morning, this master went to hire laborers for the day. He agreed to pay them for a full day. The work day was typically divided into four three-hour increments, running from 6:00 a.m. to 6:00 p.m. At each increment, the master hired more laborers for his vineyard so that some worked twelve hours, some worked nine, some worked six, and others worked three. He even hired some an hour before six.

At the end of the day, all the laborers were paid a full day's wage regardless of their work hours. One who worked longer complained, "These last worked only one hour, you have made them equal to us who have borne the burden of the day and the scorching heat." The master replied to him, "Friend, I am doing you no wrong. Did you not agree with me for a denarius?" (a full days wage). "Take what belongs to you and go. I choose to give to this last worker as I give to you. Am I not allowed to do what I choose with what belongs to me? Or do you begrudge my generosity?" (Matt. 20:1-15).

Here, Jesus levels the playing field (or the work field) with the point of the story—that whoever is called by Jesus will come to Him on equal grounds. Although some come earlier than others and some come through more toil, all come equally and receive equally from God, the gifts that He gives. Thus Jesus concludes with the famous statement: "So the last will be first, and the first last" (Matt. 20:16). This is not how I once understood the meaning of the verse. When I was young, my teacher wanted me to put others first. Rather than being first in line at the snow-cone stand, I was told to go to the back of the line. That was fine with me because somehow, I knew I would be first (although I never quite understood how).

All will come to Christ the same way and receive the same grace.

But that is not the point here. By saying that the last will be first and the first will be last, Jesus is saying that all will come to Him the same. No one will be first. No one will be last. All are equal. All will come to Christ the same way and receive the same grace. Jesus is not partial with His grace. No matter how long you work or how much burden you bear, at the end of the day everyone will receive the same eternal reward.

Faith, if it is truly of God, will show no partiality because it is rooted in the grace of Jesus Christ and the Lord has no impartialities.

Let's Play a Game

Your first inclination might be that you have no partiality. Maybe you say to yourself, "I am into equality. I treat people the same when I'm in the store and when I'm at a restaurant. I don't look down on people of different skin color at work. I'm not a racist." And maybe that is true for the most part. But underneath it all, partiality exists and we don't even see it. The Christian Jews did not see it either. So James points it out.

He does so in a way that reminds me of a game I played when I was young. It was called "Where's Waldo?" Here's how it worked. There would be a giant picture crammed with people doing all sorts of things. For instance, it might be the scene of a crowded marketplace. The picture was hand-drawn and vibrant with colors; filled with objects and things happening. Hundreds, sometimes thousands, of people would appear in the picture. And at the top would be the question, "Can you find Waldo?" Waldo was a small man dressed in a red and white striped shirt, wearing a beanie. The goal was to time yourself to see how long it took you to find him in the crowd.

The next passage found in James reminds me of this game. Rather than finding Waldo, we are to find the partiality. Let's play. You can time yourself.

Here is the picture: **"a man wearing a gold ring and fine clothing comes into your assembly, and a poor man in shabby clothing also comes in, and if you pay attention to the one who wears the fine clothing and say, 'You sit here in a good place,' while you say to the poor man, 'You stand over there,' or, 'Sit down at my feet'"** (Ja. 2:2-3). Do you see it?

Let us get a vivid picture of this. James is speaking about an **"assembly"** of believers. The word is actually translated synagogue. While Christian Gentiles were used to gathering in their homes for worship, the Jewish tradition was to meet in the synagogue (a separate building). For the most part, the Christian Jews were no longer meeting in synagogues since they were dispersed, but the idea was still communicated by when used in the Jewish context. So James essentially means the gathering of the church, as in Sunday morning worship services.

He tells us to suppose that we are all meeting to worship the Lord in our normal gatherings. We are singing songs, praying, and speaking to one another in spiritual psalms. We are encouraging each other and lifting up the Lord when two men walk in. Both are guests. Neither are said to be Christians.

The Rich Man

One is a rich man, literally. He is a **"gold-fingered man"** wearing **"bright and shiny apparel"** (Ja. 2:2, in the Greek). In other words, this fellow is wearing expensive name-brand clothing. He looks like a Hollywood superstar with gold rings adorning his hands. Young people today would say he was "blinged" out.

Let me explain why I say that. Gold rings were not so customary in that time. Jews commonly wore rings, but not gold ones because they were so expensive. Remember the story of the prodigal son? When he returned, the father put a ring on his hand? It was a sign of significance since few people could afford such. But this man who came into the assembly had gold rings. In fact, the Greek text leads us to believe that he had many gold rings—probably one on each finger. He was literally the gold-fingered-man.

In ancient times, people wore rings on every finger to be ostentatious and signify their own importance. They were also seeking the praise of others. We have sources that tell us there were even ring rental businesses in the city that enabled people to wear a ring temporarily, to herald their economic status. (If you've ever watched an award show on television, you know what occurs: actors and actresses preening themselves in front of their peers in borrowed clothes and gems.)

The Poor Man

According to James' illustration (Ja. 2.2), **"a poor man in shabby clothing also comes in"** at the same time as the rich man. They are a study in contrasts as the poor man is the total opposite of the rich man. He is called *tokos*, which means "beggar." He literally begs for clothes. The fact that he is wearing any clothes at all probably means that they are all he has. He is essentially a man from the streets with nothing to his name. The word *tokos* is used to describe the widow who put a penny in the offering (Mk. 12:43). It is also used when Jesus tells the rich man who's seeking eternal life to sell all his possessions and give the money to the poor (Matt. 19:21).

The poor man's attire is quite different from the rich man's. He is wearing dirty, filthy clothes according to the Greek translation. Because it is his only robe, he wears it all the time, sleeping in it, sweating in it, working in it. There is nothing about him that would motivate others to honor him in any way. He is a lowly person, a commoner with nothing to recommend him.

Both of these men walk into your worship gathering.

Treatment of the Rich and Poor Men

So let's see what happens. There is no sin in either man's doings. The rich man is not said to be a believer. He is not intentionally distracting people by his attire. He is likely a visitor and is wearing what he normally wears. (Otherwise, he would need no help in finding a seat.) Meanwhile the poor man is not in sin regardless of his appearance. He wears all that he has due to his circumstances. He cannot help it. He too is a visitor. So there is no problem with either of them. This is not an issue at all.

Rather, the problem is with how they are treated. Both have come into the assembly with no intent to wrong anyone. Both have sincere motives and dress according to their station in life. Both have come for the same purpose. But the church doesn't treat them both the same way. To the rich man, the church says, "You sit here in a good place." To the poor man, the church says, "You stand over there" or "Sit down at my feet."

There is obviously partiality here. On the surface, the church is showing favor to the rich man because of his appearance and social status. He looks good so he is treated accordingly. In contrast, the church is showing less grace and mercy to the poor man because of his appearance and social status. This is blatant partiality.

If you look closer, you can see even more. When the church saw the rich man, what do you think came to mind? What comes to the minds of people in most churches? Maybe something like this: "Look at him. He would be a great asset to our church. Imagine what he could do for us and the Kingdom financially. Let's seat him in a good place in order to make a good impression on him."

Synagogues (since this is still in the Jewish mind) were typically open floor. There were very few benches in the entire room, generally lining the outer wall. Sometimes a few benches were placed in front of the speaker. Most people sat cross-legged on the floor because the elevated benches were occupied by the Pharisees (Matt.12:39). Thus the room is filled with people sitting on the floor or sitting upright along the walls and toward the middle in order to see. In walks the rich man and you look across the room to find a bench, preferably one in front where he can be most comfortable and on display.

In contrast, what do you think came to mind when they noticed the poor man? Maybe they thought, "Why spend my time helping this man? He can offer us nothing. Besides, he stinks and looks bad. What will the others say about me? Let's seat him somewhere quickly and make sure he is not in our way." Or maybe they thought nothing because the poor man was not worth their time. Nevertheless, he is a visitor and it is their responsibility to help him find a seat somewhere. So they say, "You stand over there," or "Sit down at my feet." The Greek language is actually one message, "You stand over there or sit by my footstool."

The idea here is that they do not want to be bothered with this man. They do not want to invest in him in any way. By telling him to stand *over there*, it is implied that they want him to get out of their way and out of their view. It is as if they are contemptuous, certain their time is better spent on the rich man. The poor man is a bother. So, "Find yourself a place and find it quickly—just make it somewhere else." They do not guide him to a position, nor do they help him find one. They just want the poor man out of the picture.

On the other hand, they give him the option to "sit by my footstool." This is in case he cannot find a place to stand "over there." The Greek *hupo to hupopodion mou* means sit "under my footstool." The word *hupo* is more often translated "under" although it can mean "by" which is likely the case here since it is hard to sit under a footstool. Nevertheless, it is interesting to see the word in its usual context as it references a footstool. The idea might be that they are treating the poor man more like a disfavored slave. Moreover, who has a footstool when people are troubling themselves over places to sit? This usher is the worst! He has a seat and a footstool and he gives the poor man neither.

Get the Picture?

We have achieved nothing if we have not gotten the picture. James asks a rhetorical question, **"have you not then made distinctions among yourselves and become judges with evil thoughts?"** (Ja. 2:4). This is primarily where our definition of partiality is derived. Generally speaking, it is making distinctions with evil thoughts. Specifically, it is the intentional choice of people where less mercy or grace is shown for selfish benefit and for reasons that are unimportant to God.

So what do we say to James' question? Is this a picture of partiality? The answer is an emphatic, "Yes!" Therefore, we can paraphrase James' words as, "if you show one man favor and another man disfavor due to their economic status, you have shown partiality."

Friends, this is alive and at work in our churches today. It happens daily in many places throughout the world. Is that judgmental for me to say? Have I gone too far with my notions? I do not think so. It is embedded in our lives by our culture. We are trained to cultivate it in many different ways. To top it off, it is native to our sin nature, so we are born to it. Partiality runs through our veins. We practice it often and most of the time we do not even know it.

> **Partiality runs through our veins.**

Let us look at this from a different perspective. How should the rich and poor man be treated? Simply put: the same way, which is the way of honor. True faith is honoring. It shows favor and esteems others above ourselves. It was honorable to help the rich man to a good and comfortable seat (although the selfish reasons were not honorable). The same honor should have been shown to the poor man. He also should have been given a good and comfortable seat. The usher should have offered his own seat and footstool, and opted to stand. This is the idea behind the "great and first commandment" mentioned earlier (Matt. 22:34-40), which is to love your neighbor as yourself. The usher had a seat and footstool, which was him taking care of himself. The command of the Lord is to show this same love to others, even if it means you can no longer show it to yourself. The usher should have given up his seat and footstool.

Instead, these two men were shown partiality. The poor man was dishonored. In actuality, they were both dishonored by the selfish motives of the usher. It was discrimination, hateful and judgmental. It was evil, not godlike. It was sinful and worldly and has no place in the church, (the building or its people).

We Christians should be as Paul wrote:

> "We who are strong have an obligation to bear with the failings of the weak, and not to please ourselves. Let each of us please his neighbor for his good, to build him up. For Christ did not please himself, but as it is written, 'The reproaches of those who reproached you fell on me.' For whatever was written in former days was written for our instruction, that through endurance and through the encouragement granted you to live in such harmony with one another, in accord with Christ Jesus, that together you may with one voice glorify the God and Father of our Lord Jesus Christ. Therefore welcome one another as Christ has welcomed you, for the glory of God." (Rom. 15:1-7)

In light of this, we can see the gravity of our partialities. By dishonoring some we have crippled the church as a whole and suffered the "one voice" in our glorification of God. We tarnish our praise and darken our witness, if we do not destroy it entirely. Even worse, we dishonor Jesus who honored us when we needed it. In essence, we cut off the current of love. We accept it from the Lord, but it stops with us. Let us remember to show honor to all people equally and above ourselves. For true faith is honoring. Anything less should cause us to ask ourselves, "Do I have true faith?"

> **Let us remember to show honor to all people equally and above ourselves.**

True Faith is Honoring

"Are you picking up what I'm putting down?" This is a question I often ask my children whenever I am wondering if they understand what I am teaching. In the prior passage, we saw that true faith is impartial, and sprinkled throughout the chapter thus far are hints of what stands in opposition to partiality. It is the idea of honor. Did you pick it up? Because I was certainly putting it down.

Opposite of impartiality is the idea of honor, which is to show respect and esteem for everyone other than yourself. Of course there is a certain kind of esteem that belongs to particular people like the president, the peace officer, the judge, and other government officials. We should also show a certain kind of respect to elders, our parents, our providers, our teachers, and so forth. This doesn't eliminate our need to show respect or esteem toward others. Rather, we are to show all people a form of respect that is loving and honorable. As Paul writes, "In humility count others more significant than yourselves" (Phil. 2:3).

Throughout time there has been a barrier between the wealthy and the poor. The poor have always been those who are the first to be confronted, the first to be abused and ignored. They are considered lowly, both in the sense of their finances and value. On the other hand, the wealthy are the ones whose advice is sought, who win the ears and eyes of others, who enjoy special treatment and are almost never rebuked for their sins. They get the best seats in the house. They receive the smiles and polite greetings. They are included in decision making. They are considered worthy and receive honor from most people.

This has always been the case. Jesus told the common people, "Beware of the scribes, who like to walk around in long robes and like greetings in the marketplaces and have the best seats in the synagogues and the places of honor at feasts, who devour widows' houses and for a pretense make long prayers" (Mk. 12:38-40). The scribes received a higher honor among the people simply because of their vanities and status. Jesus' instructions to those who would normally honor these men above all others, was to not be deceived by their outward appearance. Their perceived honor was only skin deep. The way they dressed, their long prayers, the places they sat and ate were not reasons to set them on pedestals. Rather, the heart of a man is the true indication.

> **The heart of a man is the true indication.**

In fact, Jesus contrasted the scribes with the widow who offered very little. She came to the treasury and dropped inside "two small copper coins, which make a penny." Others were leaving large sums because they were rich. Jesus saw this and told his disciples, "Truly, I say to you, this poor widow has put in more than all those who are contributing to the offering box. For they all contributed out of their abundance, but she out of her poverty has put in everything she had, all she had to live on" (Mk. 12:41-44). Jesus draws attention to the heart of the widow. Only the heart matters.

Another place where partiality is evident is John 1:46. Jesus was calling Philip to be his disciple. Philip found Nathanael and brought him along. Nathanael, commenting on where Jesus was from, asked, "Can anything good come out of Nazareth?" Also, when Peter and John spoke with boldness and clarity, the "important" people of Jerusalem were astonished since they "perceived that they were uneducated, common men" (Acts 4:13). This was the same case on the Day of Pentecost when the Spirit of God filled the disciples. "Are not all these who are speaking Galileans?" (Acts 2:5-7), the presumption being that it is bad to be from Galilee.

Galilean Partiality

Let's put this in perspective and see how it corresponds to our time and culture. Galilee was populated by a colony of immigrants (2 Kin. 15:29; 17:24). They were from areas like Babylon and other non-Jewish sections. For this reason, the more orthodox Jews despised the Galileans (Jn. 7:52). It was like having a ghetto in your city, a place occupied by a lower class of people. They were immigrants who looked and spoke differently, and had a different culture altogether. Surely you're familiar with such an area. Every city in the United States has one. My hometown of Houston has many, often referred to as "the projects." Most people assume you are up to no good if you live there. In fact ,everyone seems to know you came from there because you have a look that is distinct from others.

These are real places and real people. It is the reality we live in. We are fractured, separated, and different. Some of us fall into the category of lower class. Some of us are categorized as upper class. Some of us are rich and some are poor. Some are educated and some are not. Some are natives and some are from other countries. Some are black and some are white. But all of these things are inconsequential to God and should be to the Christian. They have no bearing on the way anyone should be treated. Unfortunately, this is not the reality of our time—not even in the church (as we saw in the prior section).

> **We are fractured, separated and different.**

James continues his argument against partiality by making a rather forthright observation. It is staggering when you consider it and bring it into perspective. He writes:

> **"Listen, my beloved brothers, has not God chosen those who are poor in the world to be rich in faith and heirs of the kingdom, which he has promised to those who love him? But you have dishonored the poor man. Are not the rich the ones who oppress you, and the ones who drag you into court? Are they not the ones who blaspheme the honorable name by which you were called?"** (Ja. 2:5-7)

Remember this comes directly after James' indictment of partiality where he accused them of making intentional choices of people where less mercy or grace is shown for selfish benefit and for reasons that are unimportant to God. They guided the rich man to the best seat in the synagogue while they told the poor man to sit somewhere unseen. They treated the poor with dishonor. Now, he hopes to do as Jesus did and level the people again.

The Poor Are Rich

I imagine an old wise man leaning toward me confidentially to say something of great wisdom. If James were here, this might well be his stance. "Listen, my beloved brothers." What followed these words would surely be important. "Has not God chosen those who are poor in the world to be rich in faith and heirs of the kingdom, which he has promised to those who love him?" His point is forthcoming. For now the purpose is to get our attention. "You treat the poor as people of no value, as people with no soul, as people who are unimportant. Are these not the people that God chose to save and give the greatest riches?"

> **There is a divine choice for the poor.**

This may be the greatest reality check for modern America. Simply put, it says that God chose the poor people in the world to love Him and be saved. If that does not stir some deep wonder in your heart, let me say it this way: There is a divine choice for the poor. Is that a radical shift in our culture or what? Most of us believe the gospel is for those who are well-educated and financially prosperous. These are the people we tend to go to and befriend with the hidden gospel agenda. But scripturally speaking (and proven true historically) rich people feel content with their riches (Matt. 19:23-25). They feel as though they have no need for God. They can buy whatever they desire. Poor people, on the other hand, are broken and lowly in this world and naturally seek help. They can identify with being spiritually needy because they are physically needy.

Let us survey the ministry of Jesus to observe this reality so we do not get upset with James. To start with, Jesus was born in Bethlehem in an animal stable and laid in a feeding trough (Lk. 2:1-7). He was raised in Nazareth for approximately thirty years (Jn. 1:46) by parents who could not even afford an animal sacrifice, offering "two young pigeons" instead as Leviticus 12:8 commanded (Lk. 2:22-24). Growing up, Jesus worked as a carpenter which was used against him later in a derogatory manner (Mk. 6:3). To put it in today's terms, he was raised in "the projects."

During his ministry, Jesus was approached by a scribe who asked to follow Him. Jesus told him that He had no home, a lower state than the animals (Matt. 8:19-20). He also miraculously fed five thousand of His followers who were poor because neither He nor they had enough money (Mk. 6:32-44). Jesus told the rich young man who inquired about eternal life to sell all that he had and give to the poor (Matt. 19:21).

The bulk of Jesus' ministry was to the blind, the lame, the lepers, the deaf and the poor (1 Cor. 1:26).[5] This type of irony was unexpected and surprising to most people, so much so that many were upset. So Jesus said, "Blessed is the one who is not offended by me" (Matt. 11:4-6). At one point, Jesus spoke to their inability to comprehend, asking, "What then did you go out to see? A man dressed in soft clothing? Behold those who wear soft clothing are in kings' houses" (Matt. 11:7-10). In other words, they were expecting someone more presentable, more dignified by the world's standards. John the Baptist surprised them. So did Jesus. So did the disciples.

There is much more to be mentioned. The gospels are flooded with

---

[5] This is not to say that only the poor benefit from God's grace. Abraham was an extremely wealthy man (Gen. 13:2). Job was wealthy (Job 1:3). Joseph of Arimathea was a rich man who provided the tomb for Jesus' body (Jn. 19:38-42). Matthew and Zaccheus were tax collectors (Lk. 5:27). There are rich people in the church (1 Tim. 6:17-19). Philemon had man slaves and hosted an entire church assembly in his home (Philemon).

examples of Jesus' love for the poor. However, one story in particular should drive the point home. It is one of the most remarkable stories that I have read. I simply love it!

Jesus and His disciples carried around a bag of about 200 denarii (roughly eight month's wages) in order to care for the poor (Lk. 9:3; 10:4). This was all they had. In fact, Jesus sent the disciples out to proclaim the kingdom of heaven without any money for their own needs (Matt. 10:5-12).

Later, Jesus asked them, "When I sent you out with no moneybag or knapsack or sandals, did you lack anything?" The disciples replied, "Nothing." Really? Read it again and take your time. "When I sent you out [to minister] with no moneybag or knapsack or sandals, did you lack anything?" You almost have to read it slowly.

They went out to do the work of God as poor people, but they lacked absolutely nothing. They were satisfied in Jesus and trusted in God's provision. They had all that they wanted in Him. Therefore, wealth was no object to them. They were poor in the world, but rich in faith.

Paul said it this way, "You know the grace of our Lord Jesus Christ, that though he was rich, yet for your sake he became poor, so that you by his poverty might become rich" (2 Cor. 8:9). This refers to being rich in faith. The Lord and His spiritual gifts of goodness, forbearance, long suffering (Rom. 2:4), mercy, glory (Rom. 9:23), forgiveness of sin (Eph. 1:7), and Christ Himself are the riches of life and eternity (Eph. 3:8). I love how Paul words it in 2 Corinthians 6:9-10. He says that by the world "we are treated as impostors, and yet are true; as unknown, and yet well known; as dying, and behold, we live; as punished, and yet not killed; as sorrowful, yet always rejoicing; as poor, yet making many rich; as having nothing, yet possessing everything." Does that not capture it all! We have nothing in the world but we have all that we need. We have Christ.

> **We have nothing in the world but we have all that we need. We have Christ.**

These are riches we are told to work and live for while giving the world's riches to the poor (Lk. 12:15-21; 14:12-14; Matt. 6:16-21). This is consistent with God who chose the poor for salvation. Jesus

FAITH

goes so far as to say that when you serve the poor you are serving Him (Matt. 25:40). Why? Because serving the poor is the heart of God.

Psalm 72:4 says that God defends the poor and goes after their enemies. He replenishes those who give to the poor (Prov. 28:27). The rich can solve their own problems with what they have but often find it hard to see the real problem of sin. But God solves the problems of the poor (Ps. 113:7) and blesses those who consider the poor (Ps. 41:1).

God has chosen to seek out and save the poor. He chose them with a special calling to love Him and to be recipients of the riches of faith, being satisfied and content with Christ alone, and to become heirs of eternal life. They are said to be the **"poor in the world"** (Ja. 2:5). That is to say they are poor in the eyes of the world. The world says they are poor. But, they are rich in the eyes of God because they have been given the faith to believe and savor Jesus. God says they are rich. Therefore, when you dishonor the poor you are setting yourself against God (Prov. 17:8).

All of this is in the mind of James as he reminds us, **"Has not God chosen those who are poor in the world to be rich in faith and heirs of the kingdom, which he has promised to those who love him?"** (Ja. 2:5). Of course! This is the heart of God. And logically, if you love God and have His heart then you will be the same way, like Zacchaeus, whom God saved. He stood and said, "Behold, Lord, the half of my goods I give to the poor" (Lk. 19:8). This is a sign of genuine faith.

"But you…" (never words you want to hear after a summary of God's heart) **"…have dishonored the poor man"** (Ja. 2:6). You would think enough had been said already. But James goes even further to show how sinful we are when we are partial. He accuses us of siding with God's opponents and asks another rhetorical question, **"Are not the rich the ones who oppress you, and the ones who drag you into court?"** (Ja. 2:6).

Like today, money means power. The rich can have their way because they can pay for it. In the courts the rich can afford the expensive, qualified lawyer. The poor on the other hand cannot defend themselves before a judge—not even when the accusations are false. Historically this is true. The rich oppress the poor. They depreciate the value of poor people. James goes on to say that they are the **"ones who blaspheme the honorable name by which you were called"** (Ja. 2:7).

That is to say they not only depreciate your life, they also depreciate your religion. They blaspheme Jesus. This is true of all who do not consider the poor. If you set yourself against the poor, you set yourself against the Lord because He has set Himself up for the poor.

The rich are the ones who drag you into the civil court and the religious court and dishonor you and the Lord. Interestingly enough, James has changed his wording from "the poor" to "you", showing that the Christians were the poor who were oppressed. Essentially, they were siding with the enemy and helping the enemy oppress their families.

It is no coincidence then that James includes **"the honorable name by which you were called"** (Ja. 2:7). This is in contrast to the dishonoring of the poor. True faith honors the poor and thereby honors the name by which we are called to salvation. True faith honors people equally.

I am not advocating a total reversal of opinion as to how the world operates. I am not suggesting that you should no longer honor the rich and exclusively honor the poor. What I am advocating is equality in honor. The rich have no needs because of their circumstances. The poor have needs and can be honored by our gifts and considerations. Honoring all people equally does not necessarily mean that we give the same to all people. It simply means that we should hold all people in high esteem and above ourselves.

> **If you set yourself against the poor, you set yourself against the Lord**

Let me explain this with something I practice today. Mind you, I started this largely because of my studies in this passage of James. By no means is it meant to suggest any godliness on my part.

I have what I call a homeless man fund. It is money set aside in our budget for the poor who camp out under bridges or beg at intersections. It is cash I've withdrawn and set in the ash tray of my car so that when I come across a beggar, I can feed him. Now I would never take that money and give it to a rich man. And the reason is not because I am dishonoring the rich, but because the rich do not beg on street corners. They do not need my money. Therefore my intent is to show consideration for the poor. It does not mean I am inconsiderate of the rich.

Small acts of partiality can have giant repercussions. You cannot keep the faith and show unjust partiality. The two simply do not mix. If God extends a special grace to those who are poor, then we should, too—if we claim to have faith in Him. True faith is honoring.

True Faith is Merciful

James has been driving the nail into a very serious sin. He has told us that we cannot hold faith in the Lord and partiality at the same time. The two are antithetical. He has given us an example of how partiality is often seen in the church. We tend to show the popular wealthy people grace while showing the unpopular poor less grace, if any. He has also shown us that partiality is taking sides with the enemy of our souls, like switching teams in battle from God to the world, thereby warring against God.

We have also touched on the idea that partiality is not just showing more grace and less grace, meaning that we honor some while we dishonor others. It can also go in the opposite direction, meaning that we show more mercy to some while showing little or no mercy to others. This is evident when some people are overlooked for their sin while others are strongly rebuked for theirs. Those who exercise the faith given them by our Lord will show equal grace and mercy to all people. They will bestow love on all people in the same way.

> **Those who exercise the faith given them by our Lord will show equal grace and mercy to all people.**

Finally, James closes his discussion on the sin of partiality. He begins with a commendation to those who do not show partiality. Then he condemns those who do show partiality and explains the seriousness of the sin. Lastly, he leaves us with the admonition to live faithfully. He teaches that true faith is showing mercy to all and will be mercifully judged by God.

Doing Well

Earlier we considered the great commandment. Jesus, using the combination of two commandments and perhaps the summary of all the commandments, says that it is to "love the Lord your God with all your heart and with all your soul and with all your mind" and to "love your neighbor as yourself" (Matt. 22:34-40).

James recalls this great commandment as well. He says that, **"If you really fulfill the royal law according to the Scripture, 'You shall love your neighbor as yourself,' you are doing well"** (Ja. 2:8).

In the context of true faith the idea of "doing well" reminds me of the Parable of the Talents. As Jesus tells it, a master was going on a journey and he put his servants in charge of his property. He gave one five talents. To another, he gave two talents. And to another, he gave one. (A talent was about twenty years of wages for labor.) Then the master went away and left the servants with his trust. When he returned after a long period of time, he called to his servants in order to settle accounts with them. He was pleased to discover that two of the servants had made good use of the talents he had given them, doubling their amounts. To them, he said, "Well done, good and faithful servants. You have been faithful with a little; I will set you over much. Enter into the joy of your master." We will look at what he said to the third servant in a moment.

The idea here is that the master gave gifts to his servants, expecting them to be used in a profitable way. The two servants who returned double the amount given them showed the master that they could be trusted. Therefore, he gave them more. What I want to point out is that he said to them, "Well done ... enter into the joy of your master." James says that if you fulfill the royal law, you are doing well. Although these are not the same Greek words, they do communicate the same principle: You do well if you obey the law. In the end, you will be told, "Well done." Moreover, you will be able to "enter into the joy of your master." What a delight to hear!

I bring this to your attention because I believe it to be the supreme motivation to **"really fulfill the royal law"** (Ja. 2:8). What other goal is there than to please the Lord and inherit the joy of eternal life with Jesus? A psalmist wrote, "Whom have I in heaven but you? And there is nothing on earth that I desire besides you" (Ps. 73:25). This expresses the greatest joy of life and eternity—namely, the pleasure of the Lord. For this reason, we should be motivated to impartiality in our dealings with others and, by implication, we will really fulfill the royal law.

So what exactly does it mean to **"really fulfill the royal law"**? The phrase **"really fulfill"** is aimed at communicating the overall point of the arguments that follow. The Greek literally says "if you fulfill the royal law according to Scripture." There is no word to translate into "really" but it is what James is referring to in the greater context as we will see more clearly in the proceeding verses. He is making a distinction between *partially* fulfilling and *completely* fulfilling the law. Again, we will look into this momentarily. For now, understand his point: fulfilling the law in a real sense by actually and practically obeying it is doing well. It is the way to eternal life. It is the expression of true faith. It is worthy of the admonition of the Lord, "Well done."

In addition to this, the law is called **"royal"** which is the Greek word *basilikon* used to communicate the source and nature of the law. It is kingly or *of the king*. It is supreme and sovereign and non-negotiable. At the same time, it is noble to obey it. Those who act in accordance to the King's decrees are called noble, royal men. The law, therefore, is one that is supreme and most important. You might even say that it is a summary of the entire law and the reason why it is generally mentioned in context of our understanding of the Lord. He is the Lord. To love Him is to love others (Ja. 2:8; cf: Lev. 19:18).

In another way, the law is supreme in that it summarizes all of the Law. If you obey this one law, you will by default obey all of the laws. Love the Lord with all of yourself and you will love others as you love yourself (Matt. 22:34-40). This is how it works. If you love others as yourself, than you will never treat or think of others except in a way that you would treat or think of yourself. Thus you will end up honoring your parents because you honor yourself. You will not murder, you will not commit adultery, you will not steal, you will not lie, you will not covet. You will not do any of these things because you would not do these things to yourself. If you look out for your neighbor as you would look out for yourself, then you will obey all of the law. In this sense, this particular law is supreme.

> **To love Him is to love others.**

To be more precise, James says that it is the law **"according to the Scripture"** (Ja. 2:8) in opposition to the *law of the land* which says every man should look out for *number one*. Scripture, the word of the Lord, defines the supreme law and it is this law that we should fulfill in order to do well.

Doing Wrong

If we are doing well by fulfilling the royal law, then we are doing wrong by showing partiality (the antithesis of the royal law). James says **"But if you show partiality, you are committing sin and are convicted by the law as transgressors"** (Ja. 2:9). We have touched on this subject more than once already. Partiality is a sin, and, as James put it, it is a sin in two ways.

First, it is missing the mark of God's glory. Paul says that it is falling short (Rom. 3:23). This is what it means to sin. It is a disregard and a violation of the law of God. It is to aim for the target but miss it altogether. This is a description of the act in a negative sense. When you show partiality, you fail. **"You are committing sin"** (Ja. 2:9).

Second, it is going too far. James says that you **"are convicted by the law as transgressor"** (Ja. 2:9). To transgress is to go beyond the limitations of the law. It is a description of the act in a positive sense. When you show partiality, you break the boundaries. Both are a description of what we do when we disobey. We come up short and we go beyond the perfect law. Both are wrong. Both are in opposition to the idea of fulfilling the law. God has given us the law like a path to walk. If you do not walk the path you are falling short. If you walk outside of the path, you are going too far. The aim is to keep on the path and keep it perfectly until the end.

> **The aim is to keep on the path and keep it perfectly until the end.**

Remember the parable of the talents? There was a third servant that was given one talent. When his master left, he buried the talent and had nothing to offer when his master returned. Therefore, the master said to him, "You wicked and slothful servant!" He ordered the servant's talent be taken from him and given to the others. Then he said, "Cast the worthless servant into the outer darkness. In that place there will be weeping and gnashing of teeth" (Matt. 25:24-30).

This parable leads Jesus into the teaching of the Final Judgment where He will separate those who obeyed the law from those who did not. The obedient ones will hear from Him:

> "Come, you who are blessed by my Father, inherit the kingdom prepared for you from the foundation of the world. For I was hungry and you gave me food, I was thirsty and you gave me drink, I was a stranger and you

welcomed me, I was naked and you clothed me, I was sick and you visited me, I was in prison and you came to me." (Matt. 25:34-36)

If this is starting to sound like the act of being impartial, it should. Jesus said that those who fulfilled the royal law by loving others as they would love themselves will inherit eternity with Him. When these people hear this, He maintains they will ask him: "When did we see you hungry and feed you, or thirsty and give you drink?" (Matt. 25:37). And He replies, "Truly, I say to you, as you did it to one of the least of these my brothers, you did it to me" (Matt. 25:41). He is speaking about the poor. Showing the poor the same grace and mercy you show the wealthy is fulfilling the royal law.

On the other hand, to the transgressors he will say:

"Depart from me, you cursed, into the eternal fire prepared for the devil and his angels. For I was hungry and you gave me no food, I was thirsty and you gave me no drink, I was a stranger and you did not welcome me, naked and you did not clothe me, sick and in prison and you did not visit me." (Matt. 25:41-43)

Likewise, they will ask something similar as the others did: "When did we see you hungry or thirsty or a stranger or naked or sick or in prison?" (Matt. 25:44). Jesus' response is the same. "Truly, I say to you, as you did not do it to one of the least of these, you did not do it to me" (Matt. 25:45). He will then separate those who are going "away into eternal punishment" from the righteous who are going "into eternal life" (Matt. 25:46). This is the seriousness of partiality. We are talking about the gravity of this sin.

At this point, it might be best to mention something important, lest we give in to unwarranted condemnation rather than conviction. Let me also point out that the Greek verbs in this verse refer to an ongoing action. It basically says, "if you continue to show partiality, you are continually committing sin and are convicted by the law," which is in the past tense. In this sense, a continual practice of sin means that you have been convicted already for your sin and are sentenced as a transgressor. Your eternity is hell. For the one who has true faith, this will not be a practice, though it may occur. The one with such faith will repent from this act as the Lord brings him to obedience.

Grading on a Curve

You might be thinking to yourself as many Jews did at that time, "I have kept some of the law, so I'll be okay." The idea of a credit-debit system is nothing new. For hundreds of years, people have believed their good will outweigh their bad. They believed that if at least one law was perfectly kept, God would be gracious about the others. This might be the most popular belief today among professing evangelical Christians. I come across it far too much. "Sure, I've lusted a little bit, I may have lied one or two times, but I've never murdered anyone and I give donations to the church! God sees that and He honors my efforts." Does this sound familiar? Is this the way you think? Do your friends or colleagues ever express something like this?

God does see our efforts. He does see our work. And this is why we are condemned. However, it would be better if He did not see our work since it is filthy before Him (Is. 64:6; Rom. 3:20). When I was young, I would experience the relief of grading on a curve in school. I did not enjoy tests in those days. They made me anxious. I would often answer wrong even when I knew the right answer. But I recognized that if I could just get close to a passing grade, I would make it because of the grade curve.

God never grades on a curve.

This was when a teacher would grade all of the students' tests and decide that it was too hard for them corporately. Based on the top score in the class, she would raise the score as many points as necessary to reach a perfect score. The number of points she used to raise that score was then applied to all other scores. Grading on a curve saved me more than once!

However, God never grades on a curve. We often soothe our guilt by telling ourselves that God sees our heart and it is basically good since it tries to do good. But the heart is most deceitful (Jer. 17:9). It deceives even us. The Lord says, "I the Lord search the heart and test the mind, to give every man according to the fruit of his deeds" (Jer. 17:10). Does this justify our attempts to obey the law? No. Rather, it condemns us before the law. Our hearts and minds are deceiving us into thinking they are good, but they are not. When our aim is to obey the law in order to win eternal life, we fall short. Even our best efforts are sinful (Rom. 14:23).

We fool ourselves if we think that God judges on a curve. Our adoption of this idea is tragic. It weakens our view of sin and God's holiness and it strengthens our view of man and his abilities. In essence, it trains us to think that sin is not so sinful. Ask anyone on the street if they have broken any of the Ten Commandments. Most will respond negatively at first, thinking they have never murdered or cheated on their spouse. But when the commandments are explained to them, they tend to digress and admit to breaking a few. This is because most people can admit that they have once told a little white lie, or harbored unwarranted anger, or partiality towards someone and lusted in their heart. But these are small things to us Americans. These are things that everyone does. It is natural and reasonable. We are all doing these things and God understands—such is our way of thinking.

God does not use the curve. He judges us all individually and righteously. Your score does not depend on what everyone else is doing. It is true that it is natural for us to sin (Eph. 2:3). I would add that if it were not for God's mercy, we would be even more sinful. But our sinful nature is no excuse. God expects absolute perfection from each of us. He says to us all, "You therefore must be perfect, as your heavenly Father is perfect" (Matt. 5:48).

> **The is like a window and not bowling pins.**

To this end, James argues, breaking one part of the law breaks all of the law. One preacher said that the law is like a window and not bowling pins. When you bowl, you may knock down two or three or even nine pins and achieve a score. The law, however, does not work that way. There are no percentile winnings. You either knock them all down perfectly or you don't. There is no in-between. As the preacher said, the law is like a window. If you break one small part, you shatter the entire thing.

James says, **"For whoever keeps the whole law but fails in one point has become accountable for all of it"** (Ja. 2:10).

Partiality Breaks the Whole Law

James is now putting the finishing touches on his argument. He goes on to say, **"For he who said, 'Do not commit adultery,' also said, 'Do not murder.' If you do not commit adultery but do murder, you have become a transgressor of the law"** (Ja. 2:11). I do not think it is a coincidence that James uses adultery and murder as his examples. He could have used any of the commandments.

Both of these laws warrant the death penalty. They might have been the most heinous of sins in the eyes of the Jews. Earlier we saw that partiality is the root of murder. The example, then, tells us of the seriousness of the sin. Partiality is nothing to shake a stick at. It is sinful. It is serious. Even so, breaking any of the law is breaking it all. Although each of us have broken the law in one way or another, we might try to lessen our guilt by believing that we have kept at least part of the law. Here, James is saying that even part of the law is not good enough. God will judge you as if you broke all of the law. Showing partiality then will cause God to judge you as one who broke the entire law.

With all of this in mind, James concludes with a final admonition. **"So speak and so act as those who are to be judged under the law of liberty. For judgment is without mercy to one who has shown no mercy. Mercy triumphs over judgment"** (Ja. 2:12-13). In the first chapter, we looked at the phrase "law of liberty" and said that refers to the law of Christ. It is grace which is given to those who have faith, those who see the law of God as "acknowledgment of sin" (Rom. 3:20). By seeing that we are condemned by the law, we cry out to God for a savior and He responds with Christ. The perfection that God requires of us is then given to Him in Christ and on our behalf. "The righteousness of God has been manifested apart from the law" and it is manifested in the life of Jesus (Rom. 3:21). "For we hold that one is justified by faith apart from works of the law" (Rom. 3:28).

> **Breaking any of the law is breaking it all.**

The admonition is to speak and act like one who has been justified by Jesus Christ and able to now obey the law in faith. If true faith has been given to us, we will be impartial as He is impartial. We will show all people mercy because we have been shown mercy by God. Why? Because showing less mercy shows that we have yet to receive it. For those who have yet to receive the mercy of God, judgment of the law of God awaits since all of the law must be fulfilled perfectly. But it never will be. Apart from faith in Christ, there is no perfection. So be merciful because mercy wins the victory and triumphs over judgment.

Conclusion

A final thought comes to my mind and it almost mirrors that of James 2:1-13. It is a story found in Mahatma Gandhi's autobiography. It is about an experience that he had in a Christian church. While he was still a young student, he was interested in the Bible. After reading the gospels and being deeply touched, he seriously considered becoming a follower of Christ. He was thinking of converting from Hinduism because Christianity seemed to resolve the social system that was dividing the people of India.

One Sunday, he attended a church in the hopes of finding some instruction on salvation and other Christian teachings. Upon entering the sanctuary, the ushers, who noticed he was Hindu, refused to seat him and suggested that he return to his own people to worship. Walking away, he thought to himself, "If Christians have caste differences also, I might as well remain a Hindu." Gandhi left and never returned.

The truth is simple: to be partial is to be unjust. Showing partiality requires you to be judgmental. And as we judge others without mercy, we too will be judged.

It is wrong for us to think that we can show favoritism while calling ourselves Christians. So ask yourself, "Do I favor these people over others for unjust reasons?" If so, ask the Lord to help you overcome these feelings. He requires his people to "do justice, and to love kindness" (Mic. 6:8) and He will give you the grace to love all people, regardless of their status.

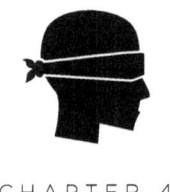

CHAPTER 4

THE TRIAL OF WORKS

JAMES 2:14-26

"I will show you my faith by my works"

On October 31, 1517, a lengthy paper was nailed to the doors of the Castle Church in Wittenberg, Germany, by a monk named Martin Luther. It was a handwritten rejection of the Roman Catholic Church's abuse of the gospel. Today it is known as the Ninety-Five Theses and its advent marked the beginning of the Protestant Reformation and the birth of Protestantism.

The primary aim of the paper was to combat the sale of indulgences—a way of purchasing a ticket to heaven. Luther pointed to the Scriptures, declaring that God's offer of salvation is by *Sola fide*, which in Latin means "faith alone". Using the gospel, he countered the prevailing "saved by purchases" philosophy of the day by preaching that man can only enter heaven by faith alone—a trusting belief in God's ability to save.

Since that time, Protestants have held fast to Luther's declaration that "justification is by faith alone, but not by the faith that is alone." Protestant scholar, Dr. John H. Gerstner underscores this belief in the book, *Justification by Faith Alone*[1] by reminding believers that it is impossible to make Jesus your Savior without making him your Lord. Thus, there is an ongoing debate between Catholics and Protestants over the purpose of works in the Christian life. Do works save or do

---

[1] John Armstrong, Joel R. Beeke, John H. Gerstner, Don Kistler, MacArthur, John F., and, R.C. Sproul. *Justification by Faith Alone: Affirming the Doctrine by Which the Church and the Individual Stands or Falls.* Morgan, PA: Soli Deo Gloria Publications, 1995. Print.

they prove that you have been saved? This is what James is after in this next test of faith.

As noted in earlier chapters, trials are God's way of maturing His people by refining their faith in Him. Sometimes, however, it reveals that their faith is not genuine. Let's follow James' logic. He begins by saying that "the testing of your faith produces steadfastness" in your walk with Christ (Ja. 1:3). Until our steadfastness (or perseverance) is fully mature, we will be tested by trials.

If we do not grow from our trials, we lack wisdom and should ask God "in faith" to help us understand what it is we should learn (Ja. 1:5-6). The one who learns from his trials and perseveres to the end receives "the crown of life," which is salvation (Ja. 1:12). Perseverance occurs when wisdom is gained. Wisdom is gained when the "word of truth" (Ja. 1:18) is "implanted" in our hearts, received with gladness, and obeyed with joy (Ja. 1:21).

The trials we undergo that mature us as Christians are also a form of works. That is to say, they require responses and actions. They spur us on to deeds of obedience.

After James states that partiality is a sin and cannot co-exist with genuine faith, he explores the topic of true faith further by defining the connection between faith and works. He addresses the problem of not working out your salvation with "fear and trembling" (Phi. 2:12), while hiding behind the idea that "a person is not justified by works of the law" (Gal. 2:16) – using it as an excuse to be lazy in the faith.

> What good is it, my brothers, if someone says he has faith but does not have works? Can that faith save him? If a brother or sister is poorly clothed and lacking in daily food, and one of you says to them, "Go in peace, be warmed and filled," without giving them the things needed for the body, what good is that? So also faith by itself, if it does not have works, is dead.
>
> But someone will say, "You have faith and I have works." Show me your faith apart from your works, and I will show you my faith by my works. You believe that God is one; you do well. Even the demons believe—and shudder! Do you want to be shown, you foolish person, that faith apart from works is useless? Was not Abraham our father justified by works when he offered up his son Isaac on the altar? You see that faith was active along with his works, and faith was completed by his works; and the Scripture was fulfilled that says, "Abraham believed

God, and it was counted to him as righteousness"—and he was called a friend of God. You see that a person is justified by works and not by faith alone. And in the same way was not also Rahab the prostitute justified by works when she received the messengers and sent them out by another way? For as the body apart from the spirit is dead, so also faith apart from works is dead. (James 2:14-26)

True Faith is Alive

All people have faith. Each time we sit in a chair or drive a car we utilize a kind of faith. We trust that the chair will hold us up and that the car will get us to our destination. However, the Bible distinguishes this kind of faith from the kind of faith that saves. Theologians make the distinction by calling one a "saving faith" since it brings about salvation. Others have distinguished the two by using the descriptive word, "divine" when referring to a saving faith, and "human" when referring to any other faith.

If you were to ask someone near you what faith is, they might respond by saying it is trust. In a spiritual context, they would suggest that it is trusting in God. Others might argue that it is the systematic collection of doctrine found in the Bible (Jude 3). It was given to us and should be protected by us. Both are true. The culmination of biblical truth and trust in God is the idea of faith. Both the knowing and the trusting are God-given abilities. They are not something we can do on our own or without being spiritually awakened by the Lord.

> **The culmination of biblical truth and trust in God is the idea of faith.**

The author of saving faith is God, not man (Heb. 12:2). Therefore, the source of this faith is God (Acts 3:16; Eph. 2:8; Gal. 2:20; Rev. 2:13). Logically, this faith is powerful and cannot be defeated. It will persevere through all trials. For this reason, Paul wrote "I am sure of this, that he who began a good work in you will bring it to completion at the day of Jesus Christ" (Phil. 1:6). If God has given you faith to believe, then you will continue to believe until the end. You will persevere because it is God who is acting in you, on your behalf.

It would make sense then that if someone had divine faith, they would show the divine source. If God is working in you, then the word of God will be seen. Picture yourself on the lawn with the water hose in hand. Standing before the flowerbed, you holler, "Son, turn on the water!" Moments later, you hear his voice, "It's on, Dad." But, after a short period of time, no water is coming out of the hose. You wait longer; still no water. Your son is now standing next to you, both of you looking into the flowerbed. The water hose is limp. No pressure. No water. Would you wonder, "Is the water *really* turned on?" I know James would—if they had water hoses back then.

Actually, he does wonder this, asking, **"What good is it, my brothers, if someone says he has faith but does not have works?"** (Ja. 2:14). In other words, "You say that the water is turned on, but I don't see any water." There is a hint of this sort of thinking in the prior chapter of James. He wrote, "If anyone thinks he is religious and does not bridle his tongue but deceives his heart, this person's religion is worthless" (Ja. 1:26). Religion that does not bring discipline in our speech is a religion that does no good. God's gifts produce God's character in us.

It is important that we get the right idea about the word *good*. Although it could imply that something is morally right or acceptable, it actually means something more. It is the word *ophelos* which means "of gain" or "profit". "What is the advantage? What is the gain? What do you profit?" This is the idea behind his use of the word. James is asking if there is any benefit for saying you have faith but not works. To him, faith is like putting a lit candle in a room. It will light the room. On the other hand, a candle with no flame lights nothing. It has no use. What good is it to stand in a dark room with a candle with no flame? There is no advantage. The candle is useless. It does nothing for you or the room. It is dormant, static and lifeless both figuratively and literally.

> **God's gifts produce God's character in us.**

To go a step further, James is not asking any random person. He is asking the professing Christian, **"my brothers"** (Ja. 2:14). He wants them to think about faith. It comes from God, and God is alive and active. He is powerful and sovereign. If we possess the faith God gives, then we should see it. It should be obvious in our works. That is to say, the things that we do should resemble the character of God. As seen in the prior chapter, we should keep ourselves pure and unstained by the world. We should care for those in need and see trials as tools of God that bring about our sanctification.

Our works before God are things that we do with a redeemed mind. They are advantageous and morally right. In fact, when you read the word *work*, appearing at least once for every verse in this passage, you can easily say "righteous behavior" in your mind. This is the idea behind the word. It refers to the characteristics of faith found before and after this passage and throughout the Bible.

So the question is posed to us who say we have faith, "What usefulness is our faith if it does not show righteous behavior?" Jesus said "My sheep hear my voice, and I know them, and they follow me" (Jn. 10:27). On the other hand, those who do not believe and follow are "not part of my flock" according to the verse before. This no suggestion, this is reality. If you are part of the flock, you have divine faith which actively reveals itself in your life by causing you to faithfully follow the Lord. To those who do, "I give them eternal life, and they will never perish, and no one will snatch them out of my hand" (Jn. 10:28). James understood these words of Christ, so the second half of his question is this: **"Can that faith save him?"** (Ja. 2:13).

A Shocking Reality

My friend, this is the matter at hand. And it is a serious matter. So read the following words carefully. Faith that shows no transformation in the heart and no signature of God is a faith that has no advantage. It has no gain. It is dormant and dead. It shows nothing of significance. Does this sound like the faith that God gives? Does it appear to be the work of God in you? Should I answer that question? Of course not! Faith that has no works is not divine faith. It is not a saving faith. It is a human and natural faith. It is nothing more than what you use to sit down or drive a car or even pick up this book and turn the pages.

> **Faith that shows no transformation in the heart and no signature of God is a faith that has no advantage.**

This might sound shocking to you but it is all through the Bible. Remember the cry of John the Baptist early in Matthew's account? He was baptizing people in the river Jordan for the repentance of their sins when Pharisees and Sadducees came to see. John noticed them and said aloud, "You brood of vipers! Who warned you to flee from the wrath to come? Bear fruit in keeping with repentance. And do not presume to say to yourselves, 'We have Abraham as our father,'" (Matt. 3:7-9). In other words, your heritage will not save you. You cannot use that as an indicator. You must demonstrate your faith by repentance and fruit.

This is also taught from the lips of Christ. To begin with, "Not everyone who says to me, 'Lord, Lord,' will enter the kingdom of heaven, but the one who does the will of my Father who is in heaven" (Matt. 7:21). He goes on to say that some will even proclaim messages from God, cast out demons, and do other mighty works. But these "works" are not righteous behavior. They are miracles, and miracles do not imply a transformed heart—righteous behavior does. The people who do these things deceive themselves and their hearers. As we are discovering, this can happen.

Nicodemus, a Pharisee who approached Jesus one evening said, "Rabbi, we know that you are a teacher come from God, for no one can do these signs that you do unless God is with him" (Jn. 3:2). He uses the word "we" to identify himself with the group in Jerusalem who "believed in his name when they saw the signs that he was doing" (Jn. 2:23). Nicodemus was one of them. He believed in Jesus. Yet, Jesus knows his heart. Jesus saw the kind of faith he had. It was dead. So he says to Nicodemus, "Truly, truly, I say to you, unless one is born of water and the Spirit, he cannot enter the kingdom of God" (Jn. 3:5). The truth is, Nicodemus had a faith that was dead and would not bring him into the eternal kingdom.

Intellectual belief is not enough to save you.

Again in John 8, the "Jews who had believed in him" were told "If you abide in my word, you are truly my disciples, and you will know the truth, and the truth will set you free" (Jn. 8:31-32). Abiding in God's word, or continuing in obedience, is a demonstration of saving faith. Those who do, reveal themselves to be true disciples. The Jews believed but not to the point of salvation.

More passages like this drive home the same point, like John 15, where we read of the abiding and non-abiding branches, and Matthew 7, with the trees that bear good or bad fruit, and the professors and possessors of faith. The writer of Hebrews commanded us to "Strive for peace with everyone, and for the holiness without which no one will see the Lord" (Heb. 12:14). Paul taught, "For we are his workmanship, created in Christ Jesus for good works, which God prepared beforehand, that we should walk in them" (Eph. 2:10).

Intellectual belief is not enough to save you. Faith, if it is given by God, is demonstrable. You could call it forensic faith. Yet this is not what these people had. They had a spoken faith. They trusted in their heritage and their words. They had belief in their minds and were persuaded that was good enough. They believed their faith to be alive, but it was dead. Forensics could not detect the faith because there was no demonstration of righteous behavior. There was no signature of God.

Can faith that does not produce righteous behavior save you? The answer that James is seeking is "No, that kind of faith cannot save him." However, in the event that one answers otherwise, James proves his point. Again, using an illustration, he imagines: **"If a brother or sister is poorly clothed and lacking in daily food, and one of you says to them, 'Go in peace, be warmed and filled,' without giving them the things needed for the body, what good is that?"** (Ja. 2:15-16). He again employs the word *ophelos* to mean benefit, asking "What is the benefit of that?"

There are two lessons to learn from this illustration. The immediate one is that wishing well to someone has no benefit to their real condition. It is like passing a poor man in the street and telling him, "I'll pray for you brother." What does this do for his nakedness and hunger? What does it accomplish? On the other hand, what does it justify to say one thing and do another?

If you express your concern but do nothing about it, do you really have a concern? John wrote something very similar to this. He said, "If anyone has the world's goods and sees his brother in need, yet closes his heart against him, how does God's love abide in him?" (1 Jn. 3:17). So it is with faith. James concludes, **"So also faith by itself if it does not have works, is dead"** (Ja. 2:17). The use of the word *dead* is to bring our mind back to the idea of uselessness and lack of benefit. It is no good. Rather, such faith is like a water hose with no water, a battery with no charge, a car with no gas, a book with no words. It is dead and good for nothing. This leads us to the second lesson to observe.

This second lesson is deeper and more grave. It is assumed that this is one who cares for the poor, who is concerned about people. He is persuaded in his own heart that he is righteous and doing well. He notices the poor man who is lacking clothes and food. In his own heart, he is convinced that he is right and justified to say to the poor man, **"Go in peace, be warmed and filled"** (Ja. 2:16) But he does nothing more. He does what clears his conscience. He does what justifies his guilt. The phrase **"go in peace"** is a Jewish expression (Mk. 5:34). It is much like we might say today, "God bless you. Hope you do well." It is pious but empty. It says to the guilty conscience, "You are so generous to take the time to think of someone else." But it deceives you. It proves nothing. These words are of no use. They have no benefit. There is no advantage to wishing someone well when they have no ability to be well. In fact, it is callous and a rejection of their needy condition.

Picture yourself driving by a terrible car wreck on the road. You approach the driver's side of the wrecked vehicle and notice the driver upside down, pinned between the steering wheel and his door. He is conscious and crying out for help in fear of losing his life. You come to a slow pace and roll down your window to utter some words of comfort, "Get out of the car and head to the hospital, they will take care of you and Godspeed!" Now forgive me for being so obvious but, what good is that? How do your words help him? He is stuck in the car. And, if he could somehow get himself out of the car, his transportation is shot. Plus, he is likely unable to walk without help. Nevertheless, in your heart you feel better. So you drive away confident that you did a good deed.

To reinforce this, the Greek verb **"be warmed and be filled"** (Ja. 2:16) can be in the middle or passive voice. It can be taken as sarcasm or caustic. It might be read in the middle voice as, "You can't have my stuff, warm and feed yourself." It would then be cruel and indifferent to another's needs. It says that you would rather not be bothered with this needful person. On the other hand, if it is read passively, it would say, "Warm and feed yourself, don't bother me with your problems." Or, at best it might read, "I hope you find someone who can help you."

James throws this back in our faces and says, "No!" This is of no use. These words are empty and lifeless. They have no benefit. The so-called concern and care that you are comforted to have is dead. It is concern without any concern. It is care without any care. It is more like a corpse, lifeless and worthless to mankind, incapable of performing good works. In like manner, **"faith by itself, if it does not have works, is dead"** (Ja. 2:17).

The reason this is so deep and grave is because it speaks directly to the faith that you profess to have. It says that the faith you have is not the same kind of faith that can save you in the end. It is faith that is worthless in every way that matters. In fact, it is only good enough to deceive you into thinking that you really do have salvation when you do not. Consider Jesus' words in this regard. He is speaking of the final judgment when man will stand before the Lord and be declared innocent or guilty.

> "When the Son of Man comes in his glory, and all the angels with him, then he will sit on his glorious throne. Before him will be gathered all the nations, and he will separate people one from another as a shepherd separates the sheep from the goats. And he will place the sheep on his right, but the goats on the left. Then the King will say to those on his right, 'Come, you who are blessed by my Father, inherit the kingdom prepared for you from the foundation of the world. For I was hungry and you gave me food, I was thirsty and you gave me drink, I was a stranger and you welcomed me, I was naked and you clothed me, I was sick and you visited me, I was in prison and you came to me.' Then the righteous will answer him, saying, 'Lord, when did we see you hungry and feed you, or thirsty and give you drink? And when did we see you a stranger and welcome you, or naked and clothe you? And when did we see you sick or in prison and visit you?' And the King will answer them, 'Truly, I say to you, as you did it to one of the least of these my brothers, you did it to me.'
>
> "Then he will say to those on his left, 'Depart from me, you cursed, into the eternal fire prepared for the devil and his angels. For I was hungry and you gave me no food, I was thirsty and you gave me no drink, I was a stranger and you did not welcome me, naked and you did not clothe me, sick and in prison and you did not visit me.' Then they also will answer, saying, 'Lord, when did we see you hungry or thirsty or a stranger or naked or sick or in prison, and did not minister to you?' Then he will answer them, saying, 'Truly, I say to you, as you did not do it to one of the least of these, you did not do it to me.' And these will go away into eternal punishment, but the righteous into eternal life." (Matt. 25:31-46)

This is a sobering thing to consider. It will not be those who have a profession of faith that will be declared righteous in the end, or those who have walked the aisle and repeated a prayer. It will not be those who attended church their entire life. Rather, it will be those who have faith that is manifested in true compassion. Without such manifestation, we should wonder whether our faith is real or not. If our faith is of God, it will be alive and useful.

True Faith is Useful

The espionage agent known as Zartan has been troublesome to G.I. Joe on many occasions. He is called the master of disguise due to his keen ability to mimic both the voices and appearances of those whom he impersonates. He does it so well, that on some occasions, the real American heroes have wondered who was real. I have seen this sort of thing occur in more than one story. The impersonator and the one who is being impersonated are so similar that it is almost impossible to tell them apart. And such is the case at times when dealing with professing Christians. They all profess to believe in Jesus Christ. But sometimes, one is an impersonator.

Living faith is useful faith. It manifests good works and godly character. It reveals a transformation within. Therefore, we see works as proof of our changed heart. We see them as evidence that God has worked first and continues to do so. Still, as in every truth there is object and argument. James puts it this way, **"But someone will say, 'You have faith and I have works.' Show me your faith apart from your works, and I will show you my faith by my works."** (Ja. 2:18).

In the original Greek, this verse is difficult to sort out. We do not know for certain if James is referring to himself or arguing with an antagonist. Considering the context, the first is most likely true. The difficulty is due to the way the Greek was written. It had no punctuation to help us sort it out. However, the point is explicitly clear. Whether it is James or the antagonist that says "You have faith and I have works," the focus is on the depth of conviction. Truth faith runs deep within. False faith is shallow.

> Truth faith runs deep within. False faith is shallow.

For the sake of consistency, let us consider the first view to be the case. Suppose then, that the "someone" in the passage is James and he says to his listeners, "You have faith, and I have works." Imagine James standing before a few others who say to him, "We are Christians. We believe and are saved." James responds to them, "You say you are Christians. You *say* you believe and are saved. Now, *prove* it to me, for I can prove my profession with my works."

Go Ahead, Show Me

The line is drawn in the sand. The narrator asks, 'Will the true faith please stand up?' Which one is impersonating true faith and which one has true faith? James says the proof is in the works.

"Show me" is the idea here. It is the word *deixon* and it refers to demonstration. It implies an exhibition that can be observed by the senses. It is something more than just a motion or a spoken word. It is manifest and evident and far more trustworthy than what we so often say, "You can take me at my word." James wants evidence. He wants demonstration. He wants to observe true faith. So he says to the antagonist, "Show me and prove to me that what you say is true, that you do have true faith and deep conviction."

Moreover, he challenges the opposition. "Show me and I will show you." In other words, "Give me your evidence and I'll give you mine." Of course, the challenge is somewhat of a rhetorical call if such a thing exists. It is a challenge that no one can answer because it is impossible to prove true faith without pointing to good works. It simply cannot be done. The reason why is that true faith is only evidenced by works. This is why he said in the verse before, "faith by itself, if it does not have works, is dead" (Ja. 2:17).

> **It is impossible to prove true faith without pointing to good works.**

This reminds me of a story found in Numbers 16. It is about the face-off between Moses and Korah's rebellion. The rebels arose one day and accused Moses of exalting himself above the nation of Israel (Num. 16:3). Moses was deeply troubled and fell to his face. He then called the rebels to a face-off. Since they wanted the position of Moses and the priests, he told them to appear in the morning with their censers of offering unto the Lord. Those whose offerings the Lord accepted would be the ones who were actually called by God. It was not that long ago that two men were killed for making unauthorized offerings to the Lord (Lev. 10:1-2). So the expectation here should have been that those who are not authorized to make offerings would die. And so it happened.

The next morning they all stood outside the tents, before the Lord, and made their offerings of fire and incense. Immediately, God opened up the ground before those who rebelled and swallowed them along with all their family, and belongings (Num. 16:31-33). The challenge to them was to prove their calling. If God called them to priestly duties then God would not kill them. But if the opposite was true, well, you get the picture.

This is what James is doing. He is calling us all to appear before the Lord and one another. Our offerings are our works, our characteristics of faith, in order to prove our genuine salvation.

The challenge really puts the impersonator on the spot. "If you have faith, show it to me." But he cannot. This is because his faith is shallow and unreal, although it may be realistic to him. He might say, "Well, I believe in Jesus Christ. I believe that he is Lord and that he died for my sins." To this, James might ask in return, "Well fine, now show me that you believe, show me that he is Lord, show me that he died for your sins. Do not tell me, show me." Scouring for evidence, he might point to the time he said a prayer out loud, or the time he walked down an aisle in service, or the time he was baptized, or the time he helped the church food drive, or the time he cried because he felt so much love for God. But this is all he has. None of these things are inherently wrong nor do they say that one is not truly saved. However, none of them say beyond a shadow of a doubt that true faith exists in the heart. We would expect things like this would accompany the true Christian but, according to Scripture, they can also accompany a false Christian (Matt. 7:21-23). James is not condemning good things, he is only requiring those things that are manifested from a genuinely changed heart—one that has been radically transformed by God and granted divine faith.

God Will Prove His Own

The question that we are faced with then is this: How do we show something that is done within us? How do we show something supernatural and spiritual? I typically give the short answer when asked these questions. It is this: *We* do nothing. *God* does something. Just like in the case of Moses and the rebellion. They all stood outside with their offerings and God proved those who were His chosen. The truth of the matter is that true faith, since it is a gift of God and empowered by God for the end that God desires, is ultimately manifested by God when and where he plans.

A good place to start would be in 1 Peter 1.

> "Blessed be the God and Father of our Lord Jesus Christ! According to his great mercy, he has caused us to be born again to a living hope through the resurrection of Jesus Christ from the dead, to an inheritance that is imperishable, undefiled, and unfading, kept in heaven for you, who by God's power are being guarded through faith for a salvation ready to be revealed in the last time" (1 Pet. 1:3-5).

Salvation is the work of God—from the beginning to the end. It was Jesus who lived the perfect life and then paid the penalty for our sins. It was also He who caused us to be saved and who keeps and guards us through faith until our inheritance is actualized. "In this you rejoice, though now for a little while, if necessary, you have been grieved by various trials, so that the tested genuineness of your faith—more precious than gold and perishes though tested by fire—may be found to result in praise and glory and honor at the revelation of Jesus Christ" (1 Pet. 1:6-7). God will manifest His own holiness in those whom He has given His gift of faith, those whom He has caused to be born again. So we should "be holy in all [our] conduct" (1 Pet. 1:15).

Salvation is the work of God—from the beginning to the end.

To some degree, we have been made new. We have overcome the wicked one and been removed from the slavery of sin. We are able to live uprightly and say "no" to the evil ways of our prior nature. We have escaped the corruption of having fallen and will not be destroyed by the world and its wickedness. So, "by this we know that we have come to know him, if we keep his commandments" because "whoever says 'I know him' but does not keep his commandments is a liar, and the truth is not in him, but whoever keeps his word, in him truly the love of God is perfected" (1 Jo. 2:3-5). The works that God does in our lives is to bring about our obedience to Him. And, as we obey, we prove to ourselves and others that we are truly saved and recipients of true faith.

To put it more plainly, John says, "By this we may know that we are in him: whoever says he abides in him ought to walk in the same way in which he walked" (1 Jn. 2:5-6). This is not only biblically true, it is logically true. If God is the one who gives us faith and the faith that He gives is from, by, and in Him, then it makes sense that we would demonstrate a Christ-likeness. When people observe our living, they should notice that we are owned and empowered by someone else—someone holy, just, and loving.

Secured by Works, Assured by Works

We sometimes confuse assurance and security. Though they both seem to mean the same thing in some instances, they are different in the more specific sense. We are secure in Christ. More specifically, we are secure in the works that He has done on our behalf. He lived perfectly, died vicariously, and rose powerfully. His works were to an end—namely, to save His people from sin. I might add the obvious; He accomplished His end by His works. His works saved us and will keep us until the end. So our security is found in the works of Christ on the cross.

Christ lived perfectly, died vicariously, and rose powerfully.

But our assurance of the secured salvation will depend on the evidence we observe. If the evidence is manifesting Christ-likeness, then we will experience the joy of assurance. On the other hand, when we (even we who are truly saved) fall to the temptations of the world, we can experience doubt and wonder if our salvation is true. So then, assurance is also found in works, but these works are done by us—at least in the immediate sense. We do good and godly works which assure us of a genuine faith. However, we should never assume that the works we do are of our own generosity or ability. Rather, they too are a gift and a work of Christ in us. Therefore, assurance is a gift. We receive it as the Lord gives it. For this reason, the Psalmist wrote, "Restore to me the joy of your salvation, and uphold me with a willing spirit" (Ps. 51:12). Assurance of our salvation is the joy that we experience when the evidence of God's work in us is observed. Therefore, as one pastor said, "Assurance is a gift. Security is a fact."

Almost as Good As Demons

Still, some will deceive themselves into thinking that security is assurance, but this is not the case. Assurance will remind us of our security in the Lord. But the fact that we are secure in the Lord should never cause us to take such truth for granted. Just because we walk the aisle and say a prayer and assume that we have been born again, this may not be real. These things are not the acid test. Obedience and holiness are. Those who believe otherwise are in danger of eternal hell. In fact, listen to these strong words appearing after our text in James, **"You believe that God is one; you do well. Even the demons believe—and shudder!"** (Ja. 2:19). Our belief, if it is only as deep as our words, is no better than the belief of demons!

Now this is worth unpacking. This is a shocker to many of us who profess to be saved and to have faith. James reminds us that even demons believe that God is one. This is sound theology. The belief that God is one is a solid belief. You do well to believe it. In fact, you do better than most in our world. However, it is not enough to just believe that God is one or, as the original text might read, "belief in one God." The Jews prided themselves in doctrine, especially believing in one God, since there were so many varieties on earth. But this does not make you a Christian any more than it makes the demons less demonic.

I get a sense that James is being sarcastic when he says, **"You do well"** (Ja. 2:19). Although it is good and biblical that we believe in one God, it is not enough. So the idea behind what James is saying might be sarcastic, as if he were saying, "Good for you!" But so do the demons. Did you catch that?

One thing we know about demons is that they all know God in a light that we do not. They know, for the most part, the truth of God. We should not think that they are unlearned and confused about God and his nature. Demons are not heretics. They are not deceitful because they do not know. I think that all demons believe in the deity and triune nature of God. They believe that Jesus is divine and the Lord of all. They believe in the death, burial, and resurrection of Christ for the sins of the elect. In fact, they can probably agree with most church statements of faith—if the statements are biblical. The point is this: demons are not heretics. They believe everything in the Bible. They know far more than we do. (They simply choose not to like it and to go against it.) In fact, they do more than just believe. As James says, they **"believe—and shudder!"** (Ja. 2:19). This is to say that demons not only believe (and believe more truth than many of us), they also tremble before God.

Trembling is an expression of fear. The circumstance of it often reminds me of the story of Jonah. Although the term Christian is a New Testament word, it essentially refers to the person who has been saved by the atoning work of Christ. A Christian then is one who is identified with Christ. So let us call Jonah a Christian. He refers to himself as a "Hebrew, and I fear the Lord, the God of heaven" (Jon. 1:9). By his own admission, Jonah is a Christian. And by implication, a Christian would fear the Lord.

However, in the entire story, Jonah never shows fear—not even once. In the beginning we find God commanding him to go to Nineveh with a message. But Jonah refuses and goes in the opposite direction. Then he is caught in a wild thunderstorm in the middle of the sea, which is identified by Jonah to be the work of God. Yet, he is fearless of God's might. On the other hand, the sailors who owned the boat and were not Christians, "were exceedingly afraid" (Jon. 1:10). After learning that Jonah was a Christian, they became even more afraid, even afraid of the Lord (Jon. 1:16). This fear motivated them to offer sacrifices to the Lord. Still Jonah was unimpressed with the mighty hand of God and feared not.

The story goes on to tell us that Jonah is cast into the sea and is drowning when God appoints a giant fish to swallow Jonah and save him. Still, in the belly of the fish, Jonah is not fearful, although, as we read in his prayer to God, he believes that God has saved him and caused the winds and storms (Jon. 2:1-9). God has the fish spit Jonah out on the shore and again commands him to deliver His message to the Ninevites. This time, Jonah cooperates. But he is still fearless.

In Nineveh, Jonah proclaims the message of the Lord, "Yet forty days, and Nineveh shall be overthrown!" (Jon. 3:4). And the people cry out in fear. They cover themselves in sorrow, mourning in their fright. They turn from food and repent for their wickedness in hopes that God will relent (Jon. 3:7-9). So God withholds his wrath and the people are saved for the time being. Still Jonah is not trembling. In fact, he is angry with the Lord and instead fears for a small plant that dies on the mountainside (Jon. 4:6).

The story of Jonah is altogether backward. The Christian who should fear the Lord is the one who shows no fear. The pagans, who do not know to fear the Lord, are the ones who do. To bring this back to the passage in James, he says that because demons believe in the Lord and fear Him, they do more than most Christians. Yet, they will never enter the kingdom of heaven.

Matthew 8 presents an excellent example of this idea. When two demon-possessed men find Jesus unexpectedly, they cry out, "What have you to do with us, O Son of God? Have you come here to torment us before the time?" (Matt. 8:29). Notice that the demons had sound theology. They knew that Jesus was the Son of God. They also knew that He had power over them and could do whatever He wanted with them. Third, they had an understanding of the end times. They knew that Jesus would at some point come to torment them. They even knew that their time of torment was not at hand. And, in case you have not noticed, they are fearful. They are trembling before God. They are shuddering. In fact, they beg Jesus not to torment them and to give them a lesser wrath (Matt. 8:30-31).

> **We should have more than a shallow conviction of biblical truth.**

Many professing Christians lack even this much belief much less fear. This is James' point. Belief, even if it is biblically sound, is only intellectual faith if it does not have demonstrative works. Demons have this much belief and more. If we are to be assured of our security in Christ, we must seek to demonstrate our professed faith. We should have more than a shallow conviction of biblical truth. We should have works that give evidence of a transformed heart and the existence of divinely given, true faith.

Must I Show You?

"Must I show you?" These are words we never like to hear from those who teach us. It implies that we do not understand. "Do you not get it? Have you not learned anything?"

Yet, this is exactly what the Jews heard from James—and by implication, we hear as well. **"Do you want to be shown that faith**

apart from works is useless?" (Ja. 2:20). The "you" in this passage is still the same. It is the antagonist. It is the person who believes to have faith without works (Ja. 2:18). This person also believes in one God (Ja. 2:19). However, he cannot show his faith nor does he tremble at the knowledge of God. He is not even qualified to be a demon much less a Christian (Ja. 2:19).

James is still in challenge mode. He challenged this person to show and prove his faith. It reminds me of the hip hop battles of the 80s and 90s. A few guys would join in a circle and begin a battle with words. They were called "freestyle battles" because the guys would make up lyrics spontaneously. They would rap words and messages that were never written or memorized. The better their lyrics, the more talent they appeared to possess. And those who seemed to have the most talent would champion the battle. When one was called to battle, he would be told to "show-and-prove" because that was what he endeavored to do.

I do not suppose James to be a rapper, but I see the similarities between the two. They are in the circle for the battle of faith. They must show-and-prove their faith. But the one who has works is the one who triumphs.

In prior verses, James called the others to show their faith without works. It was a useless call, for they cannot show what they do not have. The faith that is natural to man is shallow and dead. It has little conviction and even smaller works. They cannot show him, they can only tell him. They can only point to things they recognize and did—things that anyone can do, even demons. So they're left silent in their pride. They cannot 'show-and-prove'.

But James can. "Do you want me to show you?" he asks them. "We came to battle and you had your opportunity. You failed. Now, must I show you the truth?" It is not a coincidence that the word "show" is used in both passages. In verse 18, James tells them to show their faith. That is to say he wanted a demonstration. He was seeking something in their life that indicated true faith. He was searching for good works. Now, in verse 20, after they are unable to show him, he says he will show them.

In the Greek, the words are not the same. Though they give the same impression which is easy enough to follow, their actual meanings give us a better glimpse of what James is aiming for. To achieve his aim, remember that true faith has manifestations of God's signature: godliness, justice, impartiality, love, generosity, joy, honesty, and more. These are things that can be observed by the senses. We can see, hear, smell, feel and taste when someone acts this way. They are demonstrable. They can be measured and counted and recorded. Therefore, we can show our faith by our actions.

For this reason, James tells the others to show their faith so that he can observe it. (Not meaning that they should show him on the spot, but that they should have shown it day-by-day in their lives so that a life-observer could acknowledge it.) Now, James is going to show them. This time, the word show does not mean "to demonstrate." Rather, it means "to learn." The words are in the same family of thought. They both involve knowing by observance. The first is to show or teach by showing. The second is to learn or be taught by showing. So James is going to teach them by showing them a thing or two—actually, two exactly. He is going to show them that **"faith apart from works is useless"** (Ja. 2:20).

True Faith Is Justified

If we can follow James' progression, we would see that true faith is alive and useful for many things. For example, living faith is useful to God in that it will produce a sacrificial offering to Him and in return be of good use to mankind. Living faith produces many things. It brings about holiness, obedience, kindness, charity, long-suffering, patience, self-discipline, and more. And by these things, it is justified. Thus, in an ultimate sense, faith is useful for justification.

We left off with James in the midst of a challenge. He waited for his opponents (those who say they have faith, but have no works) to show him their true faith. But they could not. So now he is going to show them why. He is going to give them the truth about faith and works, and he is going to do it by showing them real life.

Abraham, Justified by Works

He begins with Abraham. **"Was not Abraham our father justified by works when he offered up his son, Isaac, on the altar? You see that faith was active along with his works, and faith was completed by his** works; and the Scripture was fulfilled that says, 'Abraham believed God, and it was counted to him as righteousness'—and he was called a friend of God" (Ja. 2:21-23). Since his audience is Jewish, this makes a lot of sense. Abraham was (and still is) a popular person in Jewish life. He was the father of the Jews in one sense. Speaking to Jews, Paul referred to him as "our forefather according to the flesh" (Rom. 4:1). In the same way, Jesus says Jews are the "offspring of Abraham" (Jn. 8:33). He was also a great patriarch of ancient Israel and the symbol of all that was Jewish.

By referencing Abraham as **"our father"** James is likely meaning more than simply racial identity. Abraham was not only the forefather of ethnic Israel; he was also the forefather of spiritual Israel. That is to say he is also the spiritual forefather of Christianity. In a sense he is the father of the faithful, of all who believe and are saved. In his letter to the church in Galatia (who were not Jews) Paul wrote, "…it is those of faith who are the sons of Abraham" (Gal. 3:7). He argues that God justified the Gentiles by faith when He said to Abraham, "In you shall all the nations be blessed" and thereby included the Jews and non-Jews in the blessing of salvation. "So then, those who are of faith are blessed along with Abraham, the man of faith" (Gal. 3:7-9). Therefore, since James is writing to Jewish Christians, a reminder of their natural and spiritual father of faith would do them well—as it does us. Abraham embodied faithfulness to God.

So then, "Abraham, not only your natural father but also your spiritual father, was *justified by works*." Now, if you have begun this part of the chapter without first reading all that went before, or you have forgotten what you've read, then the phrase "justified by works" might have caught your attention. It certainly did for Martin Luther. He fought tooth and nail against the Roman Catholic teachings of being justified by works. He argued for justification by faith alone from many biblical passages. He pointed to Romans 4:3, 23-24, "Abraham believed God, and it was counted to him as righteousness … But the words 'it was counted to him' were not written for his sake alone but ours also. It will be counted to us who believe in Him who raised from the dead Jesus our Lord, who was delivered up for our trespasses and raised for our justification."

So what is it? Are we justified by faith or by works? "Yes." (I love to answer that way—it is really provoking.) To be justified means "to be declared righteous" before the Lord. If you have been justified, you are in right standing with God and are not held accountable for your sins. Only the saved are justified.

James said in verse 21 that Abraham was **"justified by works"** and in verse 23 he notes that Abraham was justified after believing God. Some people may get confused by James' assertion that Abraham was justified by works because Paul denies Abraham was justified by works in Romans 4:1-12. However, James was referring to a later time in Abraham's life (Gen. 22:9-10) long after he first believed God (Gen. 15:6). James is arguing that Abraham believed and his works of obedience proved he had faith. Therefore, James uses the word "justified" to say Abraham's works demonstrated his justification—not that they actually made him righteous before God.

As Paul puts it, justification is "not a result of works, so that no one may boast," but rather that "we are his workmanship, created in Christ Jesus for good works, which God prepared beforehand, that we should walk in them" (Eph. 2:9-10). So there is no contradiction here. Both are true because the word "justification" is understood in a different sense. Salvation is by faith alone and faith is justified (or demonstrated) by works. James believed this completely, which is why he quotes Genesis 15:6 (just as Paul did) saying, **"Abraham believed God and it was counted to him as righteousness"** (Ja. 2:23).

> **Abraham believed and his works of obedience proved he had faith.**

James is showing the Christian Jews that their father and prime example of faithfulness, Abraham, was vindicated by his works. His faithfulness demonstrated his true faith. Specifically, one work stood out from the rest. It is when Abraham was told by God to offer his son Isaac as a sacrifice on the altar (Gen. 22). **"You see that faith was active along with his works, and faith was completed by his works"** (Ja. 2:21). This is James' first proof of evidence. Abraham had true faith because he obeyed the Lord even to the most difficult ends—killing his own son.

So let us familiarize ourselves with the story found in Genesis 22. The chapter begins by saying, "God tested Abraham" (Gen. 22:1). If you are like me, this sounds exactly like the place James would select for his argument on testing our salvation.

God says to Abraham, "Take your son, your only son Isaac, whom you love, and go to the land of Moriah, and offer him there as a burnt offering on one of the mountains of which I shall tell you" (Gen. 22:2). It is important to note here that God promised Abraham many descendants and it was very late in his life when his first son was born. So, this was not easy to fathom. He might have wondered why God was taking away what he promised. We do not know for certain. What we do know is that Abraham trusted God. So although he did not understand it or know the future, he obeyed.

Abraham rose up early, prepared for the sacrifice and went to the place with his son, as instructed. Isaac noticed something strange. He saw the fire and wood for the altar, but he did not see the sacrifice. "Where is the lamb for a burnt offering?" he asked his father. Abraham responded, "God will provide for Himself the lamb for a burnt offering, my son."

Upon reaching the place of offering, Abraham bound his son and laid him on the altar. Then, certainly with fear and sadness in his heart, he took his knife to slaughter his son and was interrupted by an angel. "Abraham, Abraham!" The angel said, "Do not lay your hand on the boy or do anything to him, for now I know that you fear God, seeing you have not withheld your son, your only son, from me" (Gen. 22:11-13). This was what we call a Theophany, God appearing to mankind. Of course, God did not need to know what He already knew. This serves as an illustration of being justified by works. Abraham believed and was saved. He was righteous already. In his obedience, his **"faith was completed,"** according to James. So then, **"faith was active with his works"** (Ja. 2:22). The two are inseparable. Abraham had faith and so he had works. They were both living and useful in his life. They were noticeable and evident. Therefore, his works justified, demonstrated, gave evidence of his faith. His faith was vindicated by his works.

James says that this is when **"faith was completed by his works"** and **"Scripture was fulfilled"** (Ja. 2:22-23). Both of these refer to the fruition of his faith. Think of it as a tree that, until it bears fruit, might be a kind of unknown tree. But once the fruit appears, we can determine exactly what kind of tree it is. This is not to say that the tree was not already the kind of tree we observe now. It was that kind of tree all along. Only now we are able to see it. So it is with Abraham. He was righteous before his obedience was evident to others. He became righteous the moment he believed God and was imputed righteousness from God. But, until this righteousness was manifested, he was not righteous before men. Thus we are justified by faith before God and justified by works before men.

Contrary to what some have taught, Abraham's works did not contribute to his salvation. He was not lacking something in order to be saved and counted righteous. He simply needed to believe unto salvation. So James is saying that when his works made his righteousness evident, the process of coming to full fruition was completed. To use the illustration, his faith bore fruit before man which was already before God. This is true also of the phrase **"Scripture was fulfilled"** (Ja. 2:23). James does not mean that it was prophetically perfected but that Abraham's faith was brought to fruition. John Calvin wrote that man is not justified before man "by faith alone, that is, by a bare and empty knowledge of God; he is justified by works, that is, his righteousness is known and proved by its fruit."[2]

Such fruition warranted a most dignified description. James says that Abraham was **"called a friend of God"** (Ja. 2:23). This was a rare expression of deep intimacy and communion with God. This is never mentioned in Genesis with regards to Abraham. However, in 2 Chronicles 20:7 and Isaiah 41:8, he is called the friend of God. In Isaiah it is God calling Abraham, "My friend." I wonder if there is a higher call of affection from God than that? We find in Scripture that God is love and loves all in one sense. But few are called friends of the Lord. John 15:14 might be a good indication as to why. Jesus said, "You are my friends if you do what I command you." Maybe there are few friends of God because there are few who obey Him. Friendship with God is an exclusive right of those who have genuine faith, those who love and obey Him.

> **A person is justified by faith that is not alone.**

So, as James continues, **"You see that a person is justified by works**

---

[2] Calvin, John. "Epistle of James." *Calvin's Commentaries*. Vol. XXII. Grand Rapids: Baker, 2005. Print.

and not by faith alone" (Ja. 2:24). If we could be so daring as to alter this verse just a little so that it communicates the underlying meaning, it would read: "You see that a person is justified by faith that is not alone."

Rahab, Justified by Works

"**In the same way**" may not sound like much to you now, but it will in a few moments. James has brought to our attention the great patriarch, Abraham, who proved his faith over and over, especially in the most dramatic way. He was known to the Jews as a man worthy of recognition. Abraham was one who deserved the attention and who stood as a fine example for generations to come. He was a man of supreme importance to the Jews.

On the other hand, Rahab is the opposite. She is not a patriarch nor remembered for any excellences. Her story is small and subtle, even missed at times. She is insignificant and has done little to deserve praise from anyone after her. In fact, her life does not even stand out as exemplary. She was unimportant. And, if I might add without offending, she was a female.

The prior paragraph began with "on the other hand" which is totally appropriate for my point. But James employed a phrase utterly unlike mine to make his point. Actually, in the Greek, it is the one word, *homoios*. It does not mean sitting opposite or to the contrary. It means "likewise" and "in the same manner." It means that what was true of Abraham is true of Rahab. These two were opposites in almost every way possible on earth, but spiritually speaking they stood on level ground. They were both made righteous and, as James points out, were justified by works.

Rahab was a harlot living in Jericho. She operated an inn, which also served as a brothel. So she had women prostituting in her inn as additional services to lodging. This was how she made a living.

It just so happened (by God's providential decree) that the people of God were coming to receive Canaan, the land that God was giving them. When they arrived outside of Jericho, Joshua sent two spies to survey the city before they attempted to overthrow it. The two spies took refuge in Rahab's lodge when they became aware of the King's request to find them. He sent for Rahab and told her, "Bring out the men who have come to you, who entered your house, for they have come to search out all the land." But Rahab had already hidden the spies and lied to the King, sending him in a different direction (Josh. 2:1-7).

When the King's men left to find the spies, Rahab went to the two Israelites and said:

> "I know that the Lord has given you the land, and that the fear of you has fallen upon us, and that all the inhabitants of the land melt away before you. For we have heard how the Lord dried up the water of the Red Sea before you when you came out of Egypt, and what you did to the two kings of the Amorites who were beyond the Jordan, to Sihon and Og, whom you devoted to destruction. And as soon as we heard it, our hearts melted, and there was no spirit left in any man because of you, for the Lord your God, he is God in the heavens above and on the earth beneath. Now then, please swear to me by the Lord that, as I have dealt kindly with you, you also will deal kindly with my father's house, and give me a sure sign that you will save alive my father and mother, my brothers and sisters, and all who belong to them, and deliver our lives from death" (Josh. 2:8-14).

Rahab was certain that the Lord was going to give the Israelites the land. Notice her reaction to the news of what God did for the Israelites a year before. She said that "our hearts melted" and "he is God in the heavens above and on the earth beneath." She believed and, by risking her life by hiding the Israelite spies, she demonstrated her belief. These were not just words that she uttered. They were the genuine expressions of her heart and from a life of divine faith.

James says that she was **"justified by works when she received the messengers and sent them out by another way"** (Ja. 2:25). Again, this is the same picture as the prior one with Abraham. She believed and was counted righteous. She had true faith and was saved and this was vindicated by her actions when she risked it all and gave God's people refuge.

Now, you might be wondering about her actions specifically. You might have asked yourself, "Did she not lie? Is not lying a sin?" Of course it is. Rahab was not a seasoned disciple of God. She acted as she knew. She was by nature a liar and did not know what the Lord thought of it. She expressed her faith in the midst of her paganism not so much unlike us. I am confident she learned later on that we should never lie in order to protect ourselves or to protect God's plan. He is certainly capable of doing that Himself. But that was all she knew.

The point here is that she was given the opportunity to demonstrate her faith, to put it on display. And, if she had dead faith, she would have failed. She would have told them where the spies were or possibly never granted them lodging. But she had faith that is living and useful. It was active in her action. She put her belief on display and risked her life for the sake of God. In fact, she hid the spies, told them to save her and accept her into the family of God, gave them an escape and desired to worship the true God. This was her faith demonstrated. This is how she was justified by her works before man.

The Body and the Spirit

These are two monumental examples of how true faith is revealed. It is not a matter of who goes to church, who attends the Bible study, who carries a Bible, or who walks the aisle. Although these things are good and should accompany those with true faith, they are not evidence of living faith. Rather, a denial of self and a surrender to God's commands whereby our actions are dramatically altered and sanctified in obedience to the Lord is where true assurance lies.

James' final word is this, **"For as the body apart from the spirit is dead, so also faith apart from works is dead"** (Ja. 2:26). This one last metaphor says it all. We exist materially and immaterially. That is to say that we have a physical body that gets old and decays and will at some time go back to the dirt from which it came. We also have a spiritual body that will eternally exist. Our physical body is lifeless without our spirit. So it is with those who have passed away. Their spirits have continued on to another place and their bodies have stopped living. They are dead. In this same way, faith, if it is separated from works, is dead. Faith does not live without works. Works walk hand-in-hand with faith. Otherwise faith is dead, useless, and unable to save.

> **Our works do not save us, but they do validate our salvation.**

True faith, at its very core, is alive. And because it is alive, it is useful to God and to the benefit of man. These many useful things assure us of the security that we have in Christ. Our works do not save us, but they do validate our salvation. In this sense they justify us, according to James.

We are saved by faith alone, but faith is never alone. Is this what you can say about yourself?

Conclusion

Martin Luther was right to address the prevailing heresy of his day (buying salvation) with gospel truth. It is critical to our salvation that we understand God's truth. The Five Solas of the Protestant Reformation state that, "According to Scripture alone, we are saved by grace alone through faith alone in Christ alone for the glory of God alone."

It is by faith that we are declared and counted righteous, just as Abraham was. Likewise, our faith, if it is from God, does not stand alone but comes with good works. These works don't save us, but they do attest to our salvation.

In closing, take time now and as you journey through life to ask yourself what your works say about your faith in God? Do you have belief but not behavior? Do you profess faith in Him but not obey Him? Do you love Jesus to the point that you are willing to risk your life? Is your faith alive? Is it useful? Is it justifying itself?

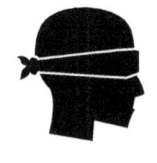

CHAPTER 5

THE TRIAL OF SPEECH

JAMES 3:1-12

"from the same mouth come blessing and cursing"

Your tongue says the most about who you are. It quite literally tells all. Since it has no boundaries or limitations, it is one of the easiest ways to sin. Anyone can misuse their tongue and, if we are honest, we speak ill more than we wish. In describing the dangers of the tongue, Pastor John MacArthur said it is, "no wonder why God has put it in a cage behind the teeth, walled in by the mouth."[1]

The tongue reveals the heart, which is where sin originates (Matt. 15:19). Jesus taught that people are like trees that are known by their fruit (Matt. 12:33-37). They either produce good fruit or bad fruit. Perhaps the most sobering thought regarding the tongue is that everyone must "give account for every careless word they speak, for by your words you will be justified, and by your words you will be condemned" (Matt. 12:36-37).

James warns believers to be careful of what they say. His counsel includes telling us to be "slow to speak" (1:19), to "bridle [your] tongue" (1:26) and to speak "as those who are to be judged under the law of liberty" (2:12). In fact, he warns us to watch our words throughout every chapter of his book! He was clearly very concerned about our ungodly speech.

In this portion of James' letter, we will explore the trial of speech. This is the test of the tongue. What would a thorough examination of

---

1 MacArthur, John. *The MacArthur New Testament Commentary: James.* Moody Press, Chicago (1998). p.144.

your words reveal?

> Not many of you should become teachers, my brothers, for you know that we who teach will be judged with greater strictness. For we all stumble in many ways. And if anyone does not stumble in what he says, he is a perfect man, able also to bridle his whole body. If we put bits into the mouths of horses so that they obey us, we guide their whole bodies as well. Look at the ships also: though they are so large and are driven by strong winds, they are guided by a very small rudder wherever the will of the pilot directs. So also the tongue is a small member, yet it boasts of great things.
>
> How great a forest is set ablaze by such a small fire! And the tongue is a fire, a world of unrighteousness. The tongue is set among our members, staining the whole body, setting on fire the entire course of life, and set on fire by hell. For every kind of beast and bird, of reptile and sea creature, can be tamed and has been tamed by mankind, but no human being can tame the tongue. It is a restless evil, full of deadly poison. With it we bless our Lord and Father, and with it we curse people who are made in the likeness of God. From the same mouth come blessing and cursing. My brothers, these things ought not to be so. Does a spring pour forth from the same opening both fresh and salt water? Can a fig tree, my brothers, bear olives, or a grapevine produce figs? Neither can a salt pond yield fresh water. (James 3:1-12)

True Faith is Mature

There is a morning kid's show that features Hip Hop Harry, a snazzy bear dressed in urban attire who raps wisdom. My kids love him. Inevitably, in each episode he says something like, "When I say 'Hip Hop' you say 'Harry'!" Naturally, he then hollers "Hip Hop" and my kids holler back, "Harry!" You know that old-school buzz tactic to get the pep rallied. I was hoping it would help me right now. "When I say 'teacher' you say …" Well, what do you say? Did any of these words come to mind: obnoxious, boring, ignorant, uninformed, worn out, unfashionable? If you were any younger, would those accurately express your immediate response?

I know that they would have come to my mind. When I was young, I thought that I was the smartest one on the planet and teachers were there to make my life miserable. I did not appreciate them. They were good for one thing: being the object of my mischief.

There is a particular day of school that I recall more vividly than others. It was the first day of my sophomore year. First days were always easygoing. There were only a few things that would happen. One was that the teachers would call role for the first time. My biology teacher prefaced it by giving us the option of telling her our nickname. There were a few students in school who were named one thing but called by another. For example, my friend Rudolph answered to Rudy.

My friends called me Toop which was short for "toupee," a word describing my super-cool skater haircut. But it was not really a nickname per se. None of my family called me that. However, the teacher asked and I was ready to be mischievous.

I was usually the first name called since names were listed in alphabetical order. "Jacob Abshire," the teacher said. "Here," I replied. "I go by Toop." She peaked over her paper, one eye cocked, and mumbled, "O ... kay." My friends knew what I was doing, so they joined in. "Derin DePalermo." He responded with "I go by Dez." She wrote it down. "David Hudgens." He told her, "Deemo is what I go by." She knew something was up but didn't say anything. It continued with a couple of others who had real nicknames, which sort of distracted her. But this was about to change.

My friend Jake didn't have a nickname, but he wanted in on the fun. So when she called his name, he said, "Please call me ..." he paused to think. "Jake the Snake!" he responded and immediately the class burst into laughter. The teacher laid her paper on the desk angrily. "We are not going to start the year off like this," she informed us. "Everyone will be called by their given name!"—which was unfortunate for Rudolph. It was equally unfortunate for the teacher, considering the year had already started in the way she'd hoped it would not. But we enjoyed it.

The Monkey Wrench

When we think of teachers today, we rarely think of noble, dignified, astute authoritarians who walk on clouds and dish out words of wisdom. Rather we view them as we did when we were young, mischievous pranksters. I know this is true in general because our society reflects it. We are, if you will pardon my English, getting dumber and dumber. Teachers are getting paid less and less. Districts are allowing learning standards to suffer, and educators are losing more and more rights. I heard my parents would receive spankings in class if they dared act as students do today. And I hear things are getting worse each year. While there are many reasons for this, one primary reason is that we have such a poor opinion of teachers. In fact, kids would rather be taught by uneducated pop stars than someone well trained in their field of education.

Are you wondering why I bring this up? Trust me, it is not because several of my friends and family members are teachers or that I hear numerous stories of kids involved in inappropriate situations even in kindergarten. I could get on a soapbox concerning teachers and how important it is for them to receive better training in the field of education, as well as more money once they become teachers. But I won't.

Rather, I bring it up because James 3:1 will throw a big monkey wrench in this entire chapter if you do not get the picture like the early Christian Jews did. I do not want that to happen on my watch. If you are like most Americans (myself included), then you have to rethink what is meant when someone brings up the word "teacher."

As mentioned earlier, James is instructing on matters of faith with regards to how it is demonstrated with our speech. An overview of the following verses say things like: the tongue controls the body, it is a fire from hell, a restless evil, forked and untamable, and like wild beasts, we should not let our tongues run wild. But, by way of introducing all of this, James says, **"Not many of you should become teachers"** (Ja. 3:1). What? What do teachers have to do with it? Exactly, and this is my point. Teachers, or at least the picture of teachers we conjure up, have little, if anything, to do with the point I am making. Ergo, the monkey wrench.

Teachers in Perspective

If we are to understand James correctly, we need to put on the Jewish mindset. Teachers to us are not the same as teachers to them. They were not objects of ridicule. They were prized persons and highly esteemed individuals. The Jews desired far more for their souls than their bodies. They cherished eternity and living for God. Unlike people of our time, they longed for eternal wisdom. Heaven was everything to them. This life was merely a place to be trained for the life hereafter. So matters of eternity were more valuable than matters of this earth.

The Talmud, a collection of Jewish commentaries and ethical wisdom, describes teachers as the most important people among men. It tells us to "Let thine esteem for thy friend border upon thy respect for thy teacher, and respect for thy teacher on reverence for God."[2] In another place it reads, "Respect for a teacher should exceed respect for a father, for both father and son owe respect to a teacher."[3] In the roster of respect and honor, God was first and teachers were second. Only after them would you place your parents and friends and officials. Even the father, though he was highly important to Jewish life, was less value than the teacher. In fact, it is suggested that if your house is burning down and both your father and teacher are inside, you should rescue the teacher first. Likewise, if they both suffer loss, the "teacher's loss has the precedence" and he "must first be assisted in recovering it." It is probably best explained this way:

> "For his father only brought him into this world. His teacher, who taught him wisdom, brings him into the life of the world to come"[4]

Think about it. In which world will you live the longest? The world to come is most important. So the bringer of world-to-come wisdom is most important and therefore worth the first and highest honor among man.

This honor used to belong to priests but by the time of the New Testament, the priests had given their responsibility of scientific law study to the Scribes and then broken trust with the people. The Scribes then took their place as the "real teachers of the people." They were overseers of Israel, "over whose spiritual life they bore complete sway."[5] That is to say that the Scribes were the most familiar with the Mosaic Law. Therefore, they were the most valuable people and worthy of everyone's attention. The Scribes were the go-to ones. When they spoke, people listened eagerly. When they finished speaking, the people obeyed earnestly.

---

[2] Pirkei Avot 4:12.

[3] Kerithoth 6:9.

[4] Baba Mezia 2:11.

[5] Schürer, Emil. "Scribism. The Scribes and Their Activity in General." *A History of the Jewish People in the Time of Jesus Christ. Second Division, Vol. 1*. Peabody, MA: Hendrickson, 2009. 313. Print.

Since the Jewish nation was theocratic, meaning that they were governed by God, the Scribes took prominence in almost all facets of society, not just the spiritual. They were found among the lawyers (Matt. 22:35; Lk. 7:30), the Pharisees (Matt. 12:38; Mk. 7:5; Lk. 6:7), the judges, the officials, the chief priests (Matt. 16:21), the aristocrats, the Sanhedrin, and were sometimes called Rabbi (Matt. 23:7). After the transfiguration, the disciples who saw Jesus with Moses and Elijah asked Jesus a question based on teachings of the Scribes (Matt. 17:10). Apparently, their teachings held that much weight. Even Jesus told the people to "practice and observe whatever they tell you" (Matt. 23:2). But with great honor came great responsibility.

Don't Rush to Moses' Seat

The role of the teacher was sometimes referred to as "Moses' seat". This is because the Israelites' heritage can be traced back to the role Moses played in leading them. God used him to deliver the Israelites from Egyptian slavery (Ex. 3:10). As God enabled, Moses led the nation out of Egypt and into the wilderness where he received the Law of God. This Law was for him to understand, teach, and use to govern the Israelites. Therefore Moses sat in the highest authority among the people, acting as God's ambassador and shepherd of the Jewish nation. He knew the Lord and so the people drew near to him for instruction on life and spiritual living. When Jethro, Moses' father-in-law, arrived, Moses explained to him that "the people come to me to inquire of God; when they have a dispute, they come to me and I decide between one person and another, and I make them know the statutes of God and his laws" (Ex. 18:15-16).

> **With great honor came great responsibility.**

This is where the Scribes come into play. They were metaphorically sitting in the seat of Moses, overseeing and shepherding the Jewish nation. Since they knew the law, they were appropriate for the position. However, their sinful nature got the best of them as it does all people. The Scribes were the object of Jesus' rebukes time and time again.

One time in particular is best known as the "Seven Woes" and is found in Matthew 23. Ironically, it is right after Jesus tells the crowd to "practice and observe whatever [the teachers] tell you." He adds one gigantic condition: "but do not what they do. For they preach, but do not practice" (Matt. 23:2-3). Jesus calls them hypocrites six times in this huge rebuke, which is almost once for every rebuke! He says that they "shut the kingdom of heaven in people's faces" and "neither enter yourselves nor allow those who would enter to go in" (Matt. 23:13). He tells them that instead of making followers of God, they make them "twice as much a child of hell as yourselves" (Matt. 23:15).

In case you are wondering, these are strong indictments. I can think of no other people that have suffered such a strong rebuke from the Lord. This is because they are more responsible, since they have been given more than others. They were given the privilege to devote their time to scientific study of the law and the ability to understand it. Of all of the people who should live according to the law, they should have. But this was not so. Instead, they were leading the people to hell. They were "blind guides" as Jesus called them (Matt. 23:16).

These kind of teachers existed after Jesus' ascension. Paul said that certain persons "have wandered away into vain discussion, desiring to be teachers of the law, without understanding either what they are saying or the things about which they make confident assertions" (1 Tim. 1:6-7).

> **The guide is guiltier than those who follow.**

They also existed long before Jesus was born. And God judged them just as intently. Remember the story of Korah, Dathan, and Abiram? They led a revolt against Moses and the repercussions were awesome to say the least. God opened up the earth below them and it "swallowed them up, with their households" and the people whom they led (Num. 16).

It is certainly bad when a leader is wrong. But consider all of those whom the leader brings with him into his error. Those who share in his error are guilty. But on the shoulder of their blind guide, the summation of their collective guilt is applied. The guide is guiltier than those who follow. The writer of Hebrews puts it this way, "they are keeping watch over your souls, as those who will have to give an account" (Heb. 13:17). For this reason, **"Not many of you should become teachers, my brothers, for you know that we who teach will**

be judged with greater strictness" (Ja. 3:1).[6] To whom much is given, much is required (Lk. 12:48). The teachers were given much, even more than the understanding of the law. They were given the trust of a nation.

The Weapon of Choice

Assuming I did well to explain, you have a better context of the passage. But one question might remain: What do teachers have to do with the trial of speech? You might see it already. If you do, allow me to affirm your assumptions. Teachers are the best examples for why our speech is so dangerous. In order to do serious damage to the soul, the weapon of choice is the tongue. With our speech, we influence a great many things. Teachers influence with their words.

In his commentary on this passage, R.C. Sproul says that the "strict judgment should restrain teachers from careless words"[7] and I would add that it would cause wannabe teachers to reconsider or at least consider more carefully. This way, only the dedicated and disciplined would pursue such a position.

Such strictness is necessary, **"For we all stumble in many ways"** (Ja. 3:2). To this matter, Paul wrote to Timothy, a fellow pastor-teacher, telling him to "keep a close watch on yourself and on your teaching. Persist in this, for by so doing you will save both yourself and your hearers" (1 Tim. 4:16). Do you see the parallel? Whether you are a Scribe or a Pastor, you are meant to handle God's Word rightly as well as the words you use to communicate.

We all stumble with our words. We say evil things more than we ought to and more than we know—some we regret and some to which we are totally oblivious. "Who can say, 'I have made my heart pure; I am clean from my sin'?" (Prov. 20:9). Second Chronicles 6:36 answers, "there is no one who does not sin." No one. "All have sinned," Paul writes (Rom. 3:23). It could not be plainer. We all stumble—especially

---

[6] It is interesting how various translations of this verse read. It might provide even more insight to James' message. The King James Version offers the most obvious, "Be not many teachers." The New International Version takes it a step further, "Not many of you should *act* as teachers" (emphasis mine) which seems to suggest that some were imitating the office of a teacher when they were never in such a position. The Living Bible goes even further and says, "Don't be eager to tell others their faults." Since the teachers were judges and discerners of people's affairs, they were in the position of exposing faults. Here, James is telling them not to be fault-finders.

[7] Sproul, R.C. *The Reformation Study Bible*. Orlando Florida: Ligonier Ministries, 2005.

with our speech.

Depending on whom you ask, the average amount of words a man speaks each day is about 7,000. A woman, on the other hand, can utter over 20,000 each day. Together, that is about the size of a 100-page book. To put it in perspective, if my wife and I were having our words transcribed for a book, we could potentially publish 365 books each year! That adds up to a whole lot of embarrassment. The opportunity to sin is there. Think of the potential. We could be locked permanently in a confessional booth, were it necessary.

The tongue is behind our words. It is the mechanism by which we speak, so it tells our tale. It puts our heart on display like an automatic, rapid-fire gun. If we were assassins of the soul, the tongue would be our weapon of choice.

The Tongue Made Me Do It

I cannot tell you how many times my son has blamed his hand or his brain for his actions. Do you know why he took my hammer without asking? He could not stop his hand. Guess why he forgot to grab his school books or could not go to sleep? Right, his brain would not let him. My son is a very intelligent boy and I am his biggest fan, but he has this all wrong. His body parts were not the culprits. His inner desires were.

Jewish writers often employ a literary device of attributing blame to a specific bodily member as if it acted autonomously. It is quite popular. In quoting a proverb, Paul said, "Their feet are swift to shed blood" (Rom. 3:15). Peter wrote, "They have eyes full of adultery" (2 Pet. 2:14). These devices can be found all through the Bible. We should understand them for the figurative language they are. Paul did not want you to think that your feet acted independently from your heart and mind. Rather, your body parts do as you will them to do. You are to blame, not your body parts. But this was a way of communicating among the Jews.

Death and life are in the power of the tongue.

James blames the tongue using this device, just as the Psalmist said that our tongues are like swords and our words like arrows (Ps. 64:3). Proverbs 18:21 goes so far as to say that "Death and life are in the power of the tongue." It is not that the devil made me do it. It is that my tongue made me do it. My son must be a Jew at heart.

The Perfect Man

A preacher once said, if you ever find a perfect church, do not join it because you will contaminate it. He said this in a joking way, but it is no joke. A perfect church is a church without people. As soon as you join it, you make it imperfect.

"For we all stumble in many ways" with our words especially (Ja. 3:2). This is to say that we all have sinned, are sinning and will sin until we join our Lord in eternity. So, there is no way of getting around it. However, we can work at making ourselves less vulnerable to stumbling. I often quote a rapper who said, "We ain't sinless, we just sin less." If you are genuinely saved and have the divine gift of faith, then this is true of you. And this is what James is after.

If the tongue is the most dangerous weapon and the easiest way to sin, then it is the most accurate gauge of our salvation. In fact, you might recall that the first expression of sin in the existence of mankind was the sin of the tongue. God found Adam hiding after he ate fruit from the forbidden tree and asked him about it. To God, he answered, "The woman whom you gave to be with me, she gave me fruit of the tree, and I ate" (Gen. 3:12). Adam had the gall to slander God for his own sin! He also blamed his wife—without using the Jewish literary device, I might add.

> **Adam had the gall to slander God for his own sin!**

There might not be anything that demonstrates our sinfulness more than our use of our tongue. It is compelling. Consider Paul's description of man's sin as he summarizes wisdom from the Psalms, "Their throat is an open grave; they use their tongues to deceive. The venom of asps is under their lips. Their mouth is full of curses and bitterness" (Rom. 3:13-14). For this reason, James writes, **"And if anyone does not stumble in what he says, he is a perfect man, able also to bridle his whole body"** (Ja. 3:2).

Does James mean to suggest that such perfection is attainable? If so, then maybe there is a perfect church somewhere that is full of perfect people. The word "perfect" in the Greek is the word *teleios* which has two possible meanings. One meaning is the idea of absolute perfection and without any flaw or error. If this is what James means, than he must be speaking hypothetically since he just said in the same verse that "all stumble in many ways" (Ja. 3:2). This could certainly be the case and would also flow with the rest of his thoughts.

On the other hand, there is a second meaning that might be more appropriate to what James is saying. The word *perfect* can also mean "mature and complete." If this is true than James is telling us that you can spot true faith at work by listening to a person's communication. If they are disciplined with their tongue, they are demonstrating a changed heart. This parallels what he wrote in the first chapter, "If anyone thinks he is religious and does not bridle his tongue but deceives his heart, this person's religion is worthless" (Ja. 1:26). Why? Because anyone who has been given the gift of divine faith will inevitably demonstrate control over the tongue. It is repeated over and over by James: people who are genuine Christians are no longer slaves to sin but able to withstand it (Rom. 6:1-14). Self-control is a characteristic of the *fruit* of the Spirit of God (Gal. 5:22-23). If the Spirit of God is working in you, then the evidence of self-control will manifest.

Whatever you take the word perfect to mean, you arrive at the same conclusion. One who is perfect will **"not stumble in what he says"** and will ultimately demonstrate perfection in all aspects of his life (Ja. 3:2).

Save the Tongue, Save the World

I was somewhat of a fan of the now-retired TV series, *Heroes*. Season one made popular a tagline that went like this: "Save the Cheerleader, Save the World." It captured the storyline pretty accurately. There was a cheerleader who was pinnacle to the salvation of the entire world. If she would be saved, so would the world. Therefore, to save her was the mission of the other heroes.

This is what I picture when I read this portion of James' letter. If we save the tongue, we can save the world. He wrote that a perfect man is one who is able to **"bridle his whole body"** because he has first bridled his tongue (Ja. 3:2 with 1:26). This is the emphasis that he places on the tongue and the reality he finds true about us all. Our speech is the hardest to control and if we can control it, we can easily control the rest of our body and thereby resist sin.

The word **"bridle"** is a word of constraint. It means to guide and restrain. It carries the idea of control and dominance. I find it interesting that this concept is present in almost every verse in this passage on speech. It is certainly a concept James wants us to understand. After the word "bridle" in verse 2, we find "bits" which is a bridling tool used with horses. It means to restrain. In the same verse is the Greek word *peithesthai* which is translated "obey us" and refers to convincing. A third word in this verse is *metagomen* which means "to turn about." The verses that follow use words that imply governing, willing, kindling, taming, and more. James wants us to think about control. Who is controlling their tongue? And who is the tongue controlling?

Bits and Rudders

I like the first two illustrations that James uses to help us imagine the power of the tongue and what it does to our whole life. They really need no explanation or interpretation. However, I would be a poor author to skip this part and pretend that we need not consider it.

"If we put bits into the mouths of horses so that they obey us, we guide their whole bodies as well" (Ja. 3:3). I have little experience in this area. My grandfather had horses when I was young but I was terrified of them. They were far too big. Occasionally, however, I would muster the courage to ride one—but only when I was accompanied by others. We would typically hop into the saddle and roam the trails behind my grandfather's property. It was fun. The trails would wind, and climb and drop. It was quite the adventure.

The horses were smart enough to follow the trail, but to keep them on course we would pull the reins—a leather strap that connected to a bit in the horse's mouth, with a small metal piece that laid on the horse's tongue. We would pull to the right to turn the horse right. Likewise, we would pull to the left to go left. Pulling back would bring the horse to a stop.

In the back of my mind, I was always aware that this large animal could toss me into the air and trample me under its hooves with a force so strong, it is used to describe the power of engines in automobiles. Yet, I could use the reins, a small strap, to guide and control it whichever way I wanted to go. This was absolutely amazing to me. James' point really made sense once I got the picture. By controlling the horse's tongue, I am controlling the horse's movements.

The second illustration is not that easy to picture, at least not from memory. "**Look at the ships also: though they are so large and are driven by strong winds, they are guided by a very small rudder wherever the will of the pilot directs**" (Ja. 3:4). There were no large ships in those times that come to my mind as being comparable to the gigantic ocean liners we have today, except maybe for Noah's ark. In Acts 27, we find Paul aboard a ship carrying cargo of wheat (Acts 27:38) from Alexandria to Rome. It was large enough to have four anchors (Acts 27:29) with an additional two or more on the bow (Acts 27:30) and a small rowboat (Acts 27:16, 30). In addition to all of this, there were 276 persons in the ship (Acts 27:38). This should give us a good perspective of size. Traditionally, we know ships were generally used for trade and war. The largest ones stretched about 150 feet long with a width of about 50 feet. Still, it is uncertain how large a ship James is referring to when he employs his illustration.

However, the nature of the illustration, as well as the fact that he has not specifically mentioned any particular ship as reference, suggests that the size is actually subject to the imagination. The word translated "so large" in our English text is the Greek word, *telikoutos*. It is used three other times in the New Testament. The first describes a kind of terrible death (2 Cor. 1:10). The second describes a valuable and endless salvation (Heb. 2:3). The third describes a powerful earthquake, the likes of which no man will ever hear on earth before it (Rev. 16:18). It is an abstract word used to refer to something bigger, older, and more powerful than you first imagine. So, I think James wants us to use our imagination.

Ships today are much larger than they were back then. They can be as large as small cities. And the illustration accommodates that. As the boat grows, the imagery grows. However, the largest ships are still controlled by rudders small enough that one person can steer. James says that though the winds move (as motors do in our time), they are "**guided by a very small rudder wherever the will of the pilot directs**" (Ja. 3:4). These pilots can usher cruise liners within a few feet of a dock without ever touching it. This is power to control.

James' point is this: the tongue, though it is small, has the power to control you and you have the power to control it, which will then control your whole body. Think of your tongue as being the small rudder. Where you want your body to go will be judged by how well you control your tongue, or worse, by how your tongue controls you.

One pastor equated the tongue to the master electric switch. I have one of these breaker boards in the back of my house. It has a bunch of switches that provide or cut the electric current to different parts of my home. They control the electric current to those appropriate rooms. But at the top of the board is something called a "master switch". By turning it off, it renders all the other breakers useless. It is the main source that controls all the other ones. This is the picture that James wants us to get. The tongue is the master switch. It controls the rest of us. Therefore, James adds, **"So also the tongue is a small member, yet it boasts of great things"** (Ja. 3:5).

> The tongue is the master switch. It controls the rest of us.

True faith is demonstrated by how well the tongue is controlled. It is a matter of maturity. You can be more or less in control, but it will be evident to you and those around you, that your tongue is becoming less a weapon and more a tool for Biblical use. True faith is mature. It is perfect in the sense that it is being made sinless, though not completely sinless. A mark of a genuine Christian is the mark of oral maturity, self-control in speech. The tongue boasts of great things. Of what does your tongue boast, may I ask?

True Faith is Disciplined

In May of 2009, *USA Today* reported statistics indicating that people were at fault for over 5,000 wildfires in Southern California in 2008 alone.[8] A week before publishing this report, the Santa Barbara area suffered a blaze that destroyed 78 homes and about 13 square miles. Apparently the fire was caused by sparks from a power tool. Two years prior, a pipe grinder accidentally ignited a 240,000-acre wildfire in the county. Another report mentioned that four out of five wildfires in the nation are caused by humans. From 1997 to 2006, these fires turned 57

---

[8] Blood, Michael R. USA Today. 14 May 2009. 16 Jan. 2011 <http://www.usatoday.com/weather/wildfires/2009-05-14-human-caused-wildfires-increasing_n.htm>.

million acres to ash.[9] That is a lot of destruction.

I played a part in starting a fire once, quite by accident. It didn't compare to the ones that appear on the news, however. I was a young boy and just getting to know the functions of the stove top. My mother taught me how to make grilled cheese sandwiches. I still make these today, though I'll probably persuade my wife to do the cooking after this story.

I was a pretty impatient lad and our stove was electric. It took longer to heat than the ones fueled by natural gas. So, typically, I would turn the stove on and sit in front of the television for a few minutes before I slapped the bread together with the cheese. Unfortunately, I forgot to check the top of the stove for pans. There was one resting right on top of the grill I was using, full of grease from breakfast.

The first thing I noticed was the smell of smoke. I looked behind me into the kitchen, saw the smoke, and panicked. I rushed into the kitchen just as the smoke alarm sounded. My mother was in her bedroom on the other side of the house and I did not want to upset her. I grabbed a glass of water and threw it on the pan which, to my surprise, splashed grease all over the stove and countertop and made the fire four times the size it had been. It happened so quick. I didn't know what to do after that since I thought water was the only fire-fighting agent. Thankfully, my mother came to my rescue. She turned off the stove, which had totally slipped my mind, then doused the flames with towels and the fire was out in a matter of minutes.

Although the fire started small, it dramatically increased in size before it was extinguished—managing to blacken an entire section of our kitchen. Furthermore the stove, countertop, wall, window curtains, cabinets and various utensils were destroyed.

It turned out that my mother was actually pleased since she was looking for a reason to ask my father if she could upgrade our kitchen. But this is often not the case when we consider fires. Fires kill and destroy. They spread without any help. They burn and move on and burn some more. Even the destruction they leave behind has its own dangers to health, farming and ecology.

James had this sort of picture in mind as he penned, **"How great a**

---

[9] Parent, Jason. Suite101.com. 3 Sep. 2009. 16 Jan. 2011 <http://www.suite101.com/content/north-american-wildfires-causes-and-prevention-a144814>.

forest is set ablaze by such a small fire!" (Ja. 3:5). You could easily substitute the word "great" with the word "large" since this is his meaning. Small fires set ablaze large forests. In other words, you do not need to light an entire forest in order to burn it down. All you need is a small flame and a little bit of patience. Fire, by nature, is a spreading element. It consumes and spreads to consume more.

This was not something hard for the Christian Jews to understand. To begin with, their land was mostly a dry place—often subject to fires. In fact, two decades after James penned this letter there was a historic wildfire in Rome. It occurred in AD 64 and lasted nearly a week. Only four out of fourteen districts of Rome managed to escape the fire. Christians are most familiar with the story since it brought about the terrible era of persecution of Jews and Christians alike because the emperor Nero blamed them for the blaze. This was a time when almost all of the apostles were killed. The persecution lasted over 200 years—all because of the fire.

James uses this picture to bring attention to the dangers of the tongue. Though it is small, it has the potential to destroy much more than it first appears—especially if it is uncontrolled.

The Tongue is a Fire

You may not realize it, but your **"tongue is a fire"** (Ja. 3:6). By this, James does not mean to refer to the gift of the Spirit (Acts 2:3). This is no gift of the Spirit. It is a natural gift inherited from Adam. It is like the small spark that flew off the power tool and into the dry grass from which the wildfire came.

As I am writing this, I am remembering the smoke and ashes from a fire I once set. It was a Sunday morning and I had just arrived home from my place of worship. Our pastor had preached a message that I thought in my heart was askew of the biblical text. I was already wound up for some reason, so I did what I typically do when my heart is beating hard. I wrote.

I did not want to bring reproach to the pastor or the church, so I simply addressed the interpretation of the text. But I wrote with great intensity, using very strong words. The sparks flew as I tapped the keyboard but I never saw them. Thirty minutes later, I published the post to my personal blog.

It was a small fire. I never saw it. In fact, I did not think anyone from my church ever read my blog. According to my website analytics, readership was low. What's more, no one in the church ever came to me to talk about any of my online writings. But I was mistaken, for there were some. And then there were more.

Months passed and the fire spread. I was now preaching at the church and my name was becoming more noticeable. I assumed this drove people to my blog. By this time I'd forgotten about the posting, never thinking that it was harmful. This all changed when I was called into the office by an associate pastor who was responsible for selecting me to teach in the church. He brought the article to my attention in a loving and gentle way, and removed me from teaching.

I found out that the small flame I had ignited had turned into a large wildfire. There were people in the church who were all but destroyed by it, losing their respect and trust in the pastor. Others felt betrayed, and others were terribly angry. Many of them took this personally and it broke their hearts. I had no idea. The fire was burning all around me and I was oblivious to it. However, now that I know of it, at least in part, I am astutely aware of the smoke and damage. I was never told the names of those who were affected by it, but every now and then I discover one or two and the stench of the smoke assaults my nose.

You need to know that I took the first opportunity to talk to the pastor whom I opposed online. He and I have a good relationship and he did not take it personally, nor was he bothered enough by it to say something to me. He knew that I was working my own weaknesses, settling the thoughts in my mind. He is a wise man to do so, and deserves the respect I nearly took away. He and I remain friends and speak openly to one another. Nevertheless, the damage tends to reappear occasionally and I am sharply reminded that my tongue is a fire.

I bring this up for five reasons. For one, I prefer you see me transparently and know that the Bible is as instructive to me as to all of us. I am not above accountability to the Word of God. I, although I am neither a scribe nor a pastor, **"will be judged with a greater strictness"** because I teach (Ja. 3:1).

Second, I want you to know that although my intention was not to hurt anyone, I did. Upon posting the article, I decided in my mind that it was not condemning to any one person or group since all names and specifics were absent. In fact, the casualties were beyond my imagination. People who I never thought would read my blog were affected by it. You might even say that it had unintentional collateral damage. My point being: the effect of our words does not discriminate based on our intentions.

Third, once the flame began to spread, it was uncontrollable. Granted, it was doused by the wisdom of the pastoral team, but this was only after a great deal of damage was done. You need not be among those connected to the flame to suffer burns. I want you to know that once the tongue sets something afire, it requires immediate and extreme action.

Fourth the extent of the damage is generally far greater than expected. The tongue hurts more than we think. In fact, I do not believe that I have heard the end of it. I am certain that more will surface as time progresses and healing takes place. The size of the tongue is never an indication of the size of the damage.

Fifth, though I mentioned that my actions were not intended to cause harm, they do reveal a deeper sin which is full of evil intentions (Jer. 17:9). Jesus said, "How can you speak good, when you are evil? For out of the abundance of the heart the mouth speaks" (Matt. 12:34). I cannot help but wonder if God allowed all of this to reveal to me a deeper sin that should be destroyed. Maybe it was purposed that I would see myself in true light in order to wage war against my own sin. Whatever the reason (only God knows), it did serve me in such a way. And I hope that it served others some way, even in its painful influence.

The effects of our words do not discriminate.

This is the nature of fire and the reason why James employs this illustration. He did not use water as his illustration. If you pour out a cup of water, it does not become a flood. There is no growth or spreading. It dissolves and goes away. Fire, on the other hand, gets hotter and bigger. It spreads until it is smothered. It requires no help to survive. Nor does it use any discretion when spreading. It burns and spreads to everything without discrimination.

The Tongue is a Cosmos

If you think that is bad, the tongue is not just a fire it is **"a world of unrighteousness"** (Ja. 3:6). This is actually an extension of the idea of the tongue being a fire. It refers to its ability to be independent of our control and the source of destruction. Think of it as being the core of the small fire that will burn down the great forest. It causes the fire to start and keeps it aflame.

Still, I like to let my imagination spin when I read this. The Greek reads *ho kosmos tes adikias* which translates "the iniquitous cosmos" or "the cosmos of iniquity." It captures the idea of a world or system of evil. The word "cosmos" should have stood out to you even in the Greek. I imagine an endless span of space and stars. I think of a galaxy that functions independently of others. Within itself it generates substance and life. It contains the elements to produce and shape and transform. It is an organism all to itself.

How It's Made marathons can keep my son and me in front of the television for hours. We love to see the company factories filled with seemingly infinite machines working together, piece by piece, to make a single product. It is like magic to us. How a bunch of little pieces pass through mechanical arms, conveyer belts and polishing liquids, and come together in the end is most fascinating. It is like a huge robot. In goes a sheet of metal and out comes a computer motherboard. Genius!

The tongue is like that. Don't let its size deceive you. It is a small manufacturing company. It manufactures evil. The word means injustice, iniquity, and wrong. When used to describe Judas' betrayal of Jesus, the ESV translates it as *wickedness* (Acts 1:18). When Simon the magician asked for the power that Peter demonstrated in Samaria, the apostle rebuked him saying that he was "in the bond of *iniquity*" (Acts 8:23, emphasis mine). There are many other passages like these where the word is understood as utter evil. It is the absence of good. Although it is not made up of matter and has no substance, we picture it as if it does because we often see its manifestations. It is sin.

While the production lines create a product for everyday living, the tongue generates a product for everyday killing. It is a system unto itself. It is wrapped up in a small bodily instrument, full of a wealth of iniquities. I think of it like the small universe on Orion's belt from the movie *Men in Black* (for my fellow sci-fi fanatics). This is what is behind the word "cosmos" and "iniquity." The tongue is a production-line machine developing words of destruction.

This is the imagery that James is employing. He is connecting the smallness of the tongue with the vastness of the world. John Calvin described it this way: "A slender portion of the flesh contains in it the whole world of iniquity."[10] The idea here is that the tongue has all it needs to function on its own as a cosmic darkness. It is both alive and dead. It lives, but it is an arrangement of death that affects the whole body and the course of life.

The Tongue is a Contaminant

By saying that the tongue is a small fire and a world of unrighteousness, James is using metaphoric language. This is not to mean that we are all running around with our mouths in flames, swallowing galaxies each time we take a sip of water. He is pointing to the tongue's ability to ruthlessly spread from a single, small system of activity. It is the Big Bang of sin!

He further explains this by saying that, **"The tongue is set among our members, staining the whole body"** (Ja. 3:6). This is what he means when referring to the tongue as a fire and cosmic ball of evil.

To begin with, the tongue is positioned among other members of the body—one of many parts. I don't know if it is James' attempt to frighten us, but it seems that way.

Placing the fiery, evil-generating tongue amidst the other members of the body will definitely give us something to think about. Being the manufacturer that it is, the tongue will actively produce evil that will burn and spread like fire. James says that it is constantly **"staining the whole body"** (Ja. 3:6) which is an ongoing action that occurs and keeps occurring. It stains and spreads to stain again. As the Greek puts it, the entire body is stained repeatedly.

> **Whatever is not burned by the fire is stained by the smoke.**

The idea of staining produces an image of what smoke leaves behind. Whatever is not burned by the fire is stained by the smoke, dark and putrid. The Greek word is *spilousa* which means "to defile or pollute" (and yes, it reads, coincidentally, like "spill on you sir").

---

[10] Calvin, John. "Epistle of James." *Calvin's Commentaries. Vol. XXII*. Grand Rapids: Baker, 2005. 320. Print.

When speaking of the matter of food that is defiling to a man, Jesus explained it is not what goes into a person that defiles him since it misses the heart and goes straight to the stomach. Food does not defile a man. On the other hand, a man is defiled by what comes out of a him.

> "For from within, out of the heart of man, come evil thoughts, sexual immorality, theft, murder, adultery, coveting, wickedness, deceit, sensuality, envy, slander, pride, foolishness. All these evil things come from within, and they defile a person." (Mk. 7:21-23)

If it is in your heart, it will come out of your mouth. The tongue reveals the condition of the heart. You can know so much about a person's inner condition by sitting and listening to them talk—especially during such daily functions as work, lunch, and communicating with close friends and family members. During such times, hints of what dwells within the depths of the heart will surface. Since the tongue is mysteriously connected to the heart, it stains the whole person.

It might benefit us to see how Jude used it in his epistle. He wrote about teachers who were leading people away from Jesus. He commands his fellow believers to "have mercy on those who doubt" and to "save others by snatching them out of the fire" and to "others show mercy with fear, hating even the garment stained by the flesh" (Jude 17-23). It is important that we watch after each other and save each other from deceptive teaching. To some we are to show mercy since they are merely doubtful of the Lord. Thus, we should guide them toward sound doctrine. Others we are to snatch quickly from false teaching before more harm comes to their faith. The third group of believers, according to Jude, is contaminated with sin. Their garment is "stained by the flesh" and therefore we should be extra careful that it does not spread to us. This is exactly the kind of evil that James is referring to. It spreads all over you and to those around you.

> **If it is in your heart, it will come out of your mouth.**

The Tongue is a Virus

One of our family's most awful experiences occurred when both of our children (we only had two at the time) caught a stomach flu that produced vomiting, diarrhea and fever. During this illness, the children didn't always make it to the bathroom in time. When they did, they needed help.

It was a fast-paced time for all of us! The kids were very weak so my wife and I would man separate toilets, each with a child. In between bouts, we would wash the towels and sheets. The second day our washer broke. Nevertheless, the sickness continued until our house was permeated with an unforgettable odor and everything we used for towels and wipes was dirty. When the horror subsided, our generous neighbors helped us recover. At the local Laundromat, it took us nearly a full day and six machines to undo the damage!

We have since found out the sickness was the *rotavirus* which began with one child and was transmitted to the other. Since my wife and I were adults our immune systems were able to fight it. But it spread throughout our house, and we had to remain secluded for almost a week until we had completely cleaned everything.

This is how the tongue works. First, it boils with iniquity. Second, it bursts into flames. Third, it burns you from within and stains your whole body. And fourth, it is **"setting on fire the entire course of life"** (Ja. 3:6). As the sickness spread, it affected the whole house—sheets, quilts, towels, clothes, wipes, floors, air, and the people within.

James tells us that the tongue is continuously staining our whole person and continuously setting on fire **"the entire course of life"** (Ja. 3:6). This is a phrase I thought I would never hear in Scripture because I first heard it on Disney's *The Lion King*. It is the phrase "circle of life." It refers to your circumference of living. It is everything around you. It is those with whom you come into contact.

Our words reach far beyond arm's length. They are distributed like bullets from an automatic weapon. They travel through the air and over computer networks. We speak our hearts through ordinary means of communication, both natural and electronic. Our words go everywhere and touch nearly everything. And since our tongue is mysteriously connected to our heart, it reveals the evil that boils within us and infects the people around us.

Do you know how this works? Our words carry meaning. When they are heard or read, they form thoughts in the minds of others who then draw conclusions and form opinions. Some of the ideas that are formed act as foundations for human behaviors and beliefs. We influence others by our words. Each time we gossip, lie, slander, accuse, spread a rumor, tell distasteful jokes or use inappropriate language, we destroy. The destruction can happen to families, communities, schools, church and more. This is how it works, whether intentional or not. We send. They receive. If the words themselves do not hurt or taint the world around us, the repercussions of those words will—even years later.

The Tongue is Wretchedness

Have you had enough of the tongue's dangers? There's one more description given by James. The tongue is a fire that stains the whole person and the whole life of the person, and it is **"set on fire by hell"** (Ja. 3:6). When I first discovered this, my mind slipped into meditation mode. I thought ... Wow! Could it be more awful? Is there anything worse? The evil that incites the tongue to spread and consume is ignited by hell!

This will definitely require some explanation. Not because I'm worried you are not getting the full picture, but because you may think, as some do, that hell is the hangout for Satan and his boys. It is not. Hell is a place of punishment for the rebelling angels (Matt. 25:41, 46) and all who rebel against God. (Rom. 6:23). In other words, demons are not using hell as a place to warm themselves over coffee or lounge while they plot their evil missions. They will suffer torment there.

> **The evil that incites the tongue to spread and consume is ignited by hell!**

James uses the word *Gehenna* here. This is the Greek word for the Hebrew valley known as Hinnom. The valley is a deep ravine southwest of Jerusalem. In earlier history, parents once sacrificed their children as burnt offerings to Molech (2 Kin. 23:10). Molech was a large bull who sat on a throne with his arms outstretched. The parents would lay their children in his arms and they would fall into the fire and die. This terrible wickedness continued until King Josiah destroyed it in order to bring the people of Israel back to God.

Hinnom gradually became the city dump where garbage and dead animals were burned. The fires burned day and night as waste was continuously fed into them. Thus it produced an ongoing hideous odor of garbage and burning flesh that became the symbol of the ever-burning fire of hell for the ungodly. Jesus was the first and only other person to use this symbol in the Bible. This would explain why James, His brother, used it. While Jesus used it to refer to a place where God would pitch the ungodly, James uses it to refer to the place from which evil is stirred.

It seems to imply the ungodly filth that is cast into the fire is spewing forth to set the tongue on fire. So the tongue is inflamed by the filthy waste of human depravity and will eventually make its way back to the burning pit. This is strong imagery!

Picture the tongue as a burning tentacle that lashes out from the fiery ground, wraps around the neck of onlookers and drags them down to the smoldering heat. This tentacle is your tongue, it is my tongue, polluting and spreading its evil to those around us; spawned by the fires of the most wretched remains.

Needless to say, this is the metaphoric reality of what the tongue is capable of if it is not bridled. It should make us more careful of our words. It should cause us to speak clearly and precisely with tenderness and mercy. We should be motivated to assure ourselves that our audience is edified with love and grace in a way that glorifies God.

> **The tongue is inflamed by the filthy waste of human depravity.**

In a lecture to his students, Charles Spurgeon said that sometimes we should "stop and take the word out of our mouth and look at it and see whether it is quite to edification." He went on to make an excellent application:

> "Brethren, far be it from us to utter a syllable which would suggest an impure thought, or raise a questionable memory. We need the Spirit of God to put bit and bridle upon us to keep us from saying that which would take the minds of our hearers away from Christ and eternal realities, and set them thinking upon the groveling things of earth."[11]

We should use our ears regularly in this attempt. The puritan preacher, Thomas Watson, said that God gave us two ears, but one

---

[11] Spurgeon, C. H. "The Holy Spirit in Connection with Our Ministry." *Lectures to My Students: Complete & Unabridged*. Grand Rapids: Ministry Resources Library, Zondervan House, 1989. 191. Print.

tongue "to show that we should be swift to hear, but slow to speak" and there is no wonder why. He went on to say that God "has set a double fence before the tongue, the teeth and the lips, to teach us to be wary that we offend not with our tongue."

I have made note in my Bible of this exact passage that reads, "Choose your words wisely and hold your tongue with great force." It reminds me of my own tendencies and dangers. I understand it is not simply I might mean something that will stir up the fires of hell. It is that I might mean something good but use inappropriate words to convey the meaning. (While my point may be heavenly, my delivery may be hellish.) The Oxford English Dictionary contains entries for more than 171,000 words. We have an immense arrangement from which we can borrow terms so there is no need to sell our listeners short. Being brief and hip is no excuse. Be biblical and godly—that is our aim if we are to be assured of our salvation. As the proverb goes, "Whoever guards his mouth preserves his life; he who opens wide his lips comes to ruin" (Prov. 13:3). True faith is disciplined.

Taming the Tongue

Fixing the tongue is never taught in the Scriptures. Rather, we learn that God imputes to us the righteousness of Jesus when we are born again. He covers us with His own works and hides the sin that we still possess. We are still sinners and we should not forget that. God has saved us from deserved wrath and sees His Son's infinite value instead of our burning evil. Yet we remain in these fleshly bodies that were born into sin and developed in sin throughout the years. So, we are hard-pressed not to sin. The tongue cannot be fixed. It must be tamed.

> **The tongue cannot be fixed. It must be tamed.**

There was a time our Lord granted us new tongues as symbolized on the day of Pentecost (Acts 2:3). But we still have the one with which we were born and it is still set on fire by hell. For this reason, James tells us to tame it, control it, and bridle it. It can be used for good, but it is a beast that has been raised in the wild. He teaches us, **"For every kind of beast and bird, of reptile and sea creature, can be tamed and has been tamed by mankind, but no human being can tame the tongue. It is a restless evil, full of deadly poison"** (Ja. 3:7-8).

So what is it? We can tame every kind of wild animal on earth and in the seas but the small muscle enclosed behind our teeth is a restless evil—wild and untamable? What does this mean? Can we tame it or not? Should we fight a battle that we can't win? "We all stumble in many ways" (Ja. 3:2). Why tell us to tame it and then tell us it cannot be tamed?

These are good questions. If we are not diligent to see James' point, we might remain confused and frustrated in our disciplines. But rest assured, the tongue can be tamed—only not by you. You are human, right? **"No human being can tame the tongue"** (Ja. 3:8). This is not to say that no human is *permitted* to tame the tongue. James says that no one *dunati*, is able to, or has the power or capability to, tame the tongue. You may want to and have permission to, you may even acknowledge that God commands you to, but you cannot tame your tongue. This is because **"it is a restless evil, full of deadly poison"** (Ja. 3:8). The tongue is a wild savage—restless and ready to break free. It hates restraint and control. The more it is held back, the more restless it becomes. And when it breaks loose, it strikes with "the venom of asps" with the intent to kill and destroy (Ps. 140:3). Remember, our Lord was murdered after a crowd of people screamed "Crucify him!" Pilate asked them "Why?" since he saw no reason. But the crowd demanded it. And the Bible says that "their voices prevailed" (Lk. 23:20-24). Also, Stephen, who was "full of grace and power" was stoned after some men "secretly instigated" and "stirred up the people and the elders and the scribes" and "set up false witnesses" (Acts 6:8-15). These and many other examples show how dangerously evil the restless tongue can be. Its poison strikes a deadly blow and it cannot be tamed by man.

> **True faith reveals the work and signature of God.**

On the other hand, James doesn't say that the tongue cannot be tamed at all. He just excludes you. "But God," someone once told me. God is able to tame the tongue. He can and will tame the tongue of the saved through His Spirit. Isn't this the overall point? Isn't this where we have been heading all along? True faith reveals the work and signature of God. If *you* could tame your tongue, then no one would see God's handiwork in your heart. Doesn't that make sense? True faith is disciplined. Our native faith is not.

Which should you exercise and which *should* you exercise? Maybe you should join me in humility and confess to our Lord, asking Him to put a bit in your mouth to control your tongue. Assurance is the goal. "Lord, help me to control my tongue so that I might experience the joy of acknowledging true faith."

True Faith is Righteous

I'm sure you've heard the old adage: "If you can't say anything good, don't say anything at all." I wonder if James had applied this command, would he have anything to say about the tongue—at all? In the greater sense, what James is teaching us is good because it is godly. But of all the things he has said in describing the tongue, very little has been good. In fact you might find it difficult to find one good thing—that is until now.

"With it we bless our Lord and Father" (Ja. 3:9). I know that it is not much, but it is really all we have. And even this is tempered with a negative. It is really only part of the statement. Still, let's hold on to it while we can. Let's look at something good about the tongue—namely, with our tongue we bless our Lord and Father.

In his letter to the Corinthian church, Paul said that "no one can say 'Jesus is Lord' except in the Holy Spirit" (1 Cor. 12:3). Although his context was the diversities of service within the unity of the church body, his point was that those with divine faith express divine credence and not the other way around. We must first have the Spirit of God if we are to speak the glories of Christ and call Him Lord.

> **Those with divine faith express divine credence.**

I mention this because we are meant to use our tongue to **"bless our Lord and Father"** (Ja. 3:9). This was very meaningful for the Jews to read. After they mentioned the name of God, it was a common practice to say "Baruch Hu!" which means "Blessed be He!" They made it a point to bless God throughout the day. Three times each typical weekday they would repeat aloud the Shmoneh Esreh, a collection of 18 prayers of blessings to God. They would conclude each one with "Blessed are you, O Lord." Of course, the Psalms are full of these blessings. One in particular stands out to me where David wrote, "I will bless the Lord at all times; his praise shall continually be in my mouth" (Ps. 34:1). You might also remember the Psalm which we sing even today, "Bless the Lord, O my soul and all that is within me, bless his holy name!" (Ps. 103:1-5).

This might seem a little tongue-in-cheek, pardon the pun. But although the tongue is a fire, a world of iniquity, a venomous snake, a restless evil, a piercing sword, it is only the mechanism by which our sinful heart is expressed. The tongue is not altogether evil. It will not be done away with when glory comes. It is made by God and for God and to God. It is called evil because it is so easily used. It is slippery, so it is easily falling. It often appears to act independently but it really does what the heart desires. For this reason we can safely say that our tongue can and should bless the Lord.

This is especially true of Christians. To reflect back to Paul's point, Christians have had a heart transplant. We have a new heart and therefore a new tongue in some mysterious and supernatural sense. We can and should utter blessings to God. I wonder sometimes if this is the idea behind the "divided tongues as of fire" that appeared on those sitting in the Upper Room on the day of Pentecost. A supernatural event happened where God filled the Christians with the Holy Spirit and they "began to speak in other tongues as the Spirit gave them utterance." In the streets were those who heard them speaking "the mighty works of God" (Acts 2:1-13). Were the fiery tongues that rested on each of them a sign that the fiery tongues they were used to had been replaced? I don't really know. Yet I can't help but notice the correlation between the two and I understand that God has made us a new creation (2 Cor. 5:17). God has redeemed us. And we can redeem our tongues with that which He has given us. I like to think this is part of what the fiery tongues meant. With these new tongues we can say "Jesus is Lord" and bless Him at all times.

Your Arms are Too Short

Consider that a commercial break. James gave us a hint of goodness before he brought us back to the reality of our tongues. Unfortunately, he didn't use a period to close the good thought. He used a comma. In fact it was only part of his thought. With our tongue, **we bless our Lord and Father, and with it we curse people who are made in the likeness of God**" (Ja. 3:9). It's kind of like giving you a sample of the tongue's good use, then pulling the rug out from under you.

The tongue is called a stumbling block, controller, manipulator, fire, restless, evil, poisonous, world of iniquity and hellish tool untamable by any human being. It causes so much destruction by what it does to other people. We use it to **"curse people"** as James puts it (Ja. 3:9). This means that we use it to wish evil on someone (Rom. 12:14) or declare someone evil and devoid of anything divine. Such is specifically reserved for God, since He knows the heart of man. It would be appropriate for Him to use the term when it applies (Matt. 25:41). But we are not to curse anyone (Rom. 12:14), not even if we are cursed first (Matt. 5:44; Lk. 6:28). Because all people were **"made in the likeness of God"** (Ja. 3:9).

The likeness we share with God is an indestructible likeness. When we say that man is totally depraved we do not mean utterly depraved. We are not as sinful as can be. We can be more sinful than we are. R.C. Sproul explains: "there is no part of us that is left untouched by sin." This means that "our minds, our wills and our bodies are affect by evil." Therefore, we "speak sinful words, do sinful deeds, have impure thoughts."[12] But in all of this, there remains a likeness of God. We are rational, personal, moral, self-conscious, and willful. We have a conscience and are able to reason. We can know, love and act on the basis of rational thought and motive and intent.[13]

When we curse someone, we are essentially cursing the Lord who made them. I liken it in a trivial way to my younger years when kids would insult each other by demeaning mothers. It was the best way to arouse anger and start a fight. You could say anything you wanted about someone, but his mom was off limits. Those were fighting words. In a similar way, when you demean another human being you are demeaning their Creator. And God does not take insults lightly. If the words are fighting words, then you are in danger. Your arms are far too short to box with God. Cursing other people is a strike in the face to the Lord. He made them and He takes it personally.

---

[12] Sproul, R. C. *Essential Truths of the Christian Faith*. Wheaton, IL: Tyndale House, 1992. 148. Print.

[13] This is a paraphrase of John MacArthur's explanation found in his sermon on James 3:5b-12 preached December 14, 1986. It can be accessed at http://www.gty.org.

This Should Not Be

No sane person wants to pick a fight with God. But each time we curse someone, it's exactly what we do. James says that we are hypocrites if this is what the Christian does. Since the Christian is born of God, transformed and made new with a new tongue capable of earnestly blessing the Lord, he should not curse God's created people whom He made in His own likeness. This should warn us that our faith is not being demonstrated appropriately, for **"from the same mouth come blessing and cursing"** (Ja. 3:10). This is absurdity. Yet it is reality.

Peter is a prime example of a person who sticks his foot in his mouth. He had a real problem with the tongue. It slipped up all the time. Remember when he told Jesus, "You are the Christ, the Son of the living God" (Matt. 16:16)? Then a few weeks later he cursed and swore, "I do not know the man" just before the rooster crowed (Matt. 26:69-75). He used the same mouth, by the way. Paul was guilty of this also. He called the high priest a "whitewashed wall" which was a metaphor that meant he was evil inside (Acts 23:3 with Matt. 23:27).

> **Cursing other people is a strike in the face to the Lord.**

We do the same and probably far worse. We use our mouths to sing songs to our Lord in worship services and bless the Lord at our dinner tables. Then we use our mouths to gossip and slander members of our family, our circle of friends, and our acquaintances at work. We are hypocrites when we do this. We say we love God, but we call Him to duel by mocking His creatures.

James says, **"My brothers, these things ought not to be so"** (Ja. 3:10). The Greek language reveals a strong negative. Throughout the entire New Testament, this type of language is only used here. James wants us to understand that it is not right; it is unacceptable. It is a compromise to the fires of hell, submission to the works of the flesh and Satan. We should not tolerate it. In fact, we should be so upset about it that we bring back the practice of cleansing our mouths with soap. It should leave an awful taste in our mouths. It is incompatible with the Christian because of the faith that dwells within.

A Spring, a Fig, and a Salt Pond

James closes his argument against unfaithful speech with three or four illustrations depending on how you count them. The first is about a spring. He asks, **"Does a spring pour forth from the same opening both fresh and salt water?"** (Ja. 3:11). He is not a simpleton. It is a rhetorical question. The answer is "No" obviously. The recipients might have responded, "Of course not! Are you dumb?" A spring does not pour forth both fresh and salt water. It is impossible. It will pour out one or the other.

In the same way, **"Can a fig tree, my brothers, bear olives?"** No. Can **"a grapevine produce figs?"** (Ja. 3:12). No. This, too, is impossible. Nature teaches us this. Moreover, **"neither can a salt pond yield fresh water"** (Ja. 3:12). These are all impossibilities. They cannot happen. What about this: Can God's gift of faith produce evil?

Did you feel the shudder down your spine like I did? It was as though he was leading us to the edge, blindfolded. Nevertheless, we have got it. True faith is righteous. It does not produce evil speech. Paul wrote, "the righteousness of God" is "through faith in Jesus Christ for all who believe" (Rom. 3:22). In Christ we are made right. Our tongues should reflect it.

We might benefit by closing this final point with the words of John Calvin:

> "There can be then no calling on God, and his praises must necessarily cease, where evil speaking prevails; for it is an impious profanation of God's name, when the tongue is virulent towards our brethren and pretends to praise him"[14] ... "He, then who truly worships and honors God, will be afraid to speak slanderously of man."[15]

Conclusion

I like what Sinclair Ferguson concluded about this passage on the tongue. He says that there seems to be two camps in Christianity: one that prefers to be silent, and one that over speaks. He argued that James is instructing both camps telling the silent ones to speak for the sake of the gospel and the over-speakers to be more gracious. Here is an excerpt:

> "When James speaks about the mastery of the tongue, he isn't just

---

[14] Calvin, John. "Epistle of James." *Calvin's Commentaries. Vol. XXII.* Grand Rapids: Baker, 2005. 323. Print.
[15] Ibid.

speaking about the words we use, he is speaking about the sensitivity to use the words that are necessary, those that are sensitive and gracious, and then to remain silent when such silence is necessary. James' words are also intended for those who are prone to remain silent, so that they would be able to speak for the sake of the gospel."[16]

With our tongue, we encourage or discourage. If we are parents, we shape our children by the words we speak. If we are pastors, we shape believers by what we say. Our tongue is incredibly powerful and influential. It can build or destroy.

Sadly, most tongues are used for destruction. This is because the tongue only speaks that which comes from the heart. Hard hearts do not speak soft words, blessings or life; but rather violence, curses and death.

True faith, which is of God, is perfect and disciplined. It does not destroy others by cursing, gossiping, being cruel, speaking ill, lying or encouraging people to sin. It is sound and righteous and it strengthens others, by speaking life over them, which is the truth of God. Consider these resolutions written by Jonathan Edwards. Maybe they can become your resolutions this year and for years to come.

> "Resolved, never to say anything against anybody except when it is acceptable to the highest degree of Christian honor and agreeable to the golden rule. Often, when I have said anything against someone, to judge it by this resolution. (#31)
>
> Resolved, in speaking narrations, to speak the pure and simple verity. (#34)
>
> Let there be something of benevolence in all that I speak. (#70)."

---

[16] Ferguson, Sinclair. Desiring God. 26 Sep. 2008. 17 Jan. 2011 <http://www.desiringgod.org/resource-library/conference-messages/the-tongue-the-bridle-and-the-blessing-an-exposition-of-james-31-12>.

CHAPTER 6

THE TRIAL OF WISDOM

JAMES 3:1-12

"wisdom from above is pure, then peaceable"

There are no self-confessed fools in our day. Everyone is an expert. Everyone has opinions. *Do it this way. Do it that way. Here is the key to success. Here are the steps to happiness.* We are bombarded with this kind of wisdom all the time. It can be difficult to weed out the good from the bad in this world. And just when we think we have it all figured out, we are blindsided by the need to discern between wisdom and foolishness in the church.

Being the most knowledgeable one is the height of human aspiration. We are like the Greeks who boast in their wisdom. Philosopher Marcus Tullius Cicero said, "Wisdom is the best gift of the gods, it is the mother of all good things. The best and that which generates all of the best."

Cicero was on to something. King Solomon asked for wisdom above all things (2 Chron. 1:10). In Proverbs we learn, "By wisdom a house is built, and by understanding it is established; by knowledge the rooms are filled with all precious and pleasant riches" (Prov. 24:3-4). Wisdom is a hot commodity. Like a diamond amidst rhinestones, knowledge is a treasure—but, as James points out, it must be tested to prove it is genuine.

> Who is wise and understanding among you? By his good conduct let him show his works in the meekness of wisdom. But if you have bitter jealousy and selfish ambition in your hearts, do not boast and be false to the truth. This is not the wisdom that comes down from above,

but is earthly, unspiritual, demonic. For where jealousy and selfish ambition exist, there will be disorder and every vile practice. But the wisdom from above is first pure, then peaceable, gentle, open to reason, full of mercy and good fruits, impartial and sincere. And a harvest of righteousness is sown in peace by those who make peace. (James 3:13-18)

True Faith is Wise

For the most part, I am a quiet guy. My friends would agree, I think. I am known to walk straight into a meeting place and never say a word. I just appear. Sometimes people don't even know I'm there. What can I say? I'm a background kind of guy.

Wisdom is like that. It's a background kind of subject. It's always there among us, but rarely addressed and noticed. It's on everyone's mind, spilling off everyone's tongue and rousing everyone's actions. It's that mysterious connection between thinking and doing. And rarely do we know it is there. "Oh, Wisdom, when did you get here?" If it were a person, it would say, "I've been here the whole time." In fact, a proverb says "wisdom cries aloud in the streets" (Prov. 1:20).

This is true of James' epistle. Wisdom has been here the whole time and we might not even know it. However, there were some hints along the way. For example, James says that if you fail at the tests of faith, then you should ask the Lord for wisdom since He gives it generously and without discrimination (Ja. 1:5). He means to say that wisdom is your greatest tool during trials. This does not somehow render all that he has equipped us with so far useless. Rather, it underscores it all. Wisdom is the rug beneath the many characteristics of faith we have been discussing since wisdom is the tool by which we conduct ourselves. Wisdom has not just been there the whole time, we have been standing and building upon it. For with wisdom, we can remain "steadfast under trial" (Ja. 1:12). The epistle of James is a book of wisdom. Is it chock-full of wisdom. It begins and ends with it. Although the emphasis is personal examination for true faith, wisdom is the smoking gun. This is because wisdom is inseparable from faith. Therefore, we should take a side trip into the world of wisdom to see the connection.

Wisdom is your greatest tool during trials.

Wisdom is a tool hidden somewhere in our immaterial person. If you probe the human body, you will come up empty-handed—no matter how sharp your scalpel. In the same way, the best hypnotic exercise will leave you puzzled. All our searches are futile. We can't find it. Yet, somehow, we all recognize that wisdom is in the room.

This is because wisdom is not an object. It is not a thing to be seen or held. It is a description of the enigmatic ability to take information and bring it to life. It is a word most often associated with age, experience and intelligence. And it is none of these things. At the same time, it is all of these things. Wisdom is something we have and something we seek. It is ever-growing and exceedingly valuable. To my knowledge, it is an esteemed premium in every culture of life. No one regards stupidity as precious. No one searches for folly. Rather, wisdom is to die for and many have died trying to attain it. So we might add that we don't just recognize wisdom to be in the room, we chase it and desire it.

Wisdom is to die for and many have died trying to attain it.

Chasing Wisdom

This is exactly what King Solomon did. Isn't he the one that most of us think of when someone mentions wisdom? I think so. In fact, one Bible dictionary calls him the "best example of a wise man."[1] I think the queen of Sheba would agree. She caught wind of his fame and went to test him with hard questions. She put them out there and he answered all of them without breaking a sweat. "There was nothing hidden from the king that he could not explain to her." The queen was so impressed with him that "there was no more breath in her." She fainted. Yeah, just like an old black-and-white film. Wrist across the forehead, weakening knees and then the slow drop to the floor. He must have been impressive because I have never seen a woman do that—not for me at least.

When she could breathe again, it is recorded that she said to the King, "The report was true that I heard in my own land of your words and of your wisdom, but I did not believe the reports until I came and my own eyes had seen it. And behold, the half was not told me. Your

---

[1] Youngblood, Ronald F., F. F. Bruce, and R. K. Harrison. *Nelson's New Illustrated Bible Dictionary*. Nashville: T. Nelson, 1995. 1316. Print.

wisdom and prosperity surpass the report that I heard. Happy are your men! Happy are your servants, who continually stand before you and hear your wisdom!" The stories she heard were not even half as good as the real thing! So she blessed the Lord and gave Solomon "120 talents of gold, and a very great quantity of spices and precious stones" because that is what you give to a man who has everything, right? The truth is, wisdom is cherished and prized. It is worth your money. It is worth your time. It is worth all that you have. This was the King's reputation. He was known as a very wise man. The queen is evidence to that (1 Kin. 10:1-13). So it was reasonable for people to lavish him for his advice.

Solomon was wise because God gave him wisdom. But, with the success that wisdom brought, he became worldly as did his wisdom. He let his sinful heart distort his wisdom and his temptations lead him away from the Lord chasing all the desires that this world could allow. You could say that his success was his downfall. Although he had wisdom to see it coming, he allowed his desires to blind him from it. The story is rather interesting, but it is also quite a downer. An overview of it will help us dig deeper into wisdom, and see the strong connection between wisdom and faith.

> **Wisdom is cherished and prized. It is worth your money.**

One night, God appeared to Solomon in a dream and told him to ask for anything of Him. (This is that one question that we all long to hear from God. I wonder what I would say.) Solomon asked the Lord for wisdom so that he could properly govern God's people as a good steward. This is an extremely noble thing to ask. God was delighted that Solomon didn't ask for selfish things like possessions, wealth, honor, long life or the death of his enemies, so he gave Solomon wisdom and riches, possessions, and honor (2 Chron. 1:7-12; 1 Kin. 3:5-13). It was like ordering the burger and getting the shake and fries for free—though on a larger scale, of course.

The Bible says that "God gave Solomon wisdom and understanding beyond measure, and breadth of mind like the sand on the seashore, so that Solomon's wisdom surpassed the wisdom of all the people of the east and all the wisdom of Egypt. For he was wiser than all other men" (1 Kin. 4:29-31). He was so wise that "people of all nations came to hear the wisdom of Solomon, and from all the kings of the earth, who had heard of his wisdom" (1 Kin. 4:34). Now that is a very wise man!

It is believed that the book of Ecclesiastes was written by Solomon. It is considered one of the five books of wisdom literature in the Old Testament.[2] But, if you want *my* wisdom, you should not follow *its* wisdom. At least not until the end. It is the kind of wisdom that James will later call "earthly, unspiritual, demonic" (Ja. 3:15) which appears to be a commentary of words describing Solomon's seeming actions of wisdom. Ironically, Solomon calls this kind of wisdom folly and foolish when writing his proverbs as well.[3] Though he didn't need to, Solomon learned this by experience. He goes the way of folly as Ecclesiastes tells us. This is true until the final verses. But I'll save that for the triumphant ending.

All is Vanity

"Vanity of vanities! All is vanity" (Ecc. 1:2). These words appear frequently throughout the entire book and even act as bookends in a sense. They encompass the main theme which is that a self-seeking life is a wasted life. It is a vapor in that it is not just short, it is empty and goes away. Solomon says this:

> "I applied my heart to seek and to search out by wisdom all that is done under heaven. It is an unhappy business that God has given to the children of man to be busy with. I have seen everything that is done under the sun, and behold, all is vanity and a striving after wind." (Ecc. 1:13-14)

He wants to find meaning in life by chasing earthly things and seeking satisfaction in attaining the riches and pleasures of this world. He admittedly says that he "acquired great wisdom, surpassing all who were over Jerusalem before me" (Ecc. 1:16). After receiving this wisdom, he then wanted more and he sought to have it by knowing the opposite which he calls "madness and folly" (Ecc. 1:17). In other words: He found no satisfaction in wisdom, so he tried hedonism (Ecc. 2:1). He found nothing in hedonism, so he tried drugs (Ecc. 2:3). He

---

[2] The five wisdom books of the Old Testament are Job, Psalms, Proverbs, Ecclesiastes, and Song of Songs.

[3] For examples of wisdom contrasting folly and foolishness, consider Proverbs 3:35; 10:8, 23; 14:1, 24; 15:5 and many more.

found nothing in drugs, so he tried realty (Ecc. 2:4-6). He found nothing in realty, so he tried business (Ecc. 2:7). He found nothing in business, so he tried money (Ecc. 2:8). He found nothing in money, so he tried music (Ecc. 2:8). He found nothing in music, so he tried sex (Ecc. 2:8). He found nothing in sex, so he tried greatness (Ecc. 2:9). He found nothing in greatness, so he tried everything else that he could imagine and desire. He kept nothing from himself (Ecc. 2:10). He exceeded all people before him in all the things that he did and attained. And in the end, he found nothing but sorrow (Ecc. 1:18). In fact, he began to hate life (Ecc. 2:17) and grow angry because all that he worked hard to attain would be given to someone else when he died—and that person would not have earned any of it (Ecc. 2:19).

At this point, it is your obvious right to think: "What a miserable and pitiful life!" It certainly sounds quite different from the wise Solomon that I once knew in Sunday School. All of his chasing left him hollow and unfulfilled. He went after everything imaginable. He lived the American dream, and lived it better than most of our great achievers. It is a sad story to hear. From the beginning to the end, it reeks of self-ambition and self-satisfaction. He started with such arrogance admitting that he was the wisest in all Jerusalem and then arrogantly toiled to reach a prize that he was confident we would find. What a waste. What a terrible life. What a loss. He sunk so low that he envied even the dead for they didn't have to live a wasted life, "I thought the dead who are already dead more fortunate than the living who were still alive" (Ecc. 4:2).

> **Fear God and keep his Commandments, for this is the duty of man.**

The takeaway of this sad story is that worldly wisdom is demonstrated by the feeble pursuit of fulfillment in earthly things. It is terribly arrogant to think that we, created beings, can find our happiness in created things. This is foolishness. It is folly. But it was what Solomon fell for. In his wisdom, he chose the things of the world and turned from the Lord and it cost him the kingdom (1 Kin. 11:1-13). You might say that it was not really wisdom. But James would say that it was earthly wisdom. It is something good tainted and used by the demons themselves. The only good part of the story is the end. I told you about the triumphant ending. Here it is. Solomon's lesson learned: "Fear God and keep his commandments, for this is the duty of man" (Ecc. 12:13). Now that is wisdom.

Fearing God and Wisdom

King Solomon was no fool. The lesson he finally learned, though it took him a long time to learn, is anything but foolish. "Fear God and keep his commandments" (Ecc. 12:13). He says that this is the whole duty of all mankind. Solomon "spoke 3,000 proverbs" and one of those is Proverbs 9:10 which reads, "The fear of the Lord is the beginning of wisdom." It certainly sounds like something he would say.

The fear of the Lord was never really described to me in a satisfying way. Not to say that any my teachers had a wrong definition. I just found their explanations to be quite ambiguous and mysterious (maybe it was my pea of a brain). They were not thoroughly spelled out. There were too many loose ends for me to tie things up. Sometimes, they were even contradictory, at least in my mind. On one hand, they would suggest that fear is reverence for God and not fright. On the other hand, they would say that it actually means fright—to be afraid of God rather than reverent. I have heard these two groups argue over it again and again.

I think the problem lies in the English vocabulary. We are abbreviated people. Just check our text messages on our cell phones. We like expedient things. We like fast food and fast cars. We even like our education and worship to be here and gone just the same. We like to keep things "short and sweet," as the saying goes. Maybe this is why we have caked up the meaning of fearing God with confusion. I don't believe that you can effectively define the fear of God with one word, even with complex words like *reverence* and *awe*. In fact, I think that the concept is somewhat foreign to the Western world which makes it even harder to convey. It would be like explaining the Internet to a Mayan tribe.

However, we in the Western world are not absent of true fear. We just fail at identifying it. In fact, it is my assessment that we unknowingly pride ourselves on being fearful people. Although we believe freedom from everything is the ultimate accomplishment, we kill ourselves trying to gain the praise of others and to gain the things of the world. I would suggest that we are quite fearful people. We just don't see our slavery to the sin as fear. However, it is exactly that. It is fearing man in an ultimate sense. So understanding the fear of God is not beyond our grasp. It will just require a little change of thinking. We are, to use a movie metaphor, in "the Matrix". It is not the truth, but we think it is. Point being, once you are out of "the Matrix", you can easily understand the fear of God. And, if the fear of God is the beginning of wisdom, then we should do our best to gain this understanding lest we miss the point of James completely. Let me also add that fear is so strongly connected to faith, your salvation depends on it.

Now, at this point, if you could see me, I would loosen my tie, roll up my sleeves, clear my throat and sit back in my chair. I am about to attempt the impossible. (Actually, I'll employ some excellent explanations from men smarter than me and pretend that I came up with them.) A deep breath. Here goes.

The Fear of God

In 1984, a small Motown artist known as Rockwell became a common name with these words, "I always feel like somebody's watching me." Truth be told, somebody *is* watching you. But that somebody is not a haunting ghost as Rockwell depicts in his music video released the same year. Rather, it is God. He sees all. "For a man's ways are before the eyes of the Lord, and he ponders all his paths" (Prov. 5:21). And as expected, God is not always delighted with what He gazes upon.

Remember the flood? Before God wiped out the planet with water, He "saw that the wickedness of man was great in the earth, and that every intention of the thoughts of his heart was only evil continually" (Gen. 6:5). David echoed this idea hundreds of years later, "The Lord looks down from heaven on the children of man, to see if there are any who understand, who seek after God. They have all turned aside; together they have become corrupt; there is none who does good not even one" (Ps. 14:2-3). In the following verse, the Lord is said to ask this rhetorical question, "Have they no knowledge?" (Ps. 14:4). This is repeated by Paul hundreds of years after in Romans 3:10-12. If the Bible was still being written today, I would argue that the same sentiment would be written yet again since it is true

> **God is always watching us.**

of our time as well.

God is always watching us. He sees the things we do. Generally speaking, mankind is up to no good—and, even worse, no god. But God's omniscience, His limitless knowledge of everything, can also be comforting. For example: When God sent Jonah to Nineveh to warn them of their evil offenses, they believed God and repented. "When God saw what they did, how they turned from their evil way, God relented of the disaster that he had said he would do to them, and he did not do it" (Jon. 3:5-10). Sin angers God, but repentance pleases Him.[4]

In a similar case, Hagar was unjustly afflicted by Sarai and so she fled. God saw her affliction and blessed her after sending her back to submit to her afflicter. Hagar, knowing that God was pitying her, says "You are a God of seeing" and "Truly here I have seen him who looks after me" (Gen. 16:13). God cared for her in her pain because He saw it. David delighted in this fact, "How precious to me are you thoughts, O God! How vast is the sum of them!" He adds, "I awake, and I am still with you" (Ps. 139:17-18). Peter said "For the eyes of the Lord are on the righteous, and his ears are open to their prayer" (1 Pet. 3:12). God is always near and observing. And more than that, He is acting.

God sees and knows all things.

Rockwell was upset that someone was not respecting his privacy. I would suggest that many feel the same way—even with regards to the Lord. In order to escape the reality of God, they train their hearts to believe that God doesn't exist (Ps. 14:1) or they reduce Him to less than a mortal (Ps. 50:21). It happened to the house of Israel. In Ezekiel, we find that they said, "The Lord has forsaken the land, and the Lord does not see" (Ez. 9:9). This way, they can live and think however they want without consequences. But the one who knows the Lord, who believes in Him, understands that He is real and really seeing everything we do. He is familiar with the realness of God's omnipresence and omniscience as Ezekiel 9:10 states the Lord's response to Israel's disregard, "As for me, my eye will not spare, nor will I have pity; I will bring their deeds

---

[4] The word "relented" in this passage is an anthropomorphic expression. God does not relent as humans do because He is omniscient and is not surprised by how things unfold. He knew beforehand that they would repent. He gave Jonah a prophetic warning to Nineveh in order to bring about such repentance. We can also see it as warning for all people. If we do not turn from our evil ways, God will bring disaster upon us.

upon their heads." God sees and knows all things. And, He can and will do whatever He wants with the things He observes. Moreover, we could be more theological and say with certainty that God is not just an observer. He put all of creation into order. He sits outside of time, sees and knows everything before it happens and yet He made it all even so.

I think David had this in mind when he wrote Psalm 139 and I am really tempted to walk through it verse by verse. But for the sake of time, let us just read it with vigor. I think that you will get the picture.

> "O LORD, you have searched me and known me! You know when I sit down and when I rise up; you discern my thoughts from afar. You search out my path and my lying down and are acquainted with all my ways. Even before a word is on my tongue, behold, O LORD, you know it altogether. You hem me in, behind and before, and lay your hand upon me. Such knowledge is too wonderful for me; it is high; I cannot attain it.

> "Where shall I go from your Spirit? Or where shall I flee from your presence? If I ascend to heaven, you are there! If I make my bed in Sheol, you are there! If I take the wings of the morning and dwell in the uttermost parts of the sea, even there your hand shall lead me, and your right hand shall hold me. If I say, 'Surely the darkness shall cover me, and the light about me be night,' even the darkness is not dark to you; the night is bright as the day, for darkness is as light with you.

> "For you formed my inward parts; you knitted me together in my mother's womb. I praise you, for I am fearfully and wonderfully made. Wonderful are your works; my soul knows it very well. My frame was not hidden from you, when I was being made in secret, intricately woven in the depths of the earth. Your eyes saw my unformed substance; in your book were written, every one of them, the days that were formed for me, when as yet there was none of them.

> "How precious to me are your thoughts, O God! How vast is the sum of them! If I would count them, they are more than the sand. I awake, and I am still with you." (Ps. 139:1-18)

The matter here is not whether or not God knows and sees all things. This is an inescapable reality. You can close your eyes and count backward, but it will still be true. The matter is what we do with this reality. Do we humble our heart and submit our entire life to Him? Do we smile and go about our way remembering it only when we fall behind on our bills, have relationship problems or land in the middle of other troubles? Or do we ignore it altogether? This is the question of fear. How concerned are you about God? Are you so concerned that you arrange your entire life around Him? If so, then you are fearing God. You are, as R.C. Sproul says, "Living Coram Deo." Living before the face of God.[5]

Coram Deo

I know you have seen it before. It is the news report where the suspect is ushered from squad car to court room. The media is pressing in, the lights are flashing, and the cameras are rolling. Surrounded by lawyers, police, and bodyguards, he stumbles with his chained hands held above his shoulders hiding his face from onlookers. Do you know why? He is hiding himself from your gaze. He does not know you, but he knows that people like you are on the other side of the camera lens.

None of us really desire to have our misdeeds exposed. We cover and hide the best way know how. This is what Adam and Eve did in the garden after they sinned. In Genesis 3:10 we find them hiding and answering God from their cover, "I heard the sound of you in the garden, and I was afraid, because I was naked, and I hid myself." In a sense, the word "nakedness" is understood as having sin on display. Adam was afraid because he sinned. His sin was perceivable. It was out in the open. It revealed Adam's inner heart toward God as rebellious. It was like his skin was suddenly transparent and inside revealed a rebellious heart against God.

I remember a phone call I had once with a friend of which I am rather ashamed (ashamed of the phone call, not the friend). I thought it was just the two of us on the phone and I started to ramble about another person saying some rather cruel things. And somewhere in the middle of my loose talk, that other person's voice chimed in, "Oh really?" At that moment I felt so naked. I was seen for what I really was. My sin was evident. I felt terrible. I imagine that this is what it must have been like for Adam, though in a much more severe sense because God was on the other line.

I make the distinction between the shame of sinning against my

---

[5] R.C. Sproul and Ligonier Ministries has made this Latin phrase popular in our day. Two articles published online explain in more detail what is meant by the phrase: http://www.ligonier.org/blog/what-does-coram-deo-mean and http://www.ligonier.org/learn/devotionals/living-coram-deo

friend and against God because that is what we all do. But the reality is: When we sin, we always sin against God. If there were no God, there would be no sin since God is the only pure Holy One. Still, we find less shame when we can remove God from the other line. Do you know how we might feel if we knew that our sin was hidden from the face of God? How different would we act if there was not a Holy One watching us? To put it plainly, we would act like the world. We would act like we naturally act and probably worse. We would do what we wanted to do without any limitations that judgement and consequences would put on us. But we would be fools, deceiving ourselves. We would be like the children who close their eyes and believe this makes them hidden from perception. What a foolish notion! It does nothing like that! We are all living before the gaze of the Lord. His face is upon on us. His eyes are intently staring—no matter what you believe.

Although everyone lives this way, only those regenerated by God's Spirit acknowledge it to the point of obedience. The person who lives coram Deo is the person who knows God is watching, is acutely aware of His sovereignty, and is sincerely offering honor to God by living a life of adoration and gratitude. A life coram Deo is a life of integrity because God is watching at all times, not just between the squad car and court room when the cameras are on. "It is a life that is open before God. It is a life in which all that is done is done as to the Lord. It is a life lived by principle, not expediency; by humility before God, not defiance."[6] It is the religious life. "It is a life lived under the tutelage of conscience that is held captive by the Word of God." It is a life that willfully says in the mind before anything is done, "What would glorify God most right now?" In short, it is the Christian life.

> **We are living before the gaze of the Lord.**

The Fear of God is Christian Living

It may come across that fearing God, or living coram Deo, sounds much like what it means to be a Christian. Hopefully it did. I don't mean to confuse you. If you thought this already, then you are right on track. You might even say that fearing God is a synonym for salvation.

---

[6] Sproul, R.C. "What Does "coram Deo" Mean?" Ligonier Ministries. Ligonier Ministries, 23 Feb. 2009. Web. 06 Apr. 2011. <http://www.ligonier.org/blog/what-does-coram-deo-mean>.

This is particularly true in the Old Testament. Those who feared the Lord, kept His commandments (Ecc. 12:13). This is what God told the Israelites through Moses, "fear the Lord your God ... by keeping his commandments ... all the days of your life" (Deut. 2:2). A Proverb says "The fear of the Lord is a hatred of evil" (Prov. 8:13). To put it in the negative, "the devising of folly is sin" (Prov. 24:9). The two go hand-in-hand. They are inseparable. If you fear the Lord, you hate evil. If you hate evil, you do not sin. Those who do not sin are those who love and fear God. They are the ones who live life coram Deo. On the other hand, if you sin, you are a fool acting in sheer folly—the opposite of wisdom.

Realistically speaking, however, we fall into sin more than we ought. What does this mean? Are you not fearing the Lord? Are you not living coram Deo? Not necessarily. It is true that God hates sin. It is also true that we should not sin and God is displeased when we do. Practically speaking, it is foolish to sin and so, when we sin, we are acting foolish. Yet, if you truly fear the Lord, you recognize your sin and turn from it by His strength. You do not continue in it.

I might have saved us all some time by repeating what a good friend of mine said when I asked him the question, "What is the fear of God?" He simply said, "It is knowing that God is God and we are not." However, if I would have thrown that at you and moved on, you may have not understood the extent of what it really means. Nevertheless, it is a great response. Knowing that God is all-seeing, all-knowing, all-powerful, and we are short-sighted, ignorant and incompetent is the grounds for coram Deo. Without it, we are speculating and making a mess of things. The more we know of the reality of God, the more fearful we become. The more fearful we become, the more Christ-like we behave.

The more fearful of God we become, the more Christ-like we behave.

So fearing God begins with knowing His powerful and holy nature in light of our feeble, limited and sinful nature. It is not necessarily the absence of sin altogether. There is one more example of this that I think we should see. After it, we might be at a good place in our understanding of the fear of God. It is found in Psalm 51. Here, we find David expressing a deep confession of sin, a heartfelt cry for mercy, and a strong affirmation of God's nature. All of these things are stirred together to make him a deeply humbled and honorable man. Remember first that David sinned with Bathsheba and though he knew it was against her, her husband, and his nation, he acknowledges that his sin was supremely against God (since all sin is against Him). The entire chapter is loaded with these things, but let us look at a few portions:

> "Have mercy on me, O God, according to your steadfast love; according to your abundant mercy blot out my transgressions. Wash me thoroughly from my iniquity, and cleanse me from my sin! For I know my transgressions, and my sin is ever before me. Against you, you only, have I sinned and done what is evil in your sight, so that you may be justified in your words and blameless in your judgment." (Ps. 51:1-4)

> "Hide your face from my sins, and blot out all my iniquities. Create in me a clean heart, O God, and renew a right spirit within me. Cast me not away from your presence, and take not your Holy Spirit from me. Restore to me the joy of your salvation, and uphold me with a willing spirit." (Ps. 51:9-12)

> "For you will not delight in sacrifice, or I would give it; you will not be pleased with a burnt offering. The sacrifices of God are a broken spirit; a broken and contrite heart, O God, you will not despise." (Ps. 51:16-17)

King David lived life in light of God. Notice that he is keenly aware of God's existence and thoroughly aware of God's nature. He affirms God as being holy, steadfast, merciful, loving, sovereign, righteous, powerful, and forgiving. At the same time, he affirms his own wretchedness, sinfulness, unfaithfulness and tendency toward sin. On one hand, he sinned against God and showed an indifference to God; but it was his sincere fear of God that brought him to his knees. He needed God to forgive him, reconcile him and restore him to the joy of salvation. He understood that God wanted humility (Ps. 51:17) rather than sacrifice (Ps. 51:16) and so that is what he offered. The penitent king wanted to be viewed with favor by the King of Kings because what mattered most to him was the opinion of the Lord. This was most important, "Against you, you only, have I sinned," he says (Ps. 51:4). He wanted a "clean heart" and a renewed "right spirit" and not to be cast away from the benevolent Lord (Ps. 51:10-11).

The take-home here is that the one who fears God will be afraid at the appropriate times and for the appropriate reasons and will be reverent in the same way. Additionally, this fear will exist at all times and in all ways. The fear of God will turn us away from sin because we know that he is the holy judge. He sins not. Nor does he tolerate sin in any way. He judges it rightly. He disposes it. In light of God, we should turn from sin because deep down inside we are fearful of God's punishment and we desperately need His affection to satisfy our souls. On the flip side, the fear of God will motivate us to repentance because we know that he is forgiving, loving, and gracious. He is willing and eager to take us back. He welcomes us and runs toward us. Additionally, the fear of God will motivate us to a great many other things. Our speech will change. Our works will change. Our giving will change. Our priorities, entertainment, values, wisdom, and views will change. This is because we are awestruck at his power, knowledge and holiness. He knows all and sees all. And nothing is bigger or stronger than Him. He can do what He wants. And, in case you are wondering, He does exactly what He wants. God is God and we are not.

> **For Christians, all things are a religious matter.**

The fear of God is more than a sudden startling. You might say that it is three things together. It is knowing God's perfect and sovereign nature, knowing our imperfect and subordinate nature, and recognizing the inferences that these two things imply. They imply that we are dependent on Him and that life, both spiritual and physical, should be lived in light of Him.

It is not a shallow, emotional stir. It is a deep, inner conviction that permeates throughout all of your life. The fear of God is living in light of God. It is being Christian. It is pure religion (Ja. 1:27). Is it being afraid? Yes. Is it not being afraid? Yes. Have I gone insane? No.

It is an awareness of God. And it is to the extent that it moves the heart to a willing and eager submission to the Sovereign Ruler. It is more than a reluctant or temporary submission. It is a state of living. It is being religious all the time and not just at church. Too often today, people will compartmentalize their lives into "religious" and "nonreligious". But those who fear God see no difference. Since God is everywhere and seeing everything, all things are a religious matter.

The Fear of God is the Beginning of Wisdom

At this point, I should digress. We have turned full circle; from faith to wisdom to fear to salvation and back to faith. These concepts are synonyms in the broad sense of their meanings. Was that hard to understand? I don't think so. I think we just needed to be awakened from "the Matrix". We needed the covering removed from our minds in order to see the real picture rather than the world's distorted one. This idea, though it is hidden from many, is so plain and so common in the Scriptures that it is practically everywhere you look. It is so plain that it is the point of the Proverbs that some have suggested picture wisdom as Jesus Himself. Keep all of this new information in mind and revisit the opening chapter of Proverbs and see it ring true, that wisdom and faith and the fear of God are inseparable:

> "Wisdom cries aloud in the street, in the markets she raises her voice; at the head of the noisy streets she cries out; at the entrance of the city gates she speaks: 'How long, O simple ones, will you love being simple? How long will scoffers delight in their scoffing and fools hate knowledge? If you turn at my reproof, behold, I will pour out my spirit to you; I will make my words known to you. Because I have called and you refused to listen, have stretched out my hand and no one has heeded, because you have ignored all my counsel and would have none of my reproof, I also will laugh at your calamity; I will mock when terror strikes you, when terror strikes you like a storm and your calamity comes like a whirlwind, when distress and anguish come upon you. Then they will call upon me, but I will not answer; they will seek me diligently but will not find me. Because they hated knowledge and did not choose the fear of the Lord, would have none of my counsel and despised all my reproof, therefore they shall eat the fruit of their way, and have their fill of their own devices. For the simple are killed by their turning away, and the complacency of fools destroys them; but whoever listens to me will dwell secure and will be at ease, without dread of disaster.'" (Prov. 1:20-33)

You know, if you are not careful, you might be reminded of a preacher of the gospel who cries out, "Repent and turn to God from your sin. Then you will have abundant life." I sure did. This is the point of parallel. It could have easily been a New Testament call to repentance. Wisdom is fearing God. It is repentance and submission to God. Wisdom cries out, "Whoever listens to me will dwell secure and will be at ease, without dread of disaster." Had we not pulled the cover from our eyes, we might not have seen this. Believe me, it is everywhere in the Bible. But, I mentioned that I would digress. So I will.

Let me summarize and return to the epistle. James is getting into the idea of godly wisdom and, for this reason, we darted out into the realm of what that actually means. We discovered that wisdom is the fruit of fearing God and fearing God is the essence of what it means to be a Christian. Wisdom, true godly wisdom, is unavailable to those who have not been regenerated by God's Spirit. It is out of grasp of those who fear not the Lord. It is something only true believers can have. It is a divine gift and spiritual resource given to God's children alone. This is why a true test of faith is the test of whether one has true wisdom or not. True faith is wise. And on that note, let's return to James 3:13 where he asks for the ones with wisdom to come forward.

Your Table is Ready

Since my wife and I have wised up, we don't go to certain restaurants on Friday nights looking to be seated quickly. We understand that the weekends are the busiest and, more than likely, we will have to sit outside and wait for a table. However, on some rare occasions, you might find us taking the risk—and it is a risk. We pay the sitter hourly and we are both exhausted from our weekly responsibilities. You may know how it goes. Waiting for a table can be an anxiety-builder if we are not careful. And extra stress doesn't help our time together.

"Rogers, party of twelve. Your table is ready." Among the multitude standing and sitting along the benches outside, no one rushes to the front. The hostess repeats the announcement, this time in the form of a question. "Rogers, party of twelve?" In our minds, we wonder where these people are. It is a bittersweet moment. On one hand, you are tempted to be upset that you have been standing for an hour waiting patiently and some goofball party that was ahead of you has bounced. These were the people holding the line up. On the other hand, these *were* the people holding the line up. Their absence means that three or more tables were just freed up and we are that much closer to being seated. If only they would call our name!

Well, unless your name is wisdom or understanding, you can stay seated. James is calling us to the rug again. **"Who is wise and understanding among you?"** (Ja. 3:13). Reading the English here, you might think you have double the chances of being called since James is asking for both the wise and understanding people rather than the wise only. But, he is only asking for one party, not two. The words "wisdom" and "understanding" are primarily the same thing. These are synonyms. He probably used them both to emphasize the idea of one, mainly wisdom. Still, there are some minor differences that might have been purposed by James though the context suggests otherwise. Let's look at them quickly.

The word "wise" is the Greek word *sophos* which is quite general in meaning. To the Greeks it meant speculative knowledge or philosophy. However, to the Jews it carried a deeper meaning. It implied an application of knowledge. It was knowledge applied to personal life. This was certainly the way James meant it to be understood since his audience was Jewish. The word "understanding" appears only once in the New Testament. It is the Greek word *epistemon* and refers to specialized knowledge. You would use it to describe a tradesman or professional. In fact, you could easily substitute it with the English word "expert" if you like. James is likely using the phrase to transition from the context of a teacher (Ja. 3:1), who is an expert in biblical knowledge, to one who uses biblical knowledge in personal life. Whatever the case, James' focus is not on knowledge per se. It is on wisdom.

> **Wisdom is the heart's application of knowledge.**

Still, there is no escaping the fact that one cannot be wise if he is not first understanding. One preacher defined *understanding* as the knowledge of principles. It is of the mind. He then defined *wisdom* as the application of principles. It is of the conduct. Proverbs 8:33 says it this way, "Apply your heart to instruction and your ear to words of knowledge." Another one reads, "Hear, my son, and be wise, and direct your heart in the way" (Prov. 23:19). This might help us draw the distinction between the two. Wisdom is the heart's application of knowledge. The Proverbs often distinguish the two. Here are a couple of other helpful proverbs. "Wisdom is in the presence of the one who has understanding" (Pr. 17:24, NASB). Again, "Wisdom rests in the heart of one who has understanding" (Pr. 14:33, NASB). Both of these teach us that wisdom comes second. On the first hand, wisdom is yours for the taking if you have understanding. On the other hand, wisdom reigns in the heart of the one who has understanding. The *knowledge* of principles must come before the *application* of principles. This is not only logical, it is natural. It is the way God made us.

James might be following the logical progression from the mind to conduct; knowledge to application. Nevertheless, his focus and our attention are on wisdom—the application of principles. He is asking those among us to come forward if you think you have it.

"Party of wise, your table is ready."

Show Your Wisdom with Good Conduct

So the hostess has called a party by name and repeated the name several times, but no one has approached the hostess booth. Evidently, the Rogers party has left the premises. Do you know what that means? It means that if we are brave (and dishonest) we could rush to the front and tell her that the rest of our party decided to leave. (I have never done this before, but it has crossed my mind a time or two.)

"Here we are. The others decided to go somewhere else," I would tell the hostess. "No problem. We will break up the tables and give you a seat. Follow me." Do you think it would be that easy? Think again. The hostess would be doing the rest of the patient crowd an injustice if she did not first confirm that we were who we say we are. This is if she didn't already recognize me as a totally different party. After all, I did give her a different name just an hour ago. Either way, she is going to put me to a test. I will have to prove to her that I am with the Rogers party.

The same is true of James. He is not going to be fooled by anyone. In fact, he doesn't even give us the opportunity to come forward until he has given us a litmus test. **"By his good conduct let him show his works in the meekness of wisdom"** (Ja. 3:13). There is no bewildering here. If you want to see if someone is wise, you must look at their conduct. Jesus said quite plainly, "Wisdom is justified by her deeds" (Matt. 11:19). The way that they apply the principles they understand will tell you whether they are wise or not. So James lays the test before them. "If you think you are wise, let us examine your personal life and see how well your wisdom shows up." This is the same idea presented in the prior chapter. If you say you have faith, show it with your works. Likewise, if you say you have wisdom, show it with your works. More specifically, show it with your good conduct. Remember, if you have true wisdom that comes from God and is given only to those who fear the Lord, then godly conduct will surface.

A quick interjection at this point is worth mentioning. My good friend and pastor would call it a "sidebar." Wisdom is applied knowledge. It is assumed at this point that the knowledge one has is biblical. Earlier in the chapter, James draws our attention to the teachers of his day. These were the religious teachers like the scribes. Of these men it was said by Jesus to "practice and observe whatever they tell you—but not what they do" (Matt. 23:2). These were men with sound instruction. They were experts in the Law. They were men of understanding. However, they apparently lacked an equal amount of wisdom since the emulation of their practice was not recommended.

James assumes his readers understand that biblical knowledge is a prerequisite. Otherwise, your conduct would show that your wisdom might not be the only thing that is worldly. The Jews were not as eclectic with their upbringings as we are. In my small cul-de-sac are six different families. Although we were all raised under the same government and in the same region of the world with the same kind of civil influences and cultures, we all express a variety of different understandings on religion. Moreover, not all of us would claim to be Christians. So you would not expect us to demonstrate wisdom the same way. This was not so for the Jews. They were a people of one religion. They were all taught the same way and from the same literature and to practice the same observances. Underneath the skin, Jews were very much alike in a general sense. Therefore, the wisdom that they possessed would be rooted in the same understanding.

> **How do you demonstrate your wisdom?**

Now what about you? How do you demonstrate your wisdom? For starters, you can see it in how you respond to trials (Ja. 1:5). Remember back in the first chapter of James, we found out that the "meeting of trials of various kinds" was for "testing of your faith" which "produces steadfastness" and then "you may be perfect and complete" (Ja. 1:2-4). We learned that these tests, though they are for our good, are not always easily endured. That is to say that we are often tempted to respond to them in an ungodly way. This is because we lack the wisdom, or the ability to apply what we understand, needed to persevere (Ja. 1:5). It then brings about our inner temptations (Ja. 1:14) and we fail the test. Therefore, one way of demonstrating wisdom is that we are steadfast throughout our trials.

Even more to this point, James doesn't just look for steadfastness in trials—he also looks for a quality of demonstration. It isn't enough that you endure only. The way you endure trials and the attitude you endure are equally important. This is what he meant by steadfast. It is to be faithful to the end. It requires a kind of faithfulness that reveals a godly understanding and heart. A good first step is to note that wisdom is to be demonstrated by **"good conduct"**, which is purposely distinguished from bad conduct. In the Greek, this refers to a noble, excellent, winsome, attractive kind of lifestyle. This is a sort of general statement that is common to the New Testament. James takes that idea and gets more specific to say that your **"works"** will sort of gleam out from your good lifestyle. Then, to be even more specific, James says that your works are to be shown **"in the meekness of wisdom"** (Ja. 3:13).

All three should be true of the Christian. He is to be wise, and wisdom is demonstrated first in a general sense as causing a noble and attractive lifestyle. This is to say that you are not an nuisance in the community. You are upright, polite, hospitable, kind, peaceable, gentle, helpful, reasonable and more. (We will dig deeper into this idea shortly.) Wisdom is also demonstrated in good works that stem from a good lifestyle. This means that you are receptive, submissive, pure, impartial, honoring, merciful, lively, useful, just, mature, disciplined, and righteous—which I hope that you have learned in covering James so far. After this, wisdom is demonstrated in your attitude in which all of these things are shown. It is the attitude of meekness.

> **Meekness is having a tender heart, but tough skin.**

Meekness is a gentle, humble attitude. My computer dictionary defines it as "soft, gentle, and easily imposed on." A humble person is not one who is doing everything to serve himself. He may have a schedule and things to do, but he will certainly do what is possible to change it for others. He is not set in his own way. He is mildly tempered. He has a tender heart, but tough skin. He is not moved by evil, but he is stirred by goodness. One thesaurus says that it is "lamblike", which paints an excellent and obvious picture.

Meekness is a characteristic of Jesus. He said to "take my yoke upon you, and learn from me, for I am gentle and lowly in heart, and you will find rest for your souls" (Matt. 11:29). He is also called humble in a prophecy of Zechariah, "Behold, your king is coming to you; righteous and having salvation is he, humble and mounted on a donkey, on a colt, the foal of a donkey" (Zach. 9:9) which was fulfilled in Jesus' triumphal entry (Matt. 21:1-11). Therefore, it is a characteristic of divine faith. It should and will be a characteristic of the faithful, those who are reborn in Christ. For "Blessed are the meek, for they shall inherit the earth" (Matt. 5:5).

Though we describe meekness with words that are in some circles today attributed to the feeble, pushover, passive, emotionally-driven man, this is far from the truth. Moses was described as being "very meek, more than all people who were on the face of the earth" (Num. 12:3). But he was not a pushover by any means. He could make decisions and "blaze with anger when the occasion arose" as one pastor put it.[7] Moses was stirred with anger when he confronted sin. He was also moved to compassion for the Lord's people. He had tough skin but a tender heart. This is precisely how William Barclay described meekness when he commented on the Greek word for it:

> **Meekness is strength under control.**

> There is a gentleness in *praus* but behind the gentleness there is the strength of steel, for the supreme characteristic of the man who is *praus* is that he is the man who is under perfect control. It is not a spineless gentleness, a sentimental fondness, a passive quietism. It is a strength under control.[8]

Meekness is strength under control, and it is always related to our interactions with others. It cannot be demonstrated in your relationship to God alone. It is shown in how you treat mankind. However, it is not by nature an action—it is an attitude. James said that we should

---

[7] MacArthur, John. "Earthly and Heavenly Wisdom, Part 1 (1/11/1987)." Grace to You. Grace Community Church, 11 July 1987. Web. 17 Feb. 2011. <http://www.gty.org/Resources/Sermons/59-19_Earthly-and-Heavenly-Wisdom-Part-1>.

[8] Barclay, William. *New Testament Words*. London: SCM, 1964. 241-42. Print.

"receive with meekness the implanted word" (Ja. 1:21). which is the understanding of the Lord and the wisdom to apply it. Meekness, then, is a gentle, humble attitude of the heart and it is central to the core of wisdom. You might say that it is the heart of wisdom. This runs parallel with the notion of fearing God. It is thinking of God as big and you as small. Meekness is the logical conclusion. So meekness and humility are at the heart of wisdom since they are the fruit of biblical fear. Fear creates a meek heart. A meek heart receives the understanding of God with great eagerness, and wisdom is established.

A Living Taste of Meekness

I recall a period in my life when this was more evident to me than other times. Sadly to say, I am in constant war against pride and getting my way. Meekness is not my strong suite. So this brief period still stands out as a unique experience. One that I long to have again, Lord willing.

It happened during an in-depth study of Romans with the Bible Study Fellowship curriculum (which I highly recommend). It was thirty-something weeks of intense learning. And, if you have studied Romans before, you know how intense it can be. If not, allow me to mention a few Christian giants of our past and how Romans affected them. In A.D. 386, Aurelius Augustine, by a rather strange but divine appointment, casually and curiously fell upon Romans 13:11-14. After reading this, he was converted to Christianity and from a life of base immorality. We know him now as the great Saint Augustine of Hippo. Years later, Martin Luther, who needs no introduction, turned toward a life of freedom in Christ alone, through faith alone, and stood against the world in the sixteenth-century Reformation. In 1738, John Wesley, who was already ordained to ministry in the Anglican church, was led to his authentic conversion by God's spirit and through the words of Paul in Romans. His life was never the same. Such encounters were the case for John Calvin, Jonathan Edwards, and many more.

This was also true for me. Much like Wesley, I thought myself to be a decent Christian even to the extent of serving in ministry (though not officially ordained). My salvation was affirmed in the walking to the altar during a benediction as well as a silent prayer I uttered in my heart before sleeping one evening. I don't discount those moments by any means, but they seemed to have a small effect on my life when compared to what God's Spirit did from the book of Romans. Some call the book the "Constitution of the Gospel" since it is the most theological book of the New Testament and the most thorough explanation of the gospel. William Tyndale called it "the principal and most excellent part of the New Testament" and "a light and a way in unto the whole scripture."[9] In it, we learn about God's holiness, justice, punishment, grace, faithfulness, and love, as well as our depravity, inability to seek and hatred toward God, unfaithfulness, sinfulness, and our desperate need for divine salvation.

To see how this progressively breaks down the soul as it did mine, consider that all people "are under sin" (Rom. 3:9) and that "none is righteous, no, not one; no one understands; no one seeks for God" (Rom. 3:10-11) and that "all have sinned and fall short of the glory of God" (Rom. 3:23). In opposition to my understanding that I was comparably a good person and a decent guy, this accused me. I had never been hit so hard from the Scriptures. I was in pieces. I finally saw myself for the first time as a terrible sinner who was accruing God's wrath and ultimately eternal judgment (Rom. 6:23). But God, took this wrath upon Himself and died on my behalf even while I was hating everything about Him (Rom. 5:6-11). Now, there is nothing that can separate me from Him (Rom. 8:31-37). In effect, Paul drug me through the dirt and opened my eyes to the wretched heart that I really had. I was not even close to being a decent person. By God's standard, I was His enemy, feebly chucking rocks at His window and hollering, "Come out and die, you idiot!"

> **In our hearts, man secretly wants God dead.**

If this is stirring some uncomfortable feelings in your inners, then I am doing well. The words we all cry out in our sin are much more hateful than these even while we believe ourselves to be so kind. In our hearts, man secretly wants God dead. I did. You did, or you might still. This is why the gospel is so grand. This is why it is so irresistible. While hurling the rocks at the divine temple of God, He is not home. Rather, He is down the road hanging on a cross and enduring the wages that our rock throwing is accumulating. And, once He finishes, He reaches

---

[9] Tyndale, William, and David Daniell. "A Prologue to the Epistle of Paul to the Romans." Tyndale's New Testament. New Haven [Conn.: Yale UP, 1989. 207. Print.

down to our hearts and changes them so that we see our own sin and put our rocks down. We see Him for who He is and ourselves for who we are. Inevitably, we fall to our knees in fear, in humility, and with a heart of meekness.

This was the travel I made as God brought me through the words found in Romans. I moved from self-righteousness to fear of God and from pride to humility. I was then experiencing the essence of meekness. God paid a debt that He did not owe; I owed a debt that I could not pay. I deserved death, but I received life. I was hateful while He was loving. I was running away while He was running toward. Despite all of my sinfulness, God saved me.

One puritan summarized this transformation of the soul in a way that I could otherwise not do. Here is an excerpt from "Man a Nothing":

O LORD, I am a shell full of dust,
> but animated with an invisible rational soul
> and made anew by an unseen power of grace;

Yet I am no rare object of valuable price,
> but one that has nothing and is nothing,
> although chosen of thee from eternity,
> given to Christ, and born again;

I am deeply convinced
> of the evil and misery of a sinful state,
> of the vanity of creatures,
> but also of the sufficiency of Christ.[10]

This deep theology that I have come to understand as the "Doctrines of Grace," put me in my place as a meek person. I remember the time. I was so Christ-and-others-seeking that it bothered people. I was intuitively aware of other people's needs and deeply bothered by my own shortcomings. I would weep at my sins and show exceeding mercy to those who sinned against me. And in all of this, I was unshakable. It was an internal disposition. I was not just saying it. My heart was really this way. And it was an era that I will forever remember and long for again. Although my life in Christ is far deeper

---

[10] Bennett, Arthur. "Man a Nothing." *The Valley of Vision: a Collection of Puritan Prayers & Devotions*. Edinburgh: Banner of Truth Trust, 2002. 166-67. Print.

than it was before and more richer than it has ever been, this one era stands alone as one of my most memorable. When I think of the far ends of meekness, I think back to that time. Oh, how I long for it again and I thank the Lord for giving it to me.

Now that I have grown more mature in my biblical understanding, it has become more tempting to be self-confident and self-righteous. Paul said that knowledge "puffs up, but love builds up" (1 Cor. 8:1). Of course, this is the temptation of all who are students of the Bible and was certainly the temptation that overcame many of the priests and teachers of Israel. Understanding the gravity of my own sin and tendency to return to my prior life of folly helps keep me from being puffed up. A daily prayer that I ask of the Lord is to take *all* sin seriously, because it is serious to sin. And knowing the seriousness of sin, that it stirs up the wrath of God since it is ultimately a transgression against Him, helps me to see my place in this world. There is no reason for me to be proud. I have nothing good to offer. Even my best is tainted by sin and from a deceitful heart. On the other hand, Christ paid my debt on the cross and has given me all of the goodness there is in Him.

> **Take me to the cross and leave me there.**

The ending of the puritan prayer mentioned earlier is most powerful, "Take me to the cross, and leave me there."[11] Wisdom begins and ends at the cross where we understand the humility of our Lord and find wisdom incarnated. I love it! I'll conclude this point with the words of Paul on this same subject:

> For the word of the cross is folly to those who are perishing, but to us who are being saved it is the power of God. For it is written, "I will destroy the wisdom of the wise, and the discernment of the discerning I will thwart."
>
> Where is the one who is wise? Where is the scribe? Where is the debater of this age? Has not God made foolish the wisdom of the world? For since, in the wisdom of God, the world did not know God through wisdom, it pleased God through the folly of what we preach to save those who believe. For Jews demand signs and Greeks seek wisdom, but we preach Christ crucified, a stumbling block to Jews and folly to Gentiles, but to those who are called, both Jews and Greeks, Christ the power of

---

[11] Ibid.

God and the wisdom of God. For the foolishness of God is wiser than men, and the weakness of God is stronger than men.

For consider your calling, brothers: not many of you were wise according to worldly standards, not many were powerful, not many were of noble birth. But God chose what is foolish in the world to shame the wise; God chose what is weak in the world to shame the strong; God chose what is low and despised in the world, even things that are not, to bring to nothing things that are, so that no human being might boast in the presence of God. And because of him you are in Christ Jesus, who became to us wisdom from God, righteousness and sanctification and redemption, so that, as it is written, "Let the one who boasts, boast in the Lord." (1 Cor. 1:18-31)

Failing the Test

If the above is not true of you, then you lack wisdom (Ja. 1:5). Humility is the heart of wisdom because wisdom begins with the fear of God. Reverence toward God is a characteristic of meekness. If you live coram Deo, you will be humble because when His glorious light is shined upon you, the darkness of your heart is revealed. James is shining the heavenly light on you now as he asks for you to announce yourself if you really have godly wisdom. If you submit yourself to the test of showing your "works in the meekness of wisdom" and show that "**you have bitter jealousy and selfish ambition in your hearts,**" then you have failed the test (Ja. 3:14). For this is the opposite of godly wisdom. It is what he will call in the following verse, worldly wisdom, and we will look at that in more detail next.

> **Humility is the heart of wisdom because wisdom begins with the fear of God.**

What does it mean, then, to "**have bitter jealousy and selfish ambition**" in your heart? My good friend would answer facetiously, "It means to be American." And, for the most part he is right in summarizing the bulk of American "celebritism" and the innate drive of the American dream. We are a country that is known for going after what we want and not being satisfied until we get it. We are a country that admires the wisdom Solomon shown in the early parts of Ecclesiastes. But it would be wrong to label Americans only. This is the way of all people. It is part of our nature. If you have children, then you know this all too well. Babies are awfully cute, but they seek solely for themselves and we don't teach them that. They come out of the womb this way. So did I. So did you. And we continue to be that way because we are sinners. We seek our own. We serve ourselves.

To really grasp what James is saying, because it is important to know so that we don't skip over it thinking it doesn't apply to us, let us look at these two descriptions more closely.

To begin with, **"bitter jealousy"** is translated from the Greek, *zehlon pikron*. The word **"bitter"** (or *pikron*) is used one other time in James and never again anywhere in the New Testament. Earlier in the same chapter, James asked, "Does a spring pour forth from the same opening both fresh and salt water?" (Ja. 3:11). He is apparently carrying the same thought when he is regarding wisdom. Those who tame their tongue are people with "strength under control" as Barclay commented. They are people with wisdom. In other words, knowing the truth and being the expert is one thing. Speaking when the time is right and speaking in an edifying way is another. This is the difference between understanding and wisdom. Those who have genuine faith will demonstrate wisdom by not having "blessing" and "cursing" come from the same mouth (Ja. 3:10) just like a spring will not have fresh water and bitter water from the same fountain. This is the idea of the word "bitter." It is salty and distasteful.

Now put bitter with envy. This word is used as an adjective describing the kind of zeal (from the Greek, *zehlos*) that is not appropriate for a Christian. Zeal is the literal translation of the word *jealousy*. It refers to the heat of a person. It is our stirring and longing. It is our excitement. Paul described himself "as to zeal, a persecutor of the church," meaning that he was heated with anger toward Christians so much so that he was searching them out to kill them wherever they were hiding (Phil. 3:6). On the other hand, Paul was comforted by hearing of the Corinthians' zeal and compassion for him during his agonizing missionary journeys (2 Cor. 7:7).

So the idea of having zeal is not inherently sinful. It is indifferent to morality. Only when it exists for evil reasons does it become sinful. For this reason, James describes a wisdom that fails the test as having "bitter zeal" which is understood as a kind of enviousness and jealousy. It is an excitedly strong feeling for something that is not yours to have. It is working hard and longing after something that only benefits yourself in this world, or at least benefits you mostly and primarily.

The second phrase, **"selfish ambition,"** is like the first. James has doubled up his terms like he did "wise and understanding." As those two are generally same thing, so are these two generally the same thing. In fact, the adjective *bitter* describes both the *zehlon* and *eritheian*, which means strife and contention. Both are distasteful. Both are self-seeking. Both are dividing. This is what worldly wisdom is. It is the zealousness for self. It is selfish ambition.

I'll stop with the vocabulary lesson for now. Let's put it all together. Failing the test of wisdom is to show that you have the opposite of godly wisdom which is characteristic of true faith. It is being excited and zealous for things that meet your own desires. It is longing after the things of the world in a way that you are aroused, and pursuing them often without regards to others as more important than yourself. You are essentially applying learned principles for your own selfish benefit. The reality is, biblical principles cannot be applied in such a way. The Scriptures teach contrary to this and, so, to show selfish ambition in your heart, is to say that you either misunderstand the Scriptures or that you are picking and choosing which ones you want to keep.

In essence, when you show this kind of wisdom, you are not honest with yourself as a Christian. You lie to yourself. You deceive yourself and possibly those who observe you (Ja. 1:16, 22). So James tells you, **"do not boast and be false to the truth"** (Ja. 3:14). In other words, be honest with yourself. Face the reality. Look yourself in the mirror and if you see dirt, clean up. Don't walk away thinking that you are clean (Ja. 1:22-25). True faith is wise. This means that it is reverent and fearful of God. It is humble and demonstrates humility in good works. The life of one who has true faith is a life of good and godly conduct. Is this true of you? Be honest. Don't be false to the truth. Don't boast of wisdom when you have not.

True Faith is Heavenly

Foreigners have a peculiar sound to their speech. I am from Texas and we have a strong accent that is easily noticeable to others around the country. But for me, it is quite normal. I can spot foreigners, whether they are from the other regions of America or across the globe, because of their speech. The way they roll their letters, position their lips or employ their gutturals. These things usually indicate that the speakers are not from Texas—we are rather lazy with our enunciations.

In the same way, wisdom can be spotted by the way it speaks—both figuratively and literally. Wisdom grows in the mind and heart and is expressed through the words we say and use, the time and tone in which we use them, and in the behavior which we put forth. Basically, you can tell where wisdom comes from by what you observe it to express. It tells us what lies in the heart. Since the fear of God is the beginning of wisdom, then one cannot have wisdom without first having God. What then is the inference here? You can have worldly wisdom by being born of flesh, and heavenly wisdom by being born of God. True wisdom is from heaven. It is from God. It is not attained through or by this world. Just ask Solomon (Ecc. 12:13).

The wisdom that James speaks about here is what you might want to call "true wisdom". It is wisdom that has eternal value. It is heavenly and God-concerned. It is a byproduct of fearing God. It marks the ones who have true faith. Those who have "bitter jealousy and selfish ambition" in their hearts do not have heavenly wisdom (Ja. 3:14). James says that, "This is not wisdom that comes down from above, but is earthly, unspiritual, demonic" (Ja. 3:15).

Pause for a moment and see if you can lift the weight of what James just said. It is easy enough to understand wisdom that is not of God is not "from above," as he puts it. He mentioned earlier that "every good gift and every perfect gift is from above, coming down from the Father of lights" (Ja. 1:17). In other words, worldly wisdom is still wisdom in some sense. It may not have eternal value, but it works in the world. Still, to God it is folly. Solomon was very wise and his wisdom worked in the world since God-given wisdom is beneficial to all of His creation. People from all over the world came to glean from his wisdom. But we have no record of any of them walking away from his palace fearing God. Eventually, Solomon's desires twisted his wisdom and made it worldly and even no good to the world as a whole—which is quite ironic when you think about it. Worldly wisdom does not benefit the world, but it does have its fruit as do most good things. But should we

Worldly wisdom does not benefit the world.

think of worldly wisdom (or folly) so kindly? Should we be so passive and casual about it? "What is it hurting really?" is what some might wonder. In my opinion, the next part of James' teaching would advise us to be more contentious with it.

Wisdom that is not from God is first of all *earthly*. This word in Greek is fairly easy to understand. It is *epigeios* and means "of and in the earth." Something that is earthly is bound to the earth. It comes from it and dwells in it. It has no existence outside of it. Whatever is earthly will never rise above the material world. Therefore, it is marked by the curse of man's fallenness. This is the antecedent to heavenly wisdom. All of the wisdom that comes from earth is full of pride and self-centeredness. It is no surprise to us that earthly wisdom always seeks its own. Like the slogan of Burger King, this wisdom says, "Have it your way." Worldly wisdom is earthbound in its extent. People who exercise it, have it their way.

Secondly, wisdom that is not from God is *unspiritual*. Not only does it not come from God, but it comes from the world and has no spiritual worth. The Greek word used here is *psuchsikos* which refers to the nature of man, his flesh. It denotes sensuality. Paul used the word in his letter to the Corinthian church saying, "The *natural* person does not accept the things of the Spirit of God, for they are folly to him, and he is not able to understand them because they are spiritually discerned" (1 Cor. 2:14, emphasis added). Being unspiritual, one cannot understand the things of God. Rather, it is folly, stupid to him. It doesn't make sense to him. One who has this kind of wisdom will joke and scoff at the wisdom of God. He will shun the idea of having less for the sake of others, or forgiving those who offend. This kind of behavior is nonsense to him. Worldly wisdom is fleshly in its drive.

> **Worldly wisdom is fleshly in its drive.**

Thirdly, wisdom that is not from God is *demonic*. Notice the progression here. First, it is from the earth. To this you might say, "Yeah, it is probably untrustworthy wisdom that we should keep our eye on." Then, it is called unspiritual. To this you might say, "Wow, I should really stop waisting my time with this worldly wisdom." Lastly, it is called demonic. Here, you would do best to show strapping contempt and say quite strongly, "Lord, help me rid myself of this wisdom and shun it with all my might!" The fact is, earthly wisdom is nothing more than demonic wisdom. Did you think of that from the get-go? Most of us do not. Most of us make light of it. But this is definitely a weighty matter.

So what does it mean that worldly wisdom is demonic? It is the Greek word *daimoniodes* and refers to being demon-like or something proceeding from an evil spirit. It is basically an adjective from the word "demon." It only appears here in the New Testament. It is meant to convey that the wisdom that comes from the mind of man, who is earthbound and sensual, really stems from the evil system of demons that are also held captive to the earth in sensuality. It is nothing more than the expression of demons. Paul had the same idea in mind when he warned Timothy that some "will depart from the faith by devoting themselves to deceitful spirits and teachings of demons" (1 Tim. 4:1). Of course, Paul is talking about teachers who will lead some Christians away from God with their wisdom. The wisdom they share will have an appeal to man's earthliness. It will make sense and so it will lure them away. But, as Paul noted, it is nothing more than doctrines of demons. Worldly wisdom is demonic in its source.

> You have no wisdom at all if you only have worldly wisdom.

James' point here is simply this: if you say that you have the wisdom of God and the wisdom you reflect is characteristic of the world—being earthbound in it extent, fleshly in its drive and demonic in its source—then you really don't have the wisdom of God. You are being false to the truth. You may seem to the world that you are spiritually wise, but you are not. If you want to get down to the grit, you have no wisdom at all if you only have worldly wisdom because it has no eternal value. Rather, it is a vacuum. It sucks in what it wants. It works everything toward its own end. As mentioned earlier, it has bitter jealousy and selfish ambition. It seeks its own. It stuffs itself. It does what is beneficial to itself. It does not benefit others in a significant way.

James follows this to its bitter end. The result of worldly wisdom is not order and humility. It is chaos and pride. **"For where jealousy and selfish ambition exist, there will be disorder and every vile practice"** (Ja. 3:16). Here, James reconnects his thought two verses before. He says that "bitter jealousy and selfish ambition" are marks of worldly wisdom (Ja. 3:14). Now, he tells us about the results of these.

You can be sure that when you find bitter jealousy and selfish ambition, you have found worldly wisdom. I can't count how many times friendships and business relationships, though they may be between two professing Christians, have crumbled due to strife brought on by worldly wisdom. It is an easy temptation since it surrounds us each day and is deeply embedded in our flesh. Even the wisest of men fall to it. Just ask Solomon. We should not be so oblivious to it. We should be alert and attentive to these temptations always asking ourself, "Is this true godly wisdom from the Bible, or does it just make sense to me?" It would also do you well to watch your relationships. If you find the marks of disorder, you will also find bitter jealousy and selfish ambition. Take a step back. Then seek the Scriptures for understanding. Ask God for wisdom for only He gives it (Ja. 1:5, 17). "For the LORD gives wisdom; from his mouth come knowledge and understanding; he stores up sound wisdom for the upright" (Prov. 26:7).

> **If you find the marks of disorder, you will also find bitter jealousy and selfish ambition.**

True faith is not earthbound, sensual or demonic. It is heavenly. It is from God and for God's glory. Where did your wisdom come from? Is it worth its weight in the life after? Does it glorify God and resemble Christ-likeness? True faith is heavenly and should reflect heaven. This is where James takes us next.

True Faith is Peaceable

"You're not from around these here parts, are ya?" Not even remotely. True faith (since it is from heaven) requires that godly wisdom (since it comes through faith) is also from heaven. So it will often stand out from the rest of the wisdom in the world. You can spot it like a foreign exchange student in school. It is so obvious at times. This is because it is so contrary to our native wisdom.

Our native wisdom, to reiterate, is earthly, unspiritual and demonic. That is to say that it makes sense to the world around us because it is earthbound and from the wisdom we collectively and experientially create. And since we have sinful hearts, the wisdom we formulate (which is highly subjective and always changing) is sensual. It is a product of bitter jealousy and selfish ambition and brings about disorder and every vile practice.

I bring this up, not because I believe you have forgotten it already. Rather, I rehash this in order to show the contrast while worldly wisdom is fresh in your mind. James sets them in opposition by saying, **"But the wisdom from above is first pure, then peaceable, gentle, open to reason, full of mercy and good fruits, impartial and sincere"** (Ja. 3:17). I don't mean to keep forcing this idea to offend your intelligence, but it is important we remember that godly wisdom is reserved for those who belong to God and that God is the only one who gives it. This is why James reminds us that "the wisdom" he is contrasting with worldly wisdom is "from above" instead of "earthly" and this is the first contrast.

Being from above does not mean that it fell from the sky and landed in your backyard. It is not a UFO. You can't see it. This is figurative language and I think you know that. The word "heaven" was a synonym for God in the Jew's mind. In Matthew 21:23-27, when the Jewish authorities interrupted Jesus teaching in the temple and questioned him, "By what authority are you doing these things, and who gave you this authority?" Jesus responds by asking, "The baptism of John, from where did it come? From heaven or from man?" They didn't like His response. They discussed among themselves saying, "If we say, 'From heaven,' he will say to us, 'Why then did you not believe him?' But if we say, 'From man,' we are afraid of the crowd, for they all hold that John was a prophet." Notice that they wanted to know the origin of Jesus' authority and who gave it to Him. Jesus knew that the people believed John to be a prophet of God, so He has them draw the inferences. If John is a prophet of God and he points to Jesus as the Messiah, then it is settled. The answer is God. But Jesus didn't mention God specifically, since the first question was related to location. Jesus mentioned heaven.

To the Jew, heaven is the presence of God. You might say that God is heaven. Heaven is where ever God's benevolent presence is. Another instance is found in Matthew 23:22 where Jesus says, "whoever swears by heaven swears by the throne of God and by him who sits upon it." The prodigal son said in his humility, "Father, I have sinned against heaven" (Lk. 15:21). Since heaven is considered to be above us (both in location and figuratively in holiness), good gifts are from above. Earlier, James mentioned that "every good gift and every perfect gift is from above, coming down from the Father of lights" (Ja. 1:17). This idea is the premise behind verses 3:15 and 3:17 here in our current text. Wisdom, a good gift, is from above because heaven is above us. This is where God is. This is what John the Baptist understood when he said, "A person cannot receive even one thing unless it is given him from heaven" (Jn. 3:27).

Wisdom from above is not earthly. It is heavenly. It is godly. And altogether foreign to us. We would expect then that heavenly wisdom manifest itself in ways that are altogether foreign to us. And it does. James says that it is "first pure, then peaceable, gentle, open to reason, full of mercy and good fruits"—none of which are demonstrated without God's involvement.

Heavenly Wisdom is Pure

Unless you eat organic, the idea of "pure foods" is not something regularly on your mind. Our foods here in America are packed with numerous other things. Even our vegetables are grown with special stimulating elements before they undergo various food processes. By the time you get your can of corn, it is less corn than the day it sprouted. This is because it has been mixed with other things. Therefore, it has lost its purity.

Something that is pure is something that has not been mixed with anything else. It is clean. With regard to morality, something that is pure is something that is without sin. It is blameless.

> **Spiritual purity is being untainted by sin.**

God is pure. He has no sin in Him. Paul admonished the church in Philippi to think about things that are true, honorable, just, lovely, commendable, excellent, praiseworthy and pure in order to have the peace of God (Phil. 4:8). When instructing his young protege Timothy, he told him to not "take part in the sins of others" which is to "keep yourself pure" (1 Tim. 4:22). John taught that believers should "be like him [God]" and that "everyone who thus hopes in him purifies himself as he is pure" (1 Jn. 3:2-3). I think the idea is clear—even if you do eat processed food. Spiritual purity is being untainted by sin. It is clean of evil. This is in contrast of being unspiritual as earlier noted as a characteristic of worldly wisdom.

We should further note that purity is not *only* the first in a list of characteristics of heavenly wisdom. It is something more. James' words are *proton men hagne estin* which translates, "is foremost indeed pure." In the English, it is quite evident that "pure" is disconnected some way from "peaceable, gentle, open to reason" and those that follow. James is making a certain emphasis that we should acknowledge so that we don't miss an important point. Basically, heavenly wisdom is first and foremost pure. After that, it is peaceable, gentle, open to reason and so forth.

Someone said to me once, "Jacob, you are a husband and a father, and what else?" I responded by saying that I am first a Christian. Then, I added the other things that I might be called (excluding the bad things, of course). Being a Christian means something far deeper than anything else that I am. I am a Christian first. And what comes from being a Christian forms and determines what I am after. I am a husband who acts and lives a certain way because I am a Christian first. I am a father who acts and lives a certain way because I am a Christian first. This is what James had in mind. Heavenly wisdom is *first* pure. It is untainted by anything. It is clean, unmixed, and undiluted. And out of this purity, the other characteristics flow. The peace that characterizes heavenly wisdom is pure. In the same way, the gentleness, humility, mercy, fruits, impartiality and sincerity are all pure since they come from purity. That is James' point. Heavenly wisdom begins from a pure state of being and all of its expressions are pure. With this in mind, we can follow it up with the other characteristics.

> **Heavenly wisdom begins from a pure state of being.**

Heavenly Wisdom is Peaceable

Contrary to worldly wisdom, which stirs up disorder, is heavenly wisdom, which brings about pure peace. This seems to be James' emphasis with his description of heavenly wisdom. If you remember how he describes folly as being divisive, restless, poisonous and disorderly, you might get the impression that he wants us to see how sinful thinking brings about sinful behavior which ultimately causes chaos and destruction. And especially here, we find him contrasting it with the idea of peace at the beginning of the list as well as the end. I believe his point here is that heavenly wisdom brings about peace. We will look at that a bit more in a minute. For now, keep that in mind as we look at these other characteristics.

Firstly, what does he mean when he says that heavenly wisdom is **"peaceable"** (Ja. 3:17)? This is the word *eirenikos* which communicates the idea of loving, bringing and promoting peace. The writer of Hebrews used this word to describe the "fruit of righteousness" that yields after God "disciplines us for our good" and we then "share in his holiness" (Heb. 12:10-11). Peace is a virtue of true faith. A person made right in the sight of God is a person who loves and promotes peace where it is possible. Jesus even preached this in the clearest way. "Blessed are the peacemakers, for they shall be called sons of God" (Matt. 5:9). Here, the term "blessed" is used to refer to an eternal state of being whereby a person is right in God's sight. Those who are peacemakers are those who are justified. Those are the ones who have true faith. It is evidenced by their love for peace.

Heavenly Wisdom is Gentle

After peaceable, heavenly wisdom is purely **"gentle"** (Ja. 3:17). In the Greek, this is the word *epieikes*. It is not an easy word to translate into English. I once read that William Barclay believed there to be no English word that completely captures its meaning. However, we might be able to capture this evasive term with more than one English word.

The difficulty lies in the fact that the word describes an attitude of the heart. This was true of the word "peaceable" and is true of the words that follow. It is a word that describes a leniency with a tender kind of motivation. We could possibly use other words to describe it if we were mindful that these words are not wooden meanings but rather descriptions of how it is expressed in one's life. These words would be long suffering, patient, kind, fair, humble, mild, forbearing, and yielding. But not one of these truly communicates the meaning of the word.

By way of preview and possibly a way of giving you a small idea of what gentleness means, think of a young boy who is perusing the park with his mother. He is just like any typical boy. He wants to climb the trees, throw the rocks, and be the king of the sand hill. When he notices a number of small ducklings swimming by in the nearby pond, he grabs one and holds it in his hand. An urge rises up inside of him to squeeze. Why? Because he can. He is stronger and bigger. He has a deep sense to conquer and show his masculinity even at such a young age. The mother, knowing full well the mind of a young boy, says politely but sincerely, "Be very gentle with the little duckling." Rather than explain how this relates to the biblical word, I'll leave you with the story. My hope is that it at least set your imagination in the proper stage so that we can form a more biblical meaning of the word.

A good place to start is with the story of Joseph when he is face-to-face with the brothers who once hated him. Although the word is never used here, the concept is evident. Joseph was sold into slavery by his brothers (though they originally wanted to kill him). God sovereignly moved Joseph into a position in Egypt whereby his brothers depended on him for their well-being. The wisdom of his time, as is our's today, would say that these brothers required justice. It would say that it is reasonable for Joseph to penalize them for their wrongdoing against him. And he was certainly in the position to do so. Frightened, the brothers said to themselves, "It may be that Joseph will hate us and pay us back for all the evil that we did to him" (Gen. 50:15). But, to their surprise, Joseph was gentle with them. He understood that they earned a good penalty but he was mindful of something greater. He said to them:

> "Do not fear, for am I in the place of God? As for you, you meant evil against me, but God meant it for good, to bring it about that many people should be kept alive, as they are today. So do not fear; I will provide for you and your little ones." (Gen. 50:19-21)

Joseph was gentle in his dealings with them. Yes, he showed long suffering, mildness, kindness, leniency, and even forgiveness. And in all of this, he dealt with them in a tender, heart-to-heart way. Here, you might see gentleness as having the book to throw at someone, yet setting it aside. Joseph knew what he could have done, but did not do it. He was satisfied with less than what was due. He understood that God was at work and that man is prone to sin. Therefore, a gentle person is ready to forgive.

One last set of examples could be found in numerous things that

Jesus did. When Peter hacked off the ear of the high priest's servant who came to capture Jesus, Jesus miraculously put it back on (Lk. 22:51). In the same scene, He points out that "twelve legions of angels" are at His disposal if He wanted a defense (Matt. 26:53). Peter was rebuked for his retaliation, not the soldiers for their injustice.

In an earlier time, King and Lord Jesus humbly knelt before His disciples and washed their feet (Jn. 13:1-20). To the woman caught in adultery, he offered hope and forgiveness. Justice would have had her stoned (Jn. 8:1-11). To the dishonest rich man named Zacchaeus, Jesus offered salvation (Lk. 19:1-10). To the world, He offers the same (Jn. 3:16). Justice, on the other hand, would have us all put to death. Gentleness is having the law on your side and the power in your hand, but the satisfaction in giving far less and especially giving good will. Gentle people know no revenge. They treat persecution with kindness.

> **Gentle people know no revenge.**

This word encompasses so much. Not only is it difficult to translate, it is equally difficult to internalize. However, with the true gift of faith, we will have heavenly wisdom and gentleness will inevitably characterize we who belong to God. The wisdom from above reflects a heart of gentleness.

Heavenly Wisdom is Yielding

The third characteristic that flows from a pure heart and characterizes heavenly wisdom is "**open to reason**" (Ja. 3:17). If you read it as is in the ESV, you might think that it refers to the willingness to see things differently. But this is not entirely accurate. It is not really being the one who doesn't argue. Rather, it is a willingness to be compliant. It carries the idea of setting your own agendas and liberties aside in order to do something expected of you. The Greek word is *eupeithes* which is the opposite of stubborn and disobedient. You may not like the rules, but you obey them nonetheless. You might not agree with everything, but you are compliant. No one has to force you because you do not speak back and object. This is what it means here. It is not to be understood as spinelessness or lack of convictions. Rather, as sinners saved by grace, we ought to have a healthy self-suspicion. We should easily recognize that we are prone to the same mistakes others make.

And this will lend to us a willingness to defer.

Being open to reason is an attitude of being reasonable. Reasonable people are easy to work with. Have you noticed that? Everyone has opinions. Everyone has a preference of doing things. But those who yield their own preferences and opinions without disputing are the ones who encourage peaceful relationships. With no disputes, there is little to quarrel over. There is no friction, no arguments. Innate to human nature, however, is the desire to be heard, to be right, and to get our way. This is the opposite of heavenly wisdom. When there are nonessential matters, the person with true faith—a faith that is heavenly and pure—will be nonconfrontation and yielding to outside rules and ideas.

You may experience opportunities to exercise your ability to be reasonable more than you think. Next time you and your friends want to meet for lunch, see if you insist on the location or yield to the others. Next time a creative idea is presented at work that you disagree with, see if you object and fight for your preference. Next time you visit a movie theater and find that they will not allow you to bring your own refreshments inside, see if you get all hot under the collar. We all know that their refreshments are way overpriced. But these are the rules. The person who is open to reason will abide to what is expected and do so in a way that is pure.

Heavenly Wisdom is Merciful

The fourth characteristic of heavenly wisdom is that it is **"full of mercy"** (Ja. 3:17). The Greek here is *meste eleous* which quite literally means bulging with mercy. It is to be full of compassion for others. King David, broken in his sin, cried out, "Have mercy on me, O God, according to your steadfast love; according to your abundant mercy blot out my transgressions" (Ps. 51:1). He begged this of the Lord because he understood God to be "a God merciful and gracious, slow to anger, and abounding in steadfast love and faithfulness" as Moses acknowledged (Ex. 34:6).

Wisdom that comes from a merciful God will reflect mercy since it is God who works it out in our lives. In other words, God's wisdom is full of mercy and James wants to see if you have it. When put to the test, the Pharisees were proven to have worldly wisdom with regards to the heart and mind of God. After calling Matthew, the tax collector, Jesus stayed to eat and "many tax collectors and sinners came and were reclining with Jesus and his disciples." The Pharisees saw this and asked the disciples, "Why does your teacher eat with tax collectors and sinners?" Jesus, overhearing it, responded, "Those who are well have no need of a physician, but those who are sick. Go and learn what this means, 'I desire mercy, and not sacrifice.' For I came not to call the righteous, but sinners" (Matt. 9:9-13). In other words, "You guys say that you have heavenly wisdom, but you have missed the entire point. God wants His people full of mercy, rather than sacrifice." A similar lesson happened in Matthew 12:1-8. It was not that sacrifice was unimportant. It was that sacrifice from a cold heart is no sacrifice at all. Besides this, the main idea is to have faith in God and live in fear of Him. God wanted obedience.

There was one Pharisee who was "not far from the kingdom of God," as Jesus said. He was close to understanding what it meant to be a genuine child of God. He said that to love God "with all the heart and with all the understanding and with all the strength, to love one's neighbor as oneself, is much more than all whole burnt offerings and sacrifices" (Mk. 12:33). This is what it means to have heavenly wisdom. One who has heavenly wisdom would know this since it was recorded in the Bible, as in Jeremiah 7:22-23, "For in the day that I brought them out of the land of Egypt, I did not speak to your fathers or command them concerning burnt offerings and sacrifices. But this command I gave them: 'Obey my voice, and I will be your God, and you shall be my people. And walk in all the way that I command you, that it may be well with you.'" God desired a people who loved Him and loved as He loves. Therefore, one who has the wisdom of God would show a heart full of mercy. As the story of the Good Samaritan teaches, the one who shows mercy is the one who loves the Lord. Jesus told the people of His day as He does so to us, "You go, and do likewise" (Lk. 10:37).

Heavenly Wisdom is Fruitful

This is the first time that James employs the word "fruit" but it is not the last. According to the original text, it also appears in the following verse. In both instances, James is teaching that heavenly wisdom has good fruits. More specifically, heavenly wisdom is *full of* good fruits (Ja. 3:17). We might say that a man is "full of hot air" when he is telling us things that are obviously untrue. When describing wisdom from above, we should say that it is full of good fruits because wisdom produces things that are good. It is full of good produce. In fact, if we skip ahead to the next verse, we find that wisdom is described as "the harvest [or fruit] of righteousness" (Ja. 3:18). It is abundantly good.

James is not talking specifically about the fruit that falls from a tree. He is pointing to something past it, something more. We understand fruit to be the purpose of the tree. It grows to bear fruit. A fig tree that bears no fig is a worthless and deceiving tree. In fact, Jesus cursed a fig tree for lacking figs when it should have them (Mk. 11:12-14). The idea of fruit carries with it a larger meaning than just tasty delights. In James 5:7 we read of an analogy of a farmer who waits patiently "for the precious fruit of the earth." James says, "You also, be patient. Establish your hearts, for the coming of the Lord is at hand" (Ja. 5:8). Here it carries the idea of waiting for the work of God, namely the coming of Jesus, but also the benefits of salvation and a transformed heart.

> **A fig tree that bears no fig is a worthless and deceiving tree.**

One more helpful use of the word in James is found a few verses later. When instructing on what most call *The Prayer of Faith*, James teaches us to pray to the Lord on our behalf and trust that He will answer our prayers. His example is Elijah. He was "a man with a nature like ours, and he prayed fervently that it might not rain, and for three years and six months it did not rain on earth. Then he prayed again, and heaven gave rain, and the earth bore its fruit" (Ja. 5:17-18). This is when Israel was worshipping a false god and Elijah the prophet was used to strip the hope of the people away from the god. Their god was the god of rain. But God alone controls the rain. Likewise, it is God alone who controls the goodness of salvation, and all things for that matter. As the fruit of the earth came forth to meet their needs, God will give us the fruit of wisdom when we ask. The idea here is that fruit serves as a picture of the good works of God. For this reason, and to get back to our text, James calls it **"good fruit"** (Ja. 3:17).

Heavenly wisdom is full of good fruit, just as it is full of mercy.

Good fruit here, could be understood as good works as we saw in James 2. He said that faith without works is not a faith that is of God. Here, he says that wisdom without fruit is not a wisdom that is of God. The parallel is clear. If you say you have heavenly wisdom, then you will demonstrate that you have good fruit. Following this logic, we could trust that good fruit is the harvest of good works. When we love God and, therefore, love people, we sow good seeds like a farmer. Then we wait patiently to see the good fruit grow from our love, for God and man. You might think of it like this: your good works might be loving your enemy, helping your neighbor, keeping your word, serving in humility, being honest and diligent and submissive. After a time of sowing these things, your good fruit might be newfound relationships, stronger family, or prosperous living. But most importantly, it will be an assurance of salvation—the joy of knowing that God has given you genuine faith to believe and obey Him and thereby inherit eternal life. Good fruits can be earthly but they will always be spiritual. According to Paul, the "fruit of the Spirit is love, joy, peace, patience, kindness, goodness, faithfulness, gentleness, self-control" (Gal. 5:22-23). These are some of the signs of heavenly wisdom.

Heavenly Wisdom is Impartial

You might have noticed that these characteristics sound very similar to the characteristics of true faith that James has been sharing since the beginning. For example, we just connected good fruits with good works as it was the subject in James 2:14-26. The matter of being open to reason might have reminded you of James 1:19-27 where we learned about being quiet and listening to God's word. The prior section on mercy might have reminded you of James 2:8-13 where we read about fulfilling the royal law. The particular characteristic that we find ourselves focusing on now is truly the most memorable one to me. In preparation for this book, it might have been the most eye-opening. It is the characteristic of impartiality. True faith is impartial. Therefore, heavenly wisdom is also impartial.

The Greek word used here is the same that we examined in chapter 3. It is just used a different way. In James 2:1 we read the command to "show no partiality"[12] and then the rhetorical question in verse 4, "have you not made distinctions among yourselves and become judges with evil thoughts?" Here, on the other hand, we are taught that heavenly wisdom is "impartial" (Ja. 3:17). Therefore, we are to be impartial. In specific, our wisdom, if it is from heaven, should show an impartial heart. Like the characteristics before it, this one is a word describing the *kind* of wisdom. It is a description of the nature of wisdom—what it is like by nature. It is not showing what it should be or what it will be, but what it is.

I need not revisit the matter of being impartial. I'll trust that you read chapter 3 of this book and understand it well enough to imagine what James might mean here. I will at least mention that his point is to show what heavenly wisdom does based on the values and worth placed on people by the world. Heavenly wisdom is indifferent to people's social status, popularity, education, skin color, living space, and so forth. In fact, it is as indifferent in its usage as it is in its reception. James began his letter by stating that "any of you" can "ask God, who gives generously to all without approach" and guess what? "It will be given him" (Ja. 1:5). Heavenly wisdom is impartial from the beginning to the end.

> **Our wisdom, if it is from heaven, should show an impartial heart.**

Heavenly Wisdom is Sincere

One of the most remarkable characteristics, in my opinion, is the final one. It is sincerity. The Greek word is *anupokritos* which means without hypocrisy or authentic. This is specifically a biblical word. It is, in a sense, a synonym to the word "pure" which began our list of characteristics. Something is pure if it is unmixed. It is also absolute sincerity. Paul used the word in Romans 12:9 when he called Christians to "let love be genuine" and then followed it with some explanation of how that pans out. Paul also told Timothy that "the aim of our charge is love that issues from a pure heart and good conscience and a sincere faith" (1 Tim. 1:5).

---

[12] Though the Greek word used here is *prosopolepsia* (respect of persons) and not *diakrino* (to show partiality), it implies the same meaning which is the way it is translated in the ESV text. Here in James 3:17, the negative participle is used. It is *adiakritos*, from the root of the latter word, and means (to be impartial).

To be hypocritical is to be illegitimate and fake. It is to be one thing, but to show another. It is like wearing a mask over your face in order to give others the impression that you are someone other than who you are. On the other hand, to be without hypocrisy is to be without disguise; to be sincere and honest. The reason that this particular characteristics strikes me as being so remarkable is that it basically describes the nature of heavenly wisdom as manifesting its authentic nature. We have just covered at least seven characteristics of heavenly wisdom. This final one says that it will manifest itself as these things all of the time. In contrast, any manifestation of the otherwise, does not have roots in heaven since it would then qualify as insincere. But, heavenly wisdom is sincere, all of the time.

Heavenly Wisdom is Orderly

I could have inserted this final characteristic with the word "peaceable" but it really had to wait until the end. From the word "pure" to the word "sincere," James subtly implies one more sense of character that we would never appreciate in the English. It is found in the alliteration of this verse. They would have a certain harmonious sound when heard orally in the original text. There are six consecutive words that begin with the Greek letter epsilon (transliterated as "e" in English) and three words beginning with the letter alpha (transliterated as "a" in English).

Could I be reading too much into the text? I don't think so. This is the nature of wisdom literature. It is often poetic in style and communicates tones through word usage much more than didactic literature. It is likely James not only wanted you to understand that heavenly wisdom is peaceable, he also wanted you to *feel* that it was peaceable. He did this by utilizing harmonious sounds in the words that come immediately after the vices describing worldly wisdom. He calls such wisdom disorderly (Ja. 3:16). The words even sound disorderly when heard—especially when they are heard in light of the more orderly words in verse 17. Point being, worldly wisdom is chaotic and heavenly wisdom is orderly. It is peaceful and harmonious.[13] This leads us to our final point on heavenly wisdom.

James finishes by saying, **"And a harvest of righteousness is sown**

---

[13] To further explore this concept, read William Varner's book entitled, *The Book of James: A New Perspective*, published by Kress Biblical Resources. It is found on page 140.

in peace by those who make peace" (Ja. 3:18). This sounds a bit obvious once the characteristics of heavenly wisdom are explored. If it is pure by nature, then it is peaceful in expression. This is why it "is first pure, then peaceable" (Ja. 3:17). We are taking a full turn once again back to true faith. This kind of authentic, divine faith is wise with a wisdom from heaven. Wisdom from heaven is given only to those who fear God—those who love and live for God. Therefore, it is for those who have true faith, for those who have been justified by Christ. That is to say, heavenly wisdom can only be found in those who are righteous. And, according to James, a "harvest of righteousness is sown in peace by those who make peace" (Ja. 3:18). The fruits of genuine faith sows seeds of peace. If you have true faith, then you will also manifest peace.

> **Heavenly wisdom can only be found in those who are righteous.**

Do you see the connection? Does your wisdom result in peace or does it stir up chaos? Do others notice that you are gentle, open to reason, full of mercy, impartial and sincere? Do you notice good fruits as the result of your wisdom? If not, then you might wonder whether the wisdom you have is heavenly. At least, some of it, according to God's word, is not. Therefore, I encourage you, as I do myself, to obey the Word of the Lord and ask God, who is the Giver of wisdom, to give generously as He says He will. But when you ask, do so in faith, trusting that He will give it and that it will be for your good; trustworthy and useful.

Conclusion

Wisdom originates from two places—here (earth) and there (heaven). We gain wisdom from earthly knowledge and experience. However, we stand to gain the most wisdom from reading and obeying God's Word which offers us untold riches in knowledge, as well as the opportunity to learn from the experiences of those whose lives and walks with God are recorded there. A believer who wants to be wise should seek to become an expert on viewing and understanding life from God's point of view.

Wisdom has manifold benefits and James underscores one of its primary blessings in chapter one when he tells us wisdom helps us learn from our tests. As believers, we are always in a cycle of godly growth. Life has trials. Wisdom helps us learn from our trials. Then, life has more trials. This is the perfecting work of God that makes us mature in the faith He has given us. True faith is wise.

Allow me to close with words from a Puritan author. "Help me to carry into ordinary life portions of divine truth and use them on suitable occasions, so that its doctrines may inform, its warnings caution, its rules guide, its promises comfort me."[14]

---

[14] Bennett, Arthur. "Spiritual Growth." *The Valley of Vision: A Collection of Puritan Prayers & Devotions*. Edinburgh: Banner of Truth Trust, 2002. 201. Print.

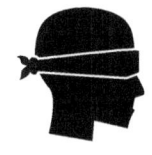

CHAPTER 7

THE TRIAL OF LOYALTY

JAMES 4:1-12

"submit yourselves therefore to God"

We have all been asked, "Whose side are you on?" Unable to make a decision, we vacillate between the two—knowing that to choose one is to abandon the other. When a Christian is struggling between choosing God's side or the world's side, James calls it "double-mindedness" (Ja. 1:8; 4:8).

The Bible repeatedly calls us to choose God's side. Joshua challenged the wayward and ever-wandering Israelites to, "choose this day whom you will serve" (Josh. 24:15). Jesus said, "No one can serve two masters, for either he will hate the one and love the other, or he will be devoted to the one and despise the other" (Matt. 6:24).

In Deuteronomy, Moses outlines the consequences of the choice God has laid before us, "...I have set before you life and death, blessing and curses. Therefore choose life, that you and your offspring may live, loving the LORD your God, obeying his voice and holding fast to him, for he is your life..." (Deut. 30:19-30). This is the call of the gospel message—choose God and you choose life.

Unfortunately, we believers don't always declare as Joshua did, "as for me and my house, we will serve the Lord" (Josh. 24:15), at least not by our actions. More often than not we choose to submit to the world and its fleeting pleasures, indulging our selfish natures in the sin that dwells in our hearts. At the core of making the correct choice lies the issue of loyalty.

What causes quarrels and what causes fights among people? Is it that their passions are at war within them? They desire and do not have, so they murder? They covet and cannot obtain, so they argue and fight?

You do not have, because you do not ask. You ask and do not receive, because you ask wrongly, to spend it on your passions. You adulterous people! Do you not know that friendship with the world is enmity with God? Therefore whoever wishes to be a friend of the world makes himself an enemy of God. Or do you suppose it is to no purpose that the Scripture says, "He yearns jealously over the spirit that he has made to dwell in us"? But he gives more grace. Therefore it says, "God opposes the proud, but gives grace to the humble." Submit yourselves therefore to God. Resist the devil, and he will flee from you. Draw near to God, and he will draw near to you. Cleanse your hands, you sinners, and purify your hearts you double-minded. Be wretched and mourn and weep. Let your laughter be turned to mourning and your joy to gloom. Humble yourselves before the Lord, and he will exalt you.

Do not speak evil against one another, brothers. For the one who speaks against a brother or judges his brother, speaks evil against the law and judges the law. But if you judge the law, you are not a doer of the law but a judge. There is only one lawgiver and judge, he who is able to save and to destroy. Who are you to judge your neighbor? (James 4:1-12)

True Faith is Selfless

Context is highly important in just about everything you read. This is especially true of the New Testament letters. And if you are one of those who skipped to this chapter for whatever reason (and I can think of many), let me mention a few things. In our prior chapter, we read about wisdom. James described it in two ways. One was worldly wisdom that was passionately self-seeking, resulting in disorder and chaos (Ja. 3:14-16). The other was described as heavenly wisdom that came down from God. It was pure, beneficial to others, and resulted in peace (Ja. 3:17-18). His point was this: If you are Christians, then you should have peace among you since Christians have Christ who is the wisdom of God. Put more succinctly: Wisdom brings peace. Christ is wisdom. Christians have Christ. Therefore, Christians have peace among them.

To the same church folks, he asks, "**What causes quarrels and what** causes fights among you?" (Ja. 4:1). Now that is a strange thing to ask Christians who profess to be wise. If you have Christ, and God has given you His wisdom, and heavenly wisdom is peaceable, where in the world did these quarrels and fights come from? James is certainly making his point rather strongly. He could have come right out and told them, "You appear to be worldly people, not heavenly people. You act like you don't have Christ at all. You act like the same people who deny Christ." I'm sure this was difficult to hear. I can almost sense the shock: "Christians, quarreling and fighting? Really!"

James used the words *polemoi* and *machai* to describe their feuds. The first word quite literally refers to war. It is where we get our English word "polemic." In the Bible, it is mostly used in the book of Revelation since battles and wars are mentioned as end-time events. Nowhere does it appear to refer to simple arguments or disagreements, nor screaming matches. It is meant to describe prolonged states of conflict. The second word, *machai*, describes individual squabbles. Both terms are in the present-plural tense meaning that there are multiple wars and fights going on continuously among them. This ... means ... war!

Paul faced a similar situation when dealing with the Corinthian church. He told them, "But I, brothers, could not address you as spiritual people, but as people of the flesh, as infants in Christ. I fed you with milk, not solid food, for you were not ready for it. And even now you are not yet ready, for you are still of the flesh. For while there is jealousy and strife among you, are you not of the flesh and behaving only in a human way?" (1 Cor. 3:1-3). Evidently, Paul addressed things the same way James did—with heavenly wisdom (1 Cor. 3:13). They both identified worldliness with selfishness and fighting. Paul said that they were acting like newborns, not fully grown in the wisdom of God. They were "of the flesh," still much like the world and in need of more development. Years later, Paul wrote them again and they were still in conflict. "For I fear that perhaps when I come I may find you not as I wish, and that you may find me not as you wish—that perhaps there may be quarreling, jealousy, anger, hostility, slander, gossip, conceit, and disorder" (2 Cor. 12:20).

This is not the way God intended His church to be. Jesus told the disciples, "A new commandment I give to you, that you love one another: just as I have loved you, you also are to love one another. By this all people will know that you are my disciples, if you have love for one another" (Jn. 13:34-35). Contrary to how some interpret this passage, Jesus is teaching that the demonstration of love among Christians is how all people (implying unbelievers primarily) will know that Christians belong to Christ. The opposite therefore is true: quarrels and fights among Christians indicate they do not belong to God—at least as perception indicates. Jesus also expressed a desire for unity among believers "that they may all be one, just as you, Father, are in me, and I in you, that they also may be in us, so that the world may believe that you have sent me" (Jn. 17:21).

This was not a far-reaching idea. The church was well unified when the Spirit of God appeared at Pentecost. Luke records, "Now the full number of those who believed were of one heart and soul, and no one said that any of the things that belonged to him was his own, but they had everything in common (Acts 4:32). It was true of the Philippians at the time Paul wrote to them. "Only let your manner of life be worthy of the gospel of Christ, so that whether I come and see you or am absent, I may hear of you that you are standing firm in one spirit, with one mind, striving side by side for the faith of the gospel" (Phil. 1:27).

God designed His church to dwell in unity.

Scripture is consistent. God designed and desires that His Church dwell in unity. The Psalmist expressed the goodness of such, "Behold, how good and pleasant it is when brothers dwell in unity!" (Ps. 133:1). Unity not only pleases God, it proves that those who dwell in it are genuinely saved. Conflicts, on the other hand, are a sign of worldliness and confuse the inner work of salvation. Moreover, they lead to far worse things—as we will see shortly.

Conflicts are bad for the body and the world. But the real problem here is far deeper, and James is searching for it. The verse reads quite literally, "*From where come* quarrels and *from where come* fights among you?" (emphasis is mine). In other words, "What is their source?" Of course, he is not asking them because he wants to know; he already knows where they come from. His intent is to help them understand and, in turn, to help us understand. So let's get to the real source of conflicts.

Getting to the Source of Conflict

Like the prior chapter when James gets to the source of wisdom that brings about "disorder and every vile practice" (Ja. 3:16), namely the world, he gets to the source of "quarrels" and "fights" (Ja. 4:1), by posing a second question. This time he is not so gentle. **"Is it not this, that your passions are at war within you?"** (Ja. 4:2). Can you imagine that anyone would disagree? Who could argue a legitimate case to the contrary? Worldly wisdom is self-seeking. When people are influenced by the world, each one seeking his own, what else can happen? It's like throwing a piece of meat in the midst of hungry dogs. Everyone is out for himself and if the self is not happy, problems arise (Ja. 3:17). One person wants something so he takes it from another person, who wants it back naturally. Neither of them is seeking the benefit of the other, so a fight ensues and continues until something disastrous occurs. We've seen this all our lives: children fighting over toys, athletes fighting over fouls, employees fighting over positions, spouses fighting over money, nations fighting over land.

> **In the game of life, you may be part of the world's team but you are a spiritual loser on your own.**

Let's look deeper, closer to home. Remember James began the search by asking about the source of the fighting "among you" (Ja. 4:1). This is understood to mean the church, the local body in particular. Then he rhetorically wonders if the fights stem from the passions at war **"within you"** (Ja. 4:2). This is a more finely-tuned sense of the word "you." Picture a much younger you with your friends, when your father confronts you, wagging his finger in disappointment. Collectively, all of you have broken his trust. Yet you maintain a level of confidence, assuming the judgment will be equally divided. That is, until his finger points directly at you. Suddenly you feel completely alone. Why? Because you are the object of judgment and you are taking it all. This is what James is doing. The truth is, in the game of life, you may be a part of the world's team but you are a spiritual loser on your own. The external conflicts we collectively experience begin as internal conflicts we experience alone. In one sense, you are guilty by association. In another sense, you are simply guilty. Therefore, when we sin, the fault is not the worlds. The fault is ours.

Let's be honest. Worldly wisdom is all around us, but we do not have to succumb to it. Yet, when we cause conflict, that is exactly what we do. Our passions take control. Our inner heart runs amok and we make a mess of things. The world cries out, "Do what you like!" And like obedient lackeys, we become slaves to our passions.

Satisfaction Slaves

Have you heard the word *hedonism*? It means "the pursuit of pleasure", generally referring to sensual self-indulgence. In the words of the Apostle Paul in 2 Timothy 3:4, worldly people are "lovers of pleasure rather than lovers of God." One who pursues his or her own corrupt desires is called a *hedonist*. The word is transliterated from the Greek, *hedone*, which is exactly what is used here in verse one, "Is it not this, that your [hedonism] is at war within you?"

The war begins when pursuits are manifested. Earlier James mentions that, "Each person is tempted when he is lured and enticed by his own desire" (Ja. 1:14). Paul wrote about this in his letter to the Romans. Though his war is not exactly the same as what we find here in James, there is a parallel. "I see in my members another law waging war against the law of my mind and making me captive to the law of sin that dwells in my members" (Rom. 7:23). When Paul speaks of "members" he is referring to his bodily members, particularly his inner yearnings and will. He sees a war within himself. It is the part of him, a kind of residue that remains from his old life prior to his spiritual transformation. The parallel falls short when Paul says that he does not want to do what is sinful (Rom. 7:15). Rather, he has the "desire to do what is right, but not the ability to carry it out" apart from God's Spirit (Rom. 7:18). "I delight in the law of God, in my inner being," that is, in his heart (Rom. 7:22). Concluding, he says "I myself serve the law of God with my mind, but with my flesh I serve the law of sin" (Rom. 7:25).

In case I've confused you, let me clarify. Paul identified that before he was regenerated by God's Spirit, he was a slave to sin. The war he suffered in his body was a war of uncontrolled passions. Now that he is spiritually regenerated, he identifies the sin residue that wars against his new desires. His desire is for the law but he finds himself breaking it. On the other hand, James is saying that, rather than having good desires yet incidentally doing wrong, worldly people have evil desires and do evil. There is no war between righteous and wrongful intentions in the heart. Therefore, he implies an unregenerate state. This is not to say that Christians do not ever have worldly desires. Paul attested to that. It is to say that a desire to please God, yet failing to do so, is far different from a desire to please yourself and consequently failing God.

I make this distinction to clarify the passage. James is teaching that love of the world is the source of the wars. It is not the love of God. The passions that are "at war within you" are not the godly passions, but the worldly passions Paul described. The word *hedone* cannot refer to good passions. In the Parable of the Sower, Jesus said that the *hedone* prevents salvation in the thorny ground (Lk. 8:14). The pursuit of pleasures is sinful and nothing more. It is not welcome in the regenerated life. In fact, it is in strong opposition to the faith that James has been describing in this entire epistle.

Now you might say that this distinction is too rigid. You might argue that Paul and James are saying exactly the same thing. My guess is that you might want to believe it is common for Christians to love the world, either to get yourself off the hook or as an excuse for someone dear to you. This is the temptation we all face, myself included. But I do not want to ignore the language here. I believe that James (and indirectly, God) wants us to know that a love for the world is not characteristic of a follower of Jesus (Matt. 19:21). A person who has faith cannot also entertain affection for the world. This is not only clear in the immediate text of James 4:1-2, it is also clear in the surrounding text and, for that matter, the entire text.

> **Love for the world is not characteristic of a follower of Jesus.**

Let us review the words leading up to this point. "Does a spring pour forth from the same opening both fresh and salt water? Can a fig tree, my brothers, bear olives, or a grapevine produce figs? Neither can a salt pond yield fresh water" (Ja. 3:11-12). James then contrasts heavenly wisdom with worldly wisdom. If you say you have heavenly wisdom but the fruit of your wisdom is "bitter jealousy and selfish ambition" then you lie (Ja. 3:14). In the chapter before this, James says that "faith apart from works is dead" (Ja. 2:26).

What am I saying? That Christians who don't act like Christians are not really Christians? It would appear that way, until chapter 4.

James might be okay with you wondering if it is possible for Christians to act worldly. And to some extent, it would be biblically true to say that Christians still sin. But the aim here is to draw Christians back to the ways of God; to bring them back to righteous living; to cause them to repent and fall into line. James does this by relating that worldly behavior indicates a worldly nature. Though his language is strong enough, the implication is somewhat subtle. However, here in chapter 4, he gets down to the basic heart-wrenching truth: "Look, you who love the world do not love God and are not saved."

James is relating to the passions that control and enslave a person, not an incidental failure to act according to the new nature. He is saying that your nature is still old. It is not necessarily that worldly passions wage war against godly passions as we might think. Rather, it is enough to have worldly passions alone. In other words, you don't have to be saved to have war in your soul with sinful desires. Sinful desires can war with themselves, with the reality of not being satisfied. They are like people who try to arouse anger in others but never find fulfillment. Worldly passions that remain unfulfilled become more and more vexing. Even worse, these desires are consuming.

Worldly behavior indicates a worldly nature.

It is said that passion is a cruel master. Obsessions control and ultimately destroy. For example: No matter what the Surgeon General says about unprotected sex, people continue to ignore the warning because they are overwhelmed by their physical lusts. They cannot make rational decisions, so they disregard the dangers. "Whoever isolates himself [makes himself unfriendly] seeks his own desire; he breaks out against all sound judgment" (Prov. 18:1). Consequently, people are enslaved by drugs, alcohol, pornography, cars, work, food, comfort, video games, the praise of men, and countless other things. John Owen coined the phrase "Be killing sin or sin will be killing you," which was apparently taken from Romans 8:13, "For if you live according to the flesh you will die." Having a pursuit for self-indulgence is living according to the flesh, synonymous with living according to the world. Again, the war is waged as the obsession goes unfulfilled and it doesn't stop there. It wars to the end.

FAITH

War to the End

Passion is a cruel master. So is sin. And it wages war to the end (Rom. 6:23). **"You desire and do not have, so you murder. You covet and cannot obtain, so you fight and quarrel. You do not have ..."** (Ja. 4:2-3). The Greek gets a little tricky over the next few verses. It will benefit us to look at it in depth. Make sure your thinking cap is on. The original Greek didn't have separations between words or punctuation marks to simplify complete thoughts. So, depending on your translation, you might find these verses handled quite differently. To my understanding, the Greek in this passage lends itself to a more poetic flow with a much stronger emphasis and pattern. The New King James is closer to what I imagine makes more sense. Ultimately, we will arrive at the same point. But for the sake of explanation, we will present the Greek this way:

> You lust, and do not have.
> You hate and covet, and cannot obtain.
> You fight and war, and do not have.
>   ... because...
> You forbid to ask.
> You ask and do not receive.
>   Because you ask wrongly,
>   to spend it on your own passions.

For those of you who wonder about my reasoning, I chose to separate the two broader thoughts with the word "because". The Greek word is *dia*, which is a preposition. It indicates agency, a channel of action. So you could translate it "because of this, for this reason, through this, by this, due to this," etc. It is not joining two equal thoughts. It is communicating a *channel* of reason in this text. The first thought *comes from and through* the second thought. James accuses and then gives reason. It is as if James declared the problem and the source of the problem, and now provides the details—giving us good reason to believe him. Plainly put, he is arguing logically.

Now that you know why I've changed the English reading of these verses, let's look more closely at the first half: the accusation. Hopefully you will see why the separation makes sense.

Notice the pattern. It is both repetitive and progressive. James says, "You lust, and do not have." Then, he says, "You murder and covet, and cannot obtain." And lastly, "You fight and war, and do not have." The repetition is clear. Simply put, "You want and do not have." This same idea is repeated two more times but not simply for the purpose of emphasis. There are subtle differences in the way "want" is communicated and it suggests a progression of passion. It is this progression that reveals the danger of desire, that it wars to the end. Let's take a closer look at this progression.

First, we begin with desire. It is implied in the text. The desire, though possibly natural and seemingly innocent, turns into lust. The Greek word is *epithyeo* which means 'to long after'. King David saw Bathsheba bathing on her rooftop and he longed to see more. He could have turned away, or gone inside to avoid the view, or occupied his mind with other things. However, he chose to stay and, entertaining his desire, began to long for her, allowing his heart to imagine the affection of a beautiful woman. In point, he lusted.

Second, our desire escalates from lust to hate. James says that we *phoneuo* and *zeloo* which literally means 'to kill and covet'. By connecting these two words, we get the idea of hatred for those who have what we long for. In 1 John 3:15, we read, "Everyone who hates his brother is a murderer." When our desires become so strong that we feel like we must have and we find others who already have, we burn with envy and hate them. Granted we might not acknowledge it as hatred, but that is exactly what it is. Love, on the other hand, rejoices in the benefits of others. It does not hate them for it (1 Cor. 13:4-7). King David's lust escalated to hatred for Bathsheba's husband since he could not have her as his wife.

> **Our desire escalates from lust to hate to war.**

Thirdly, our desire escalates from lust to hate to war. Hate is acting on lust. War is acting on hate. James has brought us full circle. He started by asking, "What causes fights and wars among you?" (Ja. 4:1). He ended by answering, "Your desires do." He says that personal lusts turn to hatred and hatred turns to fights and wars (Ja. 4:2), and in between are combined passions, which is why he asked rhetorically, "Is it not this, that your passions are at war within you?" (Ja. 4:1). King David ultimately had Bathsheba's husband killed on the battlefield, enabling him to marry her—which was what he wanted all along. He desired her as his own.

Now, let's track this story again to see the progression more fully. David glanced and saw a beautiful woman. Instead of running from temptation, he entertained his desire and it became passion. He acted on his passion and committed adultery, during which a child was conceived. David's nefarious scheme to hide his deed, by summoning her husband home from the battlefield [to sleep with his wife], turned to hatred when it didn't occur. So, acting on his hatred, David sent her husband back to the front lines to be killed. If he hoped to obtain some form of satisfaction, he gained only emptiness and regret.

Remember the remarks of Solomon discussed in the prior chapter? He was blessed with wisdom beyond measure and he lacked nothing in this world. He said in his heart, "Come now, I will test you with pleasure; enjoy yourself" (Ecc. 2:1). But he doesn't find any fulfillment there. He indulges himself in every worldly thing imaginable only to conclude that it is "all vanity," empty and unsatisfying. In fact, he was so frustrated he wrote, "I hated my life" (Ecc. 2:17). Again, "I hated all my toil" (Ecc. 2:18). "So I turned about and gave my heart up to despair over all the toil of my labors under the sun" (Ecc. 2:20) because "all [my] days are full of sorrow, and [my] work is a vexation. Even in the night [my] heart does not rest" (Ecc. 2:23). Solomon indulged in the pleasures of this world and found it so unsatisfying and so frustrating that life was meaningless and he hated living.

> **When we buy into the wisdom of the world, we find ourselves empty and angry.**

Have you ever wanted something badly enough to take it? If so, were you ultimately satisfied? Or did you feel empty inside? Perhaps you thought it would make you more of a person, only you found yourself feeling less of a person. This is why passion is a cruel master. God will never allow us to fully enjoy the things that are not meant for enjoyment. It is foolish to assume what the world says is enjoyable is ultimately enjoyable, because it never is. When we buy into the wisdom of the world, we find ourselves empty and angry. And we blame it on others, and kill them, or we blame ourselves and kill ourselves.

Homicide is one way to exert the frustration of uncontrolled desire. Suicide is another. People might not go so far as to kill others.

However, they might end their own lives if they cannot obtain what it is they lust after. We not only want to have things, we also want to have a clear conscience to enjoy those things. That is why we have so many psychologists today. People struggle with inner wars. Others try alcohol, drugs, violence, pornography, and more. When we do not find enjoyment in Christ and what He offers us, we find emptiness and anger. This is true of all people. Even nonbelievers have guilt because they too have a conscience. While it is not strengthened by the Word of God, it has a level of sensitivity. In fact, our conscience acts as a warning mechanism that either turns us to Christ or to empty satisfactions. Those who deny Christ hit the snooze button on the conscience alarm. Eventually the alarm diminishes until it is no longer heard. Then passions run amok.

Passions lead to death, often spawning more passions and more death, becoming a never-ending cycle. The story of David is an example. After his initial transgression, things became more complicated. Ahithophel, Bathsheba's grandfather, joined the ranks of a conspiracy against David (2 Sam. 15:31), undoubtedly to avenge the death of Bathsheba's husband and redeem her reputation. When he attempted to kill David during the night (2 Sam. 17:1-4) his plan was thwarted and his desire for vengeance went unfulfilled. Frustrated, "he saddled his donkey and went home" and "hanged himself" (2 Sam. 17:23). What a tragic story, that a man acting on an immoral desire should bring about the death of *any* man or child. Passions war to the end. And, as James continues, passion is accompanied by pride.

> **Those who deny Christ hit the snooze button on the conscience alarm.**

Passion and Pride

Earlier, I separated the passage found in James 4:2-3 into two sections joined by the word *dia*. I suggested that section one, "you do not have," is *because of* section two, "you ask wrongly." You can call this a cause-and-effect scenario. Now, focus on the cause, **"You ask and do not receive, because you ask wrongly, to spend it on your passions"** (Ja. 4:3). Here, the pattern ends. "You want and do not have." Now, "You ask and do not have." (This is excellent literacy!)

You are probably familiar with Jesus' teaching on prayer. We commonly summarize it as "Ask. Seek. Knock." Here is what it says:

> "Ask, and it will be given to you; seek, and you will find; knock, and it will be opened to you. For everyone who asks receives, and the one who seeks finds, and to the one who knocks it will be opened. Or which one of you, if his son asks him for bread, will give him a stone? Or if he asks for a fish, will give him a serpent? If you then, who are evil, know how to give good gifts to your children, how much more will your Father who is in heaven give good things to those who ask him!" (Matt. 7:7-11)

You might be scratching your head at this moment, wondering what James means by this asking and not having situation. He's just told us that "they" have evil desires and want to have things, but they do not receive those things. Then he says, according to the ESV, "You do not have, because you do not ask" (Ja. 4:2). Immediately after this, he says, "You ask but do not receive" (Ja. 4:3). If you are confused, let me explain.

James is not contradicting himself, nor is he correcting himself. Rather he is relating to them that they are not asking *biblically*. They are asking wrongly. The adverb used here to describe the way in which they are asking is the Greek word *kakos*, which is mostly translated as "ill" in the physical or spiritual sense. For example, Matthew 4:24 says that the Syrians were bringing to Jesus "all the sick" people in order that they might be healed. On the other hand, Jesus said, "Those who are well have no need of a physician, but those who are sick" and was referring to spiritual sickness (Matt. 9:12). Whatever the case, the word denotes an ill quality of something. The crowd to which James wrote was making ill-requests of God in their prayers. He is essentially saying, "Your prayers are sick!" For this reason, they did not receive what they asked for. To that end, James argues that asking wrongly is like not asking at all. It is a waste of breath. "You ask and do not receive because you ask wrongly, which is not asking at all."

I am willing to go out on a limb and suggest the people were not asking for things particularly wicked, at least not by today's standards. More likely they were wondering why some were better off than others, and possibly asking for things to better their circumstances. Things related to eating, sleeping, transporting, etc. I doubt they were asking for immoral things in comparison to what we Americans might ask for.

James mentions that they are asking for things "to spend" on their own passions. Perhaps these things were monetarily related, things to obtain other things. The point is, the ultimate end of the request was for selfish gain (Ja. 3:14). It was not that the things they were asking were inherently evil, but their reasons for wanting those things were.

Why would God honor such requests? He sees into the hearts of men. He knows what we really want when we ask for things. We might say, "Lord, help me get a new vehicle." But we mean, "Lord, help me get a new vehicle so that others might think more highly of me." Or we might say, "God, please give me that job position." But we mean to say, "God, please give me that job position so I'll be powerful and important." Too often our hearts belie something totally different than our words imply. I call them prideful prayers. In all honesty, this is what many of us are up to today. And believe it or not, there is a name for people like this.

What'd You Call Me?

No one really appreciates being called a name—certainly not an ugly name. My wife can call me *honey* all day and my children, *daddy*. I have no quarrel with that. However, I might get upset if you look me in the eye and call me an *idiot*. How about you? If someone called you *hypocrite*, how would you react? What if that someone was your pastor? I imagine it might be hurtful, particularly coming from him. Ugly names lack power when strangers utter them, but when family, close friends and pastors use them it can sting.

As mentioned in the first chapter, James, the half-brother of Jesus, was head of the Jerusalem church. Not only did he have authority, he had history. You could call him chief pastor of the Dispersion. He had a strong platform by which he instructed his fellow Jewish believers. His word held weight and influence. To hear him call you by any name was worthy of attention. But if it was something negative, however warranted, I must admit I would have found it devastating. Apparently it was in order here, for he says to his audience quite boldly, **"You adulterous people!"** (Ja. 4:4). Imagine if he was talking to you. It would be shocking, wouldn't it?

FAITH

The Greek word *moichos* translated "adulterous" is used to refer to people who break covenant with their spouse by having sexual intimacy with another person. So why call the Dispersion such? Was he out of line? No, he was dead on. But to be fair, he was not naming all of the Dispersion. He was only referring to the ones who met the description in the prior verses—namely, those who pursue the passions of the world. Metaphorically speaking, these people broke covenant with God by pursuing the world. Adulterous people, in this case, are spiritual two-timers. In fact, anyone who professes to follow Christ while simultaneously pursuing worldly pleasures is a spiritual two-timer. That includes you and me. We cheat on God when we become intimately involved in the world.

This idea was not foreign to the Jewish audience. Jesus taught this on several occasions. For instance, the Scribes and Pharisees once asked Him for a sign. They were not really interested in seeing a sign, however, since Jesus had already performed many miracles in their midst. Rather they were seeking something to use against the Lord. Knowing their hearts, Jesus says to them, "An evil and adulterous generation seeks for a sign, but no sign will be given to it except the sign of the prophet Jonah" (Matt. 12:38-42). His response infers that they were cheating on God. This was an accurate assessment (Jer. 5:7-8) not childish name-calling, for the Scribes and Pharisees were broadly unfaithful to God while parading themselves as God's righteous ones. In another instance in the New Testament, a similar accusation is made (Matt. 16:1-4; Mk. 8:38).

> **We cheat on God when we become intimately involved in the world.**

The Old Testament relates the same concept with which the Jewish readers would be quite familiar. In 2 Chronicles 21:11, Jehoram "made high places in the hill country of Judah and led the inhabitants of Jerusalem into whoredom and made Judah go astray." That is to say he made places of idol worship and led God's people to them, making them spiritual adulterers. The prophet Jeremiah said this about the adulterous Israelites, "For long ago I broke your yoke and burst your bonds; but you said, 'I will not serve.' Yes, on every high hill and under every green tree you bowed down like a whore" (Jer. 2:20). The Lord then asks, "If a man divorces his wife and she goes from him and becomes another man's wife, will he return to her? Would not that land be greatly polluted? You have played the whore with many lovers; and would you return to me? declares the Lord" (Jer. 3:1). Ezekiel used the same metaphor saying:

> "You also played the whore with the Egyptians, your lustful neighbors, multiplying your whoring, to provoke me to anger. Behold, therefore, I stretched out my hand against you and diminished your allotted portion and delivered you to the greed of your enemies, the daughters of the Philistines, who were ashamed of your lewd behavior. You played the whore also with the Assyrians, because you were not satisfied; yes, you played the whore with them, and still you were not satisfied. You multiplied your whoring also with the trading land of Chaldea, even with this you were not satisfied." (Ezek. 16:26-29)

This kind of language permeates the latter period of Old Testament times when Israel turned away from the Lord to the world. Why? Because Israel was God's chosen people. He made covenants with them and they continuously broke them (Jer. 31:31-32). He was faithful. They were unfaithful. This is the kind of imagery that would have come to mind when reading James' words, "You adulterous people!" (Ja. 4:4). I imagine it sounded like a trumpet blast in the midst of a noisy crowd. A holy hush sweeps the gathering. Hearts skip a beat. Jaws drop. Eyes open wide. God's people are brought to attention.

Christians are called the bride of Christ, waiting for the future wedding when they come face-to-face with their groom. Until then, we are in a betrothal period. While instructing husbands to love their wives, Paul reminds them of this reality, saying, "Christ loved the church and gave himself up for her, that he might sanctify her, having cleansed her by the washing of water with the word, so that he might present the church to himself in splendor, without spot or wrinkle or any such thing, that she might be holy and without blemish" (Eph. 5:25-27). For this reason, we are to be presented "as a pure virgin to Christ" (2 Cor. 11:2). Therefore, the church should submit to Christ as a faithful bride (Eph. 5:24).

Calling a Christian a spiritual two-timer is the equivalent of saying that he has cheated on Christ, broken vows and gone his separate way. Marriage is a binding covenant that is not to be separated. So we should pay close attention to such talk. God hates divorce. He says that divorce is an act of hatred against the spouse. So, "do not be faithless" (Mal. 2:16). Do not be adulterous. Do not be a two-timer or a spiritual cheater. Bad things happen when you do.

Friend or Enemy

We introduced this chapter asking, "Whose side are you on?" Your response will depend on whether you are the adulterous one or not. James says that spiritual adulterers have chosen their side and it is not a glorious choice. Jesus said that the Pharisees and scribes honored Him with their lips, "but their heart is far from me," which was a direct quote from Isaiah 29:13 during an indictment of Israel for spiritual adultery (Matt. 15:8). People can show up for worship, sing songs to the Lord, and appear to be righteous among others, but if their hearts are in the world they are frauds. They may seem to honor God on the outside, but on the inside they embrace their real love. In an often quoted passage, Jesus says that "No one can serve two masters, for either he will hate the one and love the other, or he will be devoted to the one and despise the other" (Matt. 6:24). The lines are drawn. Whose side are you on? This is the question James poses.

> **You are either friends with the world or friends with God.**

Earlier I made a distinction between Paul's inward war while desiring to please God, and James' war with people desiring to please themselves. Adulterers broke covenant, the only grounds for divorce according to Jesus (Matt. 5:32). Adultery was an act of hatred against God. It was a declaration of opposition. You choose one or the other. The one you choose, you love. The one you do not choose, you hate. Ultimately, you fight and war, as James mentioned earlier (Ja. 4:1-2).

James makes his point further with another rhetorical question, **"Do you know that friendship with the world is enmity with God? Therefore, whoever wishes to be a friend of the world makes himself an enemy of God"** (Ja. 4:4). The line that divides is clear. You are either friends with the world or friends with God. If you are a friend of the world, you are an enemy of God. Conversely: If you are a friend of God, you are an enemy of the world.

There are two words to focus on here: friend and enemy. The Greek word *philia* is translated "friendship" in the first half of the verse. It is rooted in the Greek word *philo* which is translated "friend" in the second half. Other than tenses, these words are the same. You might recognize *philo* as we use it from time to time in our English language. Most of us are familiar with the meaning of Philadelphia. We call it "the city of brotherly love." The prefix "phila" refers to a strong bond between friends, usually an emotional connection. It is a kind of fondness, a sense of love and intense affection. Jesus used the word when talking to His disciples, "Greater love has no one than this, that someone lay down his life for his friends" (Jn. 15:13). Again, He said, "No longer do I call you servants, for the servant does not know what his master is doing; but I have called you friends, for all that I have heard from my Father I have made known to you" (Jn. 15:15). James used it when describing Abraham as a "friend of God" (Ja. 2:23). Nowhere in the Bible is anyone called a friend of God other than those who are righteous in His sight.

The second word is *echthra* in the Greek. It refers to hostility and opposition. It is the opposite of friend. Paul wrote in Romans 8:7 describing the flesh, the sinful nature of man, to be *echthra* toward God. He says that it "does not submit to God's law" and furthermore, "it cannot" submit to it. In a letter to the church in Ephasus, he described Jesus' work on the cross as killing the *echthra* between God and man.

So what do we do with these words? No sinner is called a friend of God and no Christian is called an enemy of God. Yet, we find James describing people of the Dispersion as friends of the world and enemies of God. He basically breaks it up into two statements. The first is yet another rhetorical question. The second is the obvious answer. "Don't you know what this means? You who pursue the pleasures of the world are enemies of God." This is strong language. I can't imagine what it was like reading this back then. Yet, now we are also reading this. Let us not pass over this text as though it only applies to long-ago believers. It is especially applicable to us today. More so than ever, in fact, for it's a wake-up call to all of God's people! Do you call yourself a Christian? Are you pursuing God or entertaining your worldly desires? To put it bluntly, either get down on your knees or put your dukes up. It's your choice.

Put Your Dukes Up

In case you think I'm exaggerating, allow me to point out certain passages of Scripture that should convince you exactly how serious this is. In Deuteronomy 32, we find these words of the Lord against his opponents, "If I sharpen my flashing sword and my hand takes hold on judgment, I will take vengeance on my adversaries and will repay those who hate me. I will make my arrows drunk with blood, and my sword shall devour flesh—with the blood of the slain and the captives, from the long-haired heads of the enemy" (Deut. 32:41-42). What a frightening reality!

There's more. Isaiah prophesied that "The Lord goes out like a mighty man, like a man of war he stirs up his zeal; he cries out, he shouts aloud, he shows himself against his foes" (Is. 42:13). Nahum also prophesied, "The Lord is a jealous and avenging God; the Lord is avenging and wrathful; the Lord takes vengeance on his adversaries and keeps wrath for his enemies" (Nah. 1:2). Again, "But with an overflowing flood he will make a complete end of the adversaries, and will pursue his enemies into darkness" (Nah.1:8). Even the Psalmist joins in. "Your hand will find out all your enemies; your right hand will find out those who hate you" (Ps. 21:8). "But God will strike the heads of his enemies, the hairy crown of him who walks in his guilty ways" (Ps. 68:21). God will make His enemies His footstool (Ps. 110:1).

In a parable, Jesus said, "But as for these enemies of mine, who did not want me to reign over them, bring them here and slaughter them before me" (Lk. 19:27). These are tough words, even when uttered by a mere man. But to hear such threats from a fierce and holy God is absolutely terrifying! The writer of Hebrews said it best, "It is a fearful thing to fall into the hands of the living God" (Heb. 10:31).

This is what the future looks like for the enemies of God. They have spiritually put their dukes up with the intention of taking a swing at their Creator. But the Lord Almighty makes "His enemies lick the dust!" (Ps. 72:9). Friendship with the world, affection and fondness toward the world, will make you God's enemy and you will bite the dust when Judgment comes. Read Paul's instructions on this matter:

> "For those who live according to the flesh set their minds on the things of the flesh, but those who live according to the Spirit set their minds on the

things of the Spirit. For to set the mind on the flesh is death, but to set the mind on the Spirit is life and peace. For the mind that is set on the flesh is hostile to God, for it does not submit to God's law; indeed, it cannot." (Rom. 8:5-7)

No reasonable person can read this and assume James is talking about wayward Christians. Nowhere is a Christian called God's enemy. Nowhere is a sinner called God's friend. So we cannot conclude that this is about Christians who lapse periodically into worldliness. I understand that it is possible, actually probable, that we will sin—even after our regeneration—but it cannot be said that genuine believers can have affection for the world (1 Jn. 2:15). It is one thing to behave in a worldly way but it is another to love the world. Genuine faith will always produce genuine love for God, never hatred.

This is not an exaggeration. From conflict with others to conflict with self to conflict with God, you might be able to deal with the first two. But the day will come when the bell will ring and the boxing match is over because no one wins against God. It's not that people do not want God at all. Most people are comfortable with God—at least the god they've imagined. As James points out, even people in the church wear the Christian clothes and speak the Christian words and drink the Christian's drinks, but underneath it all they have fashioned a god that fits their love for the world. In other words, they've reduced the Lord to the object of their own affection so they can have things their way. As for guilt, they set it aside by convincing themselves the god they've concocted is perfectly okay with their passions. This is why it is difficult to find these people among us. But James says there is a sure way to recognize them. He says to "Look at their desires. If they desire to have, to be, to do the things of the world, then they are two-timing fakes."

> **Genuine faith will always produce genuine love for God, never hatred.**

The World

Let us take a moment and look more closely at the world. Not in a physical sense, referencing God's creation, but in a theological sense. What is it? What does it look like? What does it include? If you lack a solid understanding of what the word entails, I assume you are at least wondering by now. Especially after discovering that God's holy anger is stored up for His enemies who, by definition, are lovers of the world. Thus we should make sure that we understand what the Bible means when it uses the word "world."

Generally when I'm writing, I like to discuss my topics with others to see what they think about certain matters and how they visualize truths. So I asked a few people what they thought worldliness meant. Their responses were not surprising at all. In fact, not so long ago I might have responded the same in a similar situation. Answers forthcoming included drinking beer, smoking cigars, doing drugs, sleeping around, going to parties, and even listening to Country music (yes, someone actually included that!). Some people were more restrictive, mentioning virtually anything that is enjoyable, such as food, recreation, cars, work, and more. They considered anything pleasing to your senses to be worldly.

I admit the concept of worldliness baffled me for a long time. It was an ambiguous term to me. However we shouldn't be confused about it, not when it is this important. Instead we need to understand exactly what it means to be worldly and to pursue the pleasures of the world.

> **The weapons we use to fight are spiritual.**

For starters, we should picture it in terms of a system, an ethical and philosophical edifice constructed in opposition to God and His revelation.

In the book of Romans we find Paul instructing his readers, "Do not be conformed to this world, but be transformed by the renewal of your mind, that by testing you may discern what is the will of God, what is good and acceptable and perfect" (Rom. 12:2). Notice he sets the renewal of the mind adjacent to conformity to the world. He also mentions that a mind renewal will allow us to discern God's will and do what is righteous. Paul makes the world a matter of the mind. In his letter to the Corinthian church, he adds, "For though we walk in the flesh [that is, physical bodies], we are not waging war according to the flesh, for the weapons of our warfare are not of the flesh but have divine power to destroy strongholds." In other words, the spiritual battle is not waged in the physical world through physical methods or human ingenuity. The weapons we use to fight sin are spiritual. They are from God. Paul continues, "We destroy arguments and every lofty opinion that is raised against the knowledge of God, and take every thought captive to obey Christ" (2 Cor. 10:3-5). Again, the war exists in the mind. With divine weapons, we destroy arguments and lofty opinions which are raised against the knowledge of God. The Greek here implies earthly reasoning, imagination and prideful ideas. Basically it refers to worldly wisdom, as James put it in the prior chapter where he describes it as "earthly, unspiritual, demonic" and full of "jealousy and selfish ambition" (Ja. 3:15-16). It is no surprise that he now says that to engage in quarrels and fights, due to strong passions for pleasure, is loyalty to the world (Ja. 4:1-4).

Worldliness is the philosophical building erected against God's revelation. It is a system of thinking. It is contrary to God's will and instruction, to God's word, and ultimately to Christ, being the word incarnate (Jn. 1:14). For this reason Paul instructed the Colossians, "See to it that no one takes you captive by philosophy and empty deceit, according to human tradition, according to the elemental spirits of the world, and not according to Christ" (Col. 2:8). Worldliness begins with the mind since the mind is the heart of life (Prov. 4:23; cf. Matt. 15:17-20). Everything we do and say comes from the mind. It forms and shapes our behaviors and desires. It molds our life entirely. That is why Paul instructs us to be renewed in our thinking. Otherwise we will remain worldly—trained and shaped by the philosophies of Satan, the ruler of this system (2 Cor. 4:4). Worldliness is an epistemological issue. It is knowledge against knowledge. Therefore, pleasures of the world cannot be reduced to the movies we watch, the things we drink, the words we speak, the feelings we have. Writer Dave Roper describes worldly desires in a practical sense as "a passion for sensual satisfaction, an inordinate desire for the finer things in life, and self-satisfaction in who we are, what we have, and what we have done."[1]

> **There is no profit in gaining the world.**

Jesus asked, "For what will it profit a man if he gains the whole world and forfeits his soul?" (Matt. 16:26). The answer is nothing, absolutely nothing. There is no profit in gaining the world. For such

---

[1] Roper, Dave. *The Strength of a Man*, quoted in Family Survival in the American Jungle, Steve Farrar, 1991, Multnomah Press, p. 68.

does not exist. It is merely an illusion of pleasure. Do not be confused. Some have understood Jesus to be referencing the entirety of creation. But in the broader context of the passage, He is speaking about denying self and taking up the cross to follow Him. The cross was a symbol of agonizing death. Jesus was saying, deny yourself all of those pleasures the world says is worthy of pursuit and follow Him to the end (Matt. 16:24). He says you lose your temporary life in order to find it eternally (Matt. 16:25). Essentially, stop seeking your own pleasures and start seeking God's.

This is not to suggest you should never do anything you prefer to do. Rather, it is to say that nothing in this world is worth more than Jesus Himself. And if Jesus requires anything from you, even if it means you must give up something pleasurable, then you should do it willingly. It might be your job, money, relationships, house, or your life. Whatever it is, Jesus is far greater and the pursuit of Him is eternally profitable. On the other hand, the pursuit of worldly pleasures is extremely pathetic, a waste of time and a waste of life. More seriously, it is an opposing force to God. "Therefore, whoever wishes to be a friend of the world makes himself an enemy of God" (Ja. 4:4). Are any of us in opposition to our Creator? Hopefully not, for that would exhibit pride —which God despises.

> **Nothing in this world is worth more than Jesus.**

Pride is a character flaw in people who think both only of themselves and too much of themselves. Even so, such people may openly condemn themselves in order to win sympathy. This is self-seeking. On the other hand, they may openly praise themselves—which is also self-seeking. Pride is just that, self-seeking. It is going after what you want first and foremost for your own edification. It is seeking to please your own passions. James says it is worldly thinking, worldly living. It is putting self in the way of God's judgment. Believe me, God packs a deadly punch.

One or the Other

Paul sometimes uses the word "flesh" as a synonym for "the world." Think about what he wrote in Romans. "For those who live according to the flesh set their minds on the things of the flesh, but those who live according to the Spirit set their minds on the things of the Spirit; For to set the mind on the flesh is death, but to set the mind on the Spirit is life and peace. For the mind that is set on the flesh is hostile to God, for it does not submit to God's law; indeed, it cannot. Those who are in the flesh cannot please God" (Rom. 8:5-8). John wrote something similar, "Do not love the world or the things in the world. If anyone loves the world, the love of the Father is not in him. For all that is in the world—the desires of the flesh and the desires of the eyes and the pride in possessions—is not from the Father but is from the world" (1 Jn. 2:15-16).

Faith is characterized by seeking first to glorify God (Matt. 6:33). One way this is accomplished is by first seeking the benefit of others, even at your own expense. Following our reasoning throughout the book, God is selfless (Jn. 3:16) and so His people should also be selfless (Jn. 15:13). Consider Paul's instruction on this very point:

> "Do nothing from selfish ambition or conceit, but in humility count others more significant than yourselves. Let each of you look not only to his own interests, but also to the interests of others. Have this mind among yourselves, which is yours in Christ Jesus, who, though he was in the form of God, did not count equality with God a thing to be grasped, but emptied himself, by taking the form of a servant, being born in the likeness of men. And being found in human form, he humbled himself by becoming obedient to the point of death, even death on a cross." (Phil. 2:3-8)

In other words, Christ put selflessness on display by becoming human, serving humanity, withholding righteous judgment and power to deliver Himself from evil men, humbling Himself to obey the Father and dying at the hands of His own creatures. This is true selflessness. Jesus, who had every right to meet His own earthly needs, met the needs of undeserving creatures who could never repay Him. Therefore, if Jesus rules our hearts, then selflessness should rule our lives.

This is why James described godly wisdom as "peaceable, gentle, open to reason, full of mercy and good fruits, impartial and sincere" (Ja. 3:17). Godly wisdom exists only in the lives of godly people, ones who have genuine faith. Therefore, these people are marked by peace and selfless living. Faithful people do not seek personal gain, not even for essentials. Rather they seek to glorify God and put His character on display by considering others more significant than themselves in all matters of life.

Is this what characterizes your life? How are your relationships in the church? Are you peaceable and gentle with others? Are you easy to get along with? Maybe you should consider praying as the Psalmist did, "Incline my heart to your testimonies, and not to selfish gain!" (Ps. 119:36). I join you in such a prayer.

True Faith is Humble

I get an eerie feeling when I pull into an intersection and discover the cars on either side of me haven't moved. This often happens to me. I stop at a red light. Cars pull up on either side of me, and we patiently wait and watch. Suddenly the light turns green.

Pressing the gas pedal I ease into the intersection only to find that the cars on either side of me haven't moved an inch. I glance into my rearview mirror, then to the left and right to make certain I'm not about to be blindsided. Seeing the street is clear, I lean forward to check the light. Sure enough, it's green.

Whenever this happens to me, my initial response is that I made a wrong decision. When circumstances prove otherwise, I continue on my way.

A similar thing occurs when I come across a passage in the Bible I find difficult to understand. I'll spend time researching it until I'm convinced I understand what it means. In most cases, I'll extend my inquiries to experts on the Bible, who either confirm or correct my interpretation. There is one passage, however, where the experts seem to disagree, which forces me to make my own decision, to pull into the intersection. Thanks to James, we're at such an intersection now. He writes, **"Or do you suppose it is to no purpose that the Scripture says, 'He yearns jealously over the spirit that he has made to dwell in us'?"** (Ja. 4:5).

Red light. What's your move?

Imagine that you are sitting before the Word of God and there are fellow students of the Word beside you. The light turns green and you are ready to go, but they are not moving. This feels most uncomfortable, especially when you realize that those other cars are occupied by great theologians and scholars. You wonder to yourself,

"Why are they not moving? Did I get something wrong?"

Don't misunderstand me. The illustration I used was designed to let you experience the discomfort I feel whenever I'm the only one entering the intersection, fearful I misread the signal, fearful of a possible collision. You see, interpreting Scripture is a serious matter. One misstep and an eternal collision can occur. So I don't take this lightly. I am convinced, however, that the interpretation I arrived at is the correct one. In the same manner, I am also aware of my own fallibility. I might not have it right, but I am confident the light is green, so to speak. This being the case, don't mistake my certainty for dogmatic assertion. There are other ways to understand this passage and I realize that no one on earth can lay claim to a meaning that is incontrovertibly true. Please keep this in mind as I approach James 4:5.

The Other Cars

Leaving the others behind, allow me to explain why this passage is so complex. Earlier, I mentioned that the original Greek did not contain punctuation or spaces between words. Neither did it have letter cases, paragraph indentations, or verse numbers. Rather, it was one long string of capital letters. The Greek Bibles we have now contain all of these things in order to formulate a sentence so that we can read and understand them today. They even have accent marks to help us know how they might have been spoken. But even in this format, the Greek language is quite different from our native tongue. There are various nuances that simply don't exist in the English mind. The work of translating the Bible is terribly difficult and I appreciate those commissioned to do it. One Greek scholar offered a word-for-word translation of James 4:5 which read like this: "Or do you presume that vainly the scripture is saying to envy is lusting the spirit which dwells in us?"

When arriving at this text, I spent some time comparing at least ten of our popular English Bibles and found the translations to vary quite a bit. Their variations are not what you might call the *common garden variety*. They are significantly different in meaning. By asking if the Scripture says "to no purpose," you imply that the following clause is true. By adding quotations to the following clause, you might wonder if James is quoting the Bible. By making God the subject of the quotation, you teach that God is envious. Thus, it might read like this: "Is the Bible accurate when it says that God envies man's spirit?" If you answer negatively, you say the Bible is not accurate. If you answer positively, you say that God is envious. Of course, there are other things in this verse that complicate the translation and, therefore, the interpretation. This is because the Greek words in this passage are ambiguous. Rather than bore you with the details, let me explain why these translations are not consistent with James' point in my opinion.

To begin, keep in mind that James has been asking a lot of rhetorical questions. In the past four verses, he has asked at least three—that's almost one per verse! Also, it is helpful to maintain his context. We want the interpretation to flow with the text, not sporadically offshoot. He is talking about worldly wisdom among people who claim to be godly. He calls them out by showing that their quarreling reveals worldliness. From there, he hones in on the matter with deep conviction. He refers to them as adulterous people. He says they are whoring on God because they are envious for the things of the world, thereby making themselves enemies of God rather than friends as their father Abraham was (Ja. 2:23). He says that it is worldly to burn with jealousy. Now, as if he is in the heat of the moment, he writes the passage we are now trying to unpack.

Would it be pertinent at this point for James to assert that God is envious? After he associates jealousy with discontentment, sensual passions, war, murder, adultery, and being an enemy of God, do you think that he would nonchalantly say, "God is envious for the spirit you have in you"? Some do. But I think it is a grave error. Not only is it inconsistent with the context, it is an absurd assumption. Granted, God identifies Himself as jealous in Exodus 20:5—but this is used in a totally different context. God is jealous for worship because He alone deserves it. Here in James, we are talking about the spirit that dwells in man. But even this is a stretch since James only uses the Greek word, *pneuma*, translated "spirit" to refer to man's eternal person, his soul (Ja. 2:26). Again, we might argue that the spirit here is the one that God gave to man, but it is not necessary for us to believe it is the Holy Spirit. Of course, this is not to mention that the Greek verb *epipothei* never takes God as its subject elsewhere in the entire Bible. Nowhere do we find God lusting or ("yearns jealously over") something. Our context is not the jealousy of God. It is the jealousy of man.

Jealousy of Man

Fighting among people is due to one thing: jealousy. Mankind is jealous. This includes you and me. We were born this way. Paul wrote to the believers in Ephesus, "And you were dead in the trespasses and sins in which you once walked, following the course of this world, following the prince of the power of the air, the spirit that is now at work in the sons of disobedience—among whom we all once lived in the passions of our flesh, carrying out the desires of the body and the mind, and were by nature children of wrath, like the rest of mankind" (Eph. 2:1-3). That is a prolonged sentence that says it all quite candidly. This is why James calls these people adulterers. Since they are behaving like those "dead in the trespasses and sins," he says that they are worldly, or "following the course of this world," as Paul put it.

Then, with strong sarcasm, he asks (I'll paraphrase), "Do you think that the Bible lies by saying that God gave you a spirit that lusts for the world?" Translating the verse to have the spirit of man as the subject, who is the one who envies, is most appropriate. Then, we can certainly find James asking the question of whether the Bible teaches such a thing. The answer is an emphatic "No!" since James already taught that God is the source of only good (Ja. 1:13-18). God did not design the human soul to long for worldly things. He designed it to long for Him.

> **God did not design the human soul to long for worldly things.**

Rhetorical questions like this are meant to be understood as statements. So you could think of it this way: "No, the Bible doesn't lie to you and tell you that God gave you a spirit that is jealous for the world."

This is a smooth interpretation of the text. The verses following it fall into place more easily. **"But he gives more grace,"** instead of more lust. **"Therefore it says, 'God opposes the proud, but gives grace to the humble'"** (Ja. 4:6). Here we find quotations again. However, while he was pretending to quote the Bible in the prior verse, he is truly quoting it in this verse. Proverbs 3:34 says, "Toward the scorners he is scornful, but to the humble he gives favor." Peter quoted the proverb similarly to James, "God opposes the proud but gives grace to the humble" (1 Pet. 5:5). This is definitely what scriptures say!

In the end, James addresses them in their sin, asking them if the Bible teaches that they should behave the way they are behaving. He expects a negative response and then tells them what the Bible really says—namely, God opposes the proud. Isn't this exactly what James called them, proud people? They refused to humbly ask. They demanded what they wanted. They expressed discontentment with God and hostility toward others. They acted like the world revolved around them. This is exactly what James is saying. This is the epitome of worldliness. This is pride!

Submit to God

God **"opposes the proud"** (Ja. 4:6). I don't care to rehash what it means to be opposed by God. We looked earlier at what an enemy of God is. Plainly put, it is someone who dangles over the wrathful vengeance of God by a burning thread. Befriending the world puts you in such a position. But while this passage stirs the soul to fear who suffers the evils of pride, it also stirs it to hope by telling us the way to become a friend of God. It says that God **"gives grace to the humble"** (Ja. 4:6).

Paul taught along the same lines. He tasted God's grace and knew that it was good. He found peace with God instead of wrath. "Since we have been justified by faith, we have peace with God through our Lord Jesus Christ. Through him we have also obtained access by faith into this grace in which we stand, and we rejoice in hope of the glory of God" (Rom. 5:1-2). This is exceptional news. Paul was the worst of sinners. He campaigned for the slaughter of innumerable Christians. But God appeared to him, and saved him (Acts 9:1-19; 26:12-18). For this reason, he confidently said, "God shows his love for us in that while we were still sinners, Christ died for us" (Rom. 5:6). He continues then by telling of how enemies of God are reconciled to Him:

> "Since, therefore, we have now been justified by his blood, much more shall we be saved by him from the wrath of God. For if while we were enemies we were reconciled to God by the death of his Son, much more, now that we are reconciled, shall we be saved by his life. More than that, we also rejoice in God through our Lord Jesus Christ, through whom we

have now received reconciliation." (Rom. 5:9-11)

Indeed, God gives more grace. These verses speak so well of God's great gifts and how He restores us to Himself by living for our righteousness and dying for our sins. But this grace is given to the humble. Pride is not the ticket to peace with God. Humility is. In light of this, James exhorts us to **"Submit yourselves therefore to God"** (Ja. 4:7). Do you want to befriend the Lord who created your soul to long for Him? Then quit lusting for the things of the world and humble yourselves before God.

This is the first of ten commands whereby James calls sinners back to the Lord (cf: Ja. 5:20). I mentioned earlier that this portion of James' letter is aimed directly at those who profess to be saved but have deceived themselves. They call themselves friends of God, but they are enemies of God. The overall purpose of his epistle was to separate true faith from false faith. He says this is one reason God sends trials our way. They will either strengthen your faith or reveal your faith to be a sham.

Jesus once told a parable of the weeds growing among the wheat. Instead of weeding the crop and possibly hurting the good grain, he leaves them together for a future harvest time in which he will separate the weeds from the wheat (Matt. 13:24-30). This is essentially what James is doing, though it is more preventive than final. Jesus' parable warns us of a future judgment when the weeds will be pulled up and bundled to be burned. Then He will gather the wheat into His barn. It is an act of God's good grace to have the written Word of God to help us examine ourselves so that, in the future, the living Word of God will not bundle us up as weeds for the fire. We should seriously meditate on the message James lays before us.

> **Pride is not the ticket to peace with God.**

His message is one of repentance. **"Submit yourself to God"** (Ja. 4:6). This is the first of ten commands found in verses 6 through 10. Although some interpret it as a call to backsliding believers, it makes more sense as a call to unbelievers to repent. Remember, these are worldly people—ones who pursue the pleasures of the world instead of God. They may like the idea of God and appreciate what He can give them, so they will pretend to follow Him. But they are not pursuers of

God. They lust for the world and are deemed adulterers and enemies of God. Mind you, Christians were never called enemies of God. Only sinners were. In fact, James calls them sinners both in this chapter and the next (Ja. 4:8; 5:20). So he is calling sinners to repentance.

Submission is based on the military order of rank. If you are told to submit, you are told to get in line where you belong. It is a voluntary action of conformity. No one can be saved without submission to God. We must willfully get to the place He desires, fitting ourselves to His sovereign will and rule. It is a place of complete surrender. "Whoever does not bear his own cross and come after me cannot be my disciple," Jesus said (Lk. 14:27). This is the first step in humility, relinquishing all the plans, attitudes, choices, behaviors, thoughts, words, and deeds you have, and adopting the will of God.

Resist the Devil

The second command is to resist. But not to resist God like we do when we are pursuing the world. Rather we are to resist the prince of the world, the devil. **"Resist the devil,"** James says (Ja. 4:7). This is essentially what happens when you submit to God. "No one can serve two masters, for either he will hate the one and love the other, or he will be devoted to the one and despise the other" (Matt. 6:24). Consequently, to love and devote yourself to God is to hate and despise the devil.

To resist means to oppose. It carries the same connotation James used in verse 4 where the worldly people are opposing God. He essentially is saying, "Turn the tables, stop opposing God and start opposing Satan." Salvation modifies your alliance. It changes your master. John wrote, "Whoever makes a practice of sinning is of the devil, for the devil has been sinning from the beginning" (1 Jn. 3:8). Paul adds: "Do you not know that if you present yourselves to anyone as obedient slaves, you are slaves of the one whom you obey, either of sin, which leads to death, or of obedience, which leads to righteousness?" (Rom. 6:16). If Satan is your master, then you are his slave. However once you change masters and submit to the Lord of righteousness, you "have become slaves of righteousness" (Rom. 6:18). Either way, you are a slave. You must do the work of one master or the other. The Master Christ has eternal rewards, "the fruit you get leads to sanctification and its end, eternal life" (Rom. 6:22). What then do you receive when you practice submitting to God? You receive the sanctifying work of God's Spirit now and eternal life with Christ later.

Once you resist the devil, **"he will flee from you"** (Ja. 4:7). You can be triumphant over the passions that dwell in your heart. Satan cannot be your master when you humble yourself before God. He flees. The Greek word translated "resist" is the word *antistete*, a command to ongoing resistance. Although the devil will leave, he will also return to tempt you with the world's pleasures—enticing you to return to the world. But Jesus won the victory on the cross. He said, "Now is the judgment of this world; now will the ruler of this world be cast out. And I, when I am lifted up from the earth, will draw all people to myself" (Jn. 12:31-32). Because we belong to Jesus and are indwelled by His Spirit, we can continue in this victory each time the devil tempts us.

Draw Near to God

The third command is **"Draw near to God"** (Ja. 4:8). When we come to him as slaves and resist our former master, we come with a desire for Him rather than a desire for the world. Formerly our passions for the world were at war within us causing fights and quarrels (Ja. 4:1). Now our passions are for the Lord and peace exists in our hearts and lives.

The word "draw near" is from the Greek word *eggisate*, which denotes a nearness and intimacy. In Matthew 3:2, John the Baptist preached, "Repent, for the kingdom of heaven is at hand," meaning that it was close by. And it was, with the arrival of Jesus who is King of the heavenly kingdom. He prayed for those whom God would save, saying, "I do not ask for these only, but also for those who will believe in me through their word, that they may all be one, just as you, Father, are in me, and I in you, that they also may be in us" (Jn. 17:20-21). Nearness refers to an intimate bond. It denotes closeness, faithfulness and affection. The psalmist wrote, "But for me it is good to be near God; I have made the Lord God my refuge, that I may tell of all your works" (Ps. 73:28).

This kind of drawing near requires a growing, experiential knowledge in order to be nourished. It thrives on understanding and hungers for obedience. In the Old Testament, the priests were called to "come near to the Lord" and to "consecrate themselves" (Ex. 19:22). Jesus, our Great High Priest, has perfectly "passed through the heavens" on our behalf (Heb. 4:14). So, we should confidently "draw near to the throne of grace, that we may receive mercy and find grace to help in time of need" (Heb. 4:16).

Not simply in confidence, but in desperation should we seek and yearn for God. As James pointed out, God did not design our souls to long enviously. Rather He determined that "they should seek God, and perhaps feel their way toward him and find him. Yet he is actually not far from each one of us" (Acts 17:27). God satisfies the soul and brings joy to the heart. "O God, you are my God; earnestly I seek you; my soul thirsts for you; my flesh faints for you, as in a dry and weary land where there is no water," the Psalmist wrote (Ps. 63:1). When drawing near to God, you are blessed with the satisfaction of your soul. So when you draw near to God, James says, **"He will draw near to you"** (Ja. 4:7). When our soul longs for Him, He satisfies our longing with Himself.

> **God satisfies the soul and brings joy to the heart.**

Cleanse Your Hands

The fourth command is, **"Cleanse your hands, you sinners"** (Ja. 4:8). This is a Jewish idea. It is set in the context of the priests' ceremonial cleansing before approaching the Lord to offer sacrifices in the tabernacle.

> "You shall also make a basin of bronze, with its stand of bronze, for washing. You shall put it between the tent of meeting and the altar, and you shall put water in it, with which Aaron and his sons shall wash their hands and their feet. When they go into the tent of meeting, or when they come near the altar to minister, to burn a food offering to the Lord, they shall wash with water, so that they may not die. They shall wash their hands and their feet, so that they may not die. It shall be a statute forever to them, even to him and to his offspring throughout their generations." (Ex. 30:18-21)

This was understood as a way of washing the sin away in order to draw near to God. Isaiah spoke about the need to wash away sin in order to pray faithfully. "When you spread out your hands, I will hide my eyes from you; even though you make many prayers, I will not listen; your hands are full of blood." God will not hear the prayers of those who are covered in iniquity (Is. 1:15; cf: 59:3). "Wash yourselves; make yourselves clean; remove the evil of your deeds from before my eyes," He says. What does this mean? It means to "cease to do evil" (Is. 1:16).

The New Testament instructs us to baptize new believers in water which symbolizes the real cleansing of the soul from sin. Peter wrote that baptism "now saves you, not as a removal of dirt from the body but as an appeal to God for a good conscience, through the resurrection of Jesus Christ" (1 Pet. 3:21). That is to say that when we baptize someone, we are giving evidence to the Spirit's cleansing of sin since we are putting on the righteousness of Christ. The ceremony itself does not save, but what it represents does. Paul wrote that Christ "saved us, not because of works done by us in righteousness, but according to his own mercy, by the washing of regeneration and renewal of the Holy Spirit" (Tit. 3:5).

Cleansing your hands is essentially the same as submitting to God. It is an ongoing practice of putting off the worldliness we once submitted to and putting on the righteousness we now have in Christ. It is confessing our sins and asking for a clean conscience. It is restoring our joy of salvation. David rejoiced, "The Lord dealt with me according to my righteousness; according to the cleanness of my hands he rewarded me" (Ps. 18:20).

Purify Your Heart

The fifth command is a Hebraic Parallelism. It is a component of literary style found in poetry. You can find it all over the Psalms and Proverbs. It is when two phrases express the same idea, either by repeating it in different words or by stressing different aspects of it. "Cleanse your hands, sinners," is half of our parallelism. The other half reads, **"purify your hearts, you double-minded"** (Ja. 4:8). For this reason, we might echo much of what we have just covered. To cleanse is to purify—to make clean, to wash away all sin. Likewise, the "sinner" is equivalent to the "double-minded" person.

David said that "he who has clean hands and a pure heart" will "ascend the hill of the Lord" and "stand in his holy place" (Ps. 24:3-4).

The sinner must wash the sin from his hands, which is the expression of sin, and wash the sin from his heart, which is the source of sin. James is appealing for a complete turning away from sin, not just a religious rite or outward ceasing. We must also turn our hearts from sin. It is not enough to stop murdering, we must stop hating (cf: Matt. 5:21-22). Neither is it enough to stop committing adultery, we must stop lusting (cf: Matt. 5:27-28). Our hearts will be judged just as our deeds. Therefore, we must wash both of them. And when we do, God will make us new. Ezekiel 36:25-27 says this:

> "I will sprinkle clean water on you, and you shall be clean from all your uncleanness, and from all your idols I will cleanse you. And I will give you a new heart, and a new spirit I will put within you. And I will remove the heart of stone from your flesh and give you a heart of flesh. And I will put my Spirit within you, and cause you to walk in my statutes and be careful to obey my rules."

Be Wretched

The sixth command is to **"be wretched"** (Ja. 4:9). This is not exactly what you might expect God to command of us. At least not until you get to the meaning of it. It is the Greek word *talaiporesate* which means simply "be miserable, be afflicted." It gives the idea of toiling heavily over the realization of your own hardship and suffering. It is being broken, feeling the agony of being lost and sinful. When Paul recognized the toil he experienced when his flesh waged war with his mind and he sinned, even though he wanted to obey the law of God, he cried out, "Wretched man that I am! Who will deliver me from this body of death?" (Rom. 7:24). It was also the feeling the tax collector expressed when he was beating his chest, full of sorrow over his sin and crying out, "God, be merciful to me, a sinner!" (Lk. 18:13).

Being wretched is being full of sorrow over sin. It is feeling fragmented once the reality of sin's existence is recognized. It is rooted in the knowledge of God's holy character and understanding that sin is an act of direct opposition to it. It breaks God's heart and kindles His wrath. It shakes the soul of those who know God's law and fear His judgment. It is the appropriate response to the recognition of evil. The more holy a Christian becomes, the more dreadful he responds. The more sanctified he is, the more sinful he feels. It is not that a believer sins more as he matures, it is that he sins less while growing more sensitive to his trespasses.

Be Mourning

The seventh command is to **"mourn"** (Ja. 4:9). We might assume by reading this that the appropriate response to sin, namely feeling wretched, was not evident in the lives of those receiving James' epistle. Rather they might have been laughing and joking about their sin. When someone is in misery, they do not rejoice. Mourning is the response to brokenness. It is a desolate feeling of sorrow and regret, of self-contained, non-violent grief. James says to be miserable and show it by mourning.

People who have no inner pain due to brokenness and are thereby indifferent to their sin will not receive God's comfort. When rebuking the Corinthian believers for having sexual immorality among them, Paul says, "You are arrogant! Ought you not rather to mourn?" (1 Cor. 5:2). When anyone in the community of believers sins, the entire community should mourn—not just the guilty one. Lamenting is for the entire church because sin affects the entire church, even if it is the sin of one.

Jesus said, "Blessed are those who mourn, for they shall be comforted" (Matt. 5:4). God comforts those who lament as a response to misery for their sinfulness. Knowing the holiness, faithfulness, and goodness of God while acknowledging the sin that dwells among us should provoke us to misery, then to mourning.

Be Weeping

The eighth command is to **"weep"** (Ja. 4:9). While wretchedness is a response of the mind and mourning is a response of the spirit, weeping is a response of the body. It is the shedding of tears, a reaction of a humble Christian's recognition of sin. Inner sorrow works its way out. The Greek word *chlaio* literally means to sob and wail aloud. The story of Peter's denial of Jesus is well known. Remember what he did when he realized he had sinned? The Bible says that "he went out and wept bitterly" (Matt. 26:75). Weeping, then, is a humble response to our shame.

Genuine godly sorrow over sin leads to repentance. In Paul's second letter to the Corinthian church he reflects back to his first letter, which was full of strong correction. Apparently it brought them to grief. He says:

> "For even if I made you grieve with my letter, I do not regret it—though I did regret it, for I see that that letter grieved you, though only for a while. As it is, I rejoice, not because you were grieved, but because you were grieved into repenting. For you felt a godly grief, so that you suffered no loss through us. For godly grief produces a repentance that leads to salvation without regret." (2 Cor. 7:8-10)

For this reason, Jesus taught, "Blessed are you who weep now, for you shall laugh" (Lk. 6:21). Those called "blessed" here, are those who are saved. He says the saved ones, those with genuine faith, will weep for the sins of today. But when God consummates His kingdom and abolishes sin forever, the ones who weep will be filled with joy and laughter. "When the Lord restored the fortunes of Zion, we were like those who dream. Then our mouth was filled with laughter, and our tongue with shouts of joy" (Ps. 126:1-2). Weep now in order to laugh later.

> **Weep now in order to laugh later.**

Turn Laughter to Mourning, Joy to Gloom

The ninth command is apparently a summary of the prior two. "**Let your laughter be turned to mourning and your joy to gloom**" (Ja. 4:9). While in this world of sin and rebellion against God, it is not our place to sit and rest in its evil. We should be uncomfortable. This world is not our home, nor should it feel like it. It should not be *Your Best Life Now*[2], as one popular book was titled. If it is, then a lesser life is to be expected! What you do now counts forever. Those who dwell in this world and pursue this world, having a good time indulging in its pleasures, will not find a better life in the next world. "It is in your best interest to stop your laughter," James says.

This is not to refer to all kinds of joy. It is in the context of worldly pleasures and indifference to God's holiness and wrath. One pastor described the Greek word *gelos*, translated "laughter," this way:

> "It indicates the leisurely laughter of men indulging in their desires and

---

[2] Osteen, Joel. *Your Best Life Now*. New York: Warner, 2004.

pleasures. It is the laughter of fools who reject God. It is the silly laughter of a pleasure-loving gang of people indulging themselves up to their proverbial ears in the things of the world. It pictures people who give no thought to God, no serious thought to God, no thought to life, death, sin, judgment, holiness."[3]

When ministering to a great multitude, Jesus taught what is called the Beatitudes. He spoke of blessedness and followed it with woes. We cited one about weeping now in order to laugh later. Here Jesus compares the present life with the life to come. "Blessed are the poor, for yours is the kingdom of God" (Lk. 6:20). "But woe to you who are rich, for you have received your consolation" (Lk. 6:24). "Blessed are you who are hungry now, for you shall be satisfied" (Lk. 6:21). "Woe to you who are full now, for you shall be hungry" (Lk. 6:25). "Blessed are you who weep now, for you shall laugh" (Lk. 6:21). "Woe to you who laugh now, for you shall mourn and weep" (Lk. 6:25).

Do you really want your best life now? James implores us to turn from the vain pleasures of the world, for they make you an enemy of God. They might give the illusion of satisfaction, but will ultimately lead you away from the Lord of salvation. When we allow laughter to be turned to mourning and joy to gloom, we prepare our souls for the all-satisfying Christ who is in Heaven. Likewise, He prepares for us a place in which we'll be eternally satisfied.

Humble Yourselves

Following the same vein of thought, the tenth and final command says, **"Humble yourselves before the Lord, and he will exalt you"** (Ja. 4:10). This concludes his call to salvation. He ends where he began. Submit yourselves to God. Humble yourselves before the Lord. All of these commands reflect a contrite heart and a spirit of humility. The Greek word used here, *tapeinoō*, means to make yourself low. It does not refer to the silly put-downs some people use in order to have others build them up. It refers to a sincere recognition of unworthiness. It stands contrary to pride and arrogance. The humble one begs the Lord for mercy and grace, knowing full well he does not deserve it.

Jesus taught this same way. In Luke Jesus says, "For everyone who

---

[3] MacArthur, John. "Drawing Near to God, Part 2." Grace to You. Grace Community Church, 15 Mar. 1987. Web. 24 Nov. 2011. <http://www.gty.org/Resources/Sermons/59-25>.

exalts himself will be humbled, and he who humbles himself will be exalted" (Lk. 14:11). Exalting is to lift up. In a figurative sense, it is to be lifted toward Heaven, toward God. It is essentially a synonym of grace in this context. God "gives more grace" and "gives grace to the humble" as James wrote earlier (Ja. 4:6). It is how God draws near to you and you to Him. Jesus used this language to picture the going up to heaven and, conversely, going down to hell. He was rebuking those in Capernaum for rejecting Him when He said, "will you be exalted to heaven? You shall be brought down to Hades" (Lk. 10:15).

God is pleased when people humble themselves before Him. It honors Him and He gives them grace. He forgives them of their sins for which they become miserable, mourn and weep. The Lord said, "if my people who are called by my name humble themselves, and pray and seek my face and turn from their wicked ways, then I will hear from heaven and will forgive their sin and heal their land" (2 Chron. 7:14).

A wonderful picture of how God "gives more grace" to those who mourn over their sin is found in the story of the Prodigal Son. The son who took the blessings of his father and pursued a life in the world ultimately found himself ruined and in misery. He said to himself, "I will arise and go to my father, and I will say to him, 'Father, I have sinned against heaven and before you. I am no longer worthy to be called your son. Treat me as one of your hired servants'" (Lk. 15:18-19). His humility and repentance was rewarded by his father with enormous grace. "But the father said to his servants, 'Bring quickly the best robe, and put it on him, and put a ring on his hand, and shoes on his feet. And bring the fattened calf and kill it, and let us eat and celebrate. For this, my son, was dead, and is alive again; he was lost, and is found'" (Lk. 15:22-24).

All of this should warn us of the seriousness of pursuing the pleasures of the world. We make ourselves enemies of God. We become spiritual two-timers, adulterers, and faithless sinners. But, rest assured, God is faithful (2 Tim 2:13). If we submit to God, resist the devil, draw near to God, cleanse our hands, purify our hearts, be wretched, mourn, weep, turn our laughter to mourning and our joy to gloom, and humble ourselves before the Lord, he will save us. "Let us test and examine our ways, and return to the Lord!" (Lam. 3:40).

True Faith is Content

Have you ever shown up late to a small gathering to find yourself extremely uncomfortable when a sudden and seemingly coordinated hush sweeps over the group? I have. It's as though you were uninvited which makes you feel completely out of place. This next passage reminds me of those awkward moments. You might say that it feels a little out of place. James just asked his audience why the fights were stirring and pointed out that it was due to worldliness. And, in rather strong language, he tells them that they are children of the world and need to come back to Christ. "Here's how," he instructs. "Submit yourselves to God in humility." Then, this seemingly out-of-place part is injected, **Do not speak evil against one another, brothers. The one who speaks against a brother or judges his brother, speaks evil against the law and judges the law. But if you judge the law, you are not a doer of the law but a judge. There is only one lawgiver and judge, he who is able to save and to destroy. But who are you to judge your neighbor?"** (Ja. 4:11-12).

I'll admit this particular passage threw me for a loop, and I wasn't alone. Commentators have grouped it with the passage before, the passage after, and as disconnected from the before and after. At first glance, the passage is about speaking evil and judging one another. Did you see that? If your mind is still on the context of loving the world, it might be hard to transition from "submit to God" to "do not judge one another." This is how some commentators feel. So they naturally count this passage as a change of subject altogether. To them, James was talking about loving the world and now he is talking about being judgmental.

I think this is a unwarranted. There is no real indication that James has changed his subject, especially when the Greek is examined. The actual context of this passage is slander. Although slander is never mentioned in James per se, it is implied on numerous occasions. Slander is included with the sin of partiality (Ja. 2:1-13), the sin of gossip, false teaching (Ja. 3:1-12), and marked by those who are jealous (Ja. 3:13-18) and stirring up quarrels (Ja. 4:1-10). The quarrels and fights were aroused by slander due to worldly desires. Slander is a sin of the mouth which is the subject leading up to this passage. In other words, James is still on the same subject—worldliness. When you covet, what else do you do to the person who has what you want? You slander him. You speak evil about him because you are jealous. If this is true, the subject matter has not changed. James is still speaking to the professing Christians who act more like the the world than Christ.

This brings me to the next reason why this passage is such a struggle to "fit" with the surrounding text. (Trust me on this heady stuff. Though it may be boring, I am setting you up for the lesson.) James refers to the readers as *adelphoi* (translated "brothers") which is a term of tenderness toward those of close kinship, especially spiritual kinship. With the prior ten verses full of references like "adulterous people" (Ja. 4:4), "enemy of God" (Ja. 4:4), and "you sinners" (Ja. 4:8), you might wonder if James has other people in mind. But returning to a gentler spirit doesn't require us to think that he is speaking to different people now. We should see "brothers" as a term of endearment for those who are wandering from the truth. In fact, this is consistent with the closing of his letter, "My *brothers*, if *anyone among you* wanders from the truth and someone brings him back, let him know that whoever brings back a *sinner* from his *wandering* will save his soul from death and will cover a multitude of sins" (Ja. 5:19-20, emphasis added).

Hopefully, it is obvious to you that this passage is not out of place like it first seemed to be. In fact, it sets the stage for next part of our exploration: true faith is content and, therefore, does not slander.

Do Not Slander

How often have you heard a sermon and inappropriately decided it was for someone else? For instance, the pastor is talking about worldliness in the life of a Christian and you think, "Boy, he sure hit the nail on the head! So-and-so needed to hear this." Some go so far as to purchase the sermon audio to give to whom they had in mind. The problem here is to assume the sermon only applies to others. We shouldn't do that with this text. The fights and quarrels were due to worldly desires.

The Christian ought to rejoice in the blessings of others and be content with the things he has.

Maybe the poor were jealous of the wealthy and slandering them. Today, it might look like the fellow in need of a car who speaks evil of the fellow who just purchased one debt-free. There could be a sense of inner disappointment when he is reminded that he still has no transportation. But the Christian ought to rejoice in the blessings of others and be content with the things he has. The fellow who bitterly remarks hateful things might hear the sermon from James on worldliness and say under his breath, "This is what so-and-so who bought the car needs to hear." It doesn't occur to him that the sermon pinpoints the sin of jealousy which is obviously his problem.

So, James hones in on him in a sense. He wants to make sure those who heard his lesson are not buying the mp3 for others. Rather, he wants them to be included in this confrontation with truth. He says, **"Do not speak evil against one another, brothers"** (Ja. 4:11).

If my calculations are correct, James uses the word *adelphos* nineteen times in his letter. This is the word "brother" which you should be familiar with by now. In verse 11 alone, he uses the word three times. He does this to invoke a sense of brotherly love and a connection between the recipients. These are the very ones who are slandering each other and, as he noted earlier, fighting and quarreling among themselves. Although they are family, they have set each other up as enemies worthy of murder; acting as though they are not related in any way. This is the reason for the letter. "Brothers, you are not acting like brothers. You need to see if you are really brothers". (This includes the sisters, as well.)

He tells these possibly fraudulent family members, **"Do not speak evil against one another"** (Ja. 4:11). At this point we need to qualify what James means by **"speak evil against."** It is the Greek word *katalaleo* which means "to slander." This is important because speaking evil against someone might give you the wrong impression if taken to mean speaking negatively to someone. In fact, if James is teaching that we are not to speak negatively to someone, he is guilty of his own prohibition. Calling someone adulterous isn't exactly a positive thing to say. This is why I make the distinction. The translators want you to know that the kind of speech that James is condemning is a speech that is both: *against* and *evil in a moral sense*. It is slander. William Varner, author of a linguistic commentary applying discourse analysis to the book of James, describes it as "speech that is both inaccurate and damaging to the character and reputation of someone else."[4]

James uses the word "slander" in connection with the word *krineis* (translated "judges") which is another word that we should distinguish. Rather than referring to biblical discernment and decision making, it refers to unbiblical condemnation and false accusation. There is a kind of judging that is commanded by God to do. Those who might object to my statement might quote Matthew 7:1 where Jesus says, "Judge not, that you be not judged." This is a good place to start when getting underneath the teachings of biblical judging and unbiblical judging.

After telling His listeners to not judge someone because they will be judged, He adds this: "Why do you see the speck that is in your brother's eye, but do not notice the log that is in your own eye?" (Matt. 7:3). Contrary to what some may say, Jesus is not telling them to not judge at all. In fact, He is not even against us bringing to our brother's attention that he may have a speck in his eye (to use the metaphor). Rather, Jesus is against hypocritical judging. He is condemning the attitude of correcting other people's sin when you neglect your own sin by the same fault. Verse 5 records Him saying, "You hypocrite, first take the log out of your own eye, and then you will see clearly to take the speck out of your brother's eye." Here, judging is not bad unless it is done hypocritically.

In the same passage, though ten verses later, Jesus tells us to "Beware of false prophets," and that we "will recognize them by their fruits" (Matt. 7:15-20). This is an act of judging between what is true and what is false. And, it is commanded us by our Lord.

Jesus teaches us to judge rightly. During a feast Jesus began teaching and judging the Jews for not keeping the laws of Moses. Then, turning the tables figuratively, He opposes them for wanting to kill Him for breaking the same law. Paraphrasing, Jesus says, "You say you keep the law because you circumcise a man on the Sabbath in order to make a part of the body perfect, but you get angry with me when I make a whole body perfect on the same day?" Essentially they were judging, which was okay to do, but they were not judging rightly, which is not okay to do. Jesus followed this with, "Do not judge by appearances, but judge with right judgment" (Jn. 7:37).

---

[4] Varner, William C. "Analysis of James Four." *The Book of James a New Perspective: A Linguistic Commentary Applying Discourse Analysis*. Woodlands, TX: Kress Biblical Resources, 2010. 159. Print.

Paul, a worthy Biblical expositor and model of good works, said, "I have already pronounced judgment on the one who did such a thing" (1 Cor. 5:3). He was speaking about a man in the church who was committing sexual sins. He then asks a rhetorical question, "Is it not those inside the church whom you are to judge?" (1 Cor. 5:12). Moreover, Paul was not hesitant to name names. In his second letter to Timothy, he calls out Demas for loving the world more than the dangerous life of preaching the gospel (2 Tim. 4:10). Earlier in the same letter, he names Hymenaeus and Philetus for false teaching in the church (2 Tim. 2:17). All of this is to say that biblical judging is using Scripture to discern truth from falsehoods, and by doing so, removing evils from the life of the church. Biblical judgment is essentially biblical discernment in action. It is using the Word of God to speak to the matters of spiritual life.

The opposite of biblical judgment is unbiblical judgment. It is judging others without the Word of God. Paul has a unique way of expressing this. When teaching on a similar subject, he tells the Corinthians they are being prideful and arrogant when they judge unbiblically. He corrects them and tells them to not "go beyond what is written" (1 Cor. 4:6). In other words the Bible sets a limitation on what we can judge. There are some matters where the Bible is silent and God expects us to be silent on those same matters. There are other matters where the Bible says we are incapable of judging because we are limited in the ability to judge, or finite. For example, we are not to judge whether it is universally right for all Christians to eat certain meats or to worship on Sunday (Rom. 14:1-12). Likewise, and this is what will lead us back to James' point, we cannot ultimately judge a man's eternal destination. Why? Because eternity is the concern of God. Though we can use the Scripture to examine our life and each other's life in order to find our weaknesses and strengths, we cannot ultimately know if another person is genuinely saved. We cannot know another person's motivations, much less their heart. In fact, Jeremiah 17:9 teaches us that we cannot even know our own heart—for it deceives even us!

This is the kind of judging that James has in mind. He uses the

> **Biblical judgment is essentially biblical discernment in action.**

word slander in connection with *krino*, which has eternal condemnation in mind. It is an eschatological term dealing with the final judgment of the world by God. This, of course, is a judgment that only God can make. Therefore, when you judge someone with this kind of eternal judgment in mind, brother or not, you are treading on dangerous ground. In fact, you are usurping God's place as the Judge of all.

Get Off the Throne!

At this point, you might recall our study of James 3:1 where he says that "Not many of you should become teachers" because "we who teach will be judged with greater strictness." There we learned that teachers were in a position of judging people since teachers were the ones entrusted with the Holy Scriptures. They were the ones who sat in the seat of Moses in order to judge right from wrong among God's people. In a similar way, James is taking this a step further by saying that when we judge in an unbiblical way, especially when we determine the eternity of others, we shove Jesus off His throne and sit in His place.

James wrote, "**The one who speaks against a brother or judges his brother, speaks evil against the law and judges the law. But if you judge the law, you are not a doer of the law but a judge**" (Ja. 4:11). To get the full picture, I substituted the word "judge" with the word "condemn" to capture the context. Simply said, the person who slanders or condemns another is essentially slandering or condemning the law. If you are condemning the law you are not *under* the law, but *above* the law.

> When you judge in an unbiblical way, you position yourself above the law.

It reminds me of that one kid who was always in the middle of our games. The kid could be any of us. He was the kid who would change the rules of the game as we played. He did so because it enabled him to succeed. For instance, he might step out of bounds during a game of basketball and we would call it. He would then say, "No, the line is further out." Or he might lose two out of three games of rock-paper-scissors and then say, "No, best three out of four." You know the kid. You might have been him a time or two. This kid is the final authority. He is putting himself above the rules. James says that when you judge in an unbiblical way, you position yourself above the law. You make yourself the final condemner. You become the lawgiver, the one who wrote the law. In other words, you suppose yourself to be God!

When I was young, I understood there was to be no one in my father's recliner when he came home from work. It was his throne, positioned for television viewing and after-dinner snoozing. Jesus has a throne too—an eternal throne perfectly positioned to rule the world. A day will come when Jesus will return to rule from that throne and He will judge the living and the dead (2 Tim. 4:1). He will ultimately do what James is teaching us to do temporarily and personally within ourselves—examine our life and submit to the final Judge. Here's how Jesus spells it out:

> "When the Son of Man comes in his glory, and all the angels with him, then he will sit on his glorious throne. Before him will be gathered all the nations, and he will separate people one from another as a shepherd separates the sheep from the goats. And he will place the sheep on his right, but the goats on the left. Then the King will say to those on his right, 'Come, you who are blessed by my Father, inherit the kingdom prepared for you from the foundation of the world. For I was hungry and you gave me food, I was thirsty and you gave me drink, I was a stranger and you welcomed me, I was naked and you clothed me, I was sick and you visited me, I was in prison and you came to me.' Then the righteous will answer him, saying, 'Lord, when did we see you hungry and feed you, or thirsty and give you drink? And when did we see you a stranger and welcome you, or naked and clothe you? And when did we see you sick or in prison and visit you?' And the King will answer them, 'Truly, I say to you, as you did it to one of the least of these, my brothers, you did it to me.'
>
> Then he will say to those on his left, 'Depart from me, you cursed, into the eternal fire prepared for the devil and his angels. For I was hungry and you gave me no food, I was thirsty and you gave me no drink, I was a stranger and you did not welcome me, naked and you did not clothe me, sick and in prison and you did not visit me.' Then they also will answer, saying, 'Lord, when did we see you hungry or thirsty or a stranger or naked or sick or in prison, and did not minister to you?' Then he will answer them, saying, 'Truly, I say to you, as you did not do it to one of the least of these, you did not do it to me.' And these will go away into eternal punishment, but the righteous into eternal life." (Matt. 25:31-46)

When Jesus, the eternal King, returns to sit on His throne, you do not want to pretend that it is yours, much less pretend you are Him. Rather you want to honor the Lord by exalting the throne of Judgment as His holy throne alone and by humbling yourself to His holy rule alone. We should adhere to Paul's instructions when he wrote, "Therefore do not pronounce judgment before the time, before the Lord comes, who will bring to light the things now hidden in darkness and will disclose the purposes of the heart" (1 Cor. 4:5). These hidden matters are for the all-seeing Lord to judge. We are neither qualified (Rom. 14:4) or capable (Heb. 4:12) to do so.

The epistle of James flows nearly parallel with that of Leviticus 19:9-18. In it, God commands His people to love. Each command parallels the teachings of James. Here is one that pertains to us now:

> "You shall do no injustice in court. You shall not be partial to the poor or defer to the great, but in righteousness shall you judge your neighbor. You shall not go around as a slanderer among your people, and you shall not stand up against the life of your neighbor: I am the LORD." (Lev. 19:15-16)

James concludes this portion of his teaching by saying, **"There is only one lawgiver and judge, he who is able to save and to destroy. But who are you to judge your neighbor?"** (Ja. 4:12). This should serve us as an excellent closing. When we judge the hearts and eternities of others, we place ourselves on the eternal throne of Christ and act as the one who wrote the law. But we fool ourselves if we believe this is our right. From wise men of the world, to enemies of God to undermining the rule of Christ, we set ourselves in the worst place possible. Remember how easy it is for our passions to put us in such a place, creating conflict with others, conflict with ourselves, and conflict with God.

This world has room for only one God and He is the only lawgiver and judge. He is able to "destroy both soul and body in hell" and this is His holy right and responsibility (Matt. 10:28). Therefore, "who are you to judge your neighbor?" (Ja. 4:12). Who are you to assume the position of Judge and King? Who are you to determine the fate of another? Who are you to see within the heart of man, even your own? A fool may think he can, but, in reality, only God can. Remember this the next time you slander someone.

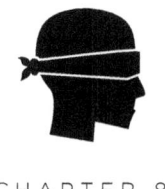

CHAPTER 8

THE TRIAL OF PLANNING

JAMES 4:13-17

"you ought to say, 'if the Lord wills'"

Jesus told this parable about presumptuous living: "The land of a rich man produced plentifully, and he thought to himself, 'What shall I do, for I have nowhere to store my crops?' And he said, 'I will do this: I will tear down my barns and build larger ones, and there I will store all my grain and my goods. And I will say to my soul, Soul, you have ample goods laid up for many years; relax, eat, drink, be merry.' But God said to him, 'Fool! This night your soul is required of you, and the things you have prepared, whose will they be?' So is the one who lays up treasure for himself and is not rich toward God" (Lk. 12:16-21).

We sometimes limit the principle of seeking first the kingdom of God (Matt. 6:33) to just our funds and provisions. While it is right to honor God with these things (this is clearly the context of Jesus' teaching) we should also put God first when it comes to our time and plans. If we seek God first in everything we do, we will reap the full benefits of His promise to add all these things to us.

We might say to each other, "I trust God to take care of us," and this is good. However, at the same time, we make plans each day, month and year without seeking God. If we are not careful, we can exclude God altogether from our lives. This is careless and presumptuous living. In James' prior instruction, he warned us not to be presumptuous over other people's lives because to do so is to be judgmental. In this passage, he continues that thought, but with a slight change of focus. This time he tells us not to be presumptuous over our own lives.

> "Come now, you who say, "Today or tomorrow we will go into such and such a town and spend a year there and trade and make a profit"— yet you do not know what tomorrow will bring. What is your life? For you are a mist that appears for a little time and then vanishes. Instead you ought to say, "If the Lord wills, we will live and do this or that." As it is, you boast in your arrogance. All such boasting is evil. So whoever knows the right thing to do and fails to do it, for him it is sin." (James 4:13-17)

True Faith is Modest

Making plans is a biblical virtue. It is wise to do. In fact, you see it in the lives of many strong biblical characters. Abraham sought to find a wife for his son Isaac in order that they would keep the way of the Lord (Gen. 24; cf: Gen. 18:19). Joseph stored and dispersed grain to help Egypt during a famine (Gen. 41). Moses learned to be a strategic thinker when he was struggling to lead Israel. His father-in-law, Jethro, taught him how to delegate the workload in order to handle the burdens of an entire nation (Ex. 18). Joshua effectively planned the entrance into the Promised Land where the Israelites faced their first enemy (Josh. 6). Solomon strategically built God's temple (1 Kings 5-7). Nehemiah tactically rebuilt the walls of Jerusalem (Neh. 1-6). In the New Testament, Jesus trained up men to establish the church throughout the known world (Acts 1:8). Of course, in the beginning He strategically created all things for His end (John 1:1-18; cf: Gen. 1:1). Paul planned his missionary journeys with a focus on key cities where he planned to establish beachheads for ministry (Acts 13:28). The list goes on.

It is wicked to plan without God.

These examples are demonstrations not only of simple strategic planning but also of good and godly strategic planning. Isaiah wrote, "He who is noble plans noble things, and on noble things he stands" (Is. 32:8). To the contrary, it is dishonorable and careless to jump into things without plans. Even worse, it is wicked to plan without God. Contrasting the noble men who plan, Isaiah says that the fool is "busy with iniquity," and the scoundrel "plans wicked schemes" (Is. 32:6-7). There are numerous examples of this kind of bad planning, and I am sure that your imagination can run with many more. For now, consider more words from the prophet Isaiah who spoke of the arrogant Babylonian king whom many liken to Satan himself. The king says, "I will ascend to heaven; above the stars of God. I will set my throne on high; I will sit on the mount of assembly in the far reaches of the north; I will ascend above the heights of the clouds; I will make myself like the Most High" (Is. 14:13-14). What a vile arrogance! Notice the repetition of "I will ... I will ... I will ..." and the indifference and defiance toward God. The king was certainly not concerned with what God thought or if God even existed.

Unfortunate for the king—and for Satan, too—God has a plan, and nothing thwarts it. A proverb reminds us of this, saying, "Many are the plans in the mind of a man, but it is the purpose of the Lord that will stand" (Prov. 19:21). Again, "No wisdom, no understanding, no counsel can avail against the Lord" (Prov. 21:30). God's plan will always happen the way He plans it (Rom. 8:28; Eph. 1:11). It was established before time (Eph. 1:4), so it is eternal (Eph. 3:11). Plainly put, God is "declaring the end from the beginning and from ancient times things not yet done, saying, 'My counsel shall stand, and I will accomplish all my purpose'" (Is. 46:10).

My will is not always in step with God's will.

When we speak about good planning and bad planning, we must identify the underlying matter which is the issue of the will. When we *will* to do something, we are saying that we intend or want to do it. We are speaking to something in the future sense, things to occur. I will finish this book, and I will eat breakfast (though not in that order). When I stood before my beautiful bride-to-be, slipped a ring on her finger, and said, "I do," I was doing as many others have done before me and will continue to do after me. I was responding positively to a question from the minister. He asked me if I promised to sacrificially love and care for her for the rest of my life. "I do promise this. I will do it." That was my commitment to her and the audience. Of course, I am prone to break promises and, sadly to say, do so all the time.. I have failed my wife on many occasions by not being loving as I should. This is because I cannot make a promise of certainty regarding the future. I can only express my intention of doing so. Essentially, my response is that "I intend on committing the rest of my life to sacrificially loving my wife at all times." It is not that I most definitely will. Why? Because my will is not always in step with God's will. The plans that I make, even with the best intentions, fall short more often than I wish.

In the above passages, we see that God makes plans too. But unlike us, God always succeeds with His plans. What He plans to happen will happen exactly the way He planned. This is because He sovereignly set up everything for this end. We are unable to change or undo His plan. Author and preacher A. W. Pink wrote it rather eloquently, "He fixed all the circumstances in the lot of individuals, and all the particulars which will comprise the history of the human race from its commencement to its close."[1] He goes on to say that God not only purposed the general laws for the government of the world, but He also established the application of those laws. All things will ultimately work out the way God purposed from eternity.

> Unlike us, God always succeeds with His plans.

I mention this not to divert your attention to such a complex doctrine of God's sovereignty, but to establish the concept of God's will. God has a will. And we should be mindful of His will when we consider our own. We have intentions, wants and plans. We can and will strategize and put certain things into place so that a certain outcome will occur. But, no matter how strong our strategy and how precise our plan, it will always end the way God ordained it.

This is not to suggest that all our planning is worthless and unnecessary. To the contrary, God's plan often works out through our plans, which is how He planned it to work. What I am suggesting is that when our plan conflicts with the plan of God, our plan will not happen the way we wanted. His will is bigger than ours. So, if there is a conflict of plan, His will prevail. What I am urging here is that we always include God in our plans in order to prevent the conflict. Being true, we do not want to engage God in a war of the wills.

War of the Wills

The story of Jonah might be the best illustration of this. Remember

---

[1] Pink, Arthur Walkington. "The Decrees of God." *The Attributes of God*. Grand Rapids: Baker Book House, 1975. 14. Print.

that God tells him to go to Nineveh to preach the gospel (in Old Testament terms, of course). This was God's will. He desired it and planned that it would happen. However, Jonah desired otherwise. So he traveled in the opposite direction, going by boat, and he ended up walking the plank. After splashing into the water, he sank like a rock to the bottom of the sea. Then a giant fish swallowed him whole, thereby preventing him from drowning. Disgusted with the taste of Jonah (sovereignly distasteful), the fish spat him back on land.

Jonah's experience was dreadful. He went from being God's great prophet to being half-digested fish food. He progressed from being content, to being disappointed, to being withdrawn, to being upset, to being furious, to being suicidal, to being humble, to being desperate. It was hardly progressive to him. Eventually, though grudgingly, he did as God commanded. In the end, we find that God planned every single thing to happen exactly the way it did. From the boat that took Jonah away to the fish that saved him from drowning, God's will unfolded in the way he planned.

There are three things in this story that I think will help us as it relates to our passage in James. First: Jonah ignored God's plan. He was commanded by God to go and preach to the Ninevites. But he ignored the command altogether. The Bible never records any words from Jonah expressing such, but his actions essentially said, "God who?" Jonah 1:2 records the command of God. Jonah 1:3 simply follows up with, "But Jonah," and that says it all.

Second: Jonah not only ignored God's command, he went against it. The story says that he "rose to flee to Tarshish from the presence of the Lord" (Jon. 1:3). For some strange reason, Jonah figured that God would not find him across the sea. So he hopped in a boat and set sail.

Third: Jonah not only ignored and went against God's command, he excluded God altogether. While on the boat, God caused "a great wind" to come upon the sea in order to frighten those inside. The mariners, pagans no less, were full of fear and later turned to God (Jon. 1:16). Jonah, on the other hand, was indifferent to God's power. He showed no fear and, get this, he slept (Jon. 1:5).

Jonah's story reminds us that ignoring God is never *just* ignoring God. It is practically impossible. How long can someone ignore the obvious? We have an English idiom for this. We say that there is an "elephant in the room." The idea is that an elephant, due to its enormous size, would be impossible to overlook. Yet, no one wants to acknowledge it. They all pretend it is not there. They *ignore* it as best as they can. To some, God is the elephant in the room. In Romans 1:19-20, Paul says:

> "For what can be known about God is plain to them, because God has shown it to them. For his invisible attributes, namely, his eternal power and divine nature, have been clearly perceived, ever since the creation of the world, in the things that have been made. So they are without excuse."

We are all without excuse. To ignore God is never *just* ignoring God. It is a front to His goodness, a slap to His face. And it will not go without some kind of confrontation. If there is an elephant in the room, you will eventually bump right into it and have to deal with it. Since God exists, we cannot continue living without having to deal with Him at some point. Ignoring God will eventually turn into all-out denial, if not submission. And since God is unavoidable, our denial will turn into opposition.

We begin this process when we start making plans without weaving God's will into our planning process. It might sound small in the beginning, but it ends with us at the bottom of the sea—not a good place to be. Jonah's story should remind us that engaging God in the war of the wills is never a pleasant ride. It is a futile fight. We never win. God's will always prevails.

The Secret and Moral Will of God

I have been purposely interchanging the words "will" and "plan" quite frequently, and it is not to confuse you. The two terms are very similar in the sense of intending an action. While the word "will" refers more to the desire of a certain action, the word "plan" refers to the decision of a certain action. In this context, planning implies will. First, the desire exists. Second, the desire brings about a decision. God never plans against His will. It is also absurd to think that man will do otherwise (at least, in the literal sense of determination).

That said, we should explore the idea of good and bad planning in light of God's desire. The Bible speaks about the "will of God" in two ways. On one hand, the will of God is called his *secret* will. This is what the Bible explains as His decretive will or pre-ordained purpose. It is "secret" because we do not know what it is until it happens. It is "decretive" and "pre-ordained" because God declared it to be before time existed just as He did when we spoke all things into being. And, as all things obeyed His voice, so all things decreed in His secret will obey. Therefore, it is mostly referred to as His sovereign will. God described His sovereign will in Isaiah 46:9-11:

> "I am God, and there is no other; I am God, and there is none like me, declaring the end from the beginning and from ancient times things not yet done, saying, 'My counsel shall stand, and I will accomplish all my purpose,' calling a bird of prey from the east, the man of my counsel from a far country. I have spoken, and I will bring it to pass; I have purposed, and I will do it."

God's sovereign secret will includes both good and bad things that happen. Isaiah 45:6-7 says the Lord forms light and darkness, makes well-being and creates calamity. In Acts, we find that the murder of Jesus was also planned by God—from the men who conspired against Him to the place He was nailed to the cross (Acts 2:22-23; 4:27-28). Again, this will is hidden from them. In hindsight, however, it is clear. We do not know it until it unfolds, then we can perceive it clearly.

On the other hand, the will of God is called a *moral* will. This will is not what He has planned to happen, but what he commands and in what he delights. This will has been revealed to us. We can and should learn it in order to obey it. It is a prescriptive will commanded for us to follow. Paul mentions that the Jews had the privilege to "rely on the law" of God and "know his will" in order to "approve what is excellent" because they were "instructed from the law" (Rom. 2:17-18). He told the Ephesian Christians not to "be foolish, but [to] understand what the will of the Lord is" (Eph. 5:17). He is speaking of God's moral will. It is for the purpose of understanding that we can "walk in a manner worthy of the Lord, fully pleasing to him, bearing fruit in every good work and increasing in the knowledge of God" (Col. 1:9-10). This will is a preceptive will and is discovered in God's word.

The two wills differ from each other in a few ways. The secret will is hidden from our understanding. The moral will is revealed for us to understand. The decretive will expresses everything that happens. The revealed will expresses everything that should happen. The sovereign will cannot be prevented by man. The preceptive will can be rejected by man, and often is. Both of these concepts of the will of God should be kept in mind when considering our plans for today or tomorrow. However, it is the moral will of God that we are taught to know and obey. It would be a great benefit to us if we briefly looked at that before returning to James.

Knowing the Will of God

There are a myriad of books dedicated to finding the will of God. But for every book, there are a hundred or so people who seek it. Most of these people, even some very close to you, seek it in the wrong places. They might be searching their inner heart, chasing a modern "prophet," or simply interpreting the feelings they have in their lower abdomen. But none of these things have the answer. God gave us the Bible to know what His will is. Already, we know that God has a sovereign will that is preordained and unchangeable. But what can we know of the will of God? What has God revealed to us that will put an end to our questioning? We, and so many others, want to know, "What is the will of God for me?"

I recognize that in our apt ability to complicate things, we Christians have made the answer to this question far too complex. The answer, however, is very simple. I admit, though, that I was once one who begged the question again and again. It might have been one of the most frustrating things that I pondered. When I came face to face with the answer, it was like a door opened to a freedom that I had not experienced before. I hope that you too will experience this freedom if you are still asking the question. I want warn you though: it is so simple that you might not even believe it. Here is an overview.

What is the will of God for me?

First, God's will is that you be saved. In 1 Timothy 2:4 we read that God "desires all people to be saved and to come to the knowledge of the truth." The word "desire" is the Greek word *thelo* which means "to will." This the first and necessary step. For this reason, God is patient with us, giving us time to surrender to Him. He is "not wishing that any should perish, but all should reach repentance" (2 Pet. 3:9). Do you want to be in the will of God? You must first be saved.

Second, God's will is that you be filled with the Spirit. That is to say, God commands us to be controlled and led by the Holy Spirit. Ephesians 5:17-18 says, "Therefore do not be foolish, but understand what the will of the Lord is. And do not get drunk with wine, for that is debauchery, but be filled with the Spirit." Every believer has the Spirit of God indwelling them (Rom. 8:9). Being filled with the Spirit, however, is an ongoing effort by which we yield to God. When we are Spirit-filled, we are manifesting Christ-likeness. We experience humility, love, submission, obedience, clarity, faithfulness, kindness, hope, peace, and more. Others will notice it by our good works and obedience to God's word.

Third, God's will is that you be sanctified. In 1 Thessalonians, we find Paul instructing us this way, "For this is the will of God, your sanctification" (1 Thess. 4:3-7). To be sanctified is to be made holy and more like Christ. It is to be purified and to remain pure. I like the correlation that the famous preacher Robert Murray McCheyne made between successful Christian ministry and purity. While ordaining Dan Edwards, he said to him:

> "Mr. Edwards, you are God's chosen instrument. According to your purity, so shall be your success. It is not great talent; it is not great ideas that God uses; it is great likeness to Jesus Christ. Mr. Edwards, a holy man is an awesome weapon in the hand of God."[2]

Fourth, God's will is that you submit to the laws of the land. This one causes many people, even Christians, to skip a breath. But it is biblical. Peter wrote, "Be subject for the Lord's sake to every human institution, whether it be to the emperor as supreme, or to governors as sent by him to punish those who do evil and to praise those who do good. For this is the will of God" (1 Pet. 2:13-15). The Lord desires that we be models of virtue whether we are being persecuted or not. We must abide by the government laws and regulations as far as they do not rule contrary to God's law. You are not in God's will if you are breaking the law of your government.

Fifth, God's will is that you suffer. (And you thought that the last one was tough!) Again, Peter wrote, "For it is better to suffer for doing good, if that should be God's will, than for doing evil" (1 Pet. 3:17).

---

[2] MacArthur, John. "The Priority of Purity." *Found: God's Will*. Wheaton, IL: Victor, 1986. 35-36. Print.

This is not to say that we should run toward danger and seek to offend those who stand against God. Rather, it means we should be so faithful, straightforward and dynamic that, when we proclaim the gospel, opposers persecute us. Of course, you may never see the kind of persecution you hear and read about in other countries—but you will suffer in one way or another. God-haters hate God's children (Jn. 15:18). Jesus said, "You will be hated by all for my name's sake. But the one who endures to the end will be saved" (Matt. 10:22). Therefore, every genuine Christ follower will suffer for Christ's sake in some way.

These are the five biblical commands revealed to us as God's will. Since you know them now, you have no excuse. You can no longer say, "But I don't know what God's will is for me!" Granted, you might wonder if you should put on your left shoe first, or fix the oldest child breakfast last, or take a job position somewhere, or attend a certain college. I understand that sort of wondering. But this is not up for you to know. This is the secret will of God. God wants us to trust Him in those decisions. Do you know how I know that? Because God did not tell you in His Word. However, He did tell you to be saved, sanctified, Spirit-filled, submissive and suffering for Him. After that, God will guide you through faith. When you trust in Him and make godly decisions and plans that are open to change, then you will be in God's secret will. You know why? Because a life that is Spirit-filled is a life that is guided by the Spirit of God, and the Spirit of God never goes the wrong way. He is always doing what is right.

> **God will guide you through faith.**

For this reason, the Psalmist wrote, "Delight yourself in the Lord, and he will give you the desires of your heart" (Ps. 37:4). Do you see how that works? If you are delighting in Christ, then you are delighting in the things He delights in. Then your heart is set on things that His heart is set on. And God will give you those things because they are within His sovereign will. I know it is obvious to say, but I will say it anyway: the Holy Spirit never does anything outside of the will of God. Submit yourself to Him, and you will be in His will.

Let us Reason

"**Come now,**" James says (Ja. 4:13). I found this short phrase pretty humorous in the Greek. It reads *Age nun* which literally means "bring now" or "lead now." In one sense, it is somewhat sarcastic when you consider the context. James is accusing some of the Jews of trying to be masters of their own futures. They presume to know what lies ahead. So, in a wooden sense of the word, James is saying, "Okay, lead us there now." In other words, "You know the future, right? Then take us there so we can see."

All humor aside, this is a commonly used phrase to grab the attention of the hearer. So "bring now" and "lead now" would be poor translations though they might serve in this context to tickle our thinking. The phrase is more forceful, direct and plain. James might have borrowed it from Isaiah 1:18 which reads, "Come now, let us reason together" since this is what James says in the full text: **"Come now, you who say,"** which expresses the idea of reasoning. The Greek words, *oi legontes*, refer to speaking intelligently or with rationale. The verb tense is active and present, making it literally read as "you who are reasoning." I think a better translation might read, "Now listen, you who are reasoning." Or in more modern language, "Pay attention, you who go on reasoning." If it were a text message, you might put NOW LISTEN in all caps. *Bring it in. Come to the table. Shut up and listen. Give me your attention. Let's reason together.*

However, James is not here to reason with them. Rather, he follows this with some strong correction and grave warning. He starts by putting on the table the essence of what he is rebuking, namely their worldly reasoning. "You who are reasoning, this is how you reason: **"Today or tomorrow we will go into such and such a town and send a year there and trade and make a profit"** (Ja. 4:13). Again, it is not bad to reason. Nor is it bad to plan in a reasonable way. Hopefully, I did a fair job of explaining this earlier. Planning is a noble thing to do. But James is not calling into question their planning or their ability to reason. In fact, there is nothing wrong with all that we see them saying. Rather, it is what they are not saying that James is questioning. There is no God in their plans.

It was quite common for Jews to be businessmen. We find this a reality even today. They are still successful in almost all noble industries. In the ancient times, a typical Jewish businessman would set out to go to a town that was flourishing and growing—especially those that were at the intersections of trade routes from various countries. These towns were ripe with opportunities. Here, as James describes, these men would plan out the operation saying, "We will go and we will stay and we will trade and we will make a profit." There is no contingency or consideration for what God might want them to do. Their planning is independent of and indifferent to God. Plainly speaking, it is presumptuous and arrogant. And, as we have learned so far, it is bad planning.

James says that they establish the time of their choice. They say **"today or tomorrow"** which is how he hypothetically describes it. Next, they establish the location of their choice. Again, hypothetically speaking, they **"will go into such and such a town."** Then, they establish the time frame of their choice for how long they will do business. They will **"spend a year there."** Continuing, they establish the operation of their choice. They will **"trade."** Lastly, they establish the objective of their choice. They will **"make a profit."** It is their choice from beginning to end, and nowhere is there a glimpse of divine contingency.

James wants you to consider that maybe God's plan is to go on a different day, to a different city, to spend a different amount of time, to perform a different action, or to have a different objective. It could be that God desires that they stay where they are now and serve the orphans and widows (Ja. 1:27) and to give instead of getting. Contrary to what many Christians believe today, God does not have to replenish your wealth. His plan might be to rid you of all you have in order to accomplish His purpose. On the other hand, God might have you do exactly what you planned. He might want you to go to another city where business is booming so that you can work and make good money. We simply do not know for sure. Regardless, leaving God out of your plans will ultimately leave you disappointed since God's plan will never be thwarted by your plan. Moreover, such planning is the mark of arrogance.

Pride in Planning

Again, pride is peaking its head. It manages to keep popping up in James' letter. This is because it is the heart of sin. Selfish thinking is how sin starts. When we plan without considering what God might want us to do and without being Spirit-led, we dethrone Jesus just like we do when we wrongly judge others (Ja. 4:11-12) and we take residence in His ruling chair. This is prideful thinking because we do not and cannot know what the future brings.

James says that you plan your future, **"yet you do not know what tomorrow will bring"** (Ja. 4:14). Have you ever debated with a young lad who thinks he knows so much more than you although there is no way he could? Now imagine you are that kid debating with God over the future. Rather, you are not just a young kid, you are a young, ignorant kid who cannot even budget your coming week's income. God, who is all knowing, even before there were created things to know, looks down at you and says, "Why you are speaking with such certainty about what you will be doing later? Do you not know that I make the plans and I do whatever I want to do?" It is almost like you are nodding your head, saying to yourself, "This God, he just doesn't get it. He doesn't know. I know what is best. I know what will happen. I am a successful businessman."

God does not waste His time with such debate. We are here and gone in a moment. Our knowledge is limited. Our life is limited. Our experience is limited. Our wisdom is limited. Our future is limited. **"What is your life?"** James asks us. **"For you are a mist that appears for a little time and then vanishes"** (Ja. 4:14). He has in mind that vapor that you see when you walk out into the cold. Your breath is warm and when it hits the icy air, it turns into mist. But as soon as it turns to mist, it is gone. Our lives are that quick. We come and we go. We are that small dash between birth and death on the tombstone. Yes, that is the extent of our lives—short and fragile. Job lamented, "My days are swifter than a weaver's shuttle and come to their end without hope" (Job 7:6). His friend said something along the same lines, "For we are but of yesterday and know nothing, for our days on earth are a shadow" (Job 8:9). The Psalms also speak of life's brevity, "My days are like an evening shadow; I wither away like grass" (Ps. 102:11).

> **No man can design or control the future.**

We should heed the proverb that reads, "Do not boast about tomorrow, for you do not know what a day may bring" (Prov. 27:1). Append this to the verse when you are committing it to memory, "much less a year." Life is complex. It is an endless complexity of events, people, affairs and forces that are all beyond our control. They are so variable that no man can design or control the future. You should "trust in the Lord with all your heart" and not "lean on your own understanding" (Prov. 3:5).

Trusting the Lord

Rather than leaning on our own understanding, we are commanded to trust in the Lord. James says, **"Instead you ought to say, 'If the Lord wills, we will live and do this or that'"** (Ja. 4:15). This might be the most practical thing you may ever hear. Continue to plan, but consider the Lord's will in your plan. Decide things that seek to accomplish the five points of God's will mentioned earlier. There are likely others around you who are involved in your plan who need to be saved. God's will can easily be included your plans, and your plans be accomplished. But even then, remember that God's will is ultimately going to win. And rather than view this as a bad thing, consider the benefits this brings you as a Christian.

> **God will orchestrate everything for our good.**

First, accepting God's makes you humble. As Haddon Robinson says "You ought to make your plans with a very strong sense of 'If,' because you don't know what the next day will hold, not to mention the next year."[3] Considering God's will and rule over your plans is the opposite of arrogance. It is humility in that you are acknowledging your own weakness and finitude, and exalting God as the sovereign, infinite and all-knowing ruler.

Second, it will make you hopeful. Knowing that God will always accomplish His plan should bring us peace when we consider that we often make a mess of things. Romans 8:28-39 teaches us that God will work things out for the good of those of us who love Him, regardless of the bad choices we tend to make. Dave Swavely, author of my favorite book on decision-making, wrote, "The Christian life is not one of perfection, but of direction. To be 'walking' is to be headed somewhere,

---

[3] Robinson, Haddon W. *Decision-Making by the Book: How to Choose Wisely in an Age of Options*. Grand Rapids: Discovery House, 1998. 63. Print.

not to have arrived"[4] (cf: Phil. 3:12-14). Our destination is heaven with our Lord in perfection. It is good to know then, that while here on earth, often making poor plans, God will orchestrate everything for our good.

Third, it will make you happy. Think of the anxiety relief this brings to you! Relinquishing the success of your spiritual growth and earthly living to God puts all of the burden on Him. Jesus taught us to live this way. "Take my yoke upon you, and learn from me, for I am gentle and lowly in heart, and you will find rest for your souls" (Matt. 11:29). Swavely calls this "the spectator principle." When we recognize that God is in control and has a plan even for our individual lives, we start to see it unfold. What a joy it is to see God at work in your own life and the lives of others. God is the Master Conductor, and all of life is a composition that is harmoniously working together for His glory and our joy.

Being modest, and therefore humbly submitting your plans to God is quite beneficial. While others are downing alcohol and popping pills to relax, we Christians can simply sit back and trust that God will take all of our plans—even the bad ones—and turn them around for our good.

True Faith is Obedient

Modesty is a character of genuine faith. Another is obedience. These planners that James calls to the rug were guilty of ignoring God. You might call them practicing atheists. In reality though, they know that God exists. They even have a deep understanding of who God is and what God wants. These were, after all, the chosen people of God, blessed with the commands and the revelations of the Lord. Nevertheless, in their sinfulness, they managed to forget about God in their plans. **"As it is, you boast in your arrogance"** (Ja. 4:16). They are more than practicing atheists. They are self-theists. Their glory is their own arrogance.

The word "boast" literally means to be loud-mouthed. In connection to the word "arrogance," he is saying that they are arrogantly and loudly bragging. The catch here is it involves arrogantly

---

[4] Swavely, David. *Decisions, Decisions: How (and How Not) to Make Them*. Phillipsburg, NJ: P&R Pub., 2003. 100. Print.

bragging about something you do not have. So it is even worse than bragging; it is *pretentious* bragging. And, **"All such boasting is evil,"** in case you were wondering (Ja. 3:16). The Greek word *poneros* from which we get "evil" is the same word used to describe Satan, the wicked one. This is what God thinks of those who make plans for the future and leave him out. This is because it was Satan's plan to usurp the authority of God and rule in His place. Essentially, when we plan without God, we are doing the same thing.

There is a small passage in the Bible that tells a story about a particular plan that goes terribly wrong. In Genesis 11:1-9, we find the people of Shinar making a grand decision. They said to themselves, "Let us build ourselves a city and a tower with its top in the heavens, and let us make a name for ourselves, lest we be dispersed over the face of the whole earth." Apparently, they were a well-educated people. It is noted that they all spoke the same language, and spoke quite well. This monument to themselves was no small feat. The Greek historian, Herodotus, said that it was eight towers stacked on each other with a spiral way running around the outside. Halfway up the monument were seats for resting from your journey. This was a enormous building and it must have required a tremendous amount of architectural genius, not to mention an outstanding talent for managing an enormous team of laborers. All of this is to say that these people were wise.

However, they were not wise with the wisdom from heaven. For they did not include the Lord in their plans. And this is where their plans went terribly wrong. They wanted to honor their own accomplishments. This tower was to tell the rest of the world that these people would not be conquered or dispersed. They had plans. They were here to stay.

God saw their plans and monuments, and knew their sin of planning without Him was just the beginning. Their impressive spiral upward was the start of a spiral downward. So God mercifully showed them their folly. He "dispersed them from there over the face of all the earth, and they left off building the city." The city was then called, "Babel, because there the LORD confused the language of all the earth." God simply changed their language and, suddenly, they were incapable of continuing their plans.

At the height of their arrogance, God showed them His will

prevails. We can choose to ignore it, deny it, and even oppose it, but, eventually, we will have to deal with it—one way or another. God will have His way. James wants us to seek the will of God in all that we do. Otherwise, we may find our plans ending suddenly.

Disobeying God's Will

James concludes with one last remark. "**So whoever knows the right thing to do and fails to do it, for him it is sin**" (Ja. 4:17). This final sweep works as a summary of this lesson. The recipients of James' words were very familiar with the Old Testament Scriptures. They understood God's sovereign will and would have easily acknowledged His moral commands for all people. They knew that God always wins the war of the wills. Yet, in their forgetfulness, they sinned by ignoring God's will in their plans. In this last statement, James says ignoring the right thing to do is disobedience and sinful.

> **God always wins the war of the wills.**

If James were to rewrite this, he might write it this way: "So, after all that we have learned, all that we now know, all that God is and we are not, if anyone still fails to involve God in his or her plans or does not seek to accomplish the will of God in his or her decisions, this person is sinning." In more personal words: You have the truth, to ignore it now is to be in sin. And, as if it is not obvious, it is out of God's will.

Obeying God's Will

Genuine faith seeks to know and obey the will of the Lord. It is an obvious mark of the Christian. "I delight to do your will, O my God; your law is within my heart," says the Psalmist (Ps. 40:8). Again, "Teach me to do your will, for you are my God! Let your good Spirit lead me on level ground!" (Ps. 143:10). Such is the attitude of the one who has been given divine faith. Jesus identified a relationship with God by doing God's will. "If anyone's will is to do God's will, he will know whether the teaching is from God or whether I am speaking on my own authority" (Jn. 7:17).

Peter also recognized this truth. "Since therefore Christ suffered in the flesh, arm yourselves with the same way of thinking, for whoever has suffered in the flesh has ceased from sin, so as to live for the rest of the time in the flesh no longer for human passions but for the will of God" (1 Pet. 4:1-2). After being regenerated by God's Spirit, a person will live for the will of God and not the desires of the world. Maybe it is best said in 1 John 2:17, "And the world is passing away along with its desires, but whoever does the will of God abides forever" (1 Jn. 2:17).

Conclusion

Planning and strategizing, even if it is for secular purposes, is wrong if we do not consider and seek God's will. As Christians, we are to live according to His plans and not our own. His will is that people be saved (1 Tim. 2:4; 2 Pet. 3:9), Spirit-filled (Eph. 5:17-18), sanctified (1 Thess. 4:3-8), submissive (1 Pet. 2:13-15) and willing to suffer for doing good (1 Pet. 3:17). Believers who demonstrate true faith acknowledge these things first and arrange their schedules and activities accordingly to make God's will their highest priority.

CHAPTER 9

THE TRIAL OF WEALTH

JAMES 5:1-6

"you have laid up treasure in the last day"

America is a country that worships wealth. We are a people whose inflated pride is intricately tied to our embarrassment of riches. Here, success is measured by the amount of wealth you have amassed. In fact, we are so famous for our wealth that this country remains the ultimate destination of untold numbers of foreigners seeking to make their fortunes. Even during an economic crisis, this is true.

Despite the fact that our money bears the phrase, "In God We Trust," our actions tell a different story. It is the dollar that is viewed as being all-powerful in this land, and it is used to purchase anything you can think of—and some you had rather not. The more you have, the more you can obtain. It's an endless cycle of ravenous consumption. In the Kingdom of God, however, this is not the case. God sovereignly rules the hearts of His people and provides for them all of their needs. True believers trust in God, not wealth.

Of course, this is not always the case in our experiences. The American dream has plagued most Americans, and those in the church are no exception. Though they have the antidote, some professing Christians betray those with whom they fellowship by loving riches more than Christ. How we handle money is, a test of genuine faith. And it is this test with which James puts believers on trial. I call it the "Trial of Wealth."

Before we get into this trial and allow it to be a tool by which the Spirit of God reveals our hearts, let us first address the matter of money, riches and wealth. Some will be quick to tell you that money is evil. But this is not true. Money is amoral, it has no inherent good or bad nature. It is nothing more than a object that we place value on for the purposes of trade. If you had a $100 bill in your hand and a new way of trade emerged as the more valuable asset, your hundred dollar bill would go back to being plain old paper. Simply put, money is only valuable if we make it valuable. Therefore, value is in the eye of the beholder—or the hand of the holder, I guess. In the same way, money has no intrinsic morality. But although money is not truly evil, in the hand of evil, it can be used for evil purposes.

It is the love of money that gets you into trouble. In Paul's letter to Timothy we read, "For the love of money is a root of all kinds of evils. It is through this craving that some have wandered away from the faith and pierced themselves with many pangs" (1 Tim. 6:10). When the Bible teaches that the *love of money is a root* of all kinds of evil, it means a number of things. In a foundational sense, to love money is to place the highest value on material things, and that which you place at the top of your value system becomes your master. You live before it and in light of it. Jesus taught that you become a servant of money when you love it. It is, therefore, your master (Matt. 6:24). As we will see here in James, if money is your master, you are betraying those around you who hear you profess to be a servant of God. And when you have another master, you essentially open yourself up to "all kinds of evil" as Paul said.

> **If money is your master, you are betraying those around you.**

In a wider sense, the love of money is really the love of worldly things. Attaining money is not the end in itself for anyone. Very few people want money just to have money. It is a means to an end. People desire to be wealthy because they desire to be comfortable, secure and popular, and because they want to buy whatever their hearts desire. This is why the trial of wealth here in James follows the trials of loyalty and planning. In fact, from the perspective of linguistics, James is now concluding a diatribe on worldliness which began back in James 4:1. Actually, he is still dealing with the same challenge—worldliness. There, he rhetorically asks about the source of church quarrels. He says that they come from worldly desires. He says that worldliness is nothing more than selfishness. He calls it pride and warns us that "God opposes the proud" by quoting Proverbs 3:34. We will discover that he concludes this by asking a final question, "Does He not oppose you?"

For this reason, we are still in the same vein of worldly living. James elaborates from the Lord's teachings that worldliness is a mark of belonging to the world and, therefore, of being a servant of Satan, not of God. Here, the test of genuine faith is not about having money, but about loving money.

> "Come now, you rich, weep and howl for the miseries that are coming upon you. Your riches have rotted and your garments are moth-eaten. Your gold and silver have corroded, and their corrosion will be evidence against you and will eat your flesh like fire. You have laid up treasure in the last days. Behold, the wages of the laborers who mowed your fields, which you kept back by fraud, are crying out against you, and the cries of the harvesters have reached the ears of the Lord of hosts. You have lived on the earth in luxury and in self-indulgence. You have fattened your hearts in a day of slaughter. You have condemned and murdered the righteous person. He does not resist you." (James 5:1-6)

True Faith is Generous

My wife and I do our best to train our children to properly understand riches. We often connect being rich with being a child of God. Instead of having great wealth, we are rich because we have great mercy and grace through our Great Lord. Prioritizing God's spiritual gifts above all earthly gifts is our aim in forming their little hearts. We desire that they see Christ as their treasure first and most supremely. If they have Christ, they need nothing else—not even money. My wife and I will tell you quite sternly that it is better to have Christ than to have breath. (Sometimes, this is how we warn our children. Kidding, of course, but not really.)

> **It is better to have Christ than to have breath.**

I do not mean to imply that we ignore earthly riches altogether. While Christ is our all-satisfying treasure, we do recognize the purpose of money and the blessings of God. Deuteronomy teaches us that God gives us the "power to get wealth" (Deut. 8:18). A proverb reminds us that "the blessing of the Lord makes rich" (Prov. 10:22). God is generous and gracious to mankind. He gives to some great wealth. So while we must train our children to love Christ, we must also train them to not speak judgmentally of those who have much. Since money has no moral nature, it is not sinful to be wealthy. A rich father cannot make his children guilty of sin by giving them his entire inheritance. Neither can a businessman become sinful the moment his income bursts to high levels. It is not sinful to possess the blessings that God grants.

In the same sense, it is not sinful to have little or to be needy. God blesses those that He wants to bless for a higher reason than we are able to know. Wealth is stewardship given by God to some. It is according to His design and purpose. He blesses all of His people in a variety of ways. To some, He gives more; to others He gives less. It is different for each person and in accordance to God's sovereign plan. We are all unique in the sense of God's blessings; however, we are all the same in the sense of responsibility of those blessings. This is where sin comes into play. We become evil doers when we misuse the blessings of God. And, as we know to be true, the more blessings you have, the more ways you are able to sin—and the stronger the temptation there is to do so. Yes, the American dream can easily turn into the American nightmare.

> **The American dream can easily turn into the American nightmare.**

Who, Me?

At this point, you might not feel like this lesson applies all that much to you. After all, you are not rich, right? There is always someone who makes more than you and has a bigger house than you, right? I understand. I have made the same assessments before. The standard by which we assess our financial status is based on an American consensus. The news reports that middle-class Americans are those who make anywhere between $25,000 to $100,000 annually. Currently, our country draws the line with tax breaks when you reach an annual income of $250,000. You might fit somewhere in those groups. If you do, you are considered to be middle class—even if you fall on the high-end. But in a global comparison, you are extremely rich—even if you fall on the low-end. And, since you likely belong to a church that has global mission funds, let us go ahead and include the global comparisons.

Expanding our consensus, you will find that you are better off than you might have thought. If you make at least $50,000 a year, you are among the top one percent of the wealthiest people in the world. That's right, you, Bill Gates and Oprah Winfrey are in the same financial club. By the world's standards you are very rich. So what if you make less than $50,000? Does that make you middle class? No. You do not qualify as middle class by the world's standards unless you make only $1,000 a year![1] Now, I understand that all things are not equal. I never included the cost of living and numerous other factors, but the point is still the same. We might not consider ourselves rich, but, in perspective, we might very well be.

Again, being rich is not necessarily evil. Joseph, a man from Arimathæa, was described as being rich and called a "disciple of Jesus" (Matt. 27:57). We know Philemon to be a great asset to the Kingdom of God as a "beloved fellow worker" of Paul and Timothy. He was a successful businessman who owned slaves, land, housing and more (Phile. 1). On the other hand, there are those who were rich in this world, but never rich in faith. The best example might be the Rich Young Man found in Matt. 19:16-22. He asked Jesus about eternal life. The answer shocked him. Jesus said, "Sell what you possess and give to the poor, and you will have treasure in heaven; and come, follow me." Matthew reports that the young man "went away sorrowful, for he had great possessions." Jesus uses this situation, as well as a few others, to teach about the difficulty it is to abandon riches for the sake of eternity. He says, "It is easier for a camel to go through the eye of a needle than for a rich person to enter the kingdom of God" (Matt. 19:23).

> **Being rich does not mean that one is evil.**

When the Bible talks about riches, it is talking about abundance. Basically, the word *rich* refers to having more than necessary. In particular, it refers to having *abundantly* more than you need. God is "rich in mercy" since He has abundantly more mercy than what we need (Eph. 2:4). Metaphorically speaking, Paul referred to Jesus as rich

---

[1] Statistics were calculated using the Global Rich List, accessed on January 2, 2010. http://www.globalrichlist.com. The calculations were based on figures from the World Bank Development Research Group according to http://www.globalrichlist.com/how.html

while in Heaven, but becoming poor when He descended to live among man (2 Cor. 8:9). Being rich does not mean that one is evil. It only means to have more than you need to sustain your family. Here in James, the attention is turned toward those who are rich, those who have more than necessary.

"**Come now, you rich**" (Ja. 5:1). Using the same language as he did in James 4:13, James calls his audience to attention. He says, *Age nun*, "Now listen!" Who, me? Yeah, you with the riches. If you were not included in the "rich" category earlier, even when compared with the rest of the world, you are still not off the hook. Though James is speaking directly to those who are rich, the poor can fall into the same traps of misusing money. It may not be as easy to fall, but it is possible. Both rich and poor people can love money and spend it incorrectly. You do not need money to love it.

> **Be a godly steward of what you have.**

The poor can be just as materialistic as the rich; however, they are not able to indulge every selfish desire quite like the wealthy can. One example might be the homeless man who receives donations, as small as they are, and blows them on liquor. He is waisting the little that he was given. This is just as wrong as the rich wasting a large amount on something useless. So the poor are not off the hook here.

Do you know what that means? If you are poor or rich, and I am confident that you are one of them, heed the message from James. Be a godly steward of what you have. True faith is generous, honest, restrained and kind, regardless of how deep your pockets may be. Let this passage be a sober reminder of the dangers of wealth and a warning of the sin of loving money.

Money to Misery

I remember a time when I was so afraid of discipline that my mother only needed to tell me what was coming. You may have been there before. "Jacob," she would say, "when we get home, you are getting a spanking." That was enough for me to hear become overwhelmed with terror. I would cry and scream immediately. You would have thought that my spanking already occurred. The same thing happens today when we have to tell our kids, "Go to your room, I'll be there in a minute." Seconds later, wailing emerges from behind a closed door on the other side of the house.

This is the idea that we need to have it mind when we hear James tell the rich to **"weep and howl for the miseries that are coming upon you"** (Ja. 5:1). It is a prophetic mode of speaking. As John Calvin wrote, "The ungodly have the punishment which awaits them set before them, and they are represented as already enduring it."[2] You might remember that James wrote something similar to this in his previous chapter. To the ones who show loyalty to the world, James reminds that "God opposes the proud, but gives grace to the humble" (Ja. 4:6), and so they ought to humble themselves before God. Submit to Him and resist the devil. Draw near to God. Cleanse your hands, purify your hearts. "Be wretched and mourn and weep. Let your laughter be turned to mourning and your joy to gloom" (Ja. 4:9). By doing so, you show humility at the reality of your sin against God. And in return, God will show you mercy and grace (Ja. 4:10). That is the promise by which sinners come to Christ and escape the wrath of God.

Here, however, there is no mention of grace; no time for repentance. The rich ought to weep and sob out loud in a lamenting way, as ones who wail for the dead (Jn. 11:31-33; Lk. 8:52). Weeping also marked the woman who, broken in her sin, washed the feet of Jesus with her tears and dried them with her hair (Lk. 7:36-38). It also seized upon Peter after he denied Jesus three times. Luke records that "he went out and wept bitterly" (Lk. 22:62). Produced by strong emotional outbursts, weeping is wailing and sobbing in a painful way. Here James says that the rich should weep as people who see the inescapable judgment that is coming.

> **Cleanse your hands, purify your hearts.**

From there, James says to add to your weeping a howl. This is the Greek word *ololuzo* which also means to lament but with a loud scream of grief. James is building the intensity since the judgment is near: "Frantically cry and shriek in despair." It is a kind of overwhelming grief and terror that strikes the heart and bursts from the mouth uncontrollably. Both "weep" and "howl" are verbs written in the present

---

[2] Calvin, John. "Epistle of James." *Calvin's Commentaries, Volumne XXII*. Grand Rapids: Baker, 2005. 343. Print.

tense indicating a continuation of action as if he is saying, "Keep on weeping and keep on howling over your impending damnation." Needless to say, these very strong words.

This text is really tough to imagine. I have had some very sad and dark times in my life. I can remember those times when I wept over tragedy. Likewise, my children weep and howl when they know that discipline is coming. But nothing really compares to the coming judgment of God. The emotions will burn with despair and sorrow. The mind will be full of unrelenting regret, and the body will ache with pain from the horrific punishment of a Holy and Sovereign God. Nothing compares to the terror this must strike in the hearts of man. The "miseries that are coming upon you" is what James is describing. It is the judgment of God. From money to misery: this is the fate of the rich who trust in their own riches rather than in God.

Your Riches are Perishing

The rich will feel the misery by first knowing that their beloved treasures are perishing. James wrote, **"Your riches have rotted and your garments are moth-eaten. Your gold and silver have corroded"** (Ja. 5:2-3). Those who set their hearts on earthly treasures will find themselves storing them up. Whether it is in the form of cash, precious metals, houses, cars, or other assets, uselessly hoarding is forbidden. It is poor stewardship of what God blesses you with since it is unused for any lasting benefit.

This is not referring to saving for a much-needed car, planning for education, and other responsible reasons for reserves (1 Tim. 5:8). It is a reference to storing up things for no end, uselessly hoarding them. This is sin. When the blessings of God go unused and stockpiled to the exclusion of its proper use, it is evil, and it will be judged as such by God Himself. Rather than fruitless storage, we are to use our money wisely by caring first for our family (1 Tim. 5:8), then the church (1 Cor. 16:2), winning the lost (Lk. 16:9), caring for the needy (1 Jn. 3:16-18), and supporting those who teach us (Gal. 6:6). As long as these things remain in need, our aim as believers should be to meet those needs. However, some love their wealth more than they love others. Rather

> **Some love their wealth more than they love others.**

than meeting needs, they are hoarding it for themselves. To these people, James says that miseries are coming. Then, in a rather troubling display, he explains himself.

First, James says that **"your riches have rotted"** (Ja. 5:2). This is likely a reference to the abundance of food like grain, wheat, barley and maybe some kinds of meat since it decays. Moreover, the Greek word *ploutos* which is translated "riches" is a word that comes from the name of an ancient Greek god of mythology. He was the god of wealth whose name meant "bounty of harvests." His mother was the goddess of agriculture. This, along with the reference of rot, lends itself to an abundance of natural food. Food will eventually rot, especially organic food. So in this case, James is alluding to the abundance of food stored up as treasure. It will rot. Or, as the text suggests, it has rotted—past tense. The slew of food has gone to waste. To the one who loves this bounty and stores it up for himself, this might be a misery all by itself. He was counting on the plenty. But it did not reward him. Rather, it wasted away, turned to poisonous and uneatable rot.

Second, James says that **"your garments are moth-eaten"** (Ja. 5:2). Like many do today, the rich of that time often purchased expensive garments. This is reference to a literal long, loose-fitting, outer robe. You might remember Jesus preaching in what we call the "Sermon on the Mount" found in Matthew 5. While on the topic of retaliation, He says if "anyone would sue you and take your tunic, let him have your cloak as well" (Matt. 5:40). The tunic was worn as an undergarment while the cloak was an outer garment and usually worn while sleeping. It served as a blanket. It was common during those times for people to have one or two tunics but only one cloak since it was more costly. In fact, Mosaic Law required borrowers to return cloaks to their proper owners "before the sun goes down, for that is his only covering, and it is his cloak for his body; in what else shall he sleep?" (Ex. 22:26-27). Here in James, we read that "your [cloaks] are moth-eaten" (Ja. 5:2) implying that the rich had more than one cloak since it was usual to have only one. Essentially, he is saying "your many cloaks are moth-eaten." These cloaks were usually embroidered with expensive yarn and jewelry making the accusation even more severe, "Your stockpile of expensive clothes are moth-eaten." Like the food, these garments are wasted away as well. It is actually eaten away by insects. The robes are nicely folded and stored in a storehouse, and the moths come and snack. Again, this is a miserable experience to the one who loves to store up expensive clothes. His closet is a room in itself, full of comfortable, fine clothing. Yet, while he is gone, insects creep into his chamber and eat the garments away.

Third, James says that **"Your gold and silver have corroded"** (Ja. 5:3). The terms "gold" and "silver" refer to the money of their day. Their coinage was not like ours. Our gold is pure and not affected by oxidation. But much of the gold in the ancient world was not pure. Rather, it was mixed with an alloy and was prone to corrode under many circumstances. Given enough time, their coins would oxidate, rust and tarnish much quicker than we see today. This too was a misery in and of itself. Those who loved their money and stored it away for themselves are now grieving because their hopes have wasted away.

When the rich see their food decay, their clothes moth-eaten, and their money turn to rust, what do they have then to show for it? Nothing. James wants us to see the foolishness in hoarding. The things of this earth fall apart in due time. Nothing here lasts forever. Most of it doesn't even last long. So it is a fool's endeavor to store it up. Moreover, it is wasting God's blessings. For this reason, the rich who are guilty of hoarding should weep and howl for the miseries that are coming. Witnessing their riches turn to waste is grievous enough, but it is not the end—nor is it the most miserable consequence. There is more.

Your Riches are Testifying

The rich will feel the misery when they find out that their storehouse is perishing. They will also feel the misery when the corrosion of their storage testifies against them. James wrote, **"Their corrosion will be evidence against you"** (Ja. 5:3). Here, he personifies the corrosion. When the gold and silver turns to rust, the rust turns against the rich. When God comes as Judge and you stand in His holy court, the witness will take the stand and speak against you. That witness will be your storehouse. This is the idea. It will testify to your ungodliness. It will testify to your hoarding. And its testimony will be irrefutable. Why? Because it exists. It is the "living" evidence.

It is the ultimate backfire. The rich hoards his treasures so that he can protect them, keep watch over them, love them, be fascinated with them. The treasures are his glory and hope. He thinks to himself, "I'll keep these here so that no one else can have them." He is a jealous and selfish man. But over time, all that he loved and cherished turns on him. It never loved him back. It never felt the connection. Rather, it took him to court and laid evidence of his privacy, his soul. This is what we might picture here. The rich will soon experience the misery from that which they loved so much.

Your Riches are Burning

This gets even more sad. Not only do the rich feel the misery of their treasure going to dirt and then exposing their ungodliness, they also feel it when their treasure is used as their executioner. James says that their storehouse **"will eat your flesh like fire"** (Ja. 5:3). It was a terrible thought to imagine that the things the rich hoard will turn on them and testify against them as if it were before the judge. But James takes it a step further. He says that it will then execute the sentence. This is strong and vivid imagery.

The notion of "fire" here reminds us of a real hell. I imagine the treasure being thrown into a pile like wood to be kindled and burned. My son and I love to start little fires. My daughters love to join in with marshmallows. Sometimes the wood will not ignite so easily due to its wetness. So we typically grab some paper from the recycling bin and maybe some leftover boxes, and we throw those in the small flames. Suddenly, they are consumed and the heat is blazing. The flames are tall. This is the picture I form in my mind when I imagine what James is communicating.

Basically, he is saying to the rich, "All that stuff you uselessly hoarded, God is going to take it and use it to support the flames of hell. Your treasure will be used as your executioner." These are very strong images and words. As one preacher said, "Hell is for hoarders." Why? Because **"You have laid up treasure in the last days"** (Ja. 5:3). This is done in disregard of the command of God. For Jesus said:

> "Do not lay up for yourselves treasures on earth, where moth and rust destroy and where thieves break in and steal, but lay up for yourselves treasures in heaven, where neither moth nor rust destroys and where thieves do not break in and steal. For where your treasure is, there your heart will be also." (Matt. 6:19-21)

Where your storehouse is, your heart is. If you live for the things in this world, your heart is earth bound. If you live for the things of heaven, your heart is heaven bound. Therefore, it is foolish to lay up treasures on earth. It is even more foolish to lay up treasures **"in the last days"** (Ja. 5:3). What does the hoarder expect to do with his riches? If these are the last days, then time is short. Jesus is returning. It is like buying up all the food in the market just before the end of the world. What for? Why would someone do such a foolish thing? The Son of God could return at any moment. And when He does, we will have to account for the things that He gave us to use. If we uselessly hoard them, we will be treated as the rich will be treated. Our gifts will corrode before us, testify against us, and execute justice on us.

If you knew that tomorrow you would die, how different would your life be today? What foods would you purchase? What clothes would you want? What would you do with the money that is left over after taking care of your needs? "As for man, his days are like grass; he flourishes like a flower of the field; for the wind passes over it, and it is gone, and its place knows it no more" (Ps. 103:15-16). And of course, in the immediate context of James, "You are a mist that appears for a little time and then vanishes" (Ja. 4:14). Hoarding is foolish.

> **If you live for the things in this world, your heart is earth bound.**

In the words of Jesus, "Take care, and be on your guard against all covetousness, for one's life does not consist in the abundance of his possessions" (Lk. 12:15). After saying these words, he told the parable:

> "The land of a rich man produced plentifully, and he thought to himself, 'What shall I do, for I have nowhere to store my crops?' And he said, 'I will do this: I will tear down my barns and build larger ones, and there I will store all my grain and my goods. And I will say to my soul, "Soul, you have ample goods laid up for many years; relax, eat, drink, be merry."' But God said to him, 'Fool! This night your soul is required of you, and the things you have prepared, whose will they be?' So is the one who lays up treasure for himself and is not rich toward God." (Lk. 12:16-21)

If the Jewish believers were not familiar with the words of Christ, they should have recalled the words of Isaiah, "I will make people more rare than fine gold, and mankind than the gold of Ophir" (Is. 13:12).

"Behold, I am stirring up the Medes against then, who have no regard for silver and do not delight in gold" (Is. 13:17). God was judging them for their abuse of gold and silver. "Wail, for the day of the Lord is near; as destruction from the Almighty it will come!" (Is. 13:6).

Useless hoarding is not only foolish, it is sinful. God's blessings are to be used for purposes that glorify Him. Selfish wasting is not one. However, generosity is. Faith that is given by God to us will reflect an extravagant generosity since this is the nature of God. When your necessities are met, where does the remainder go? Where is your heart? If someone were to observe your bank accounts, what would they conclude? Would they say that your wealth matches your profession of faith? If true faith is generous, where does your profession that you have true faith stand? Where your money is spent is where your heart can be found. Would you qualify as worldly (Ja. 4:3-5)? This is the test before you now. Compare your spending to the reality of true faith; the reality of generous faith.

A good way to summarize might be with Paul's words to Timothy:

> "As for the rich in this present age, charge them not to be haughty, nor to set their hopes on the uncertainty of riches, but on God, who richly provides us with everything to enjoy. They are to do good, to be rich in good works, to be generous and ready to share, thus storing up treasure for themselves as a good foundation for the future, so that they may take hold of that which is truly life" (1 Tim. 6:17-19).

True Faith is Honest

If theme music played while you read this book, the strings and percussions would crescendo here. James' dramatic portrayal heightens with yet another rhetorical imperative.[3] This time, he says *idou*, which means "see" or **behold.** Instead of a call to attention in the future tense like the prior use of *age nun* ("come now"), this implies a present and active perception. Rather than "come and see," it is "turn and look." There is a deeper sense of emergency. It literally refers to perceiving with the eyes. But it can also imply seeing with the mind in a figurative sense. Either way, James follows it with a picture, and it is meant to be seen with your imagination. "Picture this," is the idea. We

---
[3] See "come now" in James 4:13 and 5:1.

should envision what he is about to say. Then, we will understand it. However, things are rarely that easy. What James tells us to envision requires a bit of Jewish history to properly sketch it.

In ancient times—even more ancient than the time of James—God established a social order whereby He would provide life necessities to those in need. All people were commanded to work. We can see this as early as the Adam and Eve even before the Fall. "The Lord God took the man and put him in the garden of Eden to work it and keep it" (Gen. 2:15). Of course, God is always working in every detail of life (though He never tires). Work is an honorable duty and everyone is called to do it in one way or another. Laziness is forbidden. It is a sin. As a matter of fact, the same commandment that instructs us to rest one day out of seven also commands us to work: "Six days you shall work" (Ex. 29:9). In fact, if one does not work, he shall not eat (1 Thess. 3:10-12). However, there are times when people, though they desire to work, for various reasons cannot do so. In a similar way, there are times when people work hard but are unable to earn enough to support themselves or their families. In both situations, needs are not met—but it is not due to laziness. We experience these realities today. In fact, I have worked two jobs for several years before reaching a point where I can support my family with only one.

> **God designed work and designated it to be a meaningful part of life.**

In God's design, people who made more than enough to live were the people who were privileged to help those who did not. Now I understand that I may be treading on a thin line right now depending on your political persuasion. I promise to tread carefully. My purpose is not to convince you to vote one way or another, but to help you see God's order for the social settings of nations—particularly the Jewish nation, since it was primarily in ancient Israel where we see the order established. In America, the privilege of helping the needy is institutionalized with no spiritual accountability. It has largely turned into a way to reward laziness instead of hard work. Our nation is becoming one that honors laziness. It is the American dream to retire early, is it not? Why? Mainly because we do not see work as something of privilege or virtue. We see it much like the Greeks of the ancient world who viewed labor as something that only slaves did. This was not the plan of God. Work is a noble and honorable thing. So was giving alms. Workers were worthy of pay and protected by divine law (Lev. 19:13; Deut. 24:14-15). Jeremiah condemned those who withheld wages from their workers (Jer. 22:13), and Malachi spelled out divine judgment for the same (Mal. 3:5). God designed work and designated it to be a meaningful part of life and way to glorify Him. Those who worked also had their needs met. If not, then those who were paid in abundance were to share with those who made little or were unable to make any.

Honesty was key. In a perfectly honest community, no one goes hungry or unsheltered. Everyone has their needs met regardless of their vocation. This does not mean that all people would have the same amount of wages or resources. It just means that in God's order of life, needs are met through the community and by God's blessing. You would not find two men, both working jobs but only one able to eat. The one who was more blessed with his wages cared for the one who worked equally hard but received less. This marked the early church (Acts 2-6) just as it did the early nation of Israel.

> **In a perfectly honest community, no one goes hungry or unsheltered.**

Of course, there is presently no perfect world. Our struggle to live with sin in us and among us causes us to fall time and time again. Many of us are victims of the fallen order. Some of us are victimizers. Therefore, the rich become richer, and the poor become poorer in most cases. The list of reasons is far too long to even pretend to detail. But they are not hard to imagine. With this in mind, I wish to lay one more backdrop in order to complete our setting.

Common to this time was what we would call "day laborers." These were men who were primarily considered to be poor, though this was not prerequisite. Day laborers would arise early in the morning and stand in the marketplace in hopes that a businessman would hire them for a day. They would work for whatever was agreed and receive their payment at the end of the day. You might recall the parable that Jesus told where He used this context. Matthew records it saying, "For the kingdom of heaven is like a master of a house who went out early in the morning to hire laborers for his vineyard. After agreeing with the laborers for a denarius a day, he sent them into his vineyard" and so the story goes (Matt. 20:1-16). This was a normal aspect to the economy of Israel.

In most cases, these day workers relied heavily upon the agreed wage. If they made nothing, they ate nothing. This was why God's laws were so strict. Let's open up one of the commandments cited earlier: "You shall not oppress a hired worker who is poor and needy, whether he is one of your brothers or one of the sojourners who are in your land within your towns. You shall give him his wages on the same day, before the sun sets (for he is poor and counts on it), lest he cry against you to the Lord, and you be guilty of sin" (Deut. 24:14-15). With this in mind, let us return to James and see another perspective on the trial of wealth.

Wages Cry Out

It is a common saying: *money talks*. One person said quite humorously, "If money talks, it always tells me *goodbye*." I would agree. It says that and a great many other things. As we discovered in the prior verse, money testifies to our character (Ja. 5:3) and reveals the desires of our heart (Matt. 6:21). It can be your good help or your bad hinderer. It can enable godly deeds or unleash the godlessness of the heart. Whatever it does, it is active. And it is telling your tale almost as clearly as the tongue (Ja. 3:1-12).

James continues to personify money. He says that **"the wages of the laborers who mowed your fields … are crying out against you"** (Ja. 5:4). This is in the context of the "gold and silver" mentioned in the verse before. It has corroded and is testifying, "crying out against you" (Ja. 5:3-4). The rich who have hoarded their wealth in sin, have also acquired it in sin (Deut. 24:15). They keep it in sin probably because they acquired it in sin. The "laborers" were hired for a day. They mowed the fields and earned their wages, but their wages are now testifying against the rich businessman who hired them earlier that morning. Why? Because their wages were **"kept back by fraud"** (Ja. 5:4).

This is exactly what God commanded the Israelites not to do. Notice that he does not say that they were paid too little or too late. He says that they were paid nothing. The rich ripped the workers off and robbed them. They agreed to a day's wage and withheld that wage from them. Apparently, this was a common problem. Remember back in James 2 where he condemns the unjust exaltation of the rich over the poor? He asked them, "Are not the rich ones who oppress you, and the ones who drag you into court? Are they not the ones who blaspheme the honourable name by which you were called?" (Ja. 2:6-7). There, he condemned those who showed partiality to the rich by treating them better than they deserved while at the same time mistreating the poor. Here, he condemns the rich for mistreating the poor—something he has only addressed in passing until now.

The idea that the wages are crying out in testimony against the oppressors is not uncommon in Jewish literature. In Genesis 4, we find the blood of Abel speaking quite similarly. God confronts Cain and says, "The voice of your brother's blood is crying to me from the ground" (Gen. 4:11). Later in Genesis the sins of those in Sodom cry out against the people (Gen. 18:20; 19:13). This is not to be taken in a wooden sense. It is figurative language that refers to the evidence of an inanimate object. He needs not to voice anything in order to communicate something. It only needs to exist. If it exists, then it testifies.

> **If your workers are crying now, you will be crying later.**

Sin testifies. Blood testifies. Money testifies. They all cry out in a figurative sense and bear witness to injustice and godlessness. And, if they cry out against you, you will one day cry out yourself when justice is finally served. "Be wretched and mourn" for your sins (Ja. 4:9) or "weep and howl for the miseries that are coming upon you" (Ja. 5:1). One way or another, someone will be crying. If your workers are crying now, you will be crying later.

Workers Cry Out

The wages of those who are oppressed metaphorically cry out against injustice and the wickedness of those who love money. In a more literal sense, **"the cries of the harvesters have reached the ears of the Lord of hosts"** (Ja. 5:4). The wages tell the tale of the workers. They are the ones who suffer. They are the ones who cry out to God as they hunger and die in the night (cf: Ja. 5:6).

Since God commanded His people not to engage in this sort of fraudulent activity, it is God who will be the judge. He, therefore, will hear the crime and try the defendant. And, with full knowledge and wisdom, He will determine the sentence of the guilty and exact justice. It is a scary thought to imagine that the sins of the rich will cry out to the ears of the Holy Judge who listens intently. He not only wrote the law, He upholds it. And those who sin against it, sin against Him.

In Isaiah we read similar language to what James used. In the setting of a vineyard, figuratively referring to Israel, God speaks out in anger. He cultivated it, made it fertile, planted choice vines and watched for it to yield grapes (Is. 5:1-2). What He found, however, was wild grapes. He wanted to see justice and righteousness, but He found bloodshed and outcry (Is. 5:7). "The Lord of hosts has sworn in my hearing" (Is. 5:9).

The phrase "Lord of hosts" contains a word that is essentially untranslated into English. In some Bibles, we find the word "hosts" transliterated as "Sabbaoth." It is a reference to the armies of God, those whom He commands to execute His war (cf: 1 Sam. 17:45). Here in Isaiah, He says that He will war against His vineyard by removing its hedge and breaking down its wall in order that it will be devoured and trampled down. He continues by saying, "I will make it a waste; it shall not be pruned or hoed, and briers and thorns shall grow up; I will also command the clouds that they rain no rain upon it" (Is. 5:5-6). All of this is in light of the oppression of the poor.

What a terribly frightening thing to think about. God is the Lord of Armies. Plainly put, He is Lord of everything and will use whatever He wants as His army. To the agricultural worker who oppresses the poor, God will hold back the rain and let the insects ravage. To the realtor who oppresses the poor, He will make the housing market collapse. To the tradesman, the entrepreneur, the homemaker, the pastor, the televangelist, God will judge you if you mistreat the lowly, if you rob them of their wages, or if you lie to them to acquire their money.

"Man is humbled, and each one is brought low, and the eyes of the haughty are brought low. But the Lord of hosts is exalted in justice, and the Holy God shows himself holy in righteousness. Then shall the lambs graze as in their pasture, and nomads shall eat among the ruins of the rich" (Is. 5:15-17). Dishonest gain is not something to ignore. The cries of dishonest wages will arise and the cries of those who dishonor will also resound when the Lord executes His justice in the land. His supernatural army will come "in flaming fire, inflicting vengeance on those who do not know God and on those who do not obey the gospel of our Lord Jesus" (2 Thess. 1:8).

Sneaky business deals and tricky manipulation are sinful. They are no way to make a dime. They rob others and break the law of God. The sins will cry out against you and, eventually, you will cry out for the miseries that come upon you. Rather, we should be honest with the way we make our money. True faith is honest. It does not seek to rob others even in the smallest way or by taking advantage of other's mistakes. The one who is genuinely saved by God will show himself to be honorable in the upholding of agreements. He will work hard and give to others as the Lord gives to him.

True Faith is Restrained

So far, two dangers are said to accompany the rich: useless hoarding and dishonest gain. While both are near commonplace for the American dream, neither strike so fiercely as the next one. An honest assessment of our native culture would reveal that, for the most part, we identify with the horrors of extreme hoarding. In August 2009, for instance, television network A&E began a documentary series called *Hoarders*.[4] The Learning Channel, or TLC as most know it, followed with their own version called *Hoarding: Buried Alive* less than a year later.[5] Both shows depict real-life stories of people who suffer from "compulsive hoarding" and need assistance to help "manage their illness." From what I have seen, their lifestyle is not glorified but pitied (and probably mocked). This might indicate to us that we Americans view extreme hoarding as a kind of problem. Granted, most do not truly understand that hoarding, even when it is not extreme, is wrong just the same. Those who hoard to a lesser degree are blind to their sin.

---

[4] "Hoarders." Wikipedia, the Free Encyclopedia. 08 Jan. 2010. Web. 08 Jan. 2012. <http://en.wikipedia.org/wiki/Hoarders>.

[5] "Hoarding: Buried Alive." Wikipedia, the Free Encyclopedia. 10 Nov. 2011. Web. 08 Jan. 2012. <http://en.wikipedia.org/wiki/Hoarding:_Buried_Alive>.

The same is true of dishonest gain. In most cases, we will admit that it is wrong to withhold money from those who work for it. However, the same people who admit this will not bat an eye when cheating on taxes, sneaking food into a movie, or paying less to lower income workers than their full wages. Often when we *outwit* others, it is *smart business*. And, while the Bible calls all hoarding and all dishonest gain sin, we categorize it into moderate or excessive practices so that we might excuse ourselves from liability. Hoarding and dishonest gain, when it is done moderately, is permissible. When it is done excessively, is questionable. But rarely is it sin.

Luxurious Living

From useless hoarding to dishonest gain to luxurious living, this is the progression. Be it the development of the desire to sin or the destination of earthly treasures, there is an underlying advancement of some kind. The one who hoards is longing for more to hoard. So he seeks to gain more, even at the expense of others. He cannot acquire what he wants quickly enough, so he robs. Then, as he gains more, he spends more. But he does not spend it on spiritually beneficial things, he indulges himself in desires that parallel his evil hoarding. He stocks his storehouse full of excess and then pads his life with comfort and convenience. James says, **"You have lived on the earth in luxury and in self-indulgence"** (Ja. 5:5).

It is worth noting from the start that this is mentioned immediately after James spoke of the reality of judgment stored up in the Lord's storehouse (Ja. 5:4). Instead of laying up treasures in heaven, the rich lay up treasures **"on the earth"** (Ja. 5:5). In context, this is the beginning of the real danger. Having an earthly focus leads to all kinds of problems, one of which is unspiritual and demonic thinking (Ja. 3:15) and another of which is physical and spiritual conflict (Ja. 4:1-3). Even so, the real problem is the one you face when you stand before God who calls you His enemy (Ja. 4:4). This problem is by far the worst one to have, yet the least one that worries most people. Although "God opposes the proud" (Ja. 4:6), we praise the proud and qualify pride as confidence and success. Here, the tragedy starts. It is the sinful pursuit of earthly things. And, as we see in James, it leads to many things, one of which is luxurious living.

There are two words that are used to describe luxurious living. When translated, their distinctions are almost lost. In fact, it might appear to the English speaking person that James is being a little redundant. Depending on your translation, you might find the words *luxury* and *self-indulgent* as we find here in the ESV. When compared with other translations, these words might be reversed or substituted with synonyms. The dictionary I use to find the definitions of the original Greek words ironically defines them the same way, "to live in pleasure." But, it is when we rightly divide these two words that we uncover a deep and searing truth, one that cuts to the heart of us all.

The first word is *truphesate* which is a verb that refers to a high quality of living. It denotes an abundance of intricacy, elegancy and workmanship. It is used in connection with expensive things. You might use it to refer to a Mercedes-Benz CLS in light of a Ford Focus. The Benz is highly sophisticated and intricately designed for extreme comfort, convenience and status. The Focus was developed mainly for functionality and cost savings. While both vehicles are able to get you from point A to point B, your experience in each will be dramatically different. For this reason, the price difference will also be dramatically different. You might be able to purchase eight Fords for the same price of one Benz. The Benz is clearly a more qualitative thing.

If you are not really a car person, maybe you are a computer person like me. A more "down-to-earth" example might suffice. When you compare an Apple computer with a Hewlett-Packard, you will find several things that set these two apart. The Apple is by far the more advanced machine. It has more power, more intricacy, more craftiness, more elegance and better design. The HP, like the Ford in my prior example, is designed for functionality and immediate cost savings. And, as you probably already know, the price tag affirms it. The Apple is the more luxurious computer.

Comfort and convenience are not inherently evil. I bring these examples up in order to form a clear picture of the concept of luxury. It is somewhat relative. A Ford Focus might be called a luxurious car by someone who drives a 30-year-old Oldsmobile. Also, expensive and well crafted things are sometimes a better choice when all things are considered. For example, since I am a web and video developer, it is generally more advantageous and financially wise to spend the extra money up front on a powerful and crafty computer that will outlast the less expensive ones. But it is not necessary in most cases. It is good wisdom at best and self-indulgent at worst. This is why I say it is relative.

We make our purchasing decisions based on many things. Our reasons differ from the next person. So we cannot say that the sin of luxurious living is a one-size-fits-all sin. One man's trash is another man's luxury, you might say. We can, however, apply the *principle* to all people uniformly. Luxury is a danger to all people, even when it is not dangerous to all in the same way. One author, who was also a Belgian economist, wrote a rather interesting book on luxury where he spoke boldly against its evils. While others were troubled not to define the word *luxury*, believing that everyone knows what it means, this author wrote quite plainly of its definition. In his mind, luxury was "anything which does not answer to our primary needs, and which, since it costs much money to buy, and consequently much labour to produce, is only within the reach of the few."[6] He poses another definition by M. de Keratry, who gave it meaning in a self-condemning way, "that which creates imaginary needs, exaggerates real wants, diverts them from their true end, establishes a habit of prodigality in society, and offers through the senses a satisfaction of self-love which puffs up, but does not nourish, the heart, and which presents to others the picture of a happiness to which they can never attain."[7] I would agree with those descriptions. I think James would as well. It appears that this is what he had in mind when condemning the rich.

He says in the Greek, "You lived luxuriously." Some older manuscripts translate it as "you luxuriated," which might be the best way to understand the idea. It denotes the giving of yourself to luxury, and even more literally, to "soft-living." It is paying a high price for high experience. You might think of it as an ongoing practice of upgrading. Get the better car, the better house, the better clothes, the better food, the better job, the better bed, the better phone, in order to have a better experience of life. The person who luxuriates is constantly seeking to improve existence with earthly things. If it makes life better, get it. Even more to the spiritual point. If it makes me look more

---

[6] Laveleye, Emile De. *Luxury*. London: Swan Sonnenschein & Co., 1891. 3. Print.

[7] Ibid., 4.

fashionable, get it. What the Christian may not know is that luxuriating is developing a discontented attitude toward God's gifts, God's people and God's mission.

Material Living Deadens Missional Living

I want to diverge for a moment and consider the effects of luxuriating. You might have never noticed how prominent a role luxury plays in your own world. Did you ever consider that the microwave made cooking more convenient? What about the computerized checkouts in the grocery stores, ATM machines, cell phones, automobiles, and more? These inventions were designed to solve challenges. They essentially saved us time and money, and improved our lives. On the other hand, they also hurt our lives. How common is it that mothers disciple their young daughters in the gospel while cooking dinner? How often do we engage unbelievers behind a checkout counter or grow with a friend in person? Have any of these inventions trained us to be more patient and to seize the time for God's purposes?

These inventions are not bad in and of themselves. They truly meet needs and solve problems. They can be useful in many ways. But, if we are not careful, they can also train us to be less interested, less patient, less loving, less honest, and less truthful with others. They can form our hearts to be more cold and self-seeking. They make us brats, to put it plainly. A brat is a child that behaves wrongly because he does not get his own way. We adults can be brats as well. The more we get accustomed to having it our way, the more we expect to have it our way. We have come to epitomize the Burger King mentality. Things that inconvenience us can easily become things we will not do. Having pleasures and comforts strengthens our flesh until it takes over. Then, humility and self-denial become foreign virtues. For this reason, Jesus said that "it is easier for a camel to go through the eye of a needle than for a rich person to enter the kingdom of God" (Matt. 19:24). Why? Because luxury has won the rich person's heart. He cannot give it up. He has already given himself over. This is the idea that James has when he accuses the rich who **"lived on the earth in luxury"** (Ja. 5:5). They were living in a way that marked their lives as being given to comfort. Therefore, they would likely not give themselves to sacrificial and missional living. Physical comfort, therefore, has spiritual consequences. Believe it or not, the microwave was a mark of luxury in a not-so-distant past.

Today, the microwave can be found in just about every home in America. Almost anyone can afford one. Since it is common and affordable, its luxurious value has gone to the wayside. So has the knowledge of the spiritual effects of physical prosperity. Regardless, the fact will always remain even when it is so easily denied. Scripture stands. Some preachers today will stand with it nevertheless. Jerry Bridges, for example, commented on this subject, saying:

> "Materialism wars against our souls in a twofold manner. First it makes us discontent and envious of others. Second, it leads us to pamper and indulge our bodies so that we become soft and lazy. As we become soft and lazy in our bodies, we tend to become soft and lazy spiritually."[8]

Yes, your next purchase might have a severe effect on your walk with Christ. It might strengthen your flesh and weaken your spirit. Most of us never even entertained such a thought. Others, even now, sneer at it as though it encroaches on their happiness. My hope, however, is that some will heed the warning. When we sacrifice things necessary for things superfluous, we are making bad use of our lives and leading ourselves down a dangerous path. Luxury is never satiating; and therefore, never-ending.

Luxury is Limitless

Soft-living is rarely an end in itself. There will always be ways for a better life. John Calvin appropriately said, "For they who abound in wealth seldom keep within the bounds of moderation, but abuse their abundance by extreme indulgences."[9] The person who is given to luxury will lead himself to fulfilling all of his pleasures. This is the idea behind the second word that James uses. It is the verb *spatalesate* which denotes a profuse growing in self-indulgences. You want it. You get it.

Soft-living makes us soft in our discipline and spoils the flesh. It causes us to be unable to restrain ourselves because our desires get too strong. We are too weak to fight them, so we give into them. Therefore, getting our way makes us less competent in our war against sin—and

---

[8] Bridges, Jerry. *The Pursuit of Holiness*. Colorado Springs: Navpress, 1978. 113. Print.
[9] Calvin, John. "Epistle of James." *Calvin's Commentaries*. Vol. XXII. Grand Rapids: Baker, 2005. 345. Print.

sin becomes our master. In this case, luxury cripples us and pleasure rules us. The person who sees and gets what he wants is the person who is spiritually crippled and unable to wage war against the senses that are so strong. He gets what he wants because he cannot restrain his wanting.

Inevitably, these sensual pleasures lead to sexual pleasures. "Vanity exalts sensuality, but very often serves it to no good purpose," as the author of *Luxury* wrote.[10] The Greek word has this connotation. James is essentially saying that luxurious living leads to sexual sin. And, as Jerry Bridges points out, the luxury can be as small as tasteful food. He wrote, "The habit of always giving in to the desire for food or drink will extend to other areas. If we cannot say no to an indulgent appetite, we will be hard pressed to say no to lustful thoughts."[11] This is because "when the body is pampered and indulged, the instincts and passions of the body tend to get the upper hand and dominate our thoughts and actions."[12]

> **Luxury cripples us and pleasure rules us.**

The little things that add up matter. In fact, it is usually what we think are the trivial things in life that lead to other more significant things. Take note of some of them like sleeping in late, leaving work early, refusing to exercise, missing time in Bible study, often getting your choice in food, and so on. I have recognized this to be true in my life. In fact, my wife used to make me whatever food I wanted when we were first married. It caused me to feel entitled, and I eventually expected her to make "my" food. Also, staying up late to watch movies was a delightful experience for me. But, it would make me tired in the morning, and so I would sleep later and not spend my time in devotions and exercising. Before long, my attitude became self-centered. I snapped at the kids, was insensitive to my wife and dishonest with my boss. This is how it happens. Most of us never even consider that eating at our favorite restaurant could cause so many grave sins.

On the other hand, being mindful of others and selecting things

---

[10] Laveleye, Emile De. *Luxury*. London: Swan Sonnenschein & Co., 1891. 14. Print.

[11] Bridges, Jerry. *The Pursuit of Holiness*. Colorado Springs: Navpress, 1978. 113. Print.

[12] Ibid., 114.

that cause others delight can help us develop strong self-discipline and make us more apt to resist temptation. Moreover, it will make our joy all the more delightful and grateful when we do find our pleasures met. James' warning should deeply penetrate all of our hearts. We all have heard that the American dream is to retire early and enjoy life. There is no evil in either. But, there is a substantial danger in both. I like to call it "suicidal luxury."

Suicidal Luxury

Job said, "They spend their days in prosperity, and in peace they go down to Sheol" (Job 21:13). James parallels this quite perfectly in his own words. He says, **"You have fattened your hearts in a day of slaughter"** (Ja. 5:5). This is a proverbial expression. It was common to refer to the heart being satisfied when speaking about getting filled with earthly nourishments. For example, Paul reminded his Jewish audience that God "did not leave himself without witness, for he did good by giving you rains from heaven and fruitful seasons, satisfying your hearts with food and gladness" (Acts 14:17). Although the body is that which is filled, the heart is where the satisfaction of repletion is felt. It is a reference to earthly satisfaction. It could mean food, shelter, clothes, friendship and a myriad of other things.

> **The rich are in danger of luxuriating themselves to death.**

Still, James is not condemning them for enjoying God's gifts. He is accusing them instead of living to be satisfied with those gifts rather than with God. To make matters worse, they were seeking this satisfaction **"in a day of slaughter"** (Ja. 5:5). This phrase alludes to the slaughter of oxen or sheep for feasting. Animals that were to be food tomorrow were fattened today. No one was interested in a scrawny one —the bigger the beast, the bigger the feast.

James says that this is what the rich do when they indulge themselves with all of the luxuries of life. They satisfy and fatten themselves up for slaughter. It is to no purpose. It has no eternal reason. And if it is to be taken spiritually, it is for the feast of God's wrath. What a sobering thought! The rich are in danger of luxuriating themselves to death since by nature we can never satiate ourselves.

If we stand opposite of this, we see that true faith, since it is not recognized in these things, is retrained. It is disciplined. It seeks not to have its way. True faith is noticed in others when you see them not being so decisive about all of the trivial preferences in life. The one who has divine faith will easily and gladly accept the preferences of others first because he realizes the danger in getting his own way, and he knows the reward of putting others first.

True Faith is Kind

James warns us that those who hoard wealth, gain money by fraudulent means, live in the lap of luxury, and use money to indulge their every desire are in danger of facing God's wrath. It is a lengthy list; however, James has one last grievance regarding wealth. You might recall in *Trials of Partiality* that James addressed the church's treatment of the rich. Now, standing caddy-cornered to that subject, he addresses how the rich treat the poor. He says, **"You have condemned and murdered the righteous person. He does not resist you"** (Ja. 5:6).

This final verse, under our consideration of the trial of wealth, is a hard-hitting accusation. To tell someone that they have condemned and murdered someone is serious grounds. It is so severe that some have interpreted it figuratively just to escape the knock-out punch. Admittedly, there is a level of difficulty with the passage. It can be tricky and I will show you how.

Remember that James earlier accused some of wrongfully preferring the rich people over the poor. He said that when a person enters the worship service adorned with expensive clothing, these people find them the good seats. And, when a person enters the worship service wearing shabby clothing, the people grudgingly send them elsewhere (Ja. 2:1-4). James calls this what it is—partiality. He reminds his partisan readers that God chose "those who are poor in the world to be rich in faith and heirs to the kingdom" and thereby did a reversal of fortune. God honors the poor, but "you," he says, "you have dishonoured the poor man." He then describes how the rich treat the poor:

> "Are not the rich the ones who oppress you, and the ones who drag you into court? Are they not the ones who blaspheme the honourable name by which you were called?" (Ja. 2:6-7)

While commenting on this passage, I mentioned that the rich of that time were known to take the poor to court and, since the poor had no means to afford a defense lawyer, they would trample the poor, tribunal style. Sometimes, they bribed the judge for a sentence. I imagine that it was like it is today in many places across the world. The rich both then and now pay their way to more riches by using (and abusing) the court system. James concludes his writing on partiality by evoking the reality that hatred, particularly when it is toward the innocent and poor, is in a sense, murder (Ja. 2:11). This is used to illustrate that breaking the law with only one sin is a trespass against the entire law, not just part of it so that we might be proud of keeping the rest. Therefore, we who show hatred by being partial—even if it is all that we do—are considered law *breakers*, not law *bruisers*.

There is a sense, however, that murder, when there are several other terrible sins to use as his example, might not have been mentioned primarily for us to think of murder figuratively. In some cases, the poor were put to death for a crime that they were wrongly accused. So it is quite possible that when James calls them law breakers, since partiality is murder, he might have been speaking about actual murder. Although this was not likely true of every single case, it did happen. And since it did, James might have been lumping them all together—guilty by association.

> **Hatred leads to murder given enough time.**

This wouldn't be wrong for him to do, especially since hatred leads to murder given enough time. So those who never actually murdered the poor would still feel the weight of this severe accusation.

Cohorts with the Courts

If the rich were actually condemning and murdering the poor, then this verse takes on a more serious context. They didn't just drag the poor into the courts and pull a fast one on them. They were courted to be killed. It is our tendency to read **"you have condemned and murdered the righteous person"** and soften the sinfulness of sin. We might take it to mean that the rich were simply robbing the poor if we take it only *figuratively*. We would then say that it means that the rich are being unkind to the poor. But they were far more sinful. They would have the poor unjustly condemned in the courts and put to death. This is a kind of lust that is so selfish that it murders the innocent for the little that they have.

This extreme act of debased injustice happened often. The Romans, who generally oversaw the civil life, were not thoroughly familiar with Jewish matters so they often turned things over to the Jewish courts. Consider the mock-trial of Jesus where Pilate and the Roman-appointed Jewish authorities conspired to try and execute Jesus. Paul was also a victim of this kind of injustice. He received what we sometimes call the "thirty-nine lashes" on five different occasions at the hand of the Jewish courts (2 Cor. 11:24). Some of these beatings were not within the jurisdiction of the Jews which tells us that the Roman empire also contributed to this heinous act of maltreatment. With such power and authority, the rich would seek out, arrest and punish the Christians (Acts 4:1-3; 5:17-18). And, in some occasions, they were dragged to the Gentile courts just the same (Acts 16:19-20; 17:6). I believe that this is what James had in mind when he said, **"You have condemned and murdered the righteous person."**

The Righteous One

As my workout friend tells me, "Let's dig deeper." There is one more thing to uncover in this passage and it will make our closing all the more rewarding. In case you haven't noticed, I have subtly used "the church" and "the poor" as synonyms for what James describes as **"the righteous person"** (Ja. 5:6). This reads *ton dikaion* in the Greek. When thinking about injustice and the courts, we can easily think that the righteous person is a reference to the innocent people who are murdered at the hands of the rich. But the word is, excuse the pun, rich with redemptive meaning. The subject of righteousness is near to the message of the cross, the justice of God, and the perfection of His Son. If we can safely think of condemning and murdering in both a literal and figurative sense, might we also think of "the righteous person" the same way? Jesus was dragged to the courts to be put on a mock trial. He was innocent though accused of breaking the law. He was in every way a law abider and He obeyed the Law of God perfectly. Yet, he was condemned in the courts and murdered for sins He did not do. He was innocent. He was the righteous person—both figuratively and literally. I think that James was wanting us to see something more here.

Allow me to explain. The phrase *ton dikaion* makes an important distinction by using the definite article. It is "the" righteous person, not "a" righteous person. This is how the Greek refers to a particular quality of something. It is a distinguishing reference. We are to understand it to mean a *certain* or *specific* righteous person, not an unspecific and innocent poor person. Yet, that is exactly what we were expecting. In the past six verses, James has been talking to the rich. They love their money. They fraudulently withheld wages from their workers in order to indulge in luxury. We have no hint of the poor ever being the subject of this passage. It has always been about the rich. And with a jolting end to his diatribe, James turns his attention from the rich people to the righteous person—the person of Christ.

This is quite consistent with the flow of context. In fact, it serves as a wonderful bookend to greater point found back in same verse in the prior chapter, "God oppose the proud, but gives grace to the humble" (Ja. 4:6). Do you wonder how I put that together? In the original Greek, there were no punctuations in the text to distinguish a question from an answer. So this final part of the verse translated in most English Bibles as, "He does not resist you," reads better as a question, "Does he not resist you?" This type of rhetorical question is found over 10 times in the book of James. It is certainly consistent with his writing style and context. Think about it. James says that God opposes (or resists) those who are prideful. Then, he proves how they are full of pride. In all of this he is warning them, and so he ends with the question, "Does God not oppose you?" In other words, "Are you serious? Do you really think that God does not oppose you?"

> **Do you really think God does not oppose you?**

The Bible teaches that God is perfect, "for all his ways are justice" and "just and upright is he" (Deut. 32:4). "For the Lord is righteous; he loves righteous deeds" (Ps. 11:7). God is also called a just judge (Jer. 12:1; Ps. 7:12). He always acts justly (Gen. 18:25; Judg. 5:11; Ps. 145:17). He punishes and rewards with justice (Ps. 62:12). And, Jeremiah prophesied of Jesus, saying:

> "Behold, the days are coming, declares the LORD, when I will raise up for David a righteous Branch, and he shall reign as king and deal wisely, and shall execute justice and righteousness in the land. In his days Judah

will be saved, and Israel will dwell securely. And this is the name by which he will be called: 'The LORD is our righteousness.'"(Jeremiah 23:5-6)

Jesus was falsely accused, tried, and condemned to die on the cross by a conspiracy devised and executed by the rich Roman authorities and the aristocratic priesthood of Israel. He was by many standards a "poor" person who was condemned and murdered, quite literally. He is also said to be the caring and loving savior of the poor (Ja. 2:4). So when the poor are wrongfully condemned and put to death, Jesus is offended, and, therefore, God is offended.

By this, we can safely close James' thought—God opposes the proud. The rich who are proud with their lofty and luxurious living and are opposed and resisted by God. This is true when they condemn and murder the innocent and particularly true when they condemn and murder the righteous—the Lord and His people. Ask yourself, will God not resist them?

If this is accurate—and I think it is—then Jesus, who is the supreme righteous person, is the one who resists the ruthless rich by turning their wealth against them and unleashing His wealth of wrath upon them. And Jesus does so for the sake of His glory and the love for His righteous people. "For as by the one man's disobedience the many were made sinners, so by the one man's obedience the many will be made righteous" (Rom. 5:19). So it is taught in Scripture that "The righteous shall live by faith" (Rom. 1:17), that is, faith in Christ. Categorically speaking then, "the righteous person" is primarily Jesus and secondarily the Church, in a lesser sense.

The rich, when they sin with their useless hoarding, fraudulent gaining, luxurious living and unjust condemning, are setting themselves up against God as His enemy (Ja. 4:4). God opposes these people because they are worldly and opposers of everything that God loves. Does God not resist them? Does God not oppose them? Of course He does. And one day, they will feel the justly opposition of God at the coming of the Lord.

On the other hand, the Lord's coming will be a wonderful event for those who exercised kindness to the poor (Eph. 2:7). Jesus taught that goodness and generosity marks the "sons of the Most High, for he is kind," even to those who are evil, much more to those who are not (Lk. 6:35). Therefore, Paul commanded, "Be kind to one another, tenderhearted, forgiving one another, as God in Christ forgave you" (Eph. 4:32). It should characterize us since it characterizes the Spirit within us (Gal. 5:22). Like a robe, it should clothe us (Col. 3:12). True faith is kind.

Conclusion

Having great wealth makes living a godly life quite challenging, especially since rich people undergo trials that others do not; however, we are all subject to the same temptations. We are all capable of being seduced by materialism. We can hoard wealth, cheat others, and seek to live a life spent indulging our every whim.

James has taught us that believers who demonstrate true faith are generous with treasures, honest in acquiring them, restrained in spending, and provide for those in need. Let us close this lesson by meditating on the wise words Paul wrote to Timothy:

> "As for the rich in this present age, charge them not to be haughty, nor to set their hopes on the uncertainty of riches, but on God, who richly provides us with everything to enjoy. They are to do good, to be rich in good works, to be generous and ready to share, thus storing up treasure for themselves as a good foundation for the future, so that they may take hold of that which is truly life." (1 Timothy 6:17-19)

CHAPTER 10

THE TRIAL OF SUFFERING

JAMES 5:1-6

"you have laid up treasure in the last day"

In the prior chapter, James rebuked the rich for oppressing the poor. The poor were suffering under the merciless hands of the rich, who were craftily using the court systems to take away what little the poor had. This cycle of injustice led to more and more suffering for the poor, who were practically defenseless against the rich. Thus, the poor were being conquered again and again.

Although not everyone faces this specific type of injustice, all people suffer. This is a reality of life that we all face. Job said that as sure as sparks fly upward, "man is born for trouble" (Job 5:7). Jesus guaranteed that "in the world you will have tribulation" (Jn. 16:33). This is true for believers and nonbelievers. However, there are certain troubles that are stored up just for Christians (Acts 14:22; 2 Tim. 1:8; 3:12).

Suffering is a trial. It can lead to various temptations. As James points out, in response to a trial, true faith will be patient, cheerful, steadfast, and reliable.

> Be patient, therefore, brothers, until the coming of the Lord. See how the farmer waits for the precious fruit of the earth, being patient about it, until it receives the early and the late rains. You also, be patient. Establish your hearts, for the coming of the Lord is at hand. Do not grumble against one another, brothers, so that you may not be judged; behold, the Judge is standing at the door. As an example of suffering and patience, brothers, take the prophets who spoke in the

name of the Lord. Behold, we consider those blessed who remained steadfast. You have heard of the steadfastness of Job, and you have seen the purpose of the Lord, how the Lord is compassionate and merciful.

But above all, my brothers, do not swear, either by heaven or by earth or by any other oath, but let your "yes" be yes and your "no" be no, so that you may not fall under condemnation. (James 5:7-12)

True Faith is Patient

After visiting James, Paul found himself in a quandary. Some Jews, burning with hatred of his preaching, stirred the locals against him. It got so bad that the Roman commander, called a tribune, intervened. The uproar made it impossible for him to make sense of things, so he had Paul thrown into the barracks (Acts 21:27-37; 22:24). The next day, the tribune attempted to get to the bottom of this. He brought Paul and the accusing Jews together (Acts 22:30). Standing before them, Paul said, "Brothers, I have lived my life before God in all good conscience up to this day." Ananias, who unbeknownst to Paul was the high priest, ordered those next to Paul to strike him on the mouth. I imagine that Paul surged with anger and frustration as he exclaimed in response, "God is going to strike you, you whitewashed wall! Are you sitting to judge me according to the law, and yet contrary to the law you order me to be struck?" As quickly as he exploded, those who raised their hands to strike him said, "Would you revile God's high priest?" Immediately, Paul simmered back down, his anger now regret. He gently replied, "I did not know, brothers, that he was the high priest, for it is written, 'You shall not speak evil of a ruler of your people'" (Acts 23:1-5).

I am hesitant to say this, especially when I consider all of the suffering that Paul endured in the name of the Lord, but Paul was out of place. He grew impatient with the Jewish leaders. They were sinful. There is no doubt about that. But they were still his leaders. This was especially true of the one who commanded Paul to be beaten. Paul's frustration must have been accumulating for quite some time. He was always facing the opposition of the Jewish priests and councils. They were indeed stiff-necked and proud, and were the cause of significant suffering for Paul; however, the apostle was supposed to be patient in order to honor God. He failed the test. His frustrations got the best of him. Yet, serving as a wonderful example, he immediately repented.

If we were to compare ourselves with Paul, what would we say about our attitude during suffering? I would venture to say that many of us would do as Paul, only we would do it more often and with greater fervor. There have been times in my life when this was true of me. In fact, I have gone so far as to snap at God a time or two—to His entertainment, I'm sure!

Suffering Is Necessary for Christians

"Severe trouble in a true believer has the effect of loosening the roots of his soul earthward and tightening the anchor-hold of his heart heavenward." Oh, how I wish I had written that. Those are the words of Charles Spurgeon from a sermon on suffering.[1] He was pointing out the benefits of affliction. Yes, the benefits. You read me right.

Remember that James started off on this leg. "Count it all joy, my brothers, when you meet trials of various kinds" (Ja. 1:2). We can count it joy because of the benefits that God produces through them. Now, reaching the conclusion of his letter, James in many ways has circled back to the beginning. But this time, he has a load of teachings that he is reeling in. It is like fishing, I guess. You tie a lure to the end of a wire and toss it into the water. A short time later, you reel it back in to find it much heavier and bulkier as if it had grown underwater. Scooping it up with a net and dropping it into the boat, you find a large fish. Or, as I often find in my case, a bunch of semi-decomposed trash bags and six-pack holders all tangled together. Whatever the case, the metaphor is this: James cast the hook into the water (cf. Ja. 1:2) and has been reeling back ever since 1:18, "Of [God's] own will he brought us forth by the word of truth, that we should be a kind of firstfruits of his creatures." Where true faith exists, steadfastness will manifest itself, and the reward will be the promised "crown of life" (Ja. 1:12). James is reeling in with even more truth. No decomposed trash here.

Spurgeon added, "Affliction frequently opens truths to us, and opens us to the truth."[2] Martin Luther agreed. He said:

"For as soon as God's Word becomes known through you, the devil will

---

[1] Spurgeon, Charles H. "For the Troubled." *Classic Sermons on Suffering.* Comp. Warren W. Wiersbe. Peabody, MA: Hendrickson, 1984. 56. Print.
[2] Ibid., 57.

afflict you, will make a real doctor [teacher of doctrine] of you, and will teach you by his temptations to seek and to love God's Word. For I myself ... owe my papists [Roman Catholic adversaries] many thanks for so beating, pressing, and frightening me through the devil's raging, that they have turned me into a fairly good theologian, driving me to a goal I should never have reached."[3]

Having read up to this chapter, I trust that you are acquainted with this idea: troubles build Christian character. It is simple to say; however, it is not so simple to comprehend at times, especially when you are the one enduring the troubles. Fire is a purifying agent used in many different industrial plants. But no one ever wants to be burned by it. Carrying this point further, author and pastor R.C. Sproul wrote:

> "Suffering is a crucible. As gold is refined in the fire, purged of its dross and impurities, so our faith is tested by fire. Gold perishes. Our souls do not. We experience pain and grief for a season. It is while we are in the fire that perplexity assails us. But there is another side to the fire. As the dross burns away, the genuineness of faith is purified unto the salvation of our souls."[4]

Sproul wonderfully captured the two reasons for this book: troubles purify the soul and reveal the true nature of faith. For those who, having divine faith, are genuinely saved, suffering can be a delight even while it tastes so very sour. "It is good for me that I was afflicted, that I might learn your statutes," says the psalmist (Ps. 119:71). And again, "Before I was afflicted I went astray, but now I keep your word" (Ps. 119:67). Paul, a man of great suffering, wrote:

> "Indeed, I count everything as loss because of the surpassing worth of knowing Christ Jesus my Lord. For his sake I have suffered the loss of all things and count them as rubbish, in order that I may gain Christ and be found in him, not having a righteousness of my own that comes from the law, but that which comes through faith in Christ, the righteousness from God that depends on faith—that I may know him and the power of his resurrection, and may share his sufferings, becoming like him in his death, that by any means possible I may attain the resurrection from the

---

[3] Quoted in Ewald M. Pass, comp., *What Luther Says: An Anthology in Three Volumes* (St. Louis: Concordia Publishing House, 1959), 3:1360.

[4] Sproul, R. C. *Surprised by Suffering: The Role of Pain and Death in the Christian Life.* Lake Mary, FL: Reformation Trust Pub., 2009. 7. Print.

dead" (Phil. 3:9-11).

The rewards of being purified and assured of our salvation can only be defeated by the more blessed reward of embracing our Lord Jesus in heaven. And with such great reward, it is no surprise that James brings us here. Trials without hope are soul shattering and lead to despair. But, for the Christian, trials are *never* without hope.

The Command of the Christian

In the recent passages, James took a sharp turn in his delivery. You might remember his letter having somewhat of a gentle, brotherly tone. This is because he was brimming with the word *adelphos* which means, brother. He referred to his readers this way at least eleven times before switching the tone in James 4. Then, he abruptly shifted to words like "adulterous people" and "enemy of God," including also a touch of "be wretched and mourn and weep" and "humble yourselves" (Ja. 4:4, 9). But, to the blessing of the reader, he has now returned to his earlier, more gentle side. In four of these six verses, he employs "brother" again. Maybe he is making up for the loss!

"**Be patient**" (Ja. 5:7). The command could not be more clear. When we are suffering, we ought to be patient. The word in the Greek is *makrothumeo*. You might identify the small English word "macro" in the original text. We use it to mean large. The second half of the word means "anger" or "temper." And, since the Greek mind thought in terms of length rather than size, it would be understood as "long-angered" or even better, "long-tempered." Though this is not a term we widely use today, it is easily understood since we are well acquainted with someone who is short-tempered. People who have a short temper are people who easily and often fly off the handle. They have a "short fuse" you might say. James, on the other hand, tells us to have a long fuse. It will burn and burn and never blow.

> **For the Christians, trials are *never* without hope.**

This is one of the characteristics found in the famous love chapter (1 Cor. 13:4). Obviously then, it is a characteristic of God. Peter wrote, "The Lord is not slow to fulfill his promise as some count slowness, but is patient toward you, not wishing that any should perish, but that all should reach repentance" (2 Pet. 3:9). If a holy God can be patient with unholy people, then we unholy people can be patient with one another too.

Paul wrote to the Philippians about this. He told them to stand firm in the gospel and not be frightened by those who opposed them. He said that patience "is a clear sign to them of their destruction, but of your salvation, and that from God. For it has been granted to you that for the sake of Christ you should not only believe in him but also suffer for his sake" (Phil. 1:28-30). Long-suffering, then, is a sign to the oppressors of God's power and their coming judgment. It is also a clear evidence that you have genuine faith. The key here is patience. Suffering without patience proves nothing good or beneficial. John Calvin comments on this passage by saying, "For persecutions are in a manner seals of adoption to the children of God, if they endure them with fortitude and patience: the wicked give a token of their condemnation, because they stumble against a stone by which they shall be bruised to pieces."[5]

For this reason, patience becomes all the more easy (though it still is difficult). This is especially true when we bank on the fact that there is a coming end to the suffering. It will not last forever. God's promise, as Peter just related, will not go unfulfilled (2 Pet. 3:9). "Vengeance is mind, and recompense, for the time when their foot shall slip; for the day of their calamity is at hand, and their doom comes swiftly" (Deut. 32:35). The promise that all things will be made right is a promise for "everyone whom the Lord our God calls to himself" (Acts 2:39). When we manifest long-tempers, as James says, we assure ourselves that God has called us to Himself.

> **The suffering we face now is only momentary.**

The Coming of the Lord

Having a long fuse like our Lord is anything but easy. However, we do have some motivation. The first is that the Lord will fulfill His promise to judge. Peter again encourages us, "The end of all things is at hand; therefore be self-controlled and sober-minded" (1 Pet. 4:7). In other words, the suffering we face now is only momentary. It will soon end. We are never told to be patient forever, but **"until the coming of the**

---

[5] Calvin, John. "Epistle to Philippians." *Calvin's Commentaries*. Vol. XXI. Grand Rapids: Baker, 2005. 49. Print.

Lord" (Ja. 5:7). There will be a time when patience is not needed since suffering will cease—at least for the children of the Lord. When He so pleases, God will avenge the affliction committed against His people.

For this reason, the coming of the Lord is an important concept. Without it, we have little for which to hope. This might be why James references it at least three times in these six verses. The Lord's coming is also often cited throughout the New Testament—another reason to believe its importance. For example, Jesus spoke about His future coming. While warning the disciples about their imminent persecution, "some of you they will put to death," He encourages them to be long-suffering, "By your endurance you will gain your lives" (Lk. 21:16-17). Why? Because "they will see the Son of Man coming in a cloud." Therefore, they should "straighten up and raise your heads, because your redemption is drawing near" (Lk. 21:27-28). The coming of the Lord is our salvation from the sinful suffering we face here on Earth.

After the gospels, we find more references to the coming of the Lord. For instance, Paul instructed the Thessalonians to "establish your hearts blameless in holiness before our God and Father, at the coming of our Lord Jesus" (1 Thess. 3:13) which is consistent with James 5:8. Again Paul writes, "May your whole spirit and soul and body be kept blameless at the coming of our Lord Jesus Christ" (1 Thess. 5:23). Peter taught this as well, only he referred to it as the last time: "According to his great mercy, he has caused us to be born again to a living hope through the resurrection of Jesus Christ from the dead, to an inheritance that is imperishable, undefiled, and unfading, kept in heaven for you, who by God's power are being guarded through faith for a salvation ready to be revealed in the last time" (1 Pet. 1:3-5). John echoed, "And now, little children, abide in him, so that when he appears we may have confidence and not shrink from him in shame at his coming" (1 Jn. 2:28).

> **The righteous will suffer now but will enjoy the eternal reward of Christ later.**

This is just a few of the many references to the future coming of the Lord. Although it implies many things to our lives today, two things consistently stand above the rest. First, the righteous will suffer now but will enjoy the eternal rewards of Christ later. Second, the righteous must "be patient," as James says, so that the coming does not shame us in our impatience. We must not be as Adam and Eve after their fall into temptation when they hid from the Lord who walked through the Garden. The day will come when the Lord will again walk through the garden called Earth, and we must be ready and upright.

We must be long-suffering as Jesus was long-suffering. "When he was reviled, he did not revile in return; when he suffered, he did not threaten, but continued entrusting himself to him who judges justly" (1 Pet. 2:23). How much more are we to do this since we deserve much more suffering than we receive? This is the perspective we should have. As Christ suffered for us, we must not waiver in our faith as we too suffer. "But rejoice insofar as you share Christ's sufferings, that you may also rejoice and be glad when his glory is revealed" (1 Pet. 4:13).

Eternity is our reward, and nothing compares to it. The reality of Christ's coming again brings the genuine believer hope and joy in this age even—no especially—during affliction. Paul said, "For I consider that the sufferings of this present time are not worth comparing with the glory that is to be revealed to us" (Rom. 8:18). He could say this confidently because he knew that "this light momentary affliction is preparing for us an eternal weight of glory beyond all comparison" (2 Cor. 4:17). The affliction is not just momentary, it is full of purpose. God uses it to prepare us for His coming in order that we will not be shamed. John said it this way, "And everyone who thus hopes in him purifies himself as he is pure" (1 Jn. 3:3). Knowing that the Lord will return brings us hope and motivates us to purify our hearts and lives just as Jesus is pure.

The Case of the Farmer

The patience that James speaks about is like a farmer. **"See how the farmer waits for the precious fruit of the earth, being patient about it, until it receives the early and the late rains"** (Ja. 5:7). Remember being a child in the backseat on your way to Grandma's? "Mom, are we there yet?" And five minutes later, "Mom, are we there yet?" Continuing until one hour has past, "Mom, will we ever get there?" The trip to Grandma's house was always the same length. You knew when you were there. You would see the house and the dogs. The car would stop, and the doors would open. You were never there when you asked, "Mom, are we there yet?"

It is kind of like that. The farmer knows when the time is right to harvest the crops. But, he has to wait through the months of rain. In the ancient Middle East, rain would typically fall heavily during October (referred to as "early rains") and February (referred to as "late rains") and periodically in between. During these seasons, he would have to wait patiently. If he didn't, he would spoil the crops.

We once had a plant growing in a small pot at our house. It was an activity for the kids. The seeds would be buried in the thick, dark dirt, and the pot was placed on the windowsill for sufficient sunlight. The kids would water it each morning. And we all waited patiently for it to sprout and grow. The kids, however, grew quite impatient. A few days had passed, and they were wondering about the delay. I'm sure they thought in their small minds, "Are we there yet?" They knew very well that it was not time. But their patience wore thin. One of the children, decided that she would speed the process ahead. So she dug her little fingers into the pot and pulled up the tiny plant that had already taken root below. You could hear the tearing of the fragile roots as she brought it up to see. The plant died, and it would never be able to grow again.

> **Be steadfast as God works in the dirt.**

The farmer knows that if he does not endure, his hard work will be jeopardized. Much like the little plant in the hands of my daughter, his reward will be lost, and his time will be wasted. The fruit of his labor requires time to mature and time to grow. So he must be steadfast and long-suffering while God works. **"You also, be patient"** (Ja. 5:8). James tells us to be like the farmer. We must be steadfast as God works in the dirt, so to speak. We should not rush the work and kill the seed or the sprout. God is using our suffering to mature our hearts and purify our deeds. If we are patient, we will enjoy the wondrous bounty that He promises He will give to those who endure.

The Closeness of the Judge

In a previous verse, James told the rich, "You have fattened your hearts in a day of slaughter" (Ja. 5:5). However, he says to the afflicted, **"Establish your hearts, for the coming of the Lord is at hand"** (Ja. 5:8). While the rich can be tempted by the luxury that their money can buy, the poor can be tempted by the vengeance that their anger can excite. For this reason, those who are suffering should establish their hearts. This is a command to make the heart firmly fixed, stable and consistent, not double-minded and unstable in its ways (Ja. 1:7-8).

Consider again the text that introduced the thrust of James' epistle, "Count it all joy, my brothers, when you meet trials of various kinds, for you know that the testing of your faith produces steadfastness. And let steadfastness have its full effect, that you may be perfect and complete, lacking in nothing" (Ja. 1:2-4). Firmly fixing your heart so that it is steadfast during trials is the key. Patience, produced by a stable heart, makes you perfect and complete. It prepares you for the coming of the Lord, which James says, is near.

In the next verse, James describes the coming of the Lord as being so close that He "is standing at the door" (a vivid picture that we will explore more in a moment). At this point, however, the Lord's coming is "at hand," nearer than you might think. As we discovered already, those who are patient now will take pleasure in a time of joy and rest when the Lord comes. His return will be to us like it is to those who are rescued from a long period of tragedy, though in a much deeper and lasting sense. Think of it as the beginning of an everlasting sigh of relief.

> **Patience, produced by a stable heart, makes you perfect and complete.**

True faith longs for this rest, and hopes that it will soon find it. However, it is patient and determined not to reach down into the dirt and uproot the work that God is doing. The Holy Spirit, working in us, knows the end of our suffering and what our hearts will be like when maturity is achieved. Therefore, He works through our suffering with steadfast faith. We, too, should be confident that the Lord will soon come and our salvation will be realized. "Let us not grow weary of doing good, for in due season we will reap, if we do not give up" (Gal. 6:9).

True Faith is Cheerful

After the resurrection, the disciples were walking with Christ along the shore. Jesus had just asked Peter three times about his holy affections. And, being almost casual about it, he told Peter some of the most shocking news that anyone could hear. "When you were young, you used to dress yourself and walk wherever you wanted, but when you are old, you will stretch out your hands, and another will dress you and carry you where you do not want to go." According to the gospels, this was a reference to the kind of death that awaited him (Jn. 21:18-19). Likely stunned by this news, Peter saw John and asked Jesus, "Lord, what about this man? Will he have it bad, too?" (paraphrasing).

Many times when we suffer, we become acutely aware of those around us who are not suffering. The opportunities to compare our lot with others are endless. After all, it is hard not to notice the friend who is doing amazingly well, the co-worker who is enjoying great success, or the fellow believer who is rejoicing in an awesome blessing. When we find ourselves tempted to compare our circumstances with others, most likely we are enduring a test of our cheerfulness. The tendency of our sinful heart, however, is to take no cheer in the wellness of others, especially when we are suffering.

The Christian Is Patient

The trial of suffering can be testing in many ways. One way is in the manner by which we respond to others who are not suffering. Experiencing distress or a misery of some kind can tempt us to resent those who are doing well. I remember a time when I was tested with this. And, to my shame, I failed it repeatedly before I learned. My father taught me that a good man is a hard-working man. And since I got married, I have been working as hard as I can—often two jobs for long periods of time. For some reason, however, my wife and I suffered numerous seasons whereby we could not afford to pay our monthly bills. I observed that friends and family, many of whom worked less than I did, seemed to be safely making it from month to month with money left over—buying new cars, upgrading houses, getting fancy televisions and more. Instead of being cheerful for their blessedness, I grew resentful and envious. I would come home from my second job, sweaty and tired, and find others hanging out, full on dinner, enjoying a movie or game, laughing it up like life had no worries. Though my face smiled, my heart grumbled. (So did my stomach.)

This is the idea that James has in mind when he says, **"Do not grumble against one another, brothers"** (Ja. 5:9). Why? Because the

Christian is patient for his own and cheerful for those who are doing well. In the direct context, James is speaking to the poor who are suffering the affliction of the rich who drag them into court, condemn and murder them (Ja. 2:6; 5:6). The afflicted can easily be tempted to grumble against each other, their leadership, their governing authorities, and more. Grumbling, or *stenazo* in the Greek, is a little different than what you might think. When I first read the passage, I thought back to the wanderings of the Israelites in the wilderness. Though God had been gracious to free them from slavery, had promised to lead them to a better land, had fed them while they were traveling, had miraculously demonstrated His power, and had trained them in the way of the Lord, they murmured and grumbled at almost every turn. This is what I think about when I see the word "grumble," and it might imply that in a broad sense.

Most translations use the word "complain" here. But, that is not entirely accurate either. The idea behind *stenazo* is an inner groan. Paul used it in Romans 8:23 to describe the expression of discomfort while Christians wait for their new heavenly, incorruptible bodies. In the prior verse, he says that "the whole creation has been groaning together in the pains of childbirth until now," longing for the day when Christ makes things new (Rom. 8:22). Groaning internally is not necessarily evil. However, when it is against another person, it most certainly is. When commenting on this passage, John Calvin wrote, "We may, indeed, groan, when any evil torments us; but [James] means an accusing groan, when one expostulates with the Lord against another."[6]

We should think of grumbling, at least in this context, as the sinful disdain that one expresses inwardly. It is what takes place before the mouth, or even the body, expresses it outwardly. Here, it refers to an internal voicing of disdain for those having a lesser degree of affliction or none at all. Basically, before the chairs are thrown, the heart is thrown—not in an outburst of anger, but in an inner hatred against someone else. And notice the deeper framework, we should not grumble **"against one another,"** making a reference to the family of faith. In other words, "You, who are having it bad now, do not have disdain for those who are not having it as bad as you." This is essentially what James is saying.

---

[6] Calvin, John. "Epistle of James." *Calvin's Commentaries*. Vol. XXII. Grand Rapids: Baker, 2005. 345. Print.

It requires a sense of envy. One who grumbles against another is inwardly expressing his resentment for another because he has it better. Does this sound familiar? It should. Earlier, James asked, "What causes quarrels and what causes fights among you? Is it not this, that your passions are at war within you? You desire and do not have ... You covet" (Ja. 4:1-2). Even the poor can be quarrelsome. This is because quarrels begin with grumbling.

To take it a step further, grumbling is judgmental. "The one who speaks against his brother or judges his brother, speaks evil against the law and judges the law," (Ja. 4:11). So, "do not speak evil against one another, brothers" (Ja. 4:10). Looking further back in James' epistle, he says that earthly wisdom is full of "jealousy and selfish ambition" which characterizes grumbling (Ja. 3:16). Again, "have you not then made distinctions among yourselves and become judges with evil thoughts?" which too characterizes grumbling (Ja. 2:4). Finally, "let every person be quick to hear, slow to speak, slow to anger" (Ja. 1:19). There are traces of grumbling throughout the letter. This is because grumbling is insensitive to others and self-seeking—the very thing that James is revealing as sin. It is envious, ungrateful, unthoughtful, discontent, hateful, insubordinate, and worthy of facing the Holy Judge.

Quarrels begin with grumbling.

The Judge Is Ready

Everyone knows what happens when the teacher leaves the classroom. It is almost inevitable. The sound of the wooden door softly hitting the frame was like the sound of a bullhorn starting a drag race. Students pick up their inter-period conversations as if they had just ended. Paper is thrown from one side to the other. Pencils are strategically tossed upward but not returning. Cell phones are out. Headphones are on. And yes, maybe there is that one kid stupid enough to jump from desk to desk for kicks and giggles. Why all the ruckus? Because the teacher is gone.

We do the same each day. Do we not? We convince ourselves that no one in authority can see us, so we get all mischievous. We break the rules. We behave badly. "The Lord isn't watching," we say to ourselves. But this is not so. In a sense, God never left the classroom. In another sense, He has left but will soon be returning. James says that not only is the Lord coming (Ja. 5:7), but He is near and is ready to judge.

Earlier we looked at the coming of the Lord and how his coming is the hope of believers especially those in serious affliction. We are motivated to be patient during suffering because the Lord is coming soon, and he will make things right. We touched on one aspect of His return, that it will be a time of joyous reunion and glorification; however, there is another aspect of the second coming of Christ that provides for us another motivation to be patient. It is the negative side of His return. James says, "Be patient … Do not grumble against one another, brothers, **so that you may not be judged**" (Ja. 5:9). On one hand, the return of Christ is good news. On the other hand, the return of Christ is bad news. James is using it in both ways so he can motivate us to be patient. Those who are not patient will be judged. Those who are patient will be rewarded.

In one of Mark's descriptions of the second coming, he records Jesus as saying that He "will send out the angels and gather his elect from the four winds, from the ends of the earth to the ends of heaven" (Mk. 13:26-27). It is clear that those with genuine faith will be gathered to the Lord. The unbelievers, on the other hand, will hear Jesus say "Depart from me, you cursed, into the eternal fire prepared for the devil and his angels." When Jesus returns to judge, the unrighteous "will go away into eternal punishment, but the righteous into eternal life" (Matt. 25:41, 46).

If that does not motivate you to stop grumbling and be patient, then what if we said that the Lord was right outside the door about to enter? This is what James says, **"Behold, the Judge is standing at the door"** (Ja. 5:9). Apparently, there were judgment halls during those times like we have today. The judgment hall would be a large room with doors through which the presiding judge would enter. When he entered, the court was in session. James uses this illustration to show how near the coming of the Lord is. This passage makes me think of an old western movie where the town tough guy stands at the doors that swing both ways. A hush comes over the crowd inside, and the doors swing open. I imagine that James had something similar in mind—minus the cowboy boots and whiskey. The Lord is at the *thupa*, gate or entrance. It suggests a sense of nearness that motivates one to be alert and ready. When He comes again, He "will bring to light the things now hidden in darkness and will disclose the purpose of the heart" (1 Cor. 4:5).

When the teacher returns, you do not want to be caught misbehaving. Think of how different the classroom would be if the students knew that the teacher was before the door ready to swing it wide open! May I suggest that there would be less pencils on the ceiling, less trash on the floor, less chatter and more undivided attentiveness. Of course there would be! No one likes to be judged. No one enjoys discipline. This is why we break the rules behind closed doors. We do not want to get caught. We understand the authority of leaders. We know that they can and should correct and chastise us. How much more authority and justice does the Lord have than His fallible creatures!

When Jesus returns, do you want to be caught grumbling against your brothers and lose your reward? Or do you want Him to see how you have waited patiently in your suffering knowing that He will fulfill His promise to you? If you have been given the divine faith that saves, then you desire to be patient and you long for the coming of the Lord in order to be rewarded with His embrace. True faith will burst with cheer when it recognizes God's blessing in others, even when such blessings are not currently with us. We can be cheerful because we know that suffering is temporal and that God is using it for our good. We can also be confident in seeing God's patience work through and in us, making us a more like Him and more pleasing in His sight. Take cheer in seeing God bless others and knowing God will bless you in His timing.

True Faith is Steadfast

Acts records a brief story about a man named Stephen who preached with great wisdom in the power of the Holy Spirit. His story is brief because as soon as he arrives in the annals of the Bible he is killed. Conspirators ended his preaching by rallying up false witnesses until the high priest had to step in and interrogate. Chapter 7 records his response over some 50 verses (the longest discourse in all of Acts) as a historical survey of the Old Testament. You get a sense that he is about tie it all together with a wonderful gospel presentation when, suddenly, he turns it all around in a gigantic rebuke to the Jewish leaders who disobeyed God by rejecting His appointed leaders. I mean, the transition is so abrupt that it makes his scolding all the more shocking.

> "You stiff-necked people, uncircumcised in heart and ears, you always resist the Holy Spirit. As your fathers did, so do you. Which of the prophets did your fathers not persecute? And they killed those who announced beforehand the coming of the Righteous One, whom you have now betrayed and murdered, you who received the law as delivered by angels and did not keep it" (Acts 7:51-53).

On that note, Stephen was violently and swiftly killed. Thereby validating his accusation, I might add. Years before Stephen was delivered from his sin, Jesus cried out similar words, "O Jerusalem, Jerusalem, the city that kills the prophets and stones those who are sent to it!" (Matt. 23:37).

The history of God's prophets is one of great tragedy. This is not to mean that their lives or messages were meaningless or that they did not wonderfully serve the Lord's purpose. Quite the contrary. In light of God's sovereign will, these men are most honorable and worthy to be called heroes as we so often do. What is tragic is that they were sent to give God's message to God's people, but were rejected and persecuted instead. This is terribly tragic. Still, in a way that only God can do, good will come from their persecution.

> **The prophets were the model of long-suffering.**

James leans back into the Old Testament and draws our attention to the patience of the prophets amidst their terrible persecution. If you are keeping count, this will be the third motivation for us to be patient. **"As an example of suffering and patience, brothers, take the prophets who spoke in the name of the Lord"** (Ja. 5:10). The prophets were the model of long-suffering. We should do as they did. We should follow their pattern.

The Example of the Prophets

Before we touch on some examples, let us first consider what James might have meant by describing the prophets as those **"who spoke in the name of the Lord"** (Ja. 5:10). I found this additive a bit strange since the audience was already submerged in the history and teachings of the prophets. What might James have meant by appending this obvious remark?

I think we leap to unnecessary conclusions if we believe James was teaching them something they already would have known. Remember, the Jews of his day were groomed in the Hebraic history. Granted, they might not have been minding the prophets as an example of suffering at this moment—but they did not need a lesson. They needed only to be reminded. I think James wanted to bring their memories of the prophets to the table to help build his point. He was not wasting papyrus. The prophets were foundational for many things, one of which was godly examples.

It is important to know that when you look to the prophets as examples of suffering and patience, you look through the lens of their significance and uniqueness. Only then will their examples strengthen and motivate our hearts. He was, in a sense, elevating the tragedy of the suffering prophets. For example, we all know it is wrong to steal from a person. But to steal from a *homeless* person, that is *terribly* wrong. In the same way, it is evil to persecute a person—but even worse to persecute a holy person. The prophets were those who spoke for God and who communicated God's message to God's people. If you cut the messenger off, you cut off the One who sent the message. These men carried the words of life. They had the most important treasure that man can receive from God—His Word. No one who ever lived, except the incarnate Word Himself, ever carried such a gracious gift. The prophets were the last people who deserved hardship and the first people who deserved honor. However, they were the first ones to be dishonored, rejected and killed, and the last ones who deserved it. They suffered affliction and were patient through it all. Today, they are doubly honorable. And with that in mind, let us briefly explore a few examples.

We might begin with Moses. He was born during a brutal era when the male Hebrew infants had been ordered by Pharaoh to be killed (Ex. 1:16, 22). By divine providence, Moses was saved, and he was reared by the Pharaoh's daughter. When the lad grew of age, he "refused to be called the son of Pharaoh's daughter, choosing rather to be mistreated with the people of God than to enjoy the fleeting pleasures of sin. He considered the reproach of Christ greater wealth than the treasures of

Egypt," according to the commentary in Hebrews 11:24-26. After that, Moses endured the ridicule and threats of the Egyptians. You know the story of the great Exodus. By God's command and power, Moses led the Hebrews out of slavery and toward the Promised Land. But he then suffered forty years of stiff-necked and rebellious people. Forty years! Yet, he was faithful and meek.

David had his share of suffering. Since God was going to make him king of Israel, the presiding king wanted him dead. "Saul took three thousand chosen men out of all Israel and went to seek David and his men" (1 Sam. 24:2). The king was hunting David (1 Sam. 24:11), but David remained faithful to God. When the opportunity arose for David to easily and quietly slay the king, he said that the Lord would avenge him instead (1 Sam. 24:12). This happened a second time and David decided to flee the country to be safe (1 Sam. 26-27). Through suffering, God trained him to be king. See if you can feel the agony in many of his songs. "My God, my God, why have you forsaken me? … I am poured out like water, and all my bones are out of joint … a company of evildoers encircles me … Deliver my soul from the sword" (Ps. 22:1, 14, 16, 20). David had an established heart. He was patient during his affliction.

The prophet Elijah was alive during the reign of King Ahab. Jezebel, the king's wife, was a tyrant who corrupted her husband and the nation by promoting pagan worship. When the prophets of God opposed her, she had them massacred (1 Kin. 18:4). Only a few survived by hiding. Elijah commanded the king to repent as God said, and things only got worse. The Lord proved Himself and had Elijah kill the pagan prophets (1 Kin. 18:4). Jezebel became even more furious. She swore to Elijah, "So may the gods do to me and more also, if I do not make your life as the life of one of them by this time tomorrow" (1 Kin. 19:2). Elijah ran for his life in fear (1 Kin. 19:3). Though he faced brutal enemies, he faithfully delivered God's words of judgment. He was indeed patient.

Jeremiah was called to be the suffering prophet, as many know him today. He was told to declare God's judgments against Jerusalem (Jer. 1:16) which will arouse them to anger (Jer. 1:19). So God tells him, "Do not be dismayed by them, lest I dismay you before them" (Jer. 1:9). In other words, "Suffer them, or you will suffer Me." However, obedience to the Lord meant that the Lord would watch over him. And so he did. Yet, for almost fifty years, Jeremiah preached an uncool message and was rejected, imprisoned, beaten and persecuted. He had few friends, if any, and no wife or children according to the command of God (Jer. 16:2). His relatives betrayed him (Jer. 12:6), his people wanted him dead (Jer. 11:19-23; 18:23; 38:4), he was excluded from the feasts (Jer. 16:8), he was one-upped by false preachers with positive sermons (Jer. 14:14; 23:16-34), he was accused of treason (Jer. 37:11-16), he was forbidden entrance to the temple (Jer. 36:5), and he was eventually stoned to death, as tradition tells us. Yet, through it all, Jeremiah remained patient and faithful to God. In his lamentations, he wrote, "Why should a living man complain, a man, about the punishment of his sin?" (Lam. 3:39). He was able to endure because he recognized himself to be a sinner deserving nothing anyway. So, Jeremiah was also patient in his suffering.

After that, I feel like there is nothing more to say. But, to the contrary, there is plenty more to say. Ezekiel suffered a great deal as well. One point of suffering might surprise you. God took the life of his wife for a sermon illustration. He wanted to show the people what he was going to do to them. Ezekiel, like those before him was patient and faithful to obey the Lord.

Then, if we can race through some others, there is Daniel. He was thrown into a lion's den to be eaten (Dan. 6). Hosea suffered a disastrous marriage to an adulterer as God commanded (Hos. 1-3). John the Baptist looked like an animal, lived in the woods, preached a hard message and was beheaded (Matt. 14:10). And, to help me summarize a few more, allow the writers of Hebrews to speak:

> "And what more shall I say? For time would fail me to tell of Gideon, Barak, Samson, Jephthah, of David and Samuel and the prophets—who through faith conquered kingdoms, enforced justice, obtained promises, stopped the mouths of lions, quenched the power of fire, escaped the edge of the sword, were made strong out of weakness, became mighty in war, put foreign armies to flight. Women received back their dead by resurrection. Some were tortured, refusing to accept release, so that they might rise again to a better life. Others suffered mocking and flogging, and even chains and imprisonment. They were stoned, they were sawn in two, they were killed with the sword. They went about in skins of sheep and goats, destitute, afflicted, mistreated—of whom the world was not

worthy—wandering about in deserts and mountains, and in dens and caves of the earth" (Heb. 11:32-38).

No, this world is not worthy of such men. It does not deserve them nor the message they carried. But God in His goodness gave them to us; gave His Word to us. And now, as we look back, God has allowed us to put skin and bones to the Word that He gives us. "Be patient," the Lord says through James. "Consider the patience of My chosen messengers. Even in their fatal affliction, they speak. Even now, they speak."

"Behold, we consider those blessed who remained steadfast" (Ja. 5:10). Indeed, we do, or we ought. Those who have gone before us, showing us what the joy of obedience to God looks like in life, are truly the ones we consider blessed. Again, to see how James is bringing his letter to summary, he uses the word *hypomeno* which means "to be steadfast." Earlier in his letter, he said, "Blessed is the man who remains steadfast under trials, for when he has stood the test he will receive the crown of life" (Ja. 1:12).

To reiterate a point more thoroughly written about in prior chapters, blessedness is chiefly understood in a spiritual sense to refer to a position in blissful eternity. The blessed person is one who finds his supreme satisfaction in God. He is a saved person, one with genuine faith. As Jesus taught:

> "Blessed are the poor in spirit, for theirs is the kingdom of heaven. Blessed are those who mourn, for they shall be comforted. Blessed are the meek, for they shall inherit the earth. Blessed are those who hunger and thirst for righteousness, for they shall be satisfied. Blessed are the merciful, for they shall receive mercy. Blessed are the pure in heart, for they shall see God. Blessed are the peacemakers, for they shall be called sons of God. Blessed are those who are persecuted for righteousness' sake, for theirs is the kingdom of heaven. Blessed are you when others revile you and persecute you and utter all kinds of evil against you falsely on my account. Rejoice and be glad, for your reward is great in heaven, for so they persecuted the prophets who were before you" (Matt. 5:3-11).

Patience during suffering is a hallmark characteristic of true faith. When you recognize it in your fellow believers, you can be confident that God is working within their hearts and minds. It is as Jesus said, a way to "recognize them by their fruits" (Matt. 7:20). And, if you are honest with yourself, steadfastness should be an encouragement that God is working within your heart and mind just the same.

The Example of Job

Of all the prophets who model patience and suffering for us, Job stands above them all. **"You have heard of the steadfastness of Job, and you have seen the purpose of the Lord, how the Lord is compassionate and merciful"** (Ja. 5:11).

Job was a righteous man. "He feared God and turned away from evil" (Job 1:1). Though not due to his upright life, he was also very wealthy. He had a large family, seven sons and three daughters, many servants and thousands of animals (Job 1:2-4). He was man of good heart and faith. He worshipped the Lord and believed that God would forgive him and his household of their sins.

Satan was convinced otherwise. So he set out to afflict Job in the most severe way. God granted him a limited space to toil the man and put him to the test. One day, a servant came running to Job crying out about a terrible calamity. He said that the Sabeans mercilessly slaughtered Job's servants, oxen and donkeys while they were eating. Mid-sentence, another servant runs in saying that the Chaldeans raided the camels and killed the servants there. Again, another servant arrives out of breath saying that all of Job's children were eating in a house when a great wind blew the walls over and crushed them to death. Bad news after bad news!

Job, emotionally torn, ripped his robe, shaved his head, fell to the ground, and worshipped. "Naked I came from my mother's womb, and naked shall I return. The Lord gave, and the Lord has taken away; blessed by the name of the Lord." What a sobering thing to hear! How crushing this must have been to Job, and yet he remained faithful and patient. He worshipped the Lord recognizing that God was the giver of good things and that all things are His to do with as He pleases. "In all this Job did not sin or charge God with wrong," the Bible says (Job 1:13-22).

Though this is almost too terrible to imagine, it was not the end. Job was struck "with loathsome sores from the sole of his foot to the crown of his head" so much that "he took a piece of broken pottery with which to scrape himself while he sat in the ashes." He was physically and emotionally full of grief. His posture was that of self-loathing and repentance (cf: Job 42:6). Then, his wife antagonized him saying, "Do you still hold fast your integrity? Curse God and die." And, for you who are married, you might understand how much more devastating this was to hear. His response to her was solid, "Shall we receive good from God, and shall we not receive evil?" Again, the Bible says that he did not sin with his lips (Job 2:1-10).

If you know the story, then you know that it is still not over. Job's friends lashed out with worldly wisdom, stupid advice, and unspiritual reasoning for days on end. Yet, Job kept his faith. "Though he slay me, I will hope in him" (Job 13:15). "And after my skin has been destroyed, yet in my flesh I shall see God" (Job 19:26). Job was patient because he was confident that the Lord had a purpose. He knew what would later be written by the Apostle Paul: "For those who love God all things work together for good, for those who are called according to his purpose" (Rom. 8:28). God had many purposes in the suffering of Job, one of which was to test his faith. Job's trials were tests designed to produce steadfastness, strengthen his faith, and assure his heart (Ja. 1:3-4). Steadfastness under trial leads to eternal life (Ja. 1:12). This is what James speaks about when he tells his audience to look at Job's suffering and patience and see **"the purpose of the Lord, how the Lord is compassionate and merciful"** (Ja. 5:11).

> **Steadfastness under trial leads to eternal life.**

Job was patient until the end. As James says, Job's steadfastness had its full effect, and he was "made perfect and complete, lacking in nothing" (Ja. 1:4). This was no exaggeration. The Lord replenished Job with all that he had before and more (Job 42:10). He lived to be an old man, "full of days," it says (Job 42:17). But nothing was worth more than the joy he received by seeing and knowing the Lord. "I had heard of you by the hearing of the ear, but now my eye sees you" (Job 42:5). Job's heart was satisfied with the goodness of knowing and having God. He delighted in all that God was, is and will be for all eternity. He tasted God's deep compassion and mercy, and his heart was full.

"Look to Job," James says. He was a model among models of suffering and patience. He exemplified true faith. He was faithful and full. He was steadfast and unwavering. He was patient. His heart was established. And in the end, he was blessed with unsurpassed joy. God will do the same to us if we do the same as Job. Whatever our trial, we must be steadfast if we are to receive the crown of life (Ja. 1:12). For God has promised it only to those who are steadfast. Therefore, true faith is steadfast.

True Faith is Reliable

If I may take a small detour to speak in a more academic style. James 5:12 can be a tricky verse to parse into discourse sections. And, I fear that if I don't explain why I interpret this passage the way I do, you might be confused. The verse reads, **"But above all, my brothers, do not swear, either by heaven or by earth or by any other oath, but let your 'yes' be yes and your 'no' be no, so that you may not fall under condemnation."** Some commentators say that this verse ends the section before it. Others argue that it initiates the section after it. A third school of thinkers hold the middle ground, pulling the verse out from its context and treating it like a short, stand-alone section. No surprise to you that I believe it to conclude the section before it since I am including it within this chapter. Whether the section began at James 5:7, as early as 4:11, 4:1, or even further back, is not my concern. We can start the "flow" of James' discourse whereever we will, but I believe it to end with James 5:12. While I may suffer your objection (pun intended), I am convinced nonetheless, and I trust that you will consider my reasoning and be open to see it valid. That is, unless you already have it right like I do!

Our immediate context is about true faith being expressed in patience during suffering. Intertwined like threads in a rope are teachings on governing your speech. For example, and these are ascending backward in the text, "the prophets who *spoke* in the name of the Lord" (Ja. 5:10), "do not *grumble*" (Ja. 5:9), "all such *boasting* is evil" (Ja. 4:16), "instead you ought to *say*" (Ja. 4:15), "come now, you who *say*" (Ja. 4:13), "do not *speak* evil" (Ja. 4:11), "you *ask* wrongly" (Ja. 4:3). Before that, James specifically taught about the dangers of the tongue and how we should tame it (Ja. 3:1-12). And briefly from the first two chapters of James, "What good is it, my brothers, if someone *says* he has faith" (Ja. 2:14) and "let every person be quick to hear, slow to *speak*" (Ja. 1:19). The topic of speech certainly threaded throughout the epistle and apparently snowballs toward the end, building momentum until we are finally taught to use our speech to be faithful in prayer (Ja. 5:13-18). Our speech is an important topic when considering the genuineness of our faith. As we touched on a few chapters back, the tongue utters the secrets of the heart. A pure heart will manifest in the purity of speech (Ja. 3:10). And this is exactly the point in James 5:12.

But some might object by pointing to the way the verse begins—namely, "but above all." One might argue that since the following instruction is on oaths, it should at least be disconnected from the prior discourse section. This objection is noted but not worthy of much consideration for several reasons. One is that James already identified the importance of obeying the royal law which single-handedly holds all other laws of God with it (Ja. 2:8-13). There is no higher law to obey, even Jesus taught that (Mk. 12:28-34). Therefore, I find it hard to believe that James is jumbling his words and confusing his point—especially since it is on speaking truthfully. He would condemn his own argument if this were true. Moreover, Peter uses the same language in 1 Peter 4:8 and no one thinks of it this way; none that I know at least. So then, it is quite safe to believe that "above all" does not require us to think in terms of the final passage being qualitatively higher than everything said before it.

Let us consider some of the reasons why it fits so well as a conclusion of the existing section, rather than an elevated pull quote. Suppose we started with James 3:1, and, this time, we moved forward with the text. First, we are instructed to watch our speech since we will be judged by what we say. Then, we are told to discipline the tongue and have pure speech (Ja. 3:1-12). Because we say what we believe, James tells us to be wise with heavenly wisdom so as not to speak wickedly. In specific, we are told that those who speak evil against another will be judged by God (Ja. 4:1-12). From there, James teaches us not to speak about things we cannot know and therefore sin with our tongue (Ja. 4:13-17). In addition, we are not to slander or falsely accuse our brothers (Ja. 5:1-6). When we suffer, we are not to grumble against our brother either (Ja. 5:7-11). Basically, we are to

Unholy speech brings condemnation on ourselves.

speak truthfully and be trustworthy with our speech. If we do not, we will condemn ourselves (Ja. 5:12). Notice that we are instructed not to condemn others with our words, and now we are told, by way of summary, that unholy speech brings condemnation on ourselves. This is not only fluid with the discourse of James, it also is a good closing to the warnings found in James 5:7-11 where he teaches us to not judge others since the Judge is coming (cf: 5:7, 8, and 9).

For these reasons and more, which we will unfold as we shuffle through the text, it might be worth translating *Pro panton de* (or, "But above all") to read, "Now in summary," at least for the sake of understanding the main instruction. "Above all" might make good sense after we have absorbed the text, so I'll leave that to your discretion. But be mindful that I continue with the belief that James 5:12 is a final summary of discourse and not a random spin-off of importance.

Reliability and Faith

There is a striking resemblance between James 5:12 and Matthew 5:34-47 in the Greek. In Matthew, we find Jesus teaching on oaths during what we call his Sermon on the Mount. It reads:

> "Again you have heard that it was said to those of old, 'You shall not swear falsely, but shall perform to the Lord what you have sworn.' But I say to you, Do not take an oath at all, either by heaven, for it is the throne of God, or by the earth, for it is his footstool, or by Jerusalem, for it is the city of the great King. And do not take an oath by your head, for you cannot make one hair white or black. Let what you say be simply 'Yes' or 'No'; anything more than this comes from evil" (Matt. 5:33-37).

The matter here is truth-telling. In our day, we find very little of it. In fact, we are so used to hearing one thing and having another. We put little stock in what many people say today. Politicians, businessmen, salesmen, lawyers, parents, friends and even preachers sometimes make promises that they rarely fulfill. Our modern media and entertainment confuse the truth by blending it with falsehoods and fantasy. Truth is so hard to find that most are suspicious it even exists. In fact, it is a quite normal today to cheat, exaggerate, and make promises that we have no intention of keeping, and generally go unchallenged. Somehow, however, we still value truth. We might bicker and gripe over it, but people generally put a premium on proven trust. Even gangs of criminals, who rely on deception and swindling, desire truth among themselves.

During the time of Jesus, the Jews revered truth-telling but lost its practice. Here in Matthew's account, Jesus explains the Mosaic teaching and emphasizes God's standard on the matter of oaths. He combines the thought of Leviticus 19:12, Numbers 30:2 and Deuteronomy 23:21 into what we read in Matthew. But an oath might be best defined in Hebrews 6:16, "For people swear by something greater than themselves, and in all their disputes an oath is final for confirmation." Oaths were essentially statements whereby one would invoke the credibility of someone (or something) higher to guarantee the promise. The first automobile that I financed required me to have a "co-signer" because I had no history of credibility. My father-in-law signed with me since he had a history of qualified credit. Since he signed, a sense of credibility was then applied to my promise to pay the car loan off within a given time.

God provided for making oaths in His name (Deut. 19:12), and many saints in the Old Testament practiced it. Abraham swore an oath when making promises to the king of Sodom (Gen. 14:22-24) and to Abimelech (Gen. 21:23-24). Jacob and Laban made oaths with each other (Gen. 31:44-53) as did David and Jonathan (1 Sam. 20:16). Even God made oaths on occasion. For instance, in Genesis 22:16-17, He said, "By myself I have sworn, declares the Lord, because you have done this and have not withheld your son, your only son, I will surely bless you, and I will surely multiply your offspring as the stars of heaven and as the sand that is on the seashore." Of course, there is no one higher or more credible than God, so He can only swear by Himself (Heb. 6:13-14). This was not to add credibility to His promise but to give a sense of urgency to it (Heb. 6:17). It was commonly assumed by man that oaths not only added credibility, they added importance. Oaths help us confirm our promises. With sinful man, whose word is worth little today, an oath can help convince.

However, oaths were not supposed to be so flippantly used. They were not to be used when people spoke falsely or without intention of fulfilling their promises. The Jews of Jesus' day were frivolously making oaths and thereby using them deceitfully. It was so commonplace, much like it is today, that no one took them seriously. Oaths became empty promises, and people had little confidence in them. For this reason, Jesus told them to stop making oaths. Now, to be fair, He was not putting an end to all oaths, since even He made oaths every time He said, "Truly, truly" (cf: Matt. 5:18, 26; 6:2; 5:16; Jn. 1:51; 3:3, 5; 5:19, 24; etc.). He was essentially reasserting Leviticus 19:12, "You shall not swear by my name falsely, and so profane the name of your God: I am the Lord."

What matters to the Lord is that our word is matched by our deeds. What we say should be trustworthy and truthful. If we are to say one thing and mean another, we ought not to say it as an oath and thereby bring reproach to the one we swear by. And, since everything belongs to the Lord, we ought not to swear by anything if we are swearing frivolously. Rather, our "yes" should be yes, and our "no" should be no. We should speak truthfully so that our profession of faith matches our walk. This is again how we make ourselves confident in our salvation, the trueness of our faith.

In our suffering, we are tempted to grumble against one another and speak lies in order to advance in life and rid ourselves of affliction. Many times, maybe due to nothing in our own lives, our words mean little to others. But, if we are to make promises, especially if we are to swear by the Lord, we must be ready to deliver. In his commentary, John Calvin put it simply, "We ought to tell the truth, and to be faithful in our words."[7] If we do not, we are hypocritical and we will **"fall under condemnation"** (Ja. 5:12). True faith is reliable and does not cave on promises—even during suffering. The point here is that an unbiblical view of suffering, troubles for no purpose, can lead to despair and all kinds of wickedness from our mouth. It can lead to grumbling, lying and worse. Since true faith is divine, we who have it will find ourselves speaking truthfully, honestly and heavenly.

Conclusion

People who demonstrate true faith are patient while suffering. They do not get jealous of others who are not suffering. Rather, they are cheerful and glad for the person who is doing well. A person who has true faith

---

[7] Calvin, John. "Epistle of James." *Calvin's Commentaries*. Vol. XXII. Grand Rapids: Baker, 2005. 354. Print.

is aware of God's will and does not make promises he cannot keep. True believers also realize that the Lord is compassionate and merciful, and that He is coming soon to avenge and to bless those who have endured.

The Lord expects us to be long-suffering and reliable regardless of the trials we endure. In fact, Paul encourages us in Romans when he says, "For I consider that the sufferings of this present time are not worth comparing with the glory that is to be revealed to us" (Rom. 8:18).

God is in control of our lives and when we grasp this truth we can rest in the knowledge that he sees our suffering and provides the comfort and strength we need to endure. As Paul said to the believers in Corinth, "For as we share abundantly in Christ's sufferings, so through Christ we share abundantly in comfort too" (2 Cor. 1:5). The Prince of Preachers, as some call Charles Spurgeon, said this that motivated me to endure suffering. I trust that it will also encourage you.

> "Be thankful then, dear brethren, be thankful for trouble; and above all, be thankful because it will soon be over, and we shall be in the land where these things will be spoken of with great joy. As soldiers show their scars and talk of battles, when they come at last to spend their old age in the country at home; so shall we in the dear land to which we are hastening, speak of the goodness and faithfulness of God, which brought us through all the trials of the way. I would not like to stand in the white-robed host and hear it said, 'These are they that come out of great tribulation, all except that one.' Would you like to be there to see yourself pointed at as the one saint who never knew a sorrow? We will be content to share the battle, for we shall soon wear the crown and wave the palm."[8]

---

[8] Spurgeon, Charles H. "For the Troubled." *Classic Sermons on Suffering*. Comp. Warren W. Wiersbe. Peabody, MA: Hendrickson, 1984. 59. Print.

CHAPTER 11

THE PRAYER OF FAITH

JAMES 5:13-20

"if he has committed sins, he will be forgiven"

There was a deep emotion that was stirred when I watched the final *Star Wars* movie for the first time. The opening scene was so big. I hate to sound like a science-fiction nut, but it was riveting. Five movies down and nearly thirty years behind, the famous prologue rolls upward in and out of the panoramic screen. The story was gigantic, and it was the moment that everyone was waiting for—the turning of the mysterious cosmic savior, Anakin Skywalker, into the most notoriously evil one, Darth Vader.

The scene opens up in the middle of a galactic battle where hundreds of thousands of ships are darting across the screen, blasting their guns, congesting space, and making it nearly impossible to make sense of things. But we all knew what was happening—stellar war. And not just any war. This was the war of wars. We all knew it would be the last time to enjoy the self-made genre, at least at this magnitude. So it was a bittersweet reality. A theatric score undergirded the scene as the camera slowly drifted through the dark sky. Sounds of explosions and lasers shot from left to right, up and down, and vice versa. Noises of ship engines, radio talk, android utterances, and a pounding heartbeat (which I added to the soundtrack at no additional charge).

So it is with this final portion of James' letter to the scattered Jewish believers named, The Dispersion. There is a heavy weight of conviction on my heart as I come to the closing, and a strong incentive as I see it getting closer. Our journey has been fraught with sharp biblical truths that have cut us deep to our core and left us vulnerable and broken, maybe even despaired. Some of us were challenged with God's commands for the first time. Others understand them more acutely. Yet, all of us were exposed to the confronting, faith-purifying, life-changing Word of God. Our hearts were laid wide open, our souls made fragile, our pride laid to waste, our wills humbled, and our passions aroused for the things of God.

If this is where you are right now, then you are exactly where you ought to be. God's Word is powerfully alive (Heb. 4:12), and it accomplishes His purpose (Is. 55:11), which, at this very moment, is to draw you to Himself (Ja. 1:18). Even so, you might feel unworthy of Him. As the brilliant light of truth shined on your failed attempts when you tried time and time again to be godly, you may feel less than qualified to adorn yourself with the love of Christ. Looking back at your life, especially after the tests of faith, you might find little that is worthy of applause and much that deserves apology. My friends, I am there with you. We are all there with you.

The prologue to the galactic faceoff with evil has rolled upward, and war is now waged in our hearts. God's Spirit is tugging on the allegiance of our souls while our flesh is gripping us tighter than ever before. We are all there in this most acute moment.

True faith has been revealed.

Do you have it?

Let us begin.

> "Is anyone among you suffering? Let him pray. Is anyone cheerful? Let him sing praise. Is anyone among you sick? Let him call for the elders of the church, and let them pray over him, anointing him with oil in the name of the Lord. And the prayer of faith will save the one who is sick, and the Lord will raise him up. And if he has committed sins, he will be forgiven. Therefore, confess your sins to one another and pray for one another, that you may be healed. The prayer of a righteous person has great power as it is working. Elijah was a man with a nature like ours, and he prayed fervently that it might not rain, and for three years and six months it did not rain on the earth. Then he prayed again, and heaven gave rain, and the earth bore its fruit.
>
> "My brothers, if anyone among you wanders from the truth and someone brings him back, let him know that whoever brings back a

sinner from his wandering will save his soul from death and will cover a multitude of sins" (James 5:13-20).

I once heard my mother call from inside the house, "Jacob, I've got your favorites." She was referring to those soft chocolate-chip cookies that only moms can make. I dropped my toys and dashed toward the house. My mouth was already full of saliva. I was like a rabid dog. Nothing could get me going more quickly than those tasty delights. Across the sidewalk and lawn, I darted to the patio door and burst through hoping to find the heavenly treats still in gooey form. Smash! The sound of thick glass hitting the tile floor stopped me dead in my tracks. Still breathing deeply, I turned to see the plate of cookies on the ground shattered and scattered. The ceramic bits covered the cookies like those ice-cream nutty cones. They were ruined. So was I. In my haste, I swung the door open too quickly and knocked the plate to the ground.

Being careless can cause great disappointments, some of which can be more devastating to the soul than the loss of cookies. (I know, it is hard to believe.) Yet, the devastation can be avoided with a little patience and carefulness. I understand that you are eager to find the light at the end of this tunnel of trials. We will get there. But, we must take good care of the text. We cannot rush to it and through it too fast lest we miss the point and find a terrible disappointment in the end.

James is closing with such a momentous finale that he doesn't even bother to end his letter formally. He just stops as if to say, *Selah*. This might be due to the strong practical nature of it. Or, he might have believed that there was really nothing more to say. Probably both. Whatever the case, his final words are extremely informative and radically simplistic. If you were humbled by the prior passages, this is the one that carries you to the great promise of divine faith that yields steadfastness until the crown of life is attained (Ja. 1:12). This is where your hopes are regained, your heart is strengthened and you are brought forth by the word of truth (Ja. 1:18). But, great things rarely come easy.

My wife usually catches the kids before they trample into the house with muddy shoes. And, in her honor, I wish to catch you before you trample into this passage with muddy shoes. Dirt can make a mess of things. Historically speaking, it has made a few messes of this final passage—and we can easily do the same if we are not careful. It would be in our best interest, metaphorically speaking, to take our dirty shoes off before approaching it. We do not want to muddy things up. You know it can happen. It happens all the time.

So, let us kick off our muddy shoes and walk into these final words with clean feet ready, willing to hear the Word of God clearly and eagerly. Trust me, you will not regret it.

Prayer

Throughout the years, so much has been taught from James 5:13-18 that the obvious intent of the text has lost its obviousness. I once heard that if you tell a lie long enough you will believe it. Those you tell might believe it as well. How many times have we believed a lie? How many times have our beliefs stopped us from seeing the obvious when it is so evident? I know that I have been guilty of this plenty of times. It can be very difficult at times to see otherwise. The clearest meaning can be perverted into the strangest ideas when pride is at work. We will refuse to believe something simply because we do not want to believe it, even if it makes more sense. I like to tell people, "If your theological toes get stepped on, you should move them."

James 5:13-18 mentions the praying over the sick, praying in faith, being healed, raising up, anointing oil, and being forgiven. Some theological circles have taught that this passage refers to healing oil, holy unction, raising the dead, forgiving sickness, and a number of other things. However, I propose to you that it says nothing of the sort. Rather, it is about prayer. You might have noticed that every verse in this passage has at least one form of the word *prayer* in it. If you did not notice, go ahead and read it again. I will wait for you.

This passage is not about healing. It is not about a miraculous oil or massage therapy. It is not about a rare spiritual gift nor raising people from the dead. It is simply about prayer, but it is not at all simplistic. It is full of rich meaning, complexity and wonder. Notice that the first command is to pray (Ja. 5:13), and this passage ends with an example of prayer (Ja. 5:18). In between, it speaks about the comforting work of prayer (Ja. 5:13), the restoring work of prayer (Ja. 5:14-15), the role of prayer in fellowship (Ja. 5:16) and the power of prayer (Ja. 16-18). This passage is inundated with prayer. This is why I say it is about prayer. In specific, it is about the prayer of faith.

As we move gently through these final verses on prayer, we will unpack some of the texts that have been "proof texts" for teachings that are really not there. You might have questions about the oil, the healing, and the sick. We will get to those in due time. For now, I want you to enter the door with clean feet and a careful mind. Your reward is near.

Prayer and Comfort

Our prior chapter dealt with the trial of suffering. We discovered that suffering has a purifying role in the Holy Spirit's work of our sanctification. God uses it as a crucible in refining our faith. And, those who have true faith will endure it to the end and thereby prove themselves worthy of salvation (Ja. 1:12). In the greater context of the epistle, suffering is a common denominator. The Dispersion, a people removed from their homeland and living as foreigners in pagan countries, were often poor and mistreated (Ja. 2:6-7). Unfortunately, they were also mistreating each other (Ja. 4:1-2, 11). Jews have always been people of suffering. Throughout history they have been persecuted and killed. Even more so were the pious Christian Jews targeted by pagans and by many of their fellow Jews who did not share their faith in Jesus. Suffering was so common that it deserved some specific attention in James' letter. He tells them to be patient, persistent, cheerful, steadfast, and not to complain but suffer affliction. "Establish your hearts," he writes (Ja. 5:8), and "Do not grumble" (Ja. 5:9). Drawing their attention to the blessed prophets who endured, he tells them that God had a purpose in their suffering. Finally, he hangs his hat on the comforting reality that the Lord is "compassionate and merciful" (Ja. 5:11). And with that in mind, he says, "**Is anyone among you suffering? Let him pray. Is anyone cheerful? Let him sing praise**" (Ja. 5:13). "Turn to the Lord, for He is compassionate and merciful," is the idea. Prayer is the first thing that comes to mind.

> **Those who have true faith will endure to the end.**

Shocked to hear this? Does it sound too easy? James is not making light of their suffering. In fact, James was known as a person of great prayer. Consider this description of him by the famous Christian historian Eusebius:

> "He alone was permitted to enter into the holy place; for he wore not woolen but linen garments. And he was in the habit of entering alone into the temple, and was frequently found upon his knees begging forgiveness for the people, so that his knees became hard like those of a camel, in consequence of his constantly bending them in his worship of God, and asking forgiveness for the people."[1]

James was a remarkably pious believer in prayer. Not even the pains produced by sustained kneeling prevented him from praying. Have you tried that before? Have you knelt on a hard floor, crouched over for hours on end? Prayer was worth the pain to him. Even more, it was worth the travel, worth the separation, and worth the time. Prayer was not a whimsical utterance in James' mind. Though he likely burst out in spontaneous intercession more often than not, his time alone in the temple was intentional and planned. Prayer was not a supplemental practice; it was a necessary application. His life depended on it.

So few Christians pray often. Even fewer pray righteously.

Unfortunately, this is not true of many of us today. Prayer is not a necessity to life. It is not even important. So few Christians pray often. Even fewer pray righteously. Instead of being full of worship and submission to God's will, much of prayer is occupied with *homo in se incurvatus*, as Martin Luther said, "man curved in on himself." Have you ever had a one-sided conversation with someone who talked about nothing but himself? That is usually the talk between believers and God. He patiently listens as we run our mouths about ourselves: "I need this. I need that."

Robert Murray McCheyne, known for his honorable prayer life, considered prayer as a "link that connects earth with heaven." He not only found it important, he found it inseparably tied to his holiness and happiness. His identity was summed up in his secret prayer time. He said that "a man is what he is on his knees before God, and nothing more." This ought to make us wonder what we are like if we do not

---

[1] Ecclesiastical History. 2.23.6.

spend time before God. If we are nothing more and we spend nothing in prayer, then maybe we are nothing like what we think we are. Sadly, this is all too common today in Christian homes and in places of worship. For the most part, we consider prayer of little or no importance. It is a gift that we have so easily taken for granted and even lost.

I remember several occasions when my life was troubled. I was pretty predictable then as I am now. My brain immediately speeds into action thinking through possibilities, reasons, self-pity, self-blame, accusations, lies, anger, worry, and anxiety. My heart is racing. My body is shaking. Muscles in my neck tighten. A migraine is forming. My head is about to burst, and I turn to my wife in desperation, "What do I do?" And almost sounding totally oblivious to what I am wrestling with, she responds rather nonchalantly, "Why don't you pray?" (I have never seen my face during those moments, but I bet it is the face of stupid.)

Prayer is not my first thought when I am troubled. And, if I may generalize for a moment, prayer is not the first thought for most people. It is too trivial and basic. We have complex problems, and we feel like we need complex solutions. Prayer is not complex. So, we think it is too small for our big problems.

Prayer is a direct line to the Lord of creation.

We are forgetting the underlying truth about prayer. Regardless of its complexity, it is conversation with God. Psalm 121:2 tells us, "My help comes from the Lord, who made the heavens and the earth." Prayer is not an end in itself. It is only a channel by which we find our help. It is simple because of the power of the Lord who hears us. The most complex trouble that could ever exist is nothing to the Lord who made the most complex cosmos. Our problems are not big. The Lord who hears our prayer is big. Should we be so arrogant to think that our troubles are more complex than the cosmos, physics, or the laws of nature that were made and are sustained by God?

Prayer is a direct line to the Lord of creation, and He is eager to help. Prayer should be the *first* thing that comes to our mind. To James, it was.

Some Should Pray. Some Should Praise.

It was very common for our basketball coach to line us up and number us off into groups. I recall an exercise where we would all split into four different corners of the gym for station training. We knew which corner to run toward by the number our coach gave us, "One, two, three, four." And repeated again, "One, two, three, four," and again until all were numbered. Those numbered "one" would run to the first corner. Those numbered "two" would run to the second. The same for "three" and "four." Once we were there, we were officially assigned to specific activities.

This is the picture I imagine when reading verses 13 and 14. James tells those who are suffering to go to the prayer corner, those who are cheerful to go to the praise corner, and those who are sick to go to the elders' corner. Let us focus our attention on the first two groups and their assignments. The phrase, **"let him pray,"** is actually just one word in the Greek, *proseukestho*. It is an imperative verb indicating the seriousness of the action, "He should pray." This is different from the command to pray in the following verse where James calls the elders to act instead of the one suffering. Maybe it suggests that the one who is suffering is able to pray. He is not beyond his own ability to express his heart to the Lord. He is troubled, but strong enough to bow, able enough to concentrate and petition. He is not yet so weakened that temptation is getting the best of him. In other words, his suffering is not yet to the extent of crippling his praying abilities. Since he is able, he ought to approach the throne of God with confidence and trust.

The second phrase, **"Let him sing praise,"** is like the first in that it is only one word in the Greek, *psalleto*. This person may not have suffered as the first. This is certainly the impression James gives us. His hopes are strengthened, and his cheer is lifted. Maybe things are going well for him. Maybe he is supernaturally satisfied in Christ and delighting in Him. Whatever the case, he is commanded to praise God. Paul used this word in his letter to the Ephesian believers telling them to be "addressing one another in psalms and hymns and spiritual songs, singing and making melody to the Lord with your heart, giving thanks always and for everything to God the Father in the name of our Lord Jesus Christ" (Eph. 5:19-20). This is evidently a reference to biblical psalms and contemporary compositions. It was very common for the

Jewish people to burst in song. So the instruction is clear. The cheerful Christian ought to rejoice in the Lord.

In these two commands, James covers both poles of the emotional context of human life: the good and the bad. I like the way Kent Hughes words this in his commentary on James:

> "His commands are a congenial attack on the universal human tendency during trouble to get angry or indulge in self-pity or complain, or on the other hand, when one is untroubled and happy, to forget God. James commands that Christians pray throughout the whole spectrum of emotions. Whether low or high, at the bottom or the top, in the pits or on the pinnacle, either prayer or praise is appropriate."[2]

Avoid the tendency we all have to lose the fear of God. When troubled, turn to God in need. When cheerful, turn to God in thanksgiving. Either way, turn to God in trembling humility. No matter how you bounce it, this is the essence of prayer—communicating to God your burdens and your blessings. By doing so, we find our comfort in Him.

Prayer and Restoration

Back to my basketball illustration. There was always an activity corner that no one wanted to go to because it was the most severe. There, the extreme workouts took place. Everyone left this corner weakened and tired. It had extreme exercise and required team help all the way. With this in mind, we continue.

The third command in James' trichotomy of reasons to pray is a unique one aimed at restoring the one who suffered the more extreme troubles. He writes, **"Is anyone among you sick? Let him call for the elders of the church, and let them pray over him, anointing him with oil in the name of the Lord. And the prayer of faith will save the one who is sick, and the Lord will raise him up. And if he has committed sins, he will be forgiven"** (Ja. 5:14-15). To reiterate, this is different from the first command to pray since it tells the suffering one to turn to the elders and have them pray, instead of praying himself. This is because the one who is "sick" has continued to suffer until he has been weakened under the stress of animosity. He has endured so much that

---

[2] Hughes, R. Kent. "A Divine Prescription for Healing." *James: Faith That Works*. Vol. 59. Wheaton: Crossway, 1991. 254. Print.

he cannot bear it any longer. And, he has likely fallen prey to temptation.

Before we unpack this any further, I promised that I would explain some of these confusing texts since I made the assertion that this passage is about prayer and not about healing or magical oil potions. I will keep my promise but ask that you keep your mind open. (Don't go pick up those muddy shoes just yet.)

To begin, I want you to know that I identify the problems with this passage. They lie within our English translations. The confusion lies in the terms *sick, anointing him with oil, prayer of faith,* and *raise him up.* All of these terms lead us to think about physical healing. I am the first to admit that. In fact, it would make a lot of sense if you thought of it in terms of physical healing. That is, unless you considered the broader context surrounding this passage and the fact that this interpretation also leads to possible contradictions with the whole of Scripture. If you take that into account, it makes very little sense. Especially troubling to this interpretation is the phrase *if he has committed sins, he will be forgiven*, followed by the commandment to "confess your sins to one another and pray for one another, that you may be healed" (Ja. 5:16). If we are not careful, we will turn this passage into a healing passage by which people are made spiritually whole and forgiven of sins simply by getting their physical illness prayed for. We might draw conclusions then that our sickness is due to sin and that divine forgiveness is found in the prayers of the elderly. But, let us not believe for a moment that any elder can cleanse you from your sin or that the removal of sickness indicates a removal of guilt. No, this is terribly wrong. Besides, it would put our medical doctors in a bad situation.

Still yet, some Protestant believers, particular those in Charismatic circles, pour this teaching into the passage. I recall watching a late-night television show where so-called ministers were selling prayer cloths that would heal you because they had been prayed over. They based their premise on "let them pray over him" in James 5:14. I think this is dangerously wrong and is not Scripturally sound. It might be akin to a Roman Catholic teaching called Extreme Unction which uses this same passage as a "proof text". They teach that the anointing oil, especially when blessed by the bishop, is for the remission of sins and the restoration of bodily health by conferring grace to the sick person.

Although many of the reformers opposed this religious rite, no one opposed it more sharply than John Calvin by saying that "this passage is wickedly and ignorantly perverted, when extreme unction is established by it, and is called a sacrament, to be perpetually observed in the Church."[3] Martin Luther classified it as a rite of human, rather than divine, invention.[4] The list goes on.

With all due respect, however, there are well-intended and well-educated preachers who hold to the view that this passage is in fact talking about physical healing. For example, Kent Hughes, whom I quoted earlier, comments on this subject by saying that although sickness is not necessarily a result of sin, as seen in John 9:3 with the blind man whom Jesus healed, there are times in other New Testament passages wherein illness and even death are sometimes associated with one's sin. For instance, some people in the Corinthian church suffered physical judgment because of unconfessed sin in their lives when they partook of the Lord's Supper (1 Cor. 11:27-32). You might also remember the paralytic in Capernaum who was healed by Jesus and was told, "See, you are well! Sin no more, that nothing worse may happen to you" (Jn. 5:14). A few more similar passages might suggest that the illness these people suffered was due to the judgment of their sin. However, this is not explicitly seen in the text. It could have been that Jesus simply used the sin as a way of showing a greater suffering if one does not surrender all to Christ. Moreover, although they conservatively present an interesting case for their views, it still does not fit all that well into rest of the context of James' letter. I mean, why talk about physical healing now and leave us to suffer in the doubts of our faith?

So while I have no reason to back away from the fellowship table and cry "Heretic!" over their slightly odd interpretation, I believe there is a more cohesive meaning behind this passage in James. And, when we finish, I trust that you will agree.

The main problem, as I see it, hits us from the very beginning of this passage. See how James asks, **"Is anyone among you sick?"** (Ja. 5:14). If you take the word *sick* to mean physical illness, then the rest of the passage will follow that reference. So it is here that I wish to present

---

[3] Calvin, John. "Epistle of James." *Calvin's Commentaries*. Vol. XXII. Grand Rapids: Baker, 2005. 355. Print.

[4] Toner, P. (1909). Extreme Unction. In The Catholic Encyclopedia. New York: Robert Appleton Company. Retrieved April 1, 2012 from New Advent: http://www.newadvent.org/cathen/05716a.htm

another option, one that will not only clear up the rest of the passage but will also put the entire passage back into context and allow us to glean all the more wisdom from James.

The Wounded Warrior

The word that is throwing us into so much theological chaos is the Greek word, *asthenei*, which literally means to be weak and feeble according to every lexicon I own. It does not require us to think in terms of illness. One can be weak and not be ill. Moreover, it does not require us to think in terms of physicality. One can be spiritually weak just as much as physically weak. To help us hone in on which way we should think when reading this word in James, let us turn to the rest of Scripture and see how it is used.

When surveying all of the uses of this Greek word in the New Testament, we find that the gospels primarily use it in reference to the healing ministry of Jesus Christ. Therefore, it should be understood as physical weakness due to some illness of the body. One verse that makes this plain is Luke 4:40, which says, "All those who had any who were *sick* with various diseases brought them to him, and he laid his hands on every one of them and healed them" (emphasis added). The phrase *with various diseases* qualifies the word *sick* as a physical weakness due to physical illness. I think that is pretty clear. For the most part, this is consistent throughout the gospels. Just substitute the word *sick* in your translation with the word *weak* and you should see what I mean.

> **One can be spiritually weak just as much as physically weak.**

When we reach the epistles, we reach an entirely different story. While the gospel writers used *asthenei* primarily in reference to illness, the other New Testament writers used it primarily for general weakness and often related it to a spiritual condition. This is very consistent with James' epistle, which is a discourse about wavering faith. Let us look at a few examples from other apostolic Scripture.

Romans 4:19 clearly sets this weakness in context of faith and adjacent to physical weakness, "He did not *weaken* in faith when he considered his own body, which was as good as dead (since he was about a hundred years old), or when he considered the barrenness of

Sarah's womb" (emphasis added). Paul is speaking about Abraham who was old and feeble in body though he was not feeble in faith. Notice that Paul used *asthenei* in connection with faith and then used a different term in reference to weakness of the body. Later in the same book, he speaks of those who are weak in faith as those who are immature in their spiritual life, and, in another parallel with James, he says that the stronger ones ought to care for them (Rom. 14:1-2, 21). Earlier in the letter, he says that the law could not save man because the flesh makes the spirit weak (Rom. 8:3), yet another parallel with James. Still, there might not be a verse closer to our context than 2 Corinthians 12:10 where Paul connects this word to the sufferings of life:

> "For the sake of Christ, then, I am content with weaknesses, insults, hardships, persecutions, and calamities. For when I am weak (*astheneil*), then I am strong."

I do not want to start counting points and see which outweighs the other. I only mention this to help you see that there is no real case to think that the word *asthenei* means "ill." What I would rather you see is that the word means "weakness," not "sickness." Moreover, I would like for you to consider the fact that in most of the New Testament letters, it refers to spiritual weakness. This is not to mean that you have to change your religious views. It only means that you ought to think a little more widely and consider for the moment that this route might be a better route to take in the quest of arriving at the true sense of James' teaching. Remember, you have little to lose. At worst, you can trash this book when you finish, right?

Due to this one word, many are divided in their interpretations and theological convictions. In my opinion, it is where so many go wrong and miss out on the truth that James uses to put our tender hearts back together. If we refrain from specifying the type of weakness based on the English translation here in James and simply let the context determine the type of weakness, then we might have a clearer understanding. How differently does it sound to hear the passage this way:

> "Is anyone among you weak? Let him call for the elders of the church, and let them pray over him, anointing him with oil in the name of the

Lord. And the prayer of the faith will save the one who is weak[5], and the Lord will raise him up. And if he has committed sins, he will be forgiven."

By all of this, I do not mean to suggest that this word ought not to include the context of being *physically* weak and be restricted to describing only *spiritual* weakness. Although the context relates a more spiritual bent, the word certainly allows both kinds of weakness. In fact, it would include emotional weakness as well. James is including a kind of weakness on many levels, both individually and collectively. Remember that James' leading context is suffering and wavering faith. One who has severely suffered the weight of the world and the sins of others might succumb to emotional and physical weakness, which may lead to spiritual defeat. One who has persevered through tremendous trials, temptations and persecutions will be in desperate need of God's power, but he may be unable to draw on it alone. It is like the wounded warrior who returns from battle. He is down. He is injured. He is distressed. He is weak and needs someone to come alongside him and pray because his spiritual well-being is in jeopardy.

The Strong Care for the Weak

With weakness in mind, rather than sickness, the doors open wide to James' tender, pastoral care. He is sympathetic and loving. And we see Eusebius' description evidently true—James was a man of prayer, one who cared deeply about the spiritual strength of the faithful.

His first call to personal prayer was for those who are in the midst of suffering. They are on the front lines of war against sin and enduring the persecution of the sinful. The second call is to those who are not enduring persecution but are comfortably enjoying life with Christ. The third call is to those who have suffered so much that they cannot fight the good fight alone. They need the care of those who are strong in faith to pick them up and carry them to the Lord.

This reminds me of the final minutes in *The Return of the King* where Frodo, who has suffered more than he can handle, falls to the ground only yards away from the spewing volcano and the place where his suffering would finally end. His vision is blurred. His muscles are feeble and limp. He is dirty, delusional, overheated, thirsty, hungry,

---

[5] Here, the translations use the word "sick" again. To follow through on my point, I changed it to "weak" as I did earlier since it is a synonymous word. Literally speaking, however, it means "weary" as we will see later.

bruised, beaten, and bloody. Although his restoration is moments away, he cannot make it. It feels like all is lost. Fortunate for him, Samwise Gamgee is nearby. And in an emotional turn of story, Samwise grabs him and cries out, "I can't carry this burden for you, Mr. Frodo, but I can carry you!" Using all of his strength, the good fellow raises the suffering hobbit up and carries him to the end.

Frodo needed to toss his burden into the volcano in order to find the restoration that he required. Yet, he could not get there on his own. His friend, who was stronger than he, could not take away his burden but was certainly able to help him carry it. This is the idea behind the passage. James wants those who are suffering, those who have endured so much that they do not have the strength to make it, to let the strong ones help them carry their burden to the Lord.

James calls the strong ones **"elders"** (Ja. 5:14). This is from the Greek word *presbuteros* which is the basis of our English word *presbyter* and of the title that some churches apply to leaders. *Presbyteros* refers quite literally to the pastors or overseers of the church community. In Paul's first letter to Timothy, he spells out the qualifications of pastors. He says that a pastor must be above reproach, faithful to his wife, sober-minded, self-controlled, respectable, hospitable, able to teach, not a drunkard, not violent but gentle, not quarrelsome, not a lover of money, managing his household well, keeping his children in submission, well thought of by outsiders and more (1 Tim. 3:1-7; cf: Tit. 3:5-9). The point is that these should be the spiritually strong people since they are to tend to the needs of the weak and lead by example the way of the faithful. Remember that the twelve disciples (the first overseers of the Church) appointed helpers so that they were able to devote themselves "to prayer and to the ministry of the word" (Acts 6:4).

> **You need a righteous person to pray for you when you are weak.**

James says that the one who is at *rock-bottom* should **"call"** (from *proskaleo*, "to call alongside") the pastors of the church, since they are strong, and **"let them pray over him"** (Ja. 5:14). As we will see a bit later, "the prayer of a righteous person has great power as it is working" (Ja. 5:16). And if you think about it, you do not want another weak person praying for you in your weakness. It just does not add up. If Samwise had been as weak as Frodo, they both would have fallen and died. Consider where James began in his letter. He said that the one who is double-minded, unstable in his faith, must "not suppose that he will receive anything from the Lord" (Ja. 1:8). Now ask yourself, do you really want a double-minded person praying for you? You might be just as well off on your own. Rather, you need a righteous person to pray for you when you are weak and easily falling into temptation.

By way of parenthesis, this is not to suggest that only pastors can pray for the weak. It simply means that the pastors are primarily the strong in faith. This is their duty. It is how God designed the local church. He dispenses his divine care through the church's leaders. However, God can, and does, care for the weak through other strong Christians who are not in pastoral positions. So let this not prevent you from seeking a strong believer for prayer if this person is not a pastor. On the other hand, if you are a pastor, this ought to be a sober reminder of your divine responsibility to the sheep you under-shepherd in Christ. By neglecting to pray, you poorly serve your Lord and should repent. Preaching is only part of your duty. Prayer is another. Both are critical for having a healthy church.

> **By neglecting to pray, you poorly serve your Lord and should repent.**

Back to our passage. James continues by saying that while the elders are praying over him, they are also **"anointing him with oil in the name of the Lord"** (Ja. 5:14). This is not a reference to a ceremony by which the pastor dots the forehead with a dab of oil and calls it emblematic of the Holy Spirit. That idea might lend itself to Old Testament times when the men were ordained as priests (Ex. 30:30; Ps. 133:2), kings (1 Sam. 10:1; 16:33) and prophets (1 Kin. 19:16), but James does not have an ordination in mind. The Greek word *aleipho* means to oil or massage someone, and it is never used in the ceremonial sense (which is the word *chrio*). Rather, it is used in the sense of washing and rubbing. The root word literally means to grease.

Oil was a base of soap during biblical times (as it is today in some places), and was used to describe washing someone. For example, Luke tells of the good Samaritan who put wine and oil on the man who was robbed, beaten and left for dead (Lk. 10:34). The wine acted as a cleansing agent, killing infection by the fermented alcohol. The oil acted as a soothing agent, helping the body heal. Likewise, athletes had their muscles rubbed down with oil to help relieve soreness. Sometimes, oil was perfumed with a fragrance to refresh the body through the senses.

James is saying that elders, after praying for those who are suffering to the extent of severe weakness, need to tend to their bodily aches and restore them to strength. Now, lest this sound a little disturbing to picture a grown man oiling another, think in terms of the big picture. Caring for another man like this was not viewed as we might today. It was not strange that Jesus knelt and washed the feet of His disciples. I understand that times are quite different today. This act of restoring a brother to strength should not be limited to just the rubbing of oil. We ought to think in terms of principle. We can care for our weak brothers in other ways and accomplish the same restoring effect. One who is emotionally weak might just need someone to share in his troubles. He might need some words of encouragement. One who is saddened by a recent loss might need someone to cry with. One who is bothered so deeply by his sin might need to hear someone pray for them.

The metaphorical sense of anointing with oil is where the real practical truth lies. It means to stimulate and encourage. Think of it as massaging another's spiritual muscle or warming one's heart. The idea is to provide strength to the weak person. Refresh them. Restore them. This is the main idea.

Isaiah paints a good picture of this when speaking about the wickedness of Jerusalem. They were spiritually weak and described as being sick, unsound, bruised and sore with raw wounds and in need of some softening of the heart:

> "Why will you still be struck down? Why will you continue to rebel? The whole head is sick, and the whole heart faint. From the sole of the foot even to the head, there is no soundness in it, but bruises and sores and raw wounds; they are not pressed out or bound up or softened with oil" (Is. 1:5-6).

The Psalmist said something along the same lines that you might find encouraging. He drew from the way shepherds cared for their sheep. When he brought the sheep into the fold after a day of grazing, the shepherd would put his staff down to block the entry and allow one sheep through at a time so that he could examine each one. He would check over its body for wounds. And when he found one, he would pour oil on it and soothe it until it was soft. This would bring comfort and allow the body to heal. Then, he would let the little sheep in. This is a beautiful picture of how Jesus, as our Chief Shepherd, tends to our wounds and cares for us. And the pastor, who is also referred to as a shepherd, should follow the Lord as example.

> "You prepare a table before me in the presence of my enemies; you anoint my head with oil; my cup overflows. Surely goodness and mercy shall follow me all the days of my life, and I shall dwell in the house of the Lord forever" (Ps. 23:5-6).

This is pastoral care for the weak, and it is done on behalf of Christ, who is the Chief Shepherd. It is consistent with Him and consistent with His character. This is what James means by saying that it is done **"in the name of the Lord"** (Ja. 5:14). What a beautiful and honorable picture! Let this be in your mind when you consider the work of the pastor, God's shepherd to His Church. "We urge you, brothers, admonish the idle, encourage the fainthearted, help the weak, be patient with them all" (1 Thess. 5:14).

Prayer Will Save the Weak

The second part of this passage digs a deeper, more difficult, hole with interpretation. James adds, **"And the prayer of faith will save the one who is sick, and the Lord will raise him up. And if he has committed sins, he will be forgiven"** (Ja. 5:15). Notice first that the word *sick* has appeared yet again. Fortunately for us, we are not caught off guard. If we have learned anything about this word, it is that we should not jump to conclusions. Since the first "sick" didn't refer to illness, we should not assume that this one does either. However, it is not entirely that easy.

There is a different Greek word here. It is not the word for "weak" like the one just a verse earlier. But by the same token, it is still not the word for illness, especially not this time. This is the word *kamno*, which is a verb meaning "to grow weary, to tire." It is used only two other times in the New Testament, and both are in the context of suffering. Hebrews 12:3 reads, "Consider him who endured from sinners such hostility against himself, so that you may not grow weary (*kamno*) or fainthearted." And Revelation 2:3 reads, "I know you are enduring patiently and bearing up for my name's sake, and you have not grown weary (*kamno*)." This is inescapably clear. The word *sick* is not the best translation for either of these verses.

This does not resolve all of the conflicts in this passage. But it does at least get us on more stable ground. Other questions might arise from "the prayer of faith" and how it will "save the one who is [weary]" and what does this have to do with "the Lord will raise him up"? Though these might look intimidating, they are quite easy to reconcile now that we are on the right track.

Follow me back to the beginning of James' letter where he describes the double-minded man. He says that he is one who asks for wisdom and yet doubts the goodness of God (Ja. 1:5-7). Either he doubts God's wisdom or he doubts God's benevolence. Either way, he does not trust in God. His prayer, then, is not in faith and is, therefore, ineffective. He receives nothing from the Lord. This is the person who is double-minded, "unstable in all his ways" (Ja. 1:7). I would suggest to you that from that point on, James unpacks various trials that reveal the double-minded man. The double-minded man shows himself to be quick to speak and to anger, partial, without godly works, having a loose tongue, bitter and selfish, divisive, worldly, gossiping, boasting about tomorrow, loving money and luxury, grumbling and impatient during afflictions. Now, arriving at the closing of his letter, James calls us to the altar saying, "If you look similar to the double-minded man, call to the elders and let them pray on your behalf for they will have faith when they pray; they will not doubt."

James says the prayer that is done in faith will be answered (cf: Ja. 1:6). If the elder is praying for the suffering Christian who is weak by the affliction of the world and feeble against the temptations of sin, the prayer **"will save the one who is sick"** (Ja. 5:15). James does not mean to suggest that the prayer will save, but that **"the Lord will raise him up"** (Ja. 5:15). This is a common saying throughout James' letter. For instance, he wrote that the Word of God "is able to save your souls" (Ja. 1:21). He asked if dead faith could save you (Ja. 2:14). The lawgiver and judge "is able to save" (Ja. 4:12). He will also close his letter with the reminder that when you help your brother turn from wandering in sin, you are participating in God's work of saving him (Ja. 5:20). The words "save" (*sozo*) and "raise up" (*egeiro*) are meant to be synonyms. They refer to a restoration of the soul. The first is a very popular word and it implies a safekeeping from danger. For example, Jesus described the purpose of His incarnation by saying, "For the Son of Man came to seek and to save the lost" (Lk. 19:10). The second word, also quite popular, refers to the action of arousing from sleep or being lifted from a lower place. Jesus used it to refer to His resurrection (cf: Matt. 17:32; 26:32; 27:63).

Putting all of this together, I hope you see that the stronger Christians are to uphold the weak Christians in prayer. The pastors, in particular, ought to be living righteously and available to carry those who have been defeated by burdens and are in need of the Lord's restoration and power. It is through the prayer of faith that God chooses to restore the weak, double-minded Christian to strength and to a life of godly living.

In a similar way, Paul encourages us to prayerfully hold up our fellow believers. He wrote, "Brothers, if anyone is caught in any transgression, you who are spiritual should restore him in a spirit of gentleness. Keep watch on yourself, lest you too be tempted" (Gal. 6:1). What a wonderful reality we have in this often overlooked gift of God. Oh, it gets better. James adds this point, **"And if he has committed sins, he will be forgiven"** (Ja. 5:15). Not only will God restore us through prayer, He will forgive us our sins. He will wash us in His blood and make us new. How extremely wonderful is this?

Might I be intrusive and encourage you at this moment to seek out your pastor or a strong Christian and ask them to help you carry your burdens to the Lord? Do you want to experience the relief of casting your cares on the Lord? Do you desire to have restored to you the joy that you once had in Christ? Call out to those who are righteous. Find your restoration in prayer to the most benevolent God.

Prayer and Community

"There is no 'i' in team," my coach used to tell us. It took me a few hearings before I finally got it. He wanted us to know that the no one on the team played alone. As a team member, you play collectively and cohesively. Good teams are unified in mind and attitude. They move and think the same. They do what is best for the shared interest. James has this in mind as he apparently turns his attention from the one who is weak to the community as a whole. In sort of an open-ended instruction, he says to them, **"Therefore, confess your sins to one another and pray for one another, that you may be healed"** (Ja. 5:16a).

I take this to be a change of address. First, he speaks to the one who is suffering; next, to the one who is cheerful; then, to the one who is weak and needs the help of the church; and finally, to the church as a whole. **"Therefore,"** he says. This is a key word when following the text. It denotes a consequential transition. It means "in accordance with" something or "based on" something. It causes us to think in a summary of thought. What James just instructed to the suffering, the cheerful, the weak and the pastors, he now relates it to the general audience—everyone else who did not categorically fall into one of those four descriptions and everyone collectively. "On account of what I just instructed, everyone ought to **confess your sins to one another and pray for one another**" (Ja. 5:16).

The question lies in what is actually related to the congregation as a whole. If the suffering ought to pray, the cheerful ought to praise, and the weak ought to seek help from the pastors, what ought the church to do? With this frame of thought, we might deduce a number of practical truths about the church in relation to these instructions to specific people. In other words, what does this mean for the church—and what implications does it have on her members? By answering these questions, I think we will make it to the meaning of the text and unveil some wonderful realities of church fellowship and how prayer relates to church growth. But, first, let us unpack the Greek language here and set the foundation on which we can stand.

By way of reminder, the order of Greek words in a sentence does not contribute to the meaning. It does, however, contribute to the emphasis and mood of the meaning. So, the first word does not necessarily have to be the subject. It can be any word that is part of the sentence. More often than not, the first word is there for purposes of emphasis. In this case, the word that is translated "therefore" is not the first word (although it is in English). Rather, it is the verb *eksomologeisthe*, a compound word, meaning "be confessing." In a contemporary sense, it would mean "be sharing it out" or "let it out, be honest." The tenses in the Greek denote an on-going confession, a continual sharing and honesty.

To confess is to admit something openly and often audibly. It is a close sister of the word "profess" though they have subtle differences. We sometimes associate profession with things positive (from the prefix "pro") and confession with things negative (from the prefix "con"). But both terms can be used in the opposite way. In fact, not all professions are true. So, a profession is more of an open claim to something. Whereas a confession is admission of something that is believed to be true and real. You can openly claim something that you disbelieve, but you would definitely not confess something that you disbelieve. Otherwise, it would not be a confession.

In the New Testament, the word "confess" is usually, though not always, connected to the admission of sins. The word first appears in the New Testament in Matthew's Gospel when people from all Jerusalem and Judea were going to John the Baptist in order to be baptized. Matthew says that they were "confessing their sins" (Matt. 3:16), which was connected with John's call for them to repent from sin (Matt. 3:2). The Apostle John related this to us as a necessary and healthy practice for the believer which holds tremendous reward. "If we confess our sins, he is faithful and just to forgive us our sins and to cleanse us from all unrighteousness" (1 Jn. 1:9).

We should confess to one another.

However, James takes this command and applies it to the church in a horizontal way. In addition to confessing our sins to God, we ought to also confess our sins to one another.

I purposely stress that it is a horizontal relation. It is not to be understood in an eternal setting primarily. James is not telling us to seek spiritual forgiveness by man in order to attain a right standing before God. Remember the encounter between Jesus, the paralytic and the scribes? After forgiving the paralytic his sins, the scribes objected to Christ saying, "This man is blaspheming." Jesus turned to them and said that He did this so "that you may know that the Son of Man has authority on earth to forgive sins" (Matt. 9:1-8). If Jesus was not God, their objections would have been honorable (Mk. 2:7). Since God is the One who is sinned against, He is the one who is able to forgive. However, there is an additional element to the matter of sin. Though we sin first and foremost against the Lord, our sins are also against others. And just as sin clouds the relationship we have with God, it clouds the relationship we have with others,—especially those in our assembly. For our relationships to be strong, we must be honest, share our sins, and let our weaknesses be known. Therefore, an additional confession is sometimes needed to one another.

This leads us to our second emphasis in the Greek. It is the word *allelois* which means **"one another"** (Ja. 5:16). It is in connection to confessing your sin. It answers the question "To whom do I confess my sin?" We should confess to one another. But this does not imply just anyone in audible reach. It implies others of the same kind. Someone like you. Someone who believes in Christ, has experienced His forgiveness, and knows the struggles of resisting sin. In other words, do not use Facebook or Twitter to announce your sins so that all people know. Be wise. Share your struggles and weaknesses with those who can identify with you and understand; those who will be willing to hold you up in prayer.

The third emphasis is what you are confessing. It is the word *amartias*, or sin, but not just sin in general. In this case, the word is accusative, meaning **"your sins"** (Ja. 5:16). These are your faults, your trespasses, and your weaknesses. Do not share the sin of others with one another. Confess your own sin with others. And, as the Greek sequence continues, **"and pray for one another"** (Ja. 5:16). We should not confess our sins to one another for the sake of getting it off our chest only. We should hold up one another in prayer just as the pastor is to hold up the weakened believer who has suffered to the extent that he cannot hold himself up (Ja. 5:14-15). There is a purpose to our confession among each other, and it is not to throw our garbage on another. We are to share openly, deeply and honestly with the intention of becoming stronger and more resistant to temptation. And by going to God with our sin and struggle, we seek to attain the strength and wisdom we need for such a battle. Confessing your sin is only part of the process. Though it is necessary that you acknowledge that you have sinned and are weak, it is not an end in itself. We must draw down power from the Lord. And, we must not only share with others to have them pray for us, we must allow others to share with us so that we can pray for them. The "one another" in the Greek carries the idea of reciprocation. It is not a one-way channel.

The result is found in the final emphasis. We should confess our sins to one another and pray for and with one another, "**that you may be healed**" (Ja. 5:16). We have discussed in great lengths the matter of weakness over sickness, as well as spirituality over physicality. This is no exception. In fact, since it is tied to the confession of sins and the prayers of one another, the context should be more than clear. The Greek word *iathete* means "to make whole" and is sometimes used to refer to curing someone. A survey of the New Testament will reveal the same results we found with the prior words that cause so much trouble in the English translation. Sometimes, *iatgete* refers to physical healing of the body, even sickness. Other times, it refers to spiritual healing of the soul. The writer of Hebrews used it in connection with striving for peace with everyone and a holiness in the Lord (Heb. 12:13). But it is most obvious in Peter's first letter when he interprets Isaiah 53:5, "He himself bore our sins in his body on the tree, that we might die to sin and live to righteousness. By his wounds you have been healed" (1 Pet. 2:24).

There is a healing that occurs when believers share their struggles with one another. It is spiritual, emotional and social. And this is where we might divert for a moment to see some of the wonderful rewards we have when we practice the sharing of our struggles with each other. I hope that these rewards spur you on to practicing godly confession.

The Reward of Relief

Sins left in secrecy cause unwanted troubles. They have a way of producing guilt that churns in our mind and pollutes our soul. It can create worry, confusion, delusion, paranoia, unjust anger, anxiety and more. And yes, these things can lead to physical problems. A person who is so consumed with guilt brought on by secret sins will eventually suffer bodily ailments that can be fatal if not treated. Why else do you think so many people resort to drugs and getting drunk in the bars? Why else do people spend so much money on counselors and doctors trying to feel better about themselves? Most of the time, these people are trying to deal with the effects of sin. Therefore, confessing your sin to another believer can be very rewarding. When we let sin out, we will enjoy relief. No more hiding. No more wondering. No more loneliness.

You can sigh a relief when sin is confessed.

The Reward of Victory

Proverbs 28:13 says, "Whoever conceals his transgressions will not prosper, but he who confesses and forsakes them will obtain mercy." Satan wants nothing more than to make you a tragic victim of sin. By concealing it, you set yourself up for loss. But, by forsaking sin and exposing it, you assure victory over it, and you win God's mercy. Although confessing sin does not ultimately rid you of your weakness to fall, it is a major win in the battle. It strengthens you each time you confess. Our mortal enemy does not want us to call sin what it is nor to expose it and bring it to light. But God does. God desires that we pull sin out and see it for what it is in order to hate it and fight it. By confessing your sins, you do just that. You become a victor in the battle and show sin that it will not master you.

The Reward of Accountability

Once sin is confessed, the battle is won. But the war is not over. Sin will return again. Next time, however, it might be a more fierce battle that you will face. Sin is stubborn and does not die easily. However, by exploiting sin and sharing it with others who also hate sin and wish it to die, you essentially join forces and fight it together. Instead of a lonely soldier combatting a ruthless and militant army, you become part of a multitude of soldiers, bound arm-in-arm. Moreover, since it is God's design that we unite in the war against sin, you should think of this multitude of soldiers as God's army. He blesses it. They kneel beside you, rise with you, march alongside you, and slay for you. Not only are they praying for you while you are apart, they strengthen your will in the fight while they are near. This is the idea of accountability—another wonderful reward brought about by confessing sin.

The Reward of Support

Kin to accountability is support. While other believers will hold us to the standard and join us in the war on sin, they also will carry our load when it is too heavy for us to bear alone. Confessing sin to others allows them to find pity in our souls and hold us up when we are weak. The Bible charges us to be "bearing with one another in love" (Eph.

4:2). This means that we ought to be patient with each other, not judgmental and cold. We should live with each other in understanding and compassion being eager to support the weakened believer. As Paul commanded, "Brothers, if anyone is caught in any transgression, you who are spiritual should restore him in a spirit of gentleness. Keep watch on yourself, lest you too be tempted. Bear one another's burdens, and so fulfill the law of Christ" (Gal. 6:1-2).

The Reward of Love

As just noted, supporting our brothers when they are overburdened is to fulfill the law of Christ (Gal. 6:2). The law of Christ is love. Jesus left us a supreme commandment to "love one another: just as I have loved you, you also are to love one another" (Jn. 13:34). John applied this principle to our lives by relating that this commandment proves love for God: "Whoever loves God must also love his brother" (1 Jn 4:21). Confessing sin is the spark that initiates deeper love and compassion. It is also a mark of true love. Confessing one to another proves that love resides in the hearts of those who are caring and holding each other up in the faith. Love, then, is a reward for confessing sin.

The Reward of Clarity

In my experience, nothing makes church fellowship harder than ungodly perception. Sin has a way of diverting blame. It manipulates your thinking in order to set you against others. It causes you to grumble (Ja. 5:9) and quarrel (Ja. 4:1). It brings division between you and other believers by convincing you that they are the enemies and that they are the ones who wronged you. But, even though they might have sinned against you, it is not they who are your enemies. Rather, the enemy is sin. It is the mischievous little child who runs from a skirmish he created and leaps into your arms pointing to others. "They are mean," it says to us. Sadly, we often believe it. Hebrews tells us, "Take care, brothers, lest there be in any of you an evil, unbelieving heart, leading you to fall away from the living God. But exhort one another every day, as long as it is called 'today,' that none of you may be hardened by the deceitfulness of sin" (Heb. 3:12-13). Confessing will clear up the obscurity of truth around us that sin causes. As Paul wrote, "Having put away falsehood, let each of you speak the truth with his neighbor" (Eph. 4:25) and "Give no opportunity to the devil" (Eph. 4:27).

The Reward of Unity

When we have love for each other and clarity of the real enemy, unity emerges. According to Paul, confessing sin shows eagerness "to maintain the unity of the Spirit in the bond of peace" (Eph. 4:3). It does so in two ways. The one who confesses shows his eagerness by removing that which would cause division and stir up trouble among the body of believers. The one who hears the confession shows his eagerness by forgiving and helping others grow in righteousness. For this reason, the writer of Hebrews tells us not to neglect meeting together, "but encouraging one another," (Heb. 10:25). Since sin aims to destroy the unity of the church, confessing sin aims to destroy the division it causes.

The Reward of Humility

Sin puffs us up full of pride. It makes us self-centered and self-absorbed. Many refuse to confess their sin because of this pride and unfortunately miss out on the reward of humility. Humility is a mark of true faith. "God opposes the proud, but gives grace to the humble" (Ja. 4:6). When we confess our sin to another believer, we tear down the stronghold of pride and build up the reward of humility. "Humble yourselves, therefore, under the mighty hand of God so that at the proper time he may exalt you" (1 Pet. 5:6). As Christians, we should be humble. When writing about bearing one another's burdens, Paul reveals this basic reality: "if anyone thinks he is something, when he is nothing, he deceives himself" (Gal. 6:3). Therefore, confessing sin is key to our humility.

The Reward of Forgiveness

Confession is also key to our forgiveness. John wrote, "If we confess our sins, he is faithful and just to forgive us our sins and to cleanse us from all unrighteousness" (1 Jn. 1:9). Since it is key to our salvation, it is key to our sanctification. Our initial forgiveness of sin requires that we repent and turn to God (Acts 3:19). Likewise, our ongoing forgiveness of sins, in terms of enjoying God's eternal mercy, is also required.

Confession initiates the joy of having been forgiven our sins (1 Jn. 1:4), and it assures us of the righteousness imparted to our account through Christ. The reward of forgiveness happens on a horizontal level as well. When we confess our sins to one another, we spur them on to forgiving us. Sometimes, we sin because we have refused to forgive and we need to have an attitude of forgiveness. Confessing our sin, since it humbles us, weakens our pride and allows us to be sensitive to others so that we may forgive from the heart. In the end, forgiveness may happen on many levels and be the pinnacle of reward since all others flow from it.

Confessing Sin Is Obedience to God

There is so much more that we can say about the rewards of confessing sin. These came to mind through a close reading of James and a bit of experience. There is no telling how many things we would find once we read other passages in the Bible with a close eye. The rewards are so numerous that I wish not to count. My aim was only to help you see some of the wonderful benefits in hopes that they will motivate you to lock arms with other believers and hold each other up.

As a last draw, however, I want to mention one more thing. Confessing sin is not just beneficial. It is necessary. James, under the inspirations of the Holy Spirit, did not *suggest* that we confess and pray together. He *commanded* us to do so. Although I briefly touched us on this before, it is worth paying closer attention to, especially if I have yet to convince you of your need for confession.

My trusty thesaurus app tells me that "to accept blame" is a synonym to the verb "confess." I would suggest that accepting blame must occur before one can genuinely confess sin, but the action of expressing your trespasses is definitely a way of telling yourself that you are guilty of sin. I admit, it is a polar opposite to the way we would like to think in the American culture. It does not help with self-esteem. But it is key to the life of the believer. We must know that we are sinners and that we still sin. This is the proper perspective if we are to see our Lord in His holy glory.

Consider the words of Jesus when explaining to the Pharisees why he sat with those who disregarded the Mosaic Law. "Those who are well have no need of a physician, but those who are sick. I came not to call the righteous, but sinners" (Mk. 12:17). Those of us who find little or no blame for the many trespasses we do are categorically those who think we have no need for a physician. Simply put, if you think you have no sin, then you need no Savior. Or, put in more serious terms, if you refuse to admit your sin, Jesus will refuse to admit your salvation. Only those who acknowledge their personal guilt of sin will be saved.

I understand that by relating the confession of sins to a refusal to admit your sin, I am treading on thin ice. After all, it is not the act of confessing sin to people that is primarily in question when dealing with our salvation. In order to be saved, we must acknowledge our sin guilt before God, as a trespassers of His law. A confession of trespasses to others is not entirely the same thing. However, we might be thinking too small if we entirely separate the two—especially after reading through James and seeing him draw connections between what we do among others and our belief in God. Let me see if we can make the connection yet again.

Remember that steadfastness in trials proves the Christian true by making him perfect and complete (Ja. 1:2-4). Likewise, the one who listens and obeys the Word of Truth assures himself of his salvation because it produces righteousness (Ja. 1:19-21). Again, a true Christian will bridle his tongue (Ja. 1:26), show impartiality (Ja. 2:8-13), do good works (Ja. 3:17), exercise godly wisdom (Ja. 3:13, 17), be humble (Ja. 4:6), be giving and content (Ja. 5:1-6), and be established during suffering (Ja. 5:8). All of these were commands, no different than the command to **"confess your sins to one another"** (Ja. 5:16). Also, they were all used to form the picture of a true Christian. To fall short is to show weakness and ultimately sin. Depending on its progression, it might reveal a lack of true faith and, therefore, a lack of true salvation. My point is not to drag you back to the pit of guilt in this final chapter. Rather, I wish only to connect the dots between confessing sins to one another and its importance to the perfecting work of the Word in your life. One way we know that we are steadfast in trials is if we confess our sins to others, and this is by God's design (cf: Ja. 1:18).

To press this fact a bit more since it is so important, consider the implications of not confessing your sin to others. If we follow James' logic, it might reveal a deeper issue about your opinion of yourself. The Bible tells us that "if we say we have no sin, we deceive ourselves, and truth is not in us" (1 Jn. 1:8). Though you might find an objection in your heart to this, thinking that your silence does not imply that you believe you are sinless, think about it more closely and honestly. Sin is strengthened in your secrecy. And if you desire to truly mortify the flesh, as genuine believers do (Rom. 8:13), you will not think of sin so lightly. Rather, you should think of sin for what it is: your mortal enemy. Imagine that you were at war. During the black of night, your fellow soldier slept as you kept watch and a slew of opposing fighters rushed into your fortress to kill you, then kill your fellows. If you said nothing about their attack, what would it imply?

Sin desires to kill you so you must kill it first. Often, crying out, "The enemy is here with me!" is the first step to position yourself and ready your fellow troops to help. Your silence might indicate that you are harboring the enemy, rather than exposing it and declaring war. If you are silent about your sin and weaknesses, maybe you are not convinced that you have sin in your life. If this is true, then you are deceiving yourself, and the genuineness of your eternal salvation is in jeopardy because the truth is not in you.

Think this is too rigid to be biblical? Follow John's thoughts as he continues:

> "If we say we have no sin, we deceive ourselves, and the truth is not in us. If we confess our sins, he is faithful and just to forgive us our sins and to cleanse us from all unrighteousness. If we say we have not sinned, we make him a liar, and his word is not in us" (1 Jn. 1:8-10).

The Bible tells us that we are sinners and we continue to sin even after our conversion. God does not take us out of the war against sin. He leaves us in it but equips us with Himself and the tools of truth. We receive not the justice we deserve for our trespasses. Rather, we receive mercy and grace. He gives us gifts like confession to bring us forth to perfection (Ja. 1:4, 18).

We are commanded to confess our sins, first to God and then to others. To reiterate this from the pen of James, **"confess your sins to one another and pray for one another, that you may be healed"** (Ja. 5:16). This is not a suggestion. This is a command from a wise man whose writing is inspired by the Supreme Wise Lord (2 Tim. 3:16). It is for your good and the good of others. And, undoubtedly, the more aware you are of your sin, the more cherished is your Savior. Confession of sin to others opens the door to rewards too numerous to count—one of which is the enjoyment of your assurance of salvation.

Prayer and Power

Earlier, I identified the serious delusion we have today about prayer. To many people, prayer is a lost cause; a way to waste breath uttering sincere words into empty air. I am no exception to the trend. I admit that for many years I trivialized prayer as well. My lack of it showed just how poor my opinion really was. But our trite disregard for prayer is not only a contemporary problem. Since the Fall, mankind has failed in his regard for holy things. His vision is near-sighted and selfish. He sees the things that happen and relates them to his own desires. He is you and me. We are this way since we are sinners.

While suffering, we might pray that God deliver us since our concern does not reach past our circle of comfort. We wonder not about the overarching plan that God has in our situation, especially if it involves our discomfort. We forget that all things work for our good, even when they are obviously evil (Rom. 8:28). We do not pray that God's hidden plan bring Him glory and that our present suffering is nothing when compared to His wonderful blessings. Rather, we pray selfishly and dishonorably. We slight God's glory for our own ease and His plan for our own ideas. Then we wonder why He does not work all things out for our good in the way that we want them to be worked out. We see bad things get worse, and we conclude that prayer is weak, a waste of time.

There is power in prayer.

This is true of man today just as it was true of man yesterday. The Jewish of the Dispersion, though they were ritualized with prayer, undoubtedly fell victim to the same temptations. Since they were people of suffering, they likely prayed for an end to their troubles and often did not find it the way they had wanted. Like any other sinners, they questioned not their own heart and intent, but the effect of prayer altogether.

It is quite obvious that James wants these notions to be put to rest. We know him to be a man confident of prayer and its effect, so it is no surprise that after he tells the suffering people to pray, knowing that they are weak and questioning its effect, he reminds them that there is power in prayer. Prayer works. He says, **"The prayer of a righteous** person has great power as it is working" (Ja. 5:16). Like the prior verses, this one lends itself to some more complexities. When digging into this passage, I found a chain of truths, each individually linking together to form a greater principle. James' goal here is to remind the people of the power of prayer, but in a specific context. He qualifies the prayer as a prayer of faith (Ja. 5:15) which is offered by a righteous person (Ja. 5:16). It is the prayer of faith that has power, but only the righteous person expresses such a prayer because only a righteous person trusts in the plan and work of God. In the end, the power is not so much in the prayer as much as it is in the One who answers it.

Of course, this is a bird's eye view of the text. A deeper look will uncover some strong encouragements to pray more fervently.

Powerful Prayer

We use adjectives to describe things. We might say that we drive a *fast* car, or we wear *black* shoes, or that we have *strong* muscles. James describes prayer as being powerful; we have powerful prayers. But he doesn't use an adjective to convey the power of prayer. He uses a verb. The Greek word is *ischuo* which means to be extraordinarily able. Additionally, he qualifies this verb with a adverb, *polu*, which tells us about the quantity of the verb—it has much. Together, you might say "being much extraordinarily able."

The reason this is important, is that there is a double emphasis on the capability to perform. At least, it appears this way. Prayer is extraordinarily able; it is greatly extraordinarily able. To my children, I would say that prayer is very, very powerful.

Notice that I am still using the word as an adjective, not a verb as it is intended. So to be even more precise, we might say: Prayer is very, very prevailing, overcoming, triumphing, conquering, powering, and working. This ought to stir up some motivation in us. The kind of prayer the Lord gives us is able to conquer, able to win, able to triumph, and it is doing so at this present time. It is capable and active. There is no suggestion of opposition or challenges. Prayer is powerfully unchallenged, perfectly able and strong.

Do you remember the story of when God was doing so many extraordinary miracles that people were being healed from the handkerchiefs and aprons that touched the skin of Paul? Luke tells us that "some of the itinerant Jewish exorcists" wanted to invoke the name of Jesus over the possessed in order to exercise the same power that they saw Paul manifesting. But, to their surprise, the evil spirits scoffed at them, and one possessed man overpowered (*ischuo*) them and ran them out of town naked and wounded. Evidently, their power was more able than that of the Jewish exorcists. But, as the story continues, their power was not able enough to withstand the gospel. As Paul preached, "fear fell upon them all, and the name of the Lord Jesus was extolled," sinners repented, and many gave up pagan practices for the sake of Christ. "So the word of the Lord continued to increase and prevail mightily (*ischuo*)" (Acts 19:11-20). This is to point out that the evil spirits overpowered the unrighteous, but the Lord overpowered the evil spirits, and the Word of God overpowered the wicked persuasions of the sinners.

In the end, the one who has the greatest power is victorious. Paul said, "I can do all things through him who strengthens me" (Phil. 4:13). That is to say that he could overcome all troubles and temptations because God gave him the power to conquer them. In Galatians, he wrote that neither circumcision nor uncircumcision has the power to save. Only faith in Christ does (Gal. 5:6; 6:15). This is what is meant here in James 5:16. The kind of prayer he is referencing is the kind that always wins. It is strong enough to push through anything that it is meant to be pushed through. You could say that it has the winning edge. It is able and powerful enough to bring about whatever the Lord has planned. It is the very idea wrapped up in 1 John 5:4, "For everyone who has been born of God overcomes the world. And this is the victory that has overcome the world—our faith."

Righteous Prayer

Before we switch the television back on and say those preachers are correct, let us qualify which prayer has the power. Prayer is not all the same. What is true here in James is not true for all prayer just the same. James qualifies powerful prayer as righteous prayer. Granted, the Greek mentions the prayer of the righteous person. But the idea here is that the righteous person says a righteous prayer. He utters the right prayer, you might say. It is right because it comes from a righteous person, but it is also right because it is biblically correct and consistent with the

Lord's will.

Very few who suffer troubles will lean on the prayers of those who openly defy God. If they do, they are mistaken in what prayer is. No one in their right mind will approach an atheist looking for divine help. It is commonly understood that if we need God's help we go to God's people. The reason is simple: God listens to His people. The Psalmist wrote, "If I had cherished iniquity in my heart, the Lord would not have listened" (Ps. 66:18). Isaiah wrote, "But your iniquities have made a separation between you and your God, and your sins have hidden his face from you so that he does not hear" (Is. 59:2). In the New Testament, we find Peter echoing with this, "For the eyes of the Lord are on the righteous, and his ears are open to their prayer. But the face of the Lord is against those who do evil" (1 Pet. 3:12).

Unless the sinner is praying a prayer of repentance, he is not heard (1 Jn. 1:9). God turns a closed ear to his futile words, and they drift with the wind. The righteous, however, pray to God and are heard. Even still, there is a sense in which the "righteous" are qualified even more. I have been in small groups before when someone prays for something that is questionable. In fact, all of us at times, pray questionable things. We do it often, and don't even know it. These prayers could not qualify as a righteous prayers or as prayers of faith. They lack in many ways and fail in their power. I bring this up because not all righteous people have powerful prayers. This is because even the righteous can and do sin when praying. So rather than lay a blanket of power across all prayers when prayed by those who are Christians, let us be more specific about the kind of prayer that James is describing as having power.

It is the prayer that is righteous, rather than the double-minded (Ja. 1:8). Granted, it must be prayed by a righteous person to be heard. But it must be prayed in faith if it is to be powerful. The key to this might be found in John 15:7. The context is abiding in Christ. Jesus calls Himself the true vine, and he calls His Father the vinedresser (Jn. 15:1). Following the metaphor, we are the branches in this vine. We are cleaned and made to bear fruit as He works in and through us. Here it is in full:

> "I am the true vine, and my Father is the vinedresser. Every branch in me that does not bear fruit he takes away, and every branch that does bear

fruit he prunes, that it may bear more fruit. Already you are clean because of the word that I have spoken to you. Abide in me, and I in you. As the branch cannot bear fruit by itself, unless it abides in the vine, neither can you, unless you abide in me. I am the vine; you are the branches. Whoever abides in me and I in him, he it is that bears much fruit, for apart from me you can do nothing. If anyone does not abide in me he is thrown away like a branch and withers; and the branches are gathered, thrown into the fire, and burned. If you abide in me, and my words abide in you, ask whatever you wish, and it will be done for you. By this my Father is glorified, that you bear much fruit and so prove to be my disciples. As the Father has loved me, so have I loved you. Abide in my love. If you keep my commandments, you will abide in my love, just as I have kept my Father's commandments and abide in his love. These things I have spoken to you, that my joy may be in you, and that your joy may be full" (John 15:1-11).

The key to powerful prayer is abiding in Christ. This is a wonderful synonym for what it means to be righteous. It is to abide in Him. Observing, following, conforming, sticking to, standing by, this is what it means to abide. In more simple terms, it is to have faith. It is to trust in Him and what He says, confident that He is able to work all things to His glory and our joy. This is how He shows us love and how we abide in it. When we do, God, the vinedresser, will bring about the fruit of God's design. Good things will occur. The impossible will happen.

> **Power is found in the prayer of faith spoken by the faithful.**

For this reason, Jesus said, "If you abide in me, and my words in you, ask whatever you wish, and it will be done for you" (Jn. 15:7). Notice the emphasis of unlimited power, "*whatever* you wish." Using some common logic, we can see that the righteous person, one who abides in Christ, will prayer a righteous prayer, having Christ's words abide in him, and, therefore, it will be one of great power. Or, to put it in other words, Christ always prays with power, and when you pray what Christ prays, you will see that power.

The key to a powerful prayer is not only a righteous person, but a righteous prayer. Power is found in the prayer of faith spoken by the faithful. When writing about the suffering of Jesus, author and pastor R.C. Sproul described this kind of prayer as authentic and modeled faithfully in Christ:

"The authentic prayer of faith is one that models Jesus' prayer. It is always uttered in a spirit of subordination. In all our prayers, we must let God be God. No one tells the Father what to do, not even the Son. Prayers are always to be requests made in humility and submission to the Father's will.

"The prayer of faith is a prayer of trust. The very essence of faith is trust. We trust that God knows what is best. The spirit of trust includes a willingness to do what the Father wants us to do. Christ embodied that kind of trust in Gethsemane."[6]

While on the Mount of Olives awaiting His betrayal and arrest, Jesus prayed so earnestly that His "sweat became like great drops of blood falling down to the ground" (Lk. 22:45). Though we do not have a record of all that He prayed, we do have these most remarkable words: "Father, if you are willing, remove this cup from me. Nevertheless, not my will, but yours, be done" (Lk. 22:42). The righteous prayer is one in which the righteous person prays that God's will be done, not his own. Otherwise, he will ask and not receive (Ja. 4:3).

Effectual Prayer

There is one last thing to note about the prayer James describes. It is effectual. The Greek is *energoumene* which is the word from which we derive the English word *energy*. In the original language it is a verb, meaning "to energize" or "to work effectually." It is used to intensify work. It works "in" something to bring it about. In connection with having perfect power, this undergirds the idea that prayer works. It is not dormant or still. The prayer of faith is powerful and makes things happen. It performs. It accomplishes. It is effective. Why? Because it is righteous and powerful. It is aligned with God's plan, and He delights in seeing it come to pass.

In Paul's letter to the Corinthians about the various spiritual gifts, he says that God *works* them all to His satisfaction (1 Cor. 12:6, 11). To the Ephesians, he said that we are "predestined according to the purpose of him who works all things according to the counsel of his will" (Eph. 1:11). He reminded the Thessalonians that God was at

---

[6] Sproul, R. C. "Walking the Via Dolorosa." *Surprised by Suffering: The Role of Pain and Death in the Christian Life*. Lake Mary, FL: Reformation Trust Pub., 2009. 18. Print.

work in them through the Word (1 Thess. 2:13).

The thing to identify in all of this is that prayer which is powerful begins and ends with God. It is the Lord who makes the person righteous, gives the person prayers, makes the prayers powerful, and works the power to press through to the end that He has in mind. This is what a prayer of faith is (Ja. 5:15). It is a prayer that is full of trust in what God can and will do. It is full of humility and submission to the divine plan of the Lord. It is not expressed with inner doubt (Ja. 1:6) or selfish intention (Ja. 4:2-3) but with confidence in God and eagerness for God's plan.

"The prayer of a righteous person has great power as it is working" because God is all over it and in it and through it. The prayer of faith is divinely planned, divinely active and divinely successful.

An Average Example

Knowing that God is interwoven throughout the prayer of faith is enough to motivate us to pray, even when times are full of trouble. But we sometimes can't get past our suffering to see it for all it is worth. We get blinded by our current worries and wonder if we are righteous enough to pray such a powerful prayer. Often times, we see our pastors as those who are the only righteous. And, to some extent, God has these men in place as those who continually abide in Him for the sake of the church, so it is good that we see them as ones on whom we may lean for prayer. However, James tells us to go to one another as well. Though we might not perceive our fellow brothers and sisters as being as altogether righteous as our elders since they never set foot in the pulpit or pray with others at the altar, if they are abiding in Christ they are every much as righteous as the pastors. For, to have Christ is to have righteousness; and to abide in Him is to think righteously.

So James gives us an example of a common man who had uncommon power when he prayed. He chose Elijah. "**Elijah was a man with a nature like ours, and he prayed fervently that it might not rain, and for three years and six months it did not rain on the earth. Then he prayed again, and heaven gave rain, and the earth bore its fruit**" (Ja. 5:17-18). Before we reflect on the Old Testament to find out just how powerful his prayer really was, we should note that James describes him as "a man with a nature like ours." The Greek says it more convincingly. It literally says that he was "just a human with similar passions." That is to say that he suffered like we do. He was hungry (1 Kin. 17:11), afraid (1 Kin. 19:3) and depressed (1 Kin. 19:4). He was an average Joe. There is nothing about Elijah that would set him apart from us. He was every bit as human as we are.

This was a good example for James to draw from since the Jewish people were well acquainted with him as the most romantic, adventurous Old Testament person. They could also identify with him as a normal man. And, because God works powerfully through the prayers of common people, Elijah **"prayed fervently,"** which is an interesting phrase in the Greek. It says that he "prayed with prayer." This is a compound way of saying that he *really* prayed.

James refers to a story found back in the Old Testament. King Ahab was ruling Israel, and he managed to botch things up quite a bit. Ahab was highly influenced by his wife, Jezebel, and decided to elevate a pagan god to equal status with the Lord. In doing so, he built a temple and erected a wooden image in honor of Baal (1 Kin. 16:32-33). Eventually, at his wife's urging, he opposed the worship of the one true God, destroying His altars and killing His prophets. As punishment of Ahab and as a way to prove Himself as the only God, the Lord brought a drought to the land through Elijah's prayer. Though 1 Kings does not record the prayer, James says that he **"prayed fervently that it might not rain, and for three years and six months it did not rain on the earth"** (Ja. 5:17).

> **God works powerfully through the prayers of common people.**

In a rather amusing display of sovereign power, God showed the people of Israel who had the real power and made a complete mockery of the pagan prophets. Then, after the nation saw the power of God, "a great rain" returned to the land as Elijah prayed (1 Kin. 18:45). James wrote, **"Then he prayed again, and heaven gave rain, and the earth bore its fruit"** (Ja. 5:18). All of this from an average Joe.

Exceptional Power for Average People

Sometimes when I read about the miracles of Peter and the boldness of Paul, I wonder to myself, "There is no way these were just regular people." It is true. When I consider my cowardice, then hear about

David slaying lions and bears (and giants) with only a sling and a few rocks, I get all messed up. When I think on my impatience, then read about Paul enduring numerous imprisonments, beatings, the 39 lashes (not once, by five times), shipwrecks, sleeplessness, and the nagging of self-centered church folk, I just want to cry as I think to myself—what a lousy Christian I have become!

No doubt, these are extraordinary things to learn about. Even the story of Elijah stopping and starting the rain boggles my mind beyond belief. But I am reminded that these extraordinary feats were not the working of extraordinary people but of an extraordinary God. They are the workings of a cosmic ruler who holds this world together while maintaining every single activity of every single molecule. God is powerful. His work is extraordinary. And His plan involves us. I may fail at just about every trial mentioned in James' letter, but I rest in the fact that Jesus is working His glorious power in my life and is turning me around for my good and His glory. And, He is working this out by the word of truth and through the prayers of average people like you and me.

If you have identified trials that have wounded your spiritual life or have been a weakness in your life, know that the Lord gives grace to the humble. Wherever you are, cast your cares upon the Lord and humble yourself before Him. Confess your sins, and find others to help bear you up in righteous prayer. Trust that God will bring you forth by His word of truth and do powerful things in your circle of influence. Maybe one day, if we are faithful to the Lord and abide in His word, someone will stand above our graves and say that we were the ones who prayed with power.

Prayer and Action

There is one last principle about prayer before we end. James, in a rather strange closing, commends the Dispersion with this: "**My brothers, if anyone among you wanders from the truth and someone brings him back, let him know that whoever brings back a sinner from his wandering will save his soul from death and will cover a multitude of sins**" (Ja. 5:19-20).

We would have cheated if we had jumped to the end of James' letter from the get-go. His motivation from the start was to urge us to bring back those of us who wander from the truth. This is not only James' desire; it is a desire of his half-brother, Jesus. The Lord is patient with us all and wishes that none of us should perish, but that all of us should reach repentance (2 Pet. 3:9). This is the heart of God and has been since the Fall. It is the reason that the Son came to earth, lived a perfect life, and died for the sins of those predestined to be saved.

We wander from the truth when we doubt the Father's power and plan (Ja. 1:6), when we hear but do not obey (Ja. 1:19-27), when we show partiality to others (Ja. 2:1-13), when we show no godly works and put our trust in dead faith (Ja. 2:14-26), when we do not tame our tongues but speak wickedly (Ja. 3:1-13), when we live according to the world's wisdom (Ja. 3:14-18), when we love the world and pursue luxurious living (Ja. 4:1-10), when we speak evil against each other (Ja. 4:11-12), when we plan arrogantly without seeking first the Lord's will (Ja. 4:13-17), when we pursue riches and defraud others (Ja. 5:1-6), when we are not patient while suffering (Ja. 5:7-11), when we make promises we do not keep (Ja. 5:12), and when we think little of prayer (Ja. 5:13-18).

> **Together, we can save each other, rescue each other from sin.**

It is not only you who wanders at times. Your fellow brothers, including myself, do too. Together, we can save each other, rescue each other from sin, and bring each other back to submissive living under the truth of Christ where grace and mercy abound. "If anyone sees his brother committing a sin not leading to death, he shall ask, and God will give him life" (1 Jn. 5:16). Oh, what a simple thing it is to throw the eternal lifeline to others who are drowning and lack the might to swim to shore. God will do so much with the little we do. He is faithful and able to keep us in grace. He forgives us and covers a multitude of sins that so often make us fall like the judge's gavel. Through prayer, our Lord sends comfort, brings restoration, builds fellowship and gives power.

This is prayer in action.

Conclusion

As we close this book of trials and contemplate its searing forthrightness, let us go humbly to the Lord and take the beggar's place.

For if our faith is anything but perfect, our need for grace is anything but optional. Even the aged Christians need the blood that flows freely from the cross. So, with every bit of candor, let us rinse His feet with our tears. Let us be crushed by our lack of faithfulness, but joyous in the fullness of His. Let us pound our chests like the tax collector, "God, be merciful to me, a sinner!" (Lk. 18:13).

There is no exception for the contrite heart. It is the humble that leave the place of God justified (Lk. 18:14). For it is God's pleasure to save the sinner and give peace to the wanderer. Though the guilt of our sins unjustly discourages us from approaching His holy throne, it is best that we do; no, it is *necessary* that we do. And, when we do, we will see true faith at work,—drawing and leading us to Christ, softening our hearts, and redeeming our ways. Oh, how good God is to refine like gold in the scorching flames we who deserve their burn!

It is my prayer that you now know how true faith looks, feels, smells, acts and speaks. I trust that you have been warned of its counterparts and commended by its characteristics. Now, let this old Puritan's prayer be your heart's cry in the days to come:

> O God,
> We bless thee,
> > our Creator, Preserver, Benefactor, Teacher,
> for opening to us the volume of nature
> > where we may read and consider thy works.
> Thou hast this day spread before us the fuller pages of revelation,
> > and in them we see what thou wouldest have us do,
> > > what thou requirest of us,
> > > what thou hast done for us,
> > > what thou hast promised to us,
> > > what thou hast given us in Jesus.
> We pray thee for a conscious experience of his salvation,
> > in our deliverance from sin,
> > in our bearing his image,
> > in our enjoying his presence,
> > in our being upheld by his free Spirit.
> Let us not live uncertain of what we are,
> > of where we are going.
> Bear witness with our spirit that we are thy children;
> And enable each one to say, 'I know my Redeemer.'
> Bless us with a growing sense of this salvation.

If already enlightened in Christ, may we see greater things;
If quickened, may we have more abundant life;
If renewed, let us go on from strength to strength.
Give us closer abiding in Jesus
    that we may bring forth more fruit,
        have a deeper sense of our obligations to him,
    that we may surrender all,
        have a fuller joy,
    that we may serve him more completely.
And may our faith work by love
    towards him who died,
    towards our fellow-believers,
    towards our fellow-men.[7]

---

[7] Bennett, Arthur. *The Valley of Vision: A Collection of Puritan Prayers & Devotions*. Edinburgh: Banner of Truth Trust, 2002. 381. Print.

APPENDIX:
JAMES, THE BROTHER OF JESUS

A Bible verse rarely goes without critics. The first verse of this epistle has certainly had its share. Here, the author identifies himself as James. However, a handful of pundits throughout history have contested this. For the most part, their objections fell on deaf ears, and rightly so. There is no viable reason to disbelieve the author. Rather, the more weighty objections have come from those who protest *which* James is the author.

There are five different people in the New Testament named James. So at least the candidates are limited. There is the son of Alphaeus (Matt. 10:3; Mk. 3:18; Lk. 6:15; Acts 1:13), whom we know only as one of the twelve disciples. There is also the son of Mary (not the mother of Jesus) and brother of Joses (Matt. 27:56; Mk. 16:1; Lk. 24:10). He is called James the Less (Mk. 15:40). For the most part, he too is hidden from the biblical accounts. There is James, the father of Judas (not Iscariot) who appears only twice in the New Testament (Lk. 6:16; Acts 1:13). He is not even an apostle.

On the other hand, James, the son of Zebedee, is a well-known disciple of Christ and one of closest of the twelve. He also witnessed the transfiguration (Matt. 17:1; Mk. 9:2; Lk. 9:28). His mother was Salome. She tended to Jesus' daily needs (Matt. 27:56; Mk. 15:40-41). His brother was John, another one of the twelve. Together, they were called the "Sons of Thunder" (Mk. 3:17). Out of all the possible candidates mentioned, he certainly wins the race. However, he was killed by Herod Agrippa I, the grandson of Herod the Great (between A.D. 42-44) according to Acts 12:2, which eliminates him as candidate and leaves us only one more.

The oldest of four younger brothers of Jesus was named James (Matt. 13:55; Mk. 6:3; 1 Cor. 9:5; Gal. 1:19; Jude 1). After the birth of our Lord, Joseph and Mary had children together (Matt. 1:25; 12:47; Lk. 2:7; Jn. 2:12; Acts 1:14). These would be the children of Joseph since Jesus had no biological father (Matt. 1:23-25; Lk. 1:34). Being a brother of the Lord would certainly qualify you as a biblical author if the details lined up. And line up they do. The New Testament has a lot to say about this James.

Before Jesus was crucified, "not even his brothers believed in him" (Jn. 7:5). They thought that he was "out of his mind" (Mk. 3:21). When hanging on the cross, Jesus didn't include them as his true brothers (Matt. 12:46-50; Mk. 3:31-35; Lk. 8:19-21). However, this changed after His crucifixion. Paul records that after the resurrection, Jesus appeared to James before appearing to any of the disciples (1 Cor. 15:7). Some believe that this is when James was converted.

In Acts, James emerges as a prominent leader of a key Christian church. When a conference was held in Jerusalem to discuss the conditions of Gentile membership in the church, a solution was proposed by James. His proposition is recorded in Acts 15:13-21 and it lends us to further confidence in him as the author. The speech found here strongly parallels speech in the epistle. For example, the Greek infinitive verb *chairein* ("greetings") appears in the New Testament only in James 1:1 and Acts 15:23 (except for its use in Acts 15:25 by a Roman, Claudius Lysias). Other parallels include "beloved" (Ja. 1:16,19; Acts 15:25), "your souls" (Ja. 1:21; Acts 15:24), "visit" (Ja. 1:27; Acts 15:14), and "turn" used in the sense of repentance (Ja. 5:19-20; Acts 15:19).

The epistle also contains distinctive Jewish quotes and allusions found in the Old Testament that are too numerous to ignore. And, it has strong parallels to Jesus' Sermon on the Mount (Matt. 5-7) which a brother of Jesus could have witnessed. With all of the evidence adding up, the particular candidate for author of the epistle is James the brother of Jesus. In fact, he is a near perfect match.

STUDY GUIDE

Truth sinks in when we meditate on it. One of the ways I have found most helpful is to answer questions about what I have learned. This is especially true in a setting of friends where it could be discussed and described in many different contexts.

Study Questions for Chapter 1

1. What about James and the Dispersion help shape the way we understand trials?

2. How do you understand trials and temptations? What is God's role and your role in them?

3. What is the purpose of trials and how does that make you feel about them?

4. If you pass or fail a spiritual test, what does it mean to you?

5. Why and how are we to ask God for wisdom? Explain.

6. What is the "crown of life" and what implications does it have?

7. Are we expected to pass every spiritual test? Why?

8. What is the good and perfect gift of God, described in James 1:17 and what implications does it have to you?

9. What part stands out the most for you?

Study Questions for Chapter 2

1. How do you typically respond to trials in your life? How should you respond to trials in your life?

2. Why does James tell believers to "be quick to hear, slow to speak, slow to anger"?

3. How does God produce righteousness in us?

4. How does the encouragement to "receive with meekness the implanted word" contrast with the warnings to abstain from "filthiness and rampant wickedness"?

5. What is the significance of the illustration in verse 23-25?

6. How can our religion (or our reverence and worship of God) become useless?

7. What does pure and undefiled religion before God look like? You may want to consider 1 John 3:10 in your answer?

8. What does James teach about the person who thinks he is a Christian, but does not restrain his speech?

9. What lesson(s) from this passage of James regarding trials and responses do you feel you need to work on?

Study Questions for Chapter 3

1. What are some examples of how partiality is shown in the modern world and church?

2. Has partiality affected your life? How so?

3. What is significant about the command in James 2:1, "show no partiality as you hold the faith in our Lord Jesus Christ"?

4. James reminds readers that God chose "those who are poor in the world to be rich in faith and heirs of the kingdom" and that these two benefits were "promised to those who love him." What does this teach about God and those who are poor?

5. Why is showing partiality a sin?

6. What does James' argument that breaking one law of God makes you "accountable for all of it" have to do with partiality?

7. James' words about judgment without mercy (2:13) mirror Jesus' words in Matthew 7:2. What do these two verses mean to you?

8. What partialities do you currently have that put you at risk for being judged by your own measure?

9. What actions should you take in light of this lesson?

Study Questions for Chapter 4

1. How would you define faith? How would you define works?

2. What is the relationship of faith and works?

3. What sort of implications are there for believing works will save you? What about believing works will prove your faith?

4. How does this topic impact your faith?

5. Explain what is meant in James 2:14: "What good is it, my brothers, if someone says he has faith but does not have works? Can that faith save him?"

6. What biblical stories can you add to James' that show us a faith that was justified by works?

7. James says that "faith by itself ... is dead" (Ja. 2:17). What does this say about faith?

8. When talking about Abraham, James wrote that his faith was both "active along with his works" and "completed by his works." What do you think this means?

9. How do faith and works impact how you live?

Study Questions for Chapter 5

1. Do you have a hard time watching what you say?

2. Have you been hurt by someone's words or hurt someone with your words before?

3. What does James caution in the first verse? Why?

4. The word "perfect" in verse James 2:3 "mature" or "complete" as in James 1:4, 17 and 25. What is the relationship between being mature in speech and being able to control your body?

5. Why does James use the illustrations of the horse bit and ship rudder? Why is this important?

6. Why do you think James says the tongue is set on "fire by hell"?

7. What does James mean when he compares humans to animals?

8. Why do you think James mentions that we are all made in the likeness of God when he is instructing us on our speech?

9. Why is it important for you to tame your tongue.

Study Questions for Chapter 6

1. In what ways are people wise?

2. How do you define wisdom?

3. What is the difference between worldly wisdom and godly wisdom?

4. What does James say is the true test of wisdom?

5. How would you describe "meekness of wisdom"?

6. What are the signs of ungodly wisdom according to James 3:14?

7. Why do you think James calls worldly wisdom *earthly, unspiritual,* and *demonic*?

8. What comes with jealousy and selfish-ambition? Why?

9. What does James mean by calling heavenly wisdom "first pure"?

10. Do you consider yourself to have godly wisdom? Why or why not?

Study Questions for Chapter 7

1. What are the top ten things to which you are loyal?

2. What things fight for your loyalty?

3. What do people commonly show loyalty to?

4. According to James, what is the main causes of believer's problems?

5. How does James describe "adulterous people"?

6. James' use of "friend" and "enemy" speaks of deep affection and hostility. How does he use these terms in connection with worldliness?

7. In James 4:7-10, we are recommended to take several actions to receive God's grace concerning our worldly desires, what are they and what do they mean?

8. What reasons does James give to stop speaking "evil against one another"?

9. What point does James make by comparing us as judges with the Lawgiver?

Study Questions for Chapter 8

1. How often do you include God in your future planning?

2. Do you find yourself yielding to God's will when it means dramatically changing your own?

3. Do you seek the purposes of God when deciding what you will do —even if it means you must do something that is uncomfortable or inconvenient?

4. According to James, what makes planning without consulting God so arrogant?

5. What does James mean by saying, "you are a mist that appears for a little time and then vanishes"?

6. The word "boast" means to speak loudly or to proudly speak about your accomplishments. What does James mean by "boast in your arrogance"?

7. What do you think James means in 4:17 when he says, "whoever knows the right thing to do and fails to do it, for him it is sin"?

8. Has this chapter changed your views? If so, how?

9. What are some practical steps you can take to put the Lord's will first in your life?

Study Questions for Chapter 9

1. What advantages are there to having great wealth? What advantages are there for having little wealth?

2. What do you think James means by his descriptions of their riches in James 5:2-3?

3. Read Jesus' story about the rich man and Lazarus in Luke 16:19-25 and compare it to James 5:1-6. What do you see?

4. James' words "you have laid up" indicates that the sin of the rich is not being wealthy, but is hoarding wealth. How does this help you understand the evils associated with having too much?

5. What are the dangers facing those who are wealthy? What are the dangers facing those who are poor?

6. Why is it important to know that the cries of the victims of fraud are heard by God?

7. The phrase "lived ... in luxury" was translated from the Greek word, *truphao*, which refers to soft, delicate living. What do you think this means?

8. What do you think James means when he says, "You have fattened your hearts in a day of slaughter"?

9. How should the rich act toward those who are poor and those who are righteous?

10. If your views have changed, how?

Study Questions for Chapter 10

1. Before reading this chapter, what did you think about suffering?

2. James commands believers to "be patient." How would you describe patience in the midst of suffering?

3. What do you think James wants us to know about patience when he described the farmer who waits?

4. In your own words, what does "establish your hearts" mean?

5. In James 5:9, what are we prone to do? What do you think this means?

6. In James 5:7-8, we are reminded that the "coming of the Lord is at hand." In the next verse, James says that the Judge is at the door. Why do you think he reminds us of Jesus' impending visit twice?

7. How should a suffering believer react to hearing that God has blessed someone else?

8. James says that the prophets serve as our examples of what to do when facing troubles. How did each of the prophets act while suffering?

9. How is it helpful to know that those who suffered and were steadfast experienced blessing?

10. What does God's blessing say about His nature?

11. What does our steadfastness say about our nature?

Study Questions for Chapter 11

1. What trials do you face most often?

2. Is there a certain trial that you often fail? If so, why?

3. When comparing the characteristics of true faith to the way you live your life, what comes to your mind?

4. What should those who are suffering do? What should the cheerful do?

5. What will the "prayer of faith" do for the one who is spiritually weak?

6. Why would the one who is sick commit sins and need forgiveness?

7. According to James, what benefits are there in praying with others about our sins?

8. What do you lean from this passage about prayer?

9. Do you feel differently about prayer? If so, how?

GENERAL INDEX

Abimelech, 338
Abiram, 141
Abraham, 24, 93, 108, 112, 125-133, 232, 241, 264, 338, 353, 388
Ahab, 109, 130, 131, 330, 378
Ahithophel, 265
Alexandria, 26, 147
Amorites, 131
Anakin Skywalker, 341
Anglican Church, 189
anointing oil, 342, 344, 349, 350, 353, 356-357
Apple Computers, 301
Arabians, 27
Arabic, 80
aristocrats, 140
Asia Minor, 26-27
assurance, of salvation, 14, 16, 120-121, 132, 161, 209, 371, of belief, 21
Augustine, Saint Aurelius, 189

Babylon, 91
Babylonians, 26, 265
See also Babylon
Barclay, William, 188, 194, 203
Bathsheba, 180, 224, 226
Bethlehem, 93
Bible Study Fellowship, 189
bishops, 350
See also elders
Braves, Mississippi, 53
Bunyan, John, 37
Burger King, 197, 303

California, 148
Calvin, John, 129, 154, 165, 189, 287, 304, 318, 324, 339, 351
Canaan, 130
Capernaum, 253, 351
Cappadocia, 27
Carrier, Chris, 29
Castle Church, 107
chairein, 28, 384
Charismatic, 350
cheimetha, *See* destiny
Chesterton, G. K., 18
Cicero, Marcus Tullius, 167
conscience, 42, 62, 114, 163, 178, 210, 226, 248, 314

coram Deo, 177-179, 193
Cretan, 27
Cyrene, 27

Dallas Theological Seminary, 15
Damascus, 26
Daniel, 24, 190, 331
Darth Vader, 341
Dathan, 141
David, 24, 161, 174-176, 179-180, 206, 224-226, 248, 310, 330-331, 338, 379
Day of Pentecost, 27, 91, 159, 162
destiny, 30
Diaspora, 26, 28
discipline, from God, 70-71, 203, from the church, 70, 74, personal, 44, 110, 125, 142, 145, 148, 159, 160, 166, 187, 304, 306-307, 336, from parents, 286, 288
disease, 352
See also sickness
Disney, 156
Dispersion, 19, 28, 228-229, 232, 341, 345, 371, 379, 385
See also Diaspora
doctrines of grace, 191
doulos, 23-24
See also slave

Edwards, Jonathan, 166, 189
Edwards, Dan, 271
Elamites, 27
elders, 90, 160, 342, 348-349, 353-357, 359, 377
Elijah, 140, 208, 330, 342, 377-379
Egypt, 26-27, 69, 131, 140, 170, 204, 207, 230, 264, 330
extreme unction, 344, 350-351
Ezekiel, 331

faith, saving, 32-33, 41-43, 58, 62, 64, 95, 109, 111, 112, 118, 131, 145, 161, 188, 194, 209, 212, 234, 279, 283 307, 316, 318, 326-327, 343, false, 113, 116, 244
favoritism, 105
fear, of God, 32, 35, 48, 59, 69-70, 122-123, 128, 131, 155, 172-174, 177-183, 186, 189, 191, 193, 195-196, 204, 207, 212, 217, 243, 249, 267, 233, 249, 373, of man, 68, 174, 330, of death, 114

Fencerider, Johnny, 37
Ferguson, Sinclair, 165-166
Five Solas, 133
flesh, 55, 64, 126, 155, 159, 164, 196-197, 198-199, 217, 220, 222, 232, 235, 237, 238, 242, 280, 303-304, 342, 353, 370
Ford, 301
friend, of God, 109, 126, 129, 231-232, 243
Frodo Baggins, 254-256

Galilee, 91
Gandhi, Mahatma, 105
Gehenna, 157
Gerstner, John H., 107
G.I. Joe, 58, 116
Gilgal, 34-35
grumble, 33, 313, 323-326, 335-336, 339, 345, 366

Hagar, 175
Heroes, 145
Hindu, 105
Hip Hop Harry, 136
Hitler, Adolf, 74
holy unction, 344
    See also extreme unction
Hosea, 331
Houston, 91
Hughes, Kent, 349, 351

India, 105
Isaac, 204, 108, 125-128, 264
Islam, 80

Jeremiah, 229, 295, 310, 330-331
Jericho, 130
Jethro, 140, 264
Job, 93, 333-335
John the Baptist, 93, 111, 201, 246, 331, 362
Jonah, 122-123, 175, 229, 266-268
Joni Eareckson Tada, 16
Jordan, 111, 131
Josephus, 26
Joshua, 24, 130, 215, 264
Josiah, 157
Judea, 27, 362
judgmental, 75, 88-89, 105, 254, 263, 284, 325, 366

kingdom of God, 25, 38, 40, 112, 207, 252, 263, 281, 285, 303

Korah, 33, 117, 141

Laban, 338
Law, of God, 69, 100, 104, 140, 220, 249, 299, 309, of Moses, 22, 139, 289, 338, 368
Libyaa, 27
Lion King, the 156
Luther, Martin, 107, 126, 133, 189, 315316, 346, 351

MacArthur, John, 135, 163
Matrix, the, 174, 182
Mayan, 173
McFerrin, Bobby, 29
Medes, 27, 293
Mediterranean, 26
Men in Black, 153
Mesopotamia, 27
Molech, 157
Moriah, 128
Mosaic Law, 22, 139, 289, 338, 368
    See Law
Moses, 22, 69, 117, 119, 140-141, 179, 188, 206, 215, 257, 259, 264, 329, 330
Motown, 174

Nazareth, 91, 93
Nicodemus, 112
Ninety-Five Theses, 107
Nineveh, 122, 175, 267

overseers, 139, 355
    See also elders
Oxford English Dictionary, 159

Pamphylia, 27
parable, of talents, 98, 100, prodigal son, 85, 200, 253
paralysis, 15
Parthians, 27
partiality, partial, *See* favoritism
pastors, 70, 166, 228, 355-356, 360-361, 377
    See also elders
perseverance, 42, 108, of the saints, 41
Pharisees, 38-39, 56, 82, 87, 111, 140, 206-207, 229, 231, 268
Pilgrim's Progress, the, 37
Pompey, 26
Pontius Pilate, 28
Pontus, 27

priests, 117, 139-140, 192, 246-247, 314, 356
presbyters, *See* elders
Protestant Reformation, 107, 133, 189
Protestantism, 107

quadriplegic, 15

rabbi, 19, 112, 140
Rahab, 109, 130-131
Rockwell, 174-175
Roman Catholic Church, 107, 126, 316, 350, 351
Rome, 27, 147, 150

Sadducees, 111
Samaria, 152
Samuel, 34-36, 331
Samwise Gamgee, 355-356
Sanhedrin, 140
Santa Barabara, 148
Sarah, 353
Saul, 34-36, 330
Scribes, 90, 139, 140, 229, 231, 362
Sermon on the Mount, 39, 289, 337, 384
Sheba, 169, 180, 224, 226
shekinah, glory, 82
shepherds, 357
    See also elders
Shishak, 26
Shmoneh Esreh, 161
sickness, illness, 156, 227, 344, 350-351, 353-354, 364
Sihon, 131
slave, 24, 39, 69, 87, 93, 119, 140, 145, 174, 204, 220, 245-246, 285, 295, 324, 330
sola fide, 107
    See also Five Solas, the
Solomon, 167, 169, 170-173, 193, 196, 199, 225, 264
Spurgeon, Charles, 158, 315, 340
Sproul, R.C., 142, 163, 177, 316, 375
Stepford Wives, the, 29
synagogue, 20, 25, 27, 84, 87, 90, 92

Twelve Tribes, 19, 28
Ten Commandments, 73, 103

America, American 23, 38, 57, 81, 92, 103, 116, 138, 172, 193, 195, 201, 227, 236, 281, 284, 294, 299, 304, 306, 368

USA Today, 148

Watson, Thomas, 158
Warriors, the, 53
Wellman, Phillip, 53-54
Westminster Confession of Faith, 41-42
Wittenberg, Germany, 107

Zacchaeus, 95, 205,
Zartan, 116

SCRIPTURE INDEX

OLD TESTAMENT

Genesis
1:1...264
2:15...294
3:6...45
3:8-12..45
3:10...177
3:12...144
3:14-15..46
4:11...297
6:5...174
13:2...93
14:22-24...338
15:6...127
16:13..175
18:19..264
18:20..297
18:25..310
19:13..297
21:23-24...338
22:1..127
22:2..128
22:9-10...127
22:11-13..128
22:16-17...338
24:1-67...264
24:14...24
26:24...24
31:44-53..338
35:23-26...28
41:1-57...264
50:15..204
50:19-21..204

Exodus
1:2-5...28
1:16..329
1:22..329
3:10..140
14:31..24
18:1-27..264
18:15-16..140
19:22..247
20:2..73
20:5..241
22:26-27..289

24:16..82
25:8..82
29:9..294
29:45-46...82
30:18-21..247
30:30..356
34:6..206

Leviticus
10:1-2..117
12:8..93
19:9-18..261
19:12..338, 339
19:13..295
19:15-16..261
19:18..99

Numbers
1:20-43...28
5:3...82
14:24..24
14:28-29...63
16..141
16:3...117
16:31-33..118
30:2...338
35:34..82

Deuteronomy
2:2...179
5:6..73
8:18...283
10:17..69
12:11..82
14:23..82
16:6..82
16:11..82
19:12..338
23:21..338
24:14-15...................................295, 296
24:15..296
26:2..82
27:19..63
29:27-28...26
30:19-30..215

32:4	310
32:35	318
32:41-42	233
33:16	82

Joshua
2:1	131
2:8-14	131
6:1-27	264
24:15	215
24:29	24

Judges
5:11.310

1 Samuel
10:1	356
10:8	34
13:5	35
13:11-13	35
13:13-14	35
16:33	356
17:45	298
20:16	338
24:2	330
24:11	330
24:12	330
26-27	330

2 Samuel
3:18	24
15:31	226
17:1-4	226
17:23	226

1 Kings
3:5-13	170
4:29-31	170
4:34	171
5-7	264
6:13	82
10:1-13	170
11:1-13	172
12:13	173
14:25-28	26
15:29	91
16:32-33	378
17:11	378
17:24	91
18:4	330
18:45	378
19:2	330

19:3	330, 378
19:4	378
19:16	356

2 Kings
23:10	157

1 Chronicles
2:2	28

2 Chronicles
1:7-12	170
1:10	167
6:36	142
7:14	253
19:7	69
20:7	129
21:11	229

Ezra
43:9	82

Nehemiah
1-6	264
1:9	82

Job
1:1	333
1:2-4	333
1:3	93
1:8	24
1:13-22	333
2:1-10	334
5:7	313
13:15	334
14:1	18
19:26	334
21:13	306
42:5	334
42:6	334
42:10	334
42:17	334

Psalms
2:4	26
7:12	310
11:7	310
14:1	175
14:2-3	174
14:4	174
17:3	30

18:20	248
21:8	233
22:1	330
22:14	330
22:16	330
22:20	330
23:5-6	358
24:3-4	248
26:1-2	31
37:4	272
39:1-18	176
40:8	279
41:1	95
50:21	175
51:1	206
51:1-4	180
51:4	180
51:9-12	180
51:10-11	180
51:12	120
51:16-17	180
63:1	247
64:3	143
66:18	374
68:21	233
72:4	95
72:9	233
73:25	98
73:28	246
89:11	26
102:11	275
103:1-5	162
103:15-16	292
110:1	233
113:7	95
119:36	239
119:67	316
119:71	316
119:97	60
121:2	347
126:1-2	251
133:1	218
133:2	356
139:17-18	175
140:3	160
143:10	279

Proverbs

1:20	168, 182
3:5	276
3:34	242, 283
3:35	171
4:23	236
5:21	174
8:33	184
9:10	173
10:8	171
10:22	283
10:23	171
13:3	159
14:1	171
14:24	171
15:5	171
17:8	95
17:24	184
18:1	222
18:21	143
19:21	265
20:9	142
21:30	265
24:3-4	167
24:9	179
26:7	199
27:1	275
28:13	365
28:27	95

Ecclesiastes

1:2	171
1:13-14	171
1:16	171
1:17	171, 172
1:18	172
2:1	225
2:19	172
2:1	171
2:3	171
2:4-6	172
2:7	172
2:8	172
2:9	172
2:10	172
2:17	225
2:18	225
2:20	225
2:23	18, 225
4:2	172
12:13	179, 196

Isaiah

1:5-6	357
1:15	248
1:16	248
1:18	273

5:1-2	298
5:5-6	298
5:7	298
5:9	298
5:15-17	299
13:6	293
13:12	292
13:17	293
14:13-14	265
20:3	24
29:1	231
32:6-7	264
32:8	264
41:8	129
42:13	233
45:6-7	269
46:9-11	269
46:10	265
53:5	364
55:11	342
59:2	374
59:3	248
64:6	102

Jeremiah

1:9	330
1:16	330
1:19	330
2:20	229
3:1	230
5:7-8	229
7:22-23	207
11:19-23	331
12:1	310
12:6	331
14:14	331
16:2	331
16:8	331
17:9	102, 152, 258
17:10	102
18:23	331
22:13	295
23:5-6	311
23:16-34	331
31:31-32	230
36:5	331
37:11-16	331
38:4	331

Lamentations

3:39	331
3:40	253

Ezekiel

5:25-27	230
9:9	175
9:10	175
16:26-29	230
28:25	24
36:25-27	249

Daniel

6	331
6:20	24

Hosea

1-3	331

Jonah

1:2	267
1:3	267
1:5	267
1:9	122
1:10	122
1:16	122, 267
2:1-9	122
3:4	122
3:7-9	122
4:6	123

Micah

6:8	105

Nahum

1:2	233
1:8	233

Haggai

1:5	31

Zechariah

2:14	82
9:9	188

Malachi

2:16	231
3:5	295

NEW TESTAMENT

Matthew
1:23..20
1:23-25..383
1:25......................................20, 383
1:46..91
2:16-18...22
3:2.......................................246, 362
3:7-9...112
3:16..362
4:24..227
5-7..384
5:3..39
5:3-11...332
5:4..250
5:5...39, 188
5:8..61
5:9..203
5:16..339
5:18..339
5:21-22...249
5:21-26...73
5:26..339
5:27-28...249
5:28..47
5:32..231
5:34-47...337
5:33-37...337
5:40..289
5:43-48...78
5:44..163
5:48..103
6:2..339
6:16-21...94
6:19-21....................................38, 291
6:21..296
6:24....................215, 231, 245, 282
6:33...............................38, 238, 263
7...112
7:1..257
7:6..275
7:7-11...227
7:15-20...257
7:20..332
7:21..112
7:21-23...118
8:9..275
8:19-20...93
8:29..123
8:30-31...123

9:1-8...362
9:9-13...207
9:12..227
10:3..383
10:5-12...94
10:22..272
10:28..260
11:19..185
11:27-28...59
11:29....................................188, 277
12:1-8...207
12:3..188
12:33-37.......................................135
12:34..152
12:36-37.......................................135
12:38..140
12:38-42.......................................229
12:39..87
12:43..86
12:46..20
12:46-50................................25, 384
12:47..383
13:55..383
13:24-30.......................................244
13:54-56...20
14:10..331
15:8..231
15:13..232
15:15..232
15:17-20.......................................236
15:19..135
16:1-4...229
16:16..164
16:21..140
16:24..237
16:25..237
16:26..236
17:1..383
17:10..140
17:32..360
18:15-20...70
19:16-22.......................................285
19:16-30...40
19:19..75
19:21...............................86, 93, 221
19:23..285
19:23-25...93
19:24..303
19:28......................................26, 28

Reference	Page
20:1-15	83
20:1-16	296
20:16	83
21:1-11	188
21:23-27	200
22:16	82
22:34-40	73, 88, 97, 99
22:35	140
23:2	140, 186
23:2-3	141
23:3	164
23:7	140
23:13	141
23:15	141
23:16	141
23:22	200
23:27	164
23:37	328
25:24-30	100
25:31-46	260
25:31-46	115
25:34-36	101
25:37	101
25:40	95
25:41	101, 157, 163
25:41-43	101
25:44	101
25:45	101
25:46	101, 157
26:32	360
26:53	205
26:69-75	164
26:75	250
27:56	383
27:57	285
27:63	360

Mark

Reference	Page
2:7	362
3:17	383
3:18	383
3:21	384
3:31	20
3:31-35	384
4:10-12	56
5:34	114
6:3	93, 383
6:32-44	93
7:5	140
7:21-23	155
8:38	229
9:2	383

Reference	Page
11:12-14	208
12:17	368
12:28-34	336
12:31	75
12:33	207
12:38-40	90
12:41-44	91
13:26-27	326
13:46	326
14:61-62	26
15:40	383
15:40-41	383
16:1	383

Luke

Reference	Page
1:34	20, 383
1:35	20
2:1-7	93
2:7	20, 383
2:22-24	93
2:47	22
4:40	352
5:27	93
6:7	140
6:15	383
6:16	383
6:20	252
6:21	251
6:24	252
6:25	252
6:28	163
6:35	311
7:30	140
7:36-38	287
8:14	221
8:19-21	384
8:52	287
9:3	94
9:28	383
10:4	94
10:15	253
10:29-37	76
10:34	357
10:37	207
12:15	292
12:15-21	94
12:16-21	263, 292
12:48	142
14:11	253
14:12-14	94
14:27	245
15:18-19	253

15:21	201
15:22-24	253
16:9	288
18:13	249, 381
18:14	381
18:19	20
19:1-10	205
19:8	95
19:20	360
19:27	233
21:16-17	319
21:27-28	319
22:51	205
22:42	376
22:45	376
22:62	287
23:20-24	160
24:10	383
24:18-24	22
24:25	74
24:27	27
24:46	27

John

1:1-18	264
1:14	236
1:46	93
1:51	339
2:12	383
2:23	112
3:2	112
3:3	339
3:5	112, 339
3:5-10	175
3:16	205, 238
5:19	339
5:24	339
7:1-10	20
7:3-4	21
7:5	21, 384
7:17	279
7:37	257
7:52	91
8:1-11	205
8:31-32	112
8:33	126
9:3	351
10:27	111
10:28	111
11:4-6	93
11:7-10	93
11:31-33	287

12:27	18
12:31-32	246
13:1-20	205
13:16	18
13:21	18
13:34	364
13:34-35	218
14:15	59, 73
15	112
15:1	374
15:1-11	375
15:7	374, 375
15:13	238
15:14	129
15:18	272
15:18-21	18
16:33	313
17:20-21	246
17:21	218
19:38-42	93
21:18-19	323

Acts

1:8	264
1:13	383
1:14	20, 383
1:18	153
2:1-13	162
2:3	150, 159
2:5	27
2:5-7	91
2:6	27
2:9-11	27
2:22-23	269
2:39	318
3:13	24
3:16	109
3:19	367
4:1-3	309
4:13	91
4:27-28	15, 26, 28, 269
4:32	218
5:17-18	309
6:4	355
6:8-15	160
7:51-53	328
8:23	153
9:1-19	243
10:34	70
12:2	383
12:17	23
13:28	264

14:17	306
14:22	313
15:13	22
15:13-21	384
15:14	384
15:19	384
15:23	23, 384
15:24	384
15:25	384
16:19-20	309
17:6	309
17:27	247
19:11-20	373
21:27-37	314
22:24	314
22:30	314
23:1-5	314
26:7	28
26:12-18	243
27:16	147
27:38	147
27:29	147
27:30	147
27:38	147

Romans
1:1	24
1:17	311
1:19-20	268
2:4	94
3:9	190
3:9-10	64
2:9-11	70
2:17-18	269
3:10-11	190
3:10-12	174
3:11-12	47
3:13-14	144
3:15	143
3:20	102, 104
3:21	104
3:22	165
3:23	47, 100, 142, 190
3:28	104
4:1-12	127
4:3	126
4:19	352
4:23-24	126
5:1-2	243
5:6	243
5:6-11	190
5:9-11	244
5:19	311
6:1-14	145
6:16	245
6:18	245
6:23	157, 190, 223
6:22	246
7:15	220
7:18	220
7:18-19	64
7:22	220
7:23	220
7:24	249
7:25	220
8:3	353
8:5-7	234
8:5-8	238
8:7	232
8:9	271
8:13	64, 222, 370
8:18	320, 340
8:22	324
8:23	324
8:28	52, 265, 276, 334, 371
8:28-30	32
8:31-37	190
9:11	78
9:23	94
11:33-34	46
12:2	235
12:9	210
12:14	163
13:10	77
13:11-14	189
14:1-2	353
14:4	261
14:1-12	258
14:21	353
14:23	64, 102
15:1-7	89

1 Corinthians
1:10	147
1:18-31	193
1:26	93
2:14	57, 197
3:1-3	217
3:13	217
4:5	261, 327
4:6	258
4:17	320
5:2	250
5:3	258

5:12...258
7:28..18
8:1...192
9:5...383
9:25-27..44
10:13..36
11:27-32..351
11:28..31
12:3..161
12:6..376
12:11..376
13:4-7...224
13:4..317
15:7..21, 384
15:47...20
16:2..288

2 Corinthians
1:5...340
4:4...236
5:17..55, 162
6:9-10..94
7:7...194
7:8-10..251
8:9..94, 286
10:3-5...236
11:2..230
11:24..309
12:10..353
12:20..217
13:5...31

Galatians
1:18-19...22
1:19...383
2:9..22
2:11..68
2:12..68
2:16...108
2:20...109
3:7...126
3:7-9..126
5:6...373
5:22...312
5:22-23...145, 209
6:1...360
6:1-2..366
6:2...366
6:3...367
6:4..31
6:6...288
6:7..26

6:9...322
6:15...373

Ephesians
1:4...265
1:4-11..78
1:7..94
1:11...265, 376
2:1-3..242
2:3..103
2:4..285
2:7..311
2:8..32, 52, 109
2:9-10...127
2:10...113
3:8..94
3:11...265
4:2..365
4:3..367
4:25...367
4:27...367
4:26..74
4:32...312
5:17...269
5:17-18..271, 280
5:19-20...348
5:24...230
5:29..76

Philippians
1:1..24
1:6...32, 109
1:27...218
1:28-30..318
2:3..90
2:3-8..238
2:12.5...9, 108
2:12-13...32
3:6..194
3:9-11..317
3:12-14...277
4:8..201
4:13...373

Colossians
1:9-10...269
2:8..236
2:9-10..26
3:12...312
4:12..24

1 Thessalonians
2:13...377
3:3...30
3:10-12..294
3:13..319
4:3-7..271
4:3-8..280
5:14..358
5:23..319

2 Thessalonians
1:8..299

1 Timothy
1:5..210
2:4..270, 280
1:6-7..141
3:1-7..355
3:9..62
4:1..198
4:16..142
4:22..201
5:3..63
5:8..63, 288
6:10..282
6:17-19..........................93, 293, 312

2 Timothy
1:8..313
2:13..253
2:17..258
3:4..220
3:16..370
3:12..313
4:1..260
4:10..258
5:20..70
5:21..70

Titus
3:5..60, 248
3:5-9..355

Philemon
1..285

Hebrews
1:1-3..82
2:3..147
3:12-13..366
4:12..261, 342
4:14..247
4:15..47
4:16..247
6:13-14..338
6:16..338
6:17..338
10:25..367
10:31..233
11:24-26..330
11:32-38..332
12:1-2..44, 45
12:2..109
12:3..358
12:10-11..203
12:13..364
12:14..112
13:17..141

James
1:1..............................20, 23, 28, 384
1:2..........................28, 29, 30, 315
1:2-4....................41, 42, 186, 322, 369
1:3..29, 30, 108
1:3-4................................33, 61, 334
1:4..334, 370
1:4-5..34
1:5............36, 168, 186, 187, 193, 199, 210
1:5-6..108
1:5-7..359
1:5-8..52
1:6............................36, 37, 359, 377, 380
1:7..359
1:7-8..37, 322
1:8......................................215, 356, 374
1:9..39
1:9-10..39
1:9-11..52
1:10-11..40
1:12..28, 41, 44, 45, 61, 108, 168, 315, 332, 334, 335, 343, 345
1:13-14..47
1:13-18..242
1:14................................47, 187, 220
1:15..48
1:16............................49, 195, 196, 384
1:16-17..48
1:17................................52, 196, 199, 201
1:18......50, 53, 58, 108, 315, 342, 343, 369, 370
1:19....................53, 62, 135, 325, 335, 384
1:19-20..53
1:19-21..369
1:19-27............................51, 52, 209, 380

Reference	Pages
1:20	54
1:21	55, 56, 57, 58, 108, 189, 359, 384
1:22	58, 59, 195
1:22-25	195
1:23	60
1:23-24	59
1:24	60
1:25	60, 61
1:26	62, 135, 145, 369
1:27	62, 64, 181, 274, 384
2:1	81, 116, 209
2:1-13	69, 105, 380
2:2	85
2:2-3	84
2:4	88, 210, 311, 325
2:5	95
2:5-7	92
2:6	95, 324
2:6-7	297, 307, 345
2:7	95, 96
2:8	98, 99
2:8-13	209, 336, 369
2:9	72, 100
2:10	103
2:11	103, 308
2:12	135
2:12-13	104
2:13	111
2:14	110, 335, 359
2:14-26	109, 209, 380
2:15-16	113
2:16	114
2:17	113, 115, 117
2:18	124
2:19	121, 122, 124
2:20	74, 124, 125
2:21	127
2:21-23	126
2:22	128
2:22-23	128
2:23	127, 129, 241, 232
2:24	130
2:25	131
2:26	59, 110, 132, 241, 221
3:1	138, 142, 151, 184, 259, 336
3:1-12	136, 254, 296, 335, 336
3:1-13	380
3:2	142, 144, 145, 160
3:3	146
3:4	147
3:5	148, 150
3:6	150, 153, 154, 156, 157
3:7-8	159
3:8	160
3:9	161, 162, 163
3:10	164, 194, 336
3:11	165, 194
3:11-12	221
3:12	165
3:13	183, 185, 187, 369
3:13-18	168, 254
3:14	193, 195, 196, 199, 221, 228
3:14-16	216
3:14-18	380
3:15	171, 201, 300
3:15-16	236
3:16	198, 211, 219, 278, 325
3:17	200, 201, 203, 205, 206, 208, 210, 212, 219, 238, 369
3:17-18	216
3:18	211, 212
3:27	201
4:1	217, 219, 224, 246, 282, 335, 366
4:1-2	221, 231, 325, 345
4:1-4	236, 300
4:1-10	25, 380
4:1-12	216, 336
4:2	219, 224, 227
4:2-3	223, 226, 377
4:3	226, 227, 335, 376
4:3-5	293
4:4	228, 230, 231, 237, 255, 300, 317
4:5	239, 240
4:6	242, 243, 244, 253, 287, 300, 367, 369
4:7	244, 245, 246, 247
4:8	215, 245, 246, 248, 255
4:9	249, 250, 251, 287, 297, 317
4:10	252, 287, 325
4:11	256, 259, 311, 325, 335, 345
4:11-12	275, 380
4:12	261, 359
4:13	272, 273, 286, 335
4:13-17	264, 336, 380
4:14	275, 292
4:15	276, 335
4:16	277, 335
4:17	279
5:1	286, 287, 297
5:1-6	283, 336, 369, 380
5:2	289
5:2-3	288
5:3	2, 90, 291, 292, 296
5:3-4	296
5:4	296, 296, 297, 300

5:5	300, 303, 306, 321
5:6	298, 307, 324
5:7	209, 317, 319, 320, 326, 335
5:7-11	336, 337, 380
5:7-12	314
5:8	209, 321, 345, 369
5:9	323, 326, 335, 345, 366
5:10	328, 332, 335
5:11	333, 334, 345
5:12	335, 336, 337, 339, 380
5:13	344, 345
5:13-14	348
5:13-18	336, 344, 380
5:13-20	343
5:14	350, 351, 355, 356, 358
5:14-15	344, 349, 363
5:15	358, 359, 360, 372, 377
5:16	344, 350, 355, 361, 363, 364, 369, 370, 372, 373
5:16-18	344
5:17	378
5:17-18	209, 377
5:18	344, 378
5:19-20	384, 379
5:20	244, 245, 360

1 Peter

1:3-5	119, 319
1:6-7	119
1:15	119
1:17	70
1:19	64
1:10	31
2:13-15	271, 280
2:23	320
2:24	364
3:12	175, 374
3:17	271, 280
3:21	248
4:1-2	280
4:6	30
4:7	318
4:12	30
4:13	320
4:19	30
5:5	243
5:6	367

2 Peter

1:1	24
2:14	143
3:9	270, 280, 317, 318, 380

1 John

1:4	368
1:8	369
1:8-10	370
1:9	362, 367, 374
2:3-5	119
2:5-6	120
2:15	234
2:15-16	238
2:17	280
2:19	43
2:28	319
3:2-3	201
3:3	320
3:8	245
3:15	224
3:16	64, 75, 288
3:17	67, 113
3:18	68
4:6	33
4:8	33
4:11	72
4:12	33
4:13	33
4:21	366
5:3	59
5:4	373
5:16	380

Jude

1	24, 33, 383
3	109
4	32
5-7	32
17-23	155
20-21	33

Revelation

1:1	24
2:3	359
2:13	109
7:4	28
16:18	147

ABOUT THE AUTHOR

Jacob Abshire is author of *Forgiveness: A Commentary on Philemon* and is co-founder of Resolute Creative, an internet marketing agency. He also contributes at the weblog, *Truth411: Biblical Answers to Christian Questions* (http://www.t411.com). His expressed vision is to bring others closer to the Scriptures in order to find the riches of God's truth and the glory of God's Son. Jacob lives with his wife, Kathy, and their four children in Houston, Texas, where they serve with their local church.

www.ingramcontent.com/pod-product-compliance
Lightning Source LLC
Chambersburg PA
CBHW070135100426
42743CB00013B/2711